Ideology and Culture in
Seventeenth-Century France

Ideology and Culture in Seventeenth-Century France

ERICA HARTH

Cornell University Press

ITHACA AND LONDON

To J. E. and A.-M. S.

Contents

Contents

Illustrations

Preface

When I first undertook this project, my intention was to explore the genesis of the modern French novel. I soon found, however, that I could no more consider one genre apart from others than I could deal with questions of genre apart from those of social and cultural development. Examination of seventeenth-century novels in connection with related genres led me to formulate the notion of a representational system that, in the course of its evolution during that century, was propelled from the seeming stability of aristocratic privilege to the upheaval of bourgeois society in its early formation. My material began to acquire a life and a momentum of its own. It imposed its own questions: How did generic distinctions, such as that between history and the novel, arise? What were the social-ideological value and function of the various seventeenth-century genres? Where were the intersections and the divergences of cultural and ideological change?

My attempt to answer these questions is at most an interpretive essay; it is neither a cultural history nor an exhaustive study. I do not survey the well-known figures of a well-known cultural era. Most of my material is relatively unfamiliar outside circles of specialists. I hope to shed some light not on those isolated representatives who have been recognized as major by subsequent generations of critics and professors, but instead on major cultural and social transformations of the time as they were lived by their participants.

Because I draw on a variety of fields, this book should ideally have been a collaborative effort. Practically, such collaboration was not feasible. Yet help and cooperation essential to the completion of the book came to me from many diverse quarters in an impressive spirit of goodwill. A fellowship from the American Council of Learned Societies provided invaluable help. Brandeis University generously supplemented it with a Mazer Award, a Sachar Faculty Grant, and other research funds. The staff of the New York Public Library and the Widener, Houghton, and Fogg libraries at Harvard University gave liberally of their time and expertise. I am particularly indebted to Susan Halpert and Anne Anninger at the Houghton Library. The theoretical discussions that took place in the New York Seminar on Dialectical Criticism, in which I participated from 1978 to 1981, were a primary stimulus for the thinking that resulted in this book. I owe thanks to all the members of the seminar, and especially to Norman Rudich, Leon Roudiez, and Carol and Andrew Remes.

Friends and colleagues contributed their advice, suggestions, and criticisms of the manuscript at all stages of its preparation. Jules Brody was of inestimable help from beginning to end with his support and his critical readings. I received much encouragement and support from Edward Engelberg, Rupert Pickens, Ellen Chances, and Natalie Z. Davis. I am grateful for the very careful readings of the entire manuscript, or parts of it, by Elizabeth Fox-Genovese, Caren Greenberg, Jan Goldstein, Michael McKeon, Harrison White, Samuel K. Cohn, Jr., and John Coughlan. Discussions with Joyce Antler, William Higgins, Pierre-Yves Jacopin, Leonard Muellner, Alan Wallach, and Robert Berger aided me substantially with important aspects of the book.

It has been a privilege to work with Bernhard Kendler of Cornell University Press. His understanding and advice were indispensable to me throughout the process of publication. My warm thanks go to Barbara H. Salazar of Cornell University Press for her meticulous editorial guidance. Preparation of the manuscript was also greatly facilitated by the patience and skill of Zina Goldman, Alix Beiers, and Brenda Sens.

Most important, this work could not have been done without the moral and personal support of my good friends Judith Auerbach, Leonard Gruenberg, Muriel Heiberger, Marian Lowe, Shoshana Pakciarz, and Ellen Schrecker.

I am grateful to the Houghton Library of Harvard University, the Harvard College Library, the Beinecke Rare Book and Manuscript Library at Yale University, the Dartmouth College Library, and the Musées Nationaux, Paris, for permission to reproduce the photographs that illustrate the text. I also thank *L'Esprit Créateur* for permission to use my article "The Ideological Value of the Portrait in Seventeenth-Century France," which was published in volume 21 of that journal (Fall 1981) and now forms part of Chapter 2 of this book.

Unless otherwise noted, translations from the French are my own.

ERICA HARTH

Cambridge, Massachusetts

Ideology and Culture in
Seventeenth-Century France

1

Preliminary Considerations

In seventeenth-century Europe we begin to recognize our own world. Suddenly, it seems, history veered toward the future. The proof is that Cartesian thought is still very much with us; the passions of Racine's tragedies are our own. We perceive in the seventeenth century the first signposts of modern Western society: the nation-state, science, and a desacralized culture. Yet the reasons that we experience this culture as modern remain obscure. Descartes had just barely shaken off the trappings of scholasticism; Racine's alexandrines belong to a long-discarded formalism. It is because European social development reached a historic juncture in the seventeenth century that we hesitate to evaluate the culture of the time. In the decisive shift from the feudal to the capitalist mode of production, the bourgeoisie entered its formative stage. "Early modern" is emergent modern. With the emergence of a new mode of production and a new class, a culture that we tentatively qualify as modern began to take shape.

Artistic representation in Europe from the sixteenth to the eighteenth century was cast in an aristocratic mold of analogy. The various arts were unified by a set of correspondences between the visual and the verbal, the historical and the mythological, the ancient and the modern. The reigning monarch, for example, was regularly portrayed, in image and in text, as Hercules. Representation was the glorification and celebration of a royal or noble subject. The dimensions of art were heroic; the tone was elevated. The seventeenth century, however, witnessed a peculiar development: representation gradually ceased to fit its mold. The correspondences persisted, but the value of the representation became debased. As individual bourgeois gained economic power, they began to challenge noble hegemony. A disparate group, not yet united in a class, these bourgeois were at once progressive and conservative. They brought with them the new, but clung to the old. As they propelled Europe forward in new commercial and industrial ventures, they looked back to the past in their yearning for nobility. The bourgeois mainsprings of capitalism were allowed to unwind with the purchase of a title. Representation became filled with new values yet did not crack the traditional mold of correspondences until the eighteenth century, by which time the strain had grown too great to bear. The cultural history of seventeenth-century France is one of progressive obsolescence: the progressive forces of a forming bourgeoisie undermined an increasingly outworn representational mold.

The Ideological Crisis of Seventeenth-Century France

G. N. Clark has seen the seventeenth century as "one of the great watersheds of modern history"; other historians have debated the nature or even the existence of a "crisis of capitalism" during that period.[1] Most agree that in the seventeenth century Europe entered a phase that was to prove crucial for the future of the West. Karl Marx dated the beginning of the capitalist era from the sixteenth century, and considered the development of merchant capital and commerce which accompanied subsequent geographical expansions as major factors in the transition from feudalism to capitalism.[2] According to E. J. Hobsbawm, the seventeenth century was the "last phase" in this transition.[3] The definitive victory of capitalism did not of course occur overnight, nor did it proceed linearly at a uniform rate. The changes were slow and uneven, but comprehensive. The commercial, technological, and scientific innovations of the early modern period were all

1. See George N. Clark, *The Seventeenth Century* (Oxford, 1969), p. ix. For a good summary of the so-called transition debates, see Rodney Hilton, ed., *The Transition from Feudalism to Capitalism* (London, 1976).
2. Karl Marx, *Capital,* vol. 1 (London, 1970), 715; vol. 3 (New York, 1967), pp. 332–33.
3. Eric J. Hobsbawm, "The General Crisis of the European Economy in the Seventeenth Century," *Past and Present* 5 (1954):33.

interdependent. The gradual displacement of handicrafts by manufacture was inseparable from changes in social and intellectual life. Capitalism transformed Europe as a whole into our immediate social forebear.

In France, where political revolution was later in coming, capitalism developed more slowly than in England and Holland, France's two maritime rivals. The contradictions between a decadent feudalism and a nascent capitalism stand out with peculiar sharpness during the reigns of Louis XIII and Louis XIV, who strengthened French absolutism by centralization and bureaucratization, thus preparing both the rise to power of bourgeois technocrats and a concomitant "feudal reaction," while adding fuel to the fire of popular revolts throughout the country. Colbert's mercantilism was progressive insofar as it spurred the development of merchant capital, yet protectionism placed fetters on free trade. "Venality of offices," part and parcel of the old system of privilege, encouraged misinvestment of capital as a substantial part of a potential bourgeoisie was diverted to the ranks of the financiers and the *noblesse de robe*. Manufacture struggled with guild prerogatives. Such contradictions reveal the formation of a new society, as Marx would have it, within the womb of the old.

The challenge of new social forces split open the upper ranks of French society. Social, economic, and political power was passing rapidly from the nobility of the sword to that of the robe. "New nobles" threatened the status of the older nobility, and intendants representing the centralized monarchy began to replace the older officials. Lucien Goldmann, in his *Hidden God*, has studied the flight into Jansenism on the part of disaffected members of the *noblesse de robe*, pushed out of positions of authority by the newly created royal *commissaires*. The formation of a new elite based on wealth rather than on privilege, or what one critic has called an "alliance of the beneficiaries of the primitive accumulation of capital,"[4] provided the foundations of a bourgeoisie.

In a climate where new arrivals were ousting established power,

4. Jean-Marie Apostolidès, *Le Roi-machine* (Paris, 1981), p. 7. Cf. Carolyn C. Lougee, *Le Paradis des Femmes: Women, Salons, and Social Stratification in Seventeenth-Century France* (Princeton, 1976), pp. 127–28. George Taylor asserts that the wealth of both the bourgeoisie and the nobility made of them one economic group, but he argues (mistakenly, I believe) that because this wealth was largely proprietary, "bourgeois" cannot be equated with "capitalist," and therefore that the French Revolution was not a bourgeois revolution. See George V. Taylor, "Noncapitalist Wealth and the Origins of the French Revolution," *The American Historical Review* 72 (January 1967):469–96.

it is not surprising that social discontent should have taken on a distinctly reactionary form. Nostalgia for the "good old days" when each order kept to its place (was there ever such a time?) suffuses the complaints of seventeenth-century nobles and permeates the art and literature of what we call "French classicism." The only significant political upheaval in France during the century, the Fronde (1648–52), had a decidedly reactionary aspect.[5] Yet there were progressive voices, too. If they were less audible than the others, it was only because the bourgeoisie as a class was still in a formative stage. We have to strain our ears in order to hear them, for in the centuries intervening between the birth of capitalism and its decline they have tended to be drowned out by the more celebrated "classical" sounds. Satirists, pamphleteers, scientists, certain historians and novelists—these are some of the people who voiced the claims and protests of the rising class in its early formation.

The bourgeois challenge to authority and tradition was one facet of what I call the ideological crisis that traversed seventeenth-century France. The crisis did not stem, however, simply from a confrontation of the hitherto dominant aristocratic ideology with that of a rising bourgeoisie. The bourgeois rise to power was accompanied by conscious imitation of the noble way of life—in dress, manners, customs, art, and literature. Norbert Elias has even spoken of a "courtly bourgeoisie."[6] The bourgeois adapted aristocratic ideology to their own needs, transforming it subtly but decisively, with the result that by the reign of Louis XIV these transformations had begun to assume some of the most fundamental characteristics of the eighteenth-century bourgeois ideology, which has become the dominant ideology of our day. I will not argue that the bourgeoisie had become consolidated as a class during the reign of the Sun King, or that its ideology had attained a dominant form by this time. I maintain only that by the end of the seventeenth century, as the lineaments of the new class became clearly outlined against the old socioeconomic formations, bourgeois ideology became clearly recognizable as that of a rising class.

5. Cf. A. D. Lublinskaya, *French Absolutism: The Crucial Phase, 1620–1629* (Cambridge, England, 1968), pp. 25–26. Other historians have pointed out the progressive aspects of the Fronde. See, for example, A. Lloyd Moote, *The Revolt of the Judges: The Parlement of Paris and the Fronde, 1648–1652* (Princeton, 1971); Boris Porshnev, *Les Soulèvements populaires en France de 1623 à 1648* (Paris, 1963).

6. Norbert Elias, *The Civilizing Process: The History of Manners,* trans. Edmund Jephcott (New York, 1978), p. 35.

Ideological change is integral with social change. Ideology is not an immaterial consciousness, distinct from its material base, but is instead ubiquitous in society. Marx commented all too briefly on ideology, and the term has long befuddled Marxist thinkers. Various meanings assigned to it have been founded on an artificial topographical division between the ideological and the socioeconomic. The concept of a reigning ideology or an "ideology of the dominant class" is an implicit disembodiment of ideology. It is as if the class disappeared behind the secretion of its ideology. Similarly, to define ideology as "false consciousness" or as a largely unconscious "system of ideas" is to locate the ideological in the mental. It is an outmoded, mechanistic Marxism that erects a barrier between the material base and the ideological superstructure, and consequently views a spiritualized ideology as "reflecting" its material base. Raymond Williams, in one of the best discussions of the subject, has emphasized that consciousness is part of the material social process, that ideology cannot be divorced from the material production and reproduction of life.[7] Ideology and material production have the same social reality. Human beings produce and reproduce their material life in institutions, in culture, in language, all of which go to form our social reality.

The diverse meanings attached to ideology acquire validity when they are reconsidered in relation to this line of thought. Thus, to the extent that one mode of production predominates in a class society, one ideological mode—the "dominant ideology"—will predominate. The social and the ideological are not even as distinct as two sides of the same coin, a metaphor that preserves the epistemological dualism of base and superstructure. Domination is simultaneously social, economic, and ideological. To the extent that we live unreflectively the reality into which we are born, ideology will be nonconscious. Willy-nilly, we move in a "system of ideas" as we move in a social and economic system. We are, as one critic has put it, "in ideology" as we are

7. See Raymond Williams, *Marxism and Literature* (Oxford, 1977), pp. 55–71. Fredric Jameson's recasting of the Althusserian notion of ideology as "a representational structure which allows the individual subject to conceive or imagine his or her lived relationship to transpersonal realities such as the social structure or the collective logic of History" has the disadvantage of preserving a dualism of representation and represented, although in according priority to the concept of mode of production, Jameson would reject such dualism. See Fredric Jameson, *The Political Unconscious: Narrative as a Socially Symbolic Act* (Ithaca, N.Y., 1981), pp. 30, 17–102. Cf. Louis Althusser, *For Marx*, trans. Ben Brewster (New York, 1970), pp. 232–36. It is extremely difficult to find a critical language for the discussion of ideology.

"in language."[8] To perceive ourselves in history, or our class as the subject of history, requires a set of historical circumstances favoring a privileged awareness. When this awareness is lacking, ideology shapes self-interest into necessity and justice, fear into longing for the past, the values of one class into universal values. Much of the dominant culture in class society is built on the mystifying distortion, analogous to the distortion that Freud discovered in dreams, of a "false consciousness," or on what I call ideological work. Analysis of ideology and culture should logically constitute a reconstruction of the passage from latent to manifest ideological content which is the inner dynamic of ideology. The manifest content is just as "real" as the latent. Ideological work is a constant, nonconscious process that informs every aspect of our social lives.[9]

When a rising class challenges the entire way of life in a given society, a kind of counterideology develops within the dominant ideology. This is exactly what happened in seventeenth-century France. The process by which the forming bourgeoisie developed a new mode of production and a new ideological mode from the old is what characterizes social relations in France at this time.

Cultural production is a specific instance of this process. In the seventeenth century, changes were accelerated in certain branches of production crucial to French culture. As printing progressed beyond its earliest stage, French booksellers were unified into a guild, thereby formally entering the world of trade. With the economic and political decline of the nobility, writers tended to depend less on aristocratic patronage and more on the market. Gradually they began to produce for money. Guild privileges, at

---

8. Claude Prévost, *Littérature, politique, idéologie* (Paris, 1973), p. 214. The Gramscian concept of hegemony provides us with a means to unify the social and the ideological. According to Gramsci, the dominant class of a state exercises both political and cultural hegemony. Ideology is then "a conception of the world that is implicitly manifest in art, in law, in economic activity and in all manifestations of individual and collective life." See Antonio Gramsci, *Selections from the Prison Notebooks*, ed. Quintin Hoare and Geoffrey Nowell Smith (New York, 1971), p. 328. See also Christine Buci-Glucksmann, *Gramsci and the State*, trans. David Fernbach (London, 1980), pp. 47–68.

9. Much recent work in literary and discursive criticism has been inspired by Freud's concept of dream-work. Terry Eagleton speaks of a "text-distortion" in his *Criticism and Ideology* (London, 1978), pp. 90–94. Hayden White, in his *Tropics of Discourse: Essays in Cultural Criticism* (Baltimore, 1978), pp. 1–25, grounds his "tropological analysis" on Freud's analytic categories. White also analyzes historical discourse in terms of a "knowledge-work" (pp. 111–12). Fredric Jameson's "political unconscious" necessitates "the unmasking of cultural artifacts as socially symbolic acts" (*Political Unconscious*, p. 20).

first a boon to booksellers, quickly became fetters on their free development. Some astute publishers took advantage of regulation by circumventing it, and even as early as the mid-seventeenth century a clandestine book trade began to thrive under freer, more nearly capitalistic conditions.[10] During the reign of Louis XIV, when censorship procedures were systematically tightened, the inevitable counterpart to regulation was subversion. An eager public began to devour a literature that circulated messages strictly forbidden by the king. As the monarchy used bourgeois skills for its own purposes, bourgeois began to appropriate this expertise for their own ends. Thus Colbert's mercantilist policies and his sponsorship of scientific talent resulted in technological advance, which aided the accumulation of merchant capital, and in the liberation of science for bourgeois culture. The modernization of the book trade, the creation of a commercial market for writers, the development of science and technology all helped to transform a culture that had blossomed under earlier, precapitalist conditions into the complex cultural formation of a bourgeois society.

The *Ut Pictura Poesis* Representational System

At the beginning of the seventeenth century, the arts possessed their own peculiar coherence. They were unified by common aesthetic laws and practices elaborated under premodern conditions of production. With the deepening ideological crisis, the unity achieved in an earlier period slowly dissolved, and artistic representation entered a critical stage.

We will be obliged to relinquish our generally received conceptual categories of art in order to appreciate its development in the seventeenth century. Literature, for example, in the specialized sense that the term has acquired since the eighteenth century of a compartmentalized discipline distinct from science, the social sciences, and sometimes even poetry, did not exist at the time.[11] The notion of imitation or representation did, however, and it could

10. Robert Darnton's studies suggest that the legal and clandestine book trades belonged respectively to two different economic systems, that of Old Regime privilege and "a kind of rampant capitalism." See his *Literary Underground of the Old Regime* (Cambridge, Mass., 1982), pp. 197–98.

11. See Robert Escarpit, "La Définition du terme 'littérature,' " in *Le Littéraire et le social*, ed. Robert Escarpit (Paris, 1970), pp. 259–72.

be applied equally to belles-lettres—various forms of fictional and discursive writing—and to the plastic arts, music, theater, and so on. "Art" consisted in the skillful practice of imitation in any one or all of these domains. No matter to which form or genre it was applied, the art remained the same. So closely interrelated were the various art forms in the rules of their practice that I have chosen to refer to them as one system of representation, a system dominant in Europe from the sixteenth to the eighteenth century. I use "representation" in its sense of an aesthetic dictum of imitation as conceived and practiced in the early modern period. By "system" I mean a dynamic set of interrelated elements, each one of which was slowly evolving in accordance with changes in conditions of cultural production.

The animating principle of this system was derived from the generally misunderstood comparison in Horace's *ars poetica* of painting with poetry: *ut pictura poesis*. Horace's image was little more than a conceit, but to it the early moderns added the saying attributed by Plutarch to Simonides that painting is mute poetry, and poetry a speaking picture. From eclectic fragments of ancient thought the moderns built an aesthetic uniting the verbal and the visual arts. Its cornerstone was Aristotelian in origin, but the theoreticians expanded Aristotle's principle of art as the imitation of human action into that of art as the imitation of nature. Following both Aristotle and Horace, they linked the aesthetic and the moral, pleasure with instruction. The *ut pictura poesis* system was essentially aristocratic. It functioned to glorify noble and royal patrons; it projected conventionalized aristocratic images.

The crisis undergone by the *ut pictura poesis* system in seventeenth-century France was both structural, or intrinsic to the system, and historical, or extrinsic to the system.[12] With changes in conditions of cultural production and changing ideological demands, elements of the system began to change: in their function within the system, in their interrelationship, in their ideological value. Because the system as such possessed inner coherence, the gradual transformation of its elements proceeded in a consistent direction. This is not to say that the changes occurred in a uniform linear manner, without contradictions. As bourgeois modifi-

12. We can learn much about the development of aesthetic systems from Thomas Kuhn's study of scientific systems. Kuhn's notion of a system in crisis is particularly applicable to the *ut pictura poesis* system. But he is concerned uniquely with structural development. See Thomas S. Kuhn, *The Structure of Scientific Revolutions*, 2d ed. (Chicago, 1970).

cations were increasingly introduced, it is as if each element began slowly to work its own subversion. Bourgeois who had at first used the tools of the representational system in the service of the nobility or the monarchy began to appropriate the various elements of *ut pictura poesis* for their own ends, undermining its ideological value for the dominant class. Slowly but surely, bourgeois artists invested the system with new ideological value: *ut pictura poesis* ended in *embourgeoisement*. Throughout the seventeenth century and well into the eighteenth, the system retained enough of its coherence to be recognizable as such, despite modification of its elements. But the day was not far off when, as each element was transformed beyond recognition as part of the system, the entire edifice would crumble, along with the ancien régime supporting it.

The system was relatively intact at the beginning of the seventeenth century, the point of departure for my study. Artistic representation based on the principle of *ut pictura poesis* has been widely analyzed.[13] My notion of a representational *system*, however, integrates a set of aesthetic elements that have not necessarily been included in discussions either of *ut pictura poesis* or of seventeenth-century representation. A brief description of the system as I view it is therefore in order.

Although the essence of the entire system—that is, the concept of art as representation or imitation—was extracted primarily from Aristotle and Horace, the moderns significantly altered this concept in theory and in practice. Aristotle's imitation, as he explained it in the *Poetics,* unified manner, means, and object of representation, but in the modern variety of imitation, manner assumed a disproportionate importance. Because, faithful to their predecessors, the moderns exemplified human action in history or mythology, their painting became the visualization of a text, their poetry (in the broad Aristotelian sense) the verbal representation of a model in mythological or historical dress. To view a painting was to decipher a text; to read the description of a character was to see a portrait. History or mythology was essential to both. The "learned painter" was accordingly obliged to be not only a skilled craftsman but also a repository of knowledge. The

13. For some of the more concise accounts, see Rensselaer W. Lee, "Ut Pictura Poesis: The Humanistic Theory of Painting," *Art Bulletin* 12 (December 1940): 197–269; William G. Howard, "Ut Pictura Poesis," *PMLA* 24, n.s. 17 (1909):40–123; Joel E. Spingarn, *A History of Literary Criticism in the Renaissance* (New York, 1963), pp. 18–30.

celebrated Le Brun was criticized by a contemporary for having neglected the conventional allegorical sources of painting in favor of his own inventions, thereby mystifying rather than enlightening and edifying his spectators.[14] Similarly, the *précieuses,* who displayed their pictorial wits in the salons of seventeenth-century France by drawing verbal portraits of one another and their friends, were cultivated women. History and mythology were regular features of their parlor games, and their portraits turned up as set pieces in the written literature of the time. Aristotle's imitation of object, then, became doubled by an imitation in manner. Painting and poetry, in their respective manners, imitated each other's means of representation as well as their respective objects of representation. The value of the representation came to consist in the "artifice," or skillful manner, of its imitation. From the ancient concept of art as imitation the moderns evolved an art *of* imitation.

The objects of representation, in poetry as in painting, were to be taken from either history or fable (poetry). Although Aristotle in the *Poetics* distinguished between poetry and history as treating respectively the universal and the particular, his discussion of tragedy pointed to the use of history in poetry, to the mingling of fact and fiction in order to achieve probability in poetic representation. Horace advised his poet to blend fact and fiction. In the practice of the *ut pictura poesis* system, history and poetry were often interwoven by allegory. Since the general perceptual and intellectual mode in early modern times was analogical, historical figures were likened to the heroes and heroines of antiquity through mythological representation, while at the same time fictional, mythological characters were given the dignity of history.[15]

14. Lee, "Ut Pictura Poesis," p. 216.

15. For an analysis of the analogical imagination that I see as underlying the *ut pictura poesis* representational system, see Michel Foucault, *The Order of Things* (New York, 1973), pp. 46–77. In Foucault's view, the Renaissance imagination functioned according to a "global system of correspondences" between words and things. In the seventeenth century, he maintains, all knowledge was related to a *mathesis* exemplified in the work of the early philosophers from Descartes to Condorcet. The basic cognitive shift from the sixteenth to the seventeenth century was, then, one from interpretation to order. Seen in these terms, what happened to the *ut pictura poesis* system in the course of the seventeenth century was that a *mathesis* became grafted onto an older set of correspondences. See below, Chapter 6. In his *Discourse of Modernism* (Ithaca, N.Y., 1982), Timothy J. Reiss discusses a discursive shift from "patterning" to the "analytico-referential," which, in his view, began to occur in the sixteenth century. Reiss's notion of discursive change differs from that of Foucault in its emphasis on continuity. I regret that I was not able to make full use of Reiss's richly suggestive book, which appeared after my own was already written.

Both artist and public needed erudition in order to master allegorical representation. Artists generally consulted one or several of the standard mythological manuals of the day, such as Cesare Ripa's *Iconologia,* in order to gain the information that Le Brun's critic accused him of overlooking. Whereas to us such imitation hardly seems faithful to reality, our seventeenth-century ancestors understood imitation as mediation. For them, imitation, in order to qualify as such, had to be artful. Allegory was another necessary component of "artifice." But allegory could not weigh too heavily on the object of representation. The allegory had to be decipherable to the restricted public that knew its language. If it was too obscure, it became pure diversion, enigma, depriving the representation of recognizable, imitative value. The absence of allegory, on the other hand, would have yielded a transparent, immediately recognizable truth.

The interposition of allegory between art and nature, representation and object of representation, yielded not truth but rather the semblance of truth, verisimilitude. The value of an artistic imitation was in direct proportion to its value as semblance of truth. Imitation was never very far removed from illusionism and trompe l'oeil.

Theoretically, verisimilitude was both a moral and an aesthetic concept. In practice, it was the locus of contradictions arising with modern application of ancient theory. From Aristotle's distinction between history as the description of what has happened and poetry as that of what might be, the moderns derived the moral idea of verisimilitude as the depiction of what ought to be. A semblance that in practice often approached illusion was not necessarily, however, the best vehicle for the expression of a moral truth. The contradictions of an aesthetic that placed value on both the truths of nature and the deceits of illusion perhaps underlay the Renaissance debate over literal versus ideal imitation. By the seventeenth century, critical opinion favored a version of Aristotle's ideal imitation. The artist was to correct the defects of nature in representing it as beautiful.[16] Horace's notion of decorum served to strengthen the semblance of truth by imposing appropriateness with respect to age, sex, social condition, and so forth, on the portrayal of character. His concept of what was appropriate for dramatization was widened to include what was morally

16. On ideal imitation in seventeenth-century France, see Bernard Tocanne, *L'Idée de nature en France dans la seconde moitié du XVIIe siècle* (Paris, 1978), pp. 325–46.

appropriate or inappropriate to representation. Filling in the moral gaps that verisimilitude may have left uncovered, decorum (*bienséance*) came to fulfill a censoring function in seventeenth-century France; it meant conformity to certain standards of decency and morality.

If successfully observed, verisimilitude and decorum could further the double artistic aim of pleasure and instruction. The goal of moving human passions seems to have been secondary. The ubiquitous use of the exemplum, especially in historical genres, epitomizes the fusion of these goals. If, following the rhetorical conventions of classical antiquity, an artist wished to hold up a contemporary historical figure as an example to posterity, presentation of this figure in the mythological disguise of an ancient god or goddess would intensify the pleasure of the moral lesson. In addition, the example would arouse the public's admiration.

It was to this system of representation that artists in seventeenth-century France almost automatically referred, even when they strove to reject it. With its supply of heroic mythology, its penchant for ideal imitation, its reliance on rules applicable to the noble genre of tragedy, it was a system well suited to the glorification of aristocratic patrons. The problem of the system's historical genesis is beyond the scope of this study. Jean Seznec's monumental *Survival of the Pagan Gods*, however, suggests some interesting possibilities. Seznec shows how classical form and subject came to be separated during the Middle Ages, when writers and manuscript copyists, painters and sculptors may have had access to either a written or a visual source, but not to both. Thus medieval and Christian characters whose representation was based on a visual model alone appeared as ancient deities, while an ancient god or goddess known solely from a written document turned up in medieval costume. One result of what Seznec calls the "strange game of changing places," in which Christian or contemporary historical figures appeared in the guise of ancient counterparts, was the development of an analogical mode of perception and representation. Lack of sources and the dispersion of manuscripts during the Middle Ages established an analogical artistic tradition so firmly that it endured beyond the synthesis of form and subject by which Seznec characterizes the Renaissance. Dynastic pride, he notes, inspired a tendency, extending from the Middle Ages onward, to seek national or royal origin in a mythological hero: the legend of the Trojan origin of the Franks was especially persistent. By the seventeenth century, both visual and verbal representation of, for example, the monarch as Hercules had become conventionalized.[17]

My study of the *ut pictura poesis* system, which encompassed all the arts in Europe from the sixteenth to the eighteenth century, is selective. My choice of artistic products was determined by considerations related to the system's social evolution rather than by deference to established masterpieces. I examine the functional development of a subset of this system in seventeenth-century France. In choosing to treat prose fiction, history, portraiture, and voyage literature, I neglect some of the more spectacular embodiments of the system: music, theater, opera, court ballet.[18] My subset, however, forms a kind of core, which I hope will serve as a starting point for future studies. The interrelationship of history and poetry, and in turn their relationship to the "sister art" of painting, formed the basis of the entire *ut pictura poesis* system. Here, then, is the logical place to begin. I have chosen to follow the system only from its full flowering at the beginning of the seventeenth century to the moment when it suffered irreversible erosion toward the end of Louis XIV's reign. The ideology that, as it developed, gradually disintegrated the system was not to become dominant until many decades after the terminating point of my study, the death of the Sun King. During the seventeenth century, the struggle for preeminence between nobles and bourgeois played a crucial role in determining the fortunes of this originally aristocratic representational system. By Louis XIV's death the system had entered its definitive decline. It was left to the France of Louis XV and Louis XVI to witness the denouement.

Art and Ideology: Some Theoretical Issues

Any study of cultural and ideological change will raise fundamental theoretical questions as to the interrelationship of culture, art, and ideology, the dynamic of cultural change, and the value of art. Recent work has opened fruitful directions for further exploration in a field where definitive answers are not readily

17. Jean Seznec, *The Survival of the Pagan Gods,* trans. Barbara F. Sessions (Princeton, 1972). See especially pp. 24–25, 212–13.

18. Margaret McGowan points out the fundamental importance of *ut pictura poesis* in court ballet and in the performing arts in France during the sixteenth and seventeenth centuries. See her *Art du ballet de cour en France, 1581–1643* (Paris, 1963), pp. 11–15.

forthcoming. I will propose no solutions, but will draw on a selection of the vast theoretical literature on these matters to suggest a ground for examining the particular historical situation that forms the subject of this book.

In focusing on the *ut pictura poesis* system, I identify what may be termed an aesthetic formation located in the cultural matrix of the ancien régime. Such formations are just as much material production as they are ideology. At once a social, economic, and technological process, art is "in ideology" at the same time that it produces it. Culture in general produces ideology anew.[19] It is a material production by and of ideology. Art as one branch of cultural production is conditioned by factors common to this production as a whole. The problem lies in discovering the distinctiveness of art in relation to ideology.

Art is no more identical to ideology than it is a reflection of it. Art as the "expression," no matter how distorted, of ideology or of social reality is merely a variation on the theme of reflection, and, like that theme, implies the dualism of superstructure and base. Interestingly enough, Marxist reflection theory, with its separation of art and "reality," has not departed significantly from the seventeenth-century version of Aristotelian mimesis. The step from mirroring nature to reflecting society is not a very large one. Marxist reflectionism has not strayed far from Aristotle.

Art produces but does not necessarily reproduce ideology; it reshapes it. Fredric Jameson, following Claude Lévi-Strauss, has defined the function of art as the provision of imaginary resolutions to contradictions unreconcilable in social reality.[20] This notion can be broadened. Art also refashions as objects of aesthetic contemplation the contradictions that it resolves. Poiesis is a remaking but not a repetition. Art reworks ideology for pleasure.

---

19. Pierre Macherey's *Pour une théorie de la production littéraire* (Paris, 1966) was a landmark in the theory of artistic production. Macherey denies the individual a primary role, because he considers that literature is produced under social-ideological conditions. Here he goes beyond Lucien Goldmann, who in his concept of intrasubjectivity introduced the social dimension but preserved the notion of creation. See "Le Sujet de la création culturelle," in Lucian Goldmann, *Marxisme et sciences humaines* (Paris, 1970), pp. 94–120. Terry Eagleton's idea of art as a production of ideology has provided an essential step in the elaboration of a dialectical-materialist view of art. See his *Criticism and Ideology*. Other critics have rightly emphasized the necessity of studying the conditions of artistic production. See, for example, Richard A. Peterson, ed., *The Production of Culture* (Beverly Hills, Calif., 1976).

20. Jameson, *Political Unconscious*, p. 79. For a very useful critique of reflection theory, see France Vernier, *L'Ecriture et les textes* (Paris, 1974), pp. 37–38, 45–47.

Critics in capitalist society have tended to view art more as product than as production. Because art has become a commodity under capitalism, the product has been severed from the process of its production, and works nominated as masterpieces have been relegated to the hallowed niche of the museum or the library. The artistic product, like any other product of human labor, is mediated by the process of its production. This process forms an individual social and economic history of the product. Provided with such a history, the inert aesthetic object springs to life, and we understand our distance from or proximity to it. Marx retrieved the living social relations of capital by analyzing its mediating conditions of production. If mediation is understood as the relationship between base and superstructure, the concept is of arguable theoretical value.[21] The concept of mediation should more properly be applied to the relations between product and conditions of production. This theoretical shift marks the distance between a Cartesian type of dualism and a materialist dialectic. The distinctiveness of art resides in the mediations between process and product resulting in an ideologically valued and valuable pleasure.

The very word "art" includes the meanings of both product and process of production. If we have specialized the meaning of product to that of a canonized work, in seventeenth-century France the sense of process was active in the sense of product, and the latter had yet to acquire its sacred aura. "Art" was just as much skill, dexterity, and "artifice" as it was their result. Art was not yet far from craft, or the product from the labor of its production.

So far I have spoken of ideological rather than of aesthetic value. If the transformation and ultimate demise of the *ut pictura poesis* system occurred along with the loss of its original ideological value, does that mean that it lost its aesthetic value as well? Certainly it did begin to do so increasingly for bourgeois artists and public in seventeenth- and eighteenth-century France. But what about us? We continue to place aesthetic value on certain products of a system that ceased to be active several centuries ago. Perhaps there will even be those among us who will hail some of the rather obscure material that I have uncovered as long-neglected works of art. I hesitate to claim this status for it. The designation of certain

---

21. Raymond Williams and Fredric Jameson are among those Marxists who have questioned the value of the concept of mediation between base and superstructure. See Williams, *Marxism and Literature*, pp. 97–100, and Jameson, *Political Unconscious*, pp. 39–41. Jameson's discussion is a particularly important contribution.

products as art has depended historically on a dialectical interaction of artistic product and social process resulting in society's selection of certain works for incorporation into an artistic canon. If we hold that changes in the canon are conditioned by social and ideological change, it is not easy to account for the survival of certain works of art beyond the stage of social development at which they were produced. We are still intimidated by the bugbear that Marx raised in the introduction to the *Grundrisse:* how to explain the transhistorical value of some works of art? This very value, however, is not static, but is revalued and changes along with changes in the mode of production. As art evolved from craft and patronized gift to commodity, for example, its exchange value came to equal if not to predominate over its use value.[22] Our valuation of seventeenth-century art is bound to the historical process whereby a new aesthetic develops dialectically from the old, with the emergence of a new ideological mode and a new mode of production. This is not to say that aesthetic value is merely relative, but that a critical understanding of it will comprehend it in a historical process.

Bourgeois artists and public did not discard the aristocratic *ut pictura poesis* system, but rather appropriated and adapted it. The seventeenth century, although it recognized individual talent, or "invention," placed yet greater value on tradition, and even a potentially revolutionary bourgeoisie respected this priority. Moreover, bourgeois were eager to adopt the ways of nobles, whom they wished to resemble. Nobles recognized themselves in the representations of *ut pictura poesis;* bourgeois wanted to recognize themselves in the same system. From this contradiction developed a new aesthetic that finally exploded the old.

A rising class appropriates and finally breaks through the traditional means of artistic and ideological production with a new culture that is nevertheless still linked to the old. In a well-known discussion of this phenomenon, Antonio Gramsci pointed to the necessity of considering how intellectuals—or artists—organically linked to the rising class use and appropriate traditional materials, institutions, and values.[23] While it struggled to adapt, transform, and finally shatter the *ut pictura poesis* system, the French bourgeoisie transmitted to posterity a fundamental aesthetic value that it inherited from a noble tradition: recognition. When this class

22. See Karl Marx, *Pre-Capitalist Economic Formations* (New York, 1965), pp. 104–5.
23. See Gramsci, *Selections from the Prison Notebooks*, pp. 5–14.

could no longer recognize itself in the *ut pictura poesis* system, it
fashioned a new mirror in bourgeois realism. The desire for a
mirror image in art has persisted centuries after the demise of the
aristocratic representational system. Even for Trotsky, art was just
as much "mirror" as it was "hammer."[24] Along with recognition,
the French bourgeoisie transmitted a new aesthetic value, organically linked to its subversive cultural activities: distancing. This
was not only the parodic process whereby through satire it removed itself from the aristocracy and the aristocratic values that it
endeavored to borrow. It was also the process whereby it saw itself
in an alien mirror. In our own world, where the bourgeois is now
the traditional, Bertolt Brecht understood how the now traditional (but not dominant) value of aesthetic distancing could be
appropriated for revolutionary ends.

The seventeenth-century French bourgeoisie preserved the traditional aesthetic value of recognition because it needed it for its
own ideological ends. If today's bourgeoisie has preserved an artistic canon along with certain aesthetic values inherited from the
past, has it not also done so for ideological ends? It seems that we
still need to see ourselves in Greek art, just as we need to measure
our distance from it. And we derive aesthetic pleasure from viewing ourselves as in but not of it. Aesthetic value is always social
value. If selected works of art have survived through different
historical periods, it is because they still resonate with ideological
meaning. This is not to reduce the aesthetic to the social and the
ideological, but to see the social reality in which it is embedded.
Only by studying the social production of art and aesthetic values
will we be able to arrive at a truly critical evaluation of art.

24. Leon Trotsky, *Literature and Revolution* (Ann Arbor, 1975), p. 137.

2

Shepherd and Madman

The big literary hit of seventeenth-century France was a novel
that hardly anyone reads today—in a modern edition its five volumes add up to more than 3,000 pages. But Honoré d'Urfé's
L'Astrée, which appeared in successive volumes from 1607 to 1627,
was a sensation, and its success resounded into the eighteenth
century. Jean-Jacques Rousseau was not above shedding a tear
over it. His *Nouvelle Héloïse* is in part a distant response to the
seventeenth-century novel. A fraction of a fraction of the French
population was responsible for *L'Astrée*'s success, for the over-
whelming majority of people in the ancien régime were illiterate.
Among the literate, it seems to have made the biggest initial impact among the nobility. They were the ones who eagerly devoured each volume as it appeared. Yet it was this tiny minority
that was to determine France's cultural preferences. If we have
more or less forgotten *L'Astrée* today, the aesthetic and literary
values to which it gave birth endured into French classicism and
beyond. Paradoxically, it was with this improbable idyll of love in
a fifth-century pastoral setting that very modern notions of artistic
truth arose. In the shepherds and shepherdesses of d'Urfé's Forez
the French nobility saw itself, and this image it called *vraisemblable.*

No sooner had all the volumes of *L'Astrée* been published than a
challenge to it appeared in the form of Charles Sorel's novel *Le
Berger extravagant* (1627–28). Sorel transforms Celadon, d'Urfé's
longsuffering hero, into Lysis, the dotty bourgeois who fancies

himself a shepherd. *Le Berger extravagant* is a demystification of the pastoral: shepherd becomes madman. Sorel, however, was satirizing not only d'Urfé but also the pastoral tradition and the aesthetic values in which a whole way of life was implicated. It is as if Sorel were saying: What you consider true to life I consider mad. In his satire Sorel suggests a new concept of artistic truth, a new form of the novel, and a different way of life. These elements of a system that eventually came to predominate in the modern novel develop dialectically from the old: the original makes the satire possible. The title of Sorel's revised edition of *Le Berger extravagant* (1633–34), *L'Anti-roman*, is richly suggestive: the "anti-novel" is itself a novel that tells us not only what a novel should not be, but also what it should be. In the confrontation of *L'Astrée* and *Le Berger extravagant* we find an incipient confrontation of two ideologies. Honoré d'Urfé, representative of the nobility of the sword, an aristocracy with a limited future, used a long-venerated tradition that was to disappear shortly after the publication of his novel. *L'Astrée* was really the last of the great pastoral novels. Sorel, the bourgeois with aristocratic pretensions, representative of a rising class, wrote not only *Le Berger extravagant,* but also *Francion*, another comic novel of a type that was to become increasingly popular. Yet it was *L'Astrée* that captured the attention of seventeenth-century France; *Le Berger extravagant* had in comparison only a modest success. How did it happen that a work representative of a literary genre and a social class that were both past their prime won out in public esteem? Why did Sorel's particular brand of realism go underground in France during most of the seventeenth century only to reemerge triumphant later on in the modern novel? How does a class whose dominance is much eroded come to impose its view of what is true to life on a rising class, and how does the rising class in turn use what it receives from the past? These are some of the issues that we will explore in confronting the shepherd with his mad travesty.

L'Astrée and Aristocratic Ideology

L'Astrée is the story of a group of shepherds and shepherdesses in the pleasant region of Forez in fifth-century Gaul. Despite a passing reference or two to sheep, the main activity carried on by the banks of the river Lignon is love—or rather not love itself, but the discourse of love. For thousands of pages these people seem to do nothing but talk. According to a form inherited from collections of tales such as *The Decameron* or *The Canterbury Tales,* there is a main or frame story (such as a pilgrimage) and subordinate or framed stories (such as the tales the pilgrims tell to pass the time). In the case of *L'Astrée,* the story-within-a-story structure becomes very intricate, with one tale leading to another so that there is often a story-within-a-story-within-a-story. The stories do not form discrete units as they do in collections of tales, but are interconnected through their characters, who end up knowing each other or being related in some way. Theirs is a small world. Technically, the connections are so rigorously interwoven that Baro, one of d'Urfé's two continuators, was able to tie up the threads with relative ease in the fourth and fifth volumes, which he completed after d'Urfé's death in 1625. The tales are interspersed with letters and with verses pertaining to the action in question. The central action and characters belong to Forez. The frame story concerns a trio of shepherdesses, Astrée, Diane, and Phillis, all good friends, who are courted with varying degrees of misfortune by three shepherds, respectively, Celadon, Silvandre, and Lycidas (Celadon and Lycidas are brothers). The main pair of lovers is Astrée and Celadon. After Astrée banishes Celadon for an imagined offense, he returns disguised as Alexis, the daughter of the local druid, Adamas. Thus protected, he is able to enjoy the somewhat inappropriate ardor of Astrée's "innocent" affections. The gallery of characters in the Forez group includes one Hylas, the Don Juan of the crowd, who seemingly violates the novel's code of love by running from woman to woman. Matched with the Platonist Silvandre, he offers material for the age-old debates on the nature of love, constancy versus inconstancy, and so on, which crop up throughout the novel. These debates, together with the "courts of love," or practice of submitting an amorous quarrel to the judgment of a higher authority, hark back to courtly medieval forms and help to create the archaic atmosphere of the novel. On the margin of the Forez group are the *nymphes* who inhabit palaces and have a higher social standing than that of the shepherds and shepherdesses. Outside the main circle of action is the "real world" of the fifth century: that of emperors and rulers, political intrigue, violence, and war. Violence and war, however, impinge on the inner or "fictional" world when the villain Polemas declares war on Amasis, a neighboring *nymphe.* We can see from this structure of social hierarchies within the novel that the pastoral group occupies the center and the "real" or historical group the outside: myth prevails over history.

D'Urfé left the frame story and many of the framed stories unresolved for thousands of pages. This fact in part accounts for the intense impatience with which the aristocratic readers of the novel awaited the publication of each successive volume. But there were other reasons as well for their avid curiosity.

Since the sixteenth century the restricted little society that composed the French nobility had carried on its cultural life in salons. Interrupted by the ravages of the Religious Wars, the salons resumed their existence in a burst of new vitality at the beginning of the seventeenth century. Following the examples of such women as Marguerite de Valois, Henri IV's repudiated wife; Madeleine de la Ferté-Sennecterre, formerly one of Catherine de Médicis's maids of honor; and Mademoiselle de Gournay, Montaigne's "adopted daughter," who was responsible for the posthumous edition of his essays, several *grandes dames* began to gather about them little circles of writers, dilettantes, and assorted *beaux esprits*. In the first decade of the seventeenth century, Catherine de Vivonne-Savella, marquise de Rambouillet; Marie Bruneau, dame des Loges; and Charlotte des Ursins, vicomtesse d'Auchy, disenchanted with court life and in any case confined at home by numerous pregnancies, opened Parisian salons that were to serve as models of the kind. The constellation of luminaries surrounding these ladies represented cliques separated by all kinds of petty intrigues and rivalries yet socially interconnected. Parisians and provincials, aristocrats and eventually even some select bourgeois, all gathered in these fashionable homes to exchange news, compose verses and epigrams, and display their wit. It has been shown that the seventeenth-century salon was a meeting place for the new and the old nobility, for robe and sword, for the ambitious bourgeois and the established aristocrat. The salon was not, however, a democratic institution, but one that helped to form a new elite.[1] Even with the admission of those whose blood was not truly blue, it was a highly restricted group. Everyone knew everyone else, and nothing was so passionately interesting as the latest gossip. What, for example, was the vicomte d'Auchy going to do about his wife's affair with the poet Malherbe? This must have been one of the most exciting questions of 1609, the year when

---

1. See Carolyn C. Lougee, *Le Paradis des Femmes: Women, Salons, and Social Stratification in Seventeenth-Century France* (Princeton, 1976), pp. 113–37.

things had come to such a pass that the enraged husband decided to lock up his wife and close her salon.[2]

Such were the readers of *L'Astrée*. If they themselves did not possess copies of the book, they borrowed one from a friend or attended a reading. In the first several centuries of printing, editions were small and books were expensive. Reading aloud was not merely a social occasion; it was a practical and sometimes, in the case of the illiterate, an imperative alternative to private reading. Henry IV supposedly had *L'Astrée* read to him. Reading aloud was a regular practice in Mme de Rambouillet's *chambre bleue,* where the playwright Pierre Corneille read his *Polyeucte,* the critic and would-be poet Jean Chapelain his *Pucelle.* Another diversion of the beau monde was dressing up in the disguise of characters from *L'Astrée* and playing at recreating the atmosphere of the novel. This game had a solid tradition behind it, since the production of amateur pastorals had been going on in many a château for some time. The habitués of the Hôtel de Rambouillet would engage in such theatricals also or even on occasion don, for example, the garb of King Arthur's knights.

In this world where to see and to be seen was the chief activity, the nobility was enthralled by the spectacle of itself. It adopted disguise in order to see itself in disguise. If *L'Astrée* became, as Mlle de Gournay said, the "breviary of the ladies and gallants of the Court,"[3] it was not only for its educational value as a manual of civility but also because its readers delighted in what they perceived as their reflected image. D'Urfé knew his audience well, because, socially, he was one of them. Like all successful authors, he could given them what they wanted.

In his preface, "L'Autheur à la bergère Astrée," d'Urfé coyly warns his readers not to look for the real-life counterparts to Astrée and Celadon. If the characters of his pastoral are not representations of real people, are they then merely ordinary shepherds and shepherdesses? Hardly, says the author. These folk speak too well; they are not poor peasants but rather well-bred people who have adopted the life-style of shepherds to get away from it all and lead a better life. To defend his representation, d'Urfé adds that he has seen shepherds and shepherdesses on stage not dressed in old rags and clodhoppers, like common villagers, but gracing the scene with golden staffs and skirts of

2. See Emile Magne, *La Vie quotidienne au temps de Louis XIII* ([Paris, 1948]), pp. 206–48.

3. Mlle de Gournay, *L'Ombre* (Paris, 1626), pp. 593–94.

taffeta. They talk not about their flocks, which could interest no one, but rather about love, as they do in Tasso. In other words, d'Urfé's shepherds and shepherdesses are nobles dressed up as if for any amateur theatrical in a local château. Moreover, says the author, his pastoral picture is in perfect conformity with the *bienséance des bergers,* or correct representation of shepherds, because to depict a plausible shepherd all you need is some sign or other indicating that he is a shepherd. Such recognizable signs, according to d'Urfé, suffice for those who engage in pastorals to represent something "as naturally as possible," so why should they not suffice for him, who is in any event creating a work not to be seen but to be heard?[4] The passage from the visual to the auditory is significant, for much of *L'Astrée* can be considered as a transposition from one realm to the other. The mirror and spectacle themes so prominent in baroque art are central to d'Urfé's novel, in which the nobility found a mirror image of itself.

D'Urfé undermines his own disclaimer. His shepherds and shepherdesses gain their plausibility not from any resemblance they may bear to real rustics but from their allegorical or metaphorical relationship to nobles. D'Urfé's readers did exactly what he told them not to do—as he must have known they would—and looked for the real person behind the disguise. *L'Astrée* is a roman à clef.

Modern criticism has tended to turn up its nose at this aspect of *L'Astrée,* as if it were irrelevant to the artistic worth of the novel. But we will not understand the art of this novel—that is, the meaning of the aesthetic it embodies—if we do not understand the relationship of the roman à clef form to the type of verisimilitude it expresses. We are concerned here not with d'Urfé's intentions but with the way in which his novel was read and the value of its verisimilitude for his readers. For there is no doubt that the novel struck its public both as a roman à clef and as true to life. Even d'Urfé's parodist, Charles Sorel, had to admit that *L'Astrée* contained stories that were *vraisemblables* and conversations that were "natural."[5] Mlle de Scudéry, in the preface to her novel *Ibrahim* (1641), declares herself an "adorer" of d'Urfé, whose work she has loved for twenty years. Everything in it is marvelous and beautiful, says she, but most important of all, everything is natural and *vraisemblable.* Now what exactly does she find *vraisemblable* in this slightly antiquated pastoral? She elaborates: You could call

---

4. See Honoré d'Urfé, *L'Astrée,* ed. Hugues Vaganay (Lyon, 1925–28), 1:5–8.
5. Charles Sorel, *La Bibliothèque françoise* (Paris, 1664), p. 158.

d'Urfé a "painter of the soul." He knows how to unearth the most intimate secrets of the heart, and in the variety of the models for his painting "everyone finds his portrait."[6]

Notice the visual imagery that Mlle de Scudéry uses. D'Urfé himself used similar language. The readers of *L'Astrée* were seeking their own portraits. In the illustrations by several of the most famous engravers of the time accompanying the 1633 edition of *L'Astrée* (the importance of which may be measured by the fact that lavishly engraved editions of novels were unusual because of the cost and the corporative restrictions involved), some readers may even have sought their physical likenesses.[7] Composing verbal portraits or thumbnail sketches in prose or verse of various real people was a salon pastime that slipped easily into literature, given that its practitioners, like the poet Voiture, were often both salon habitués and belletrists. Mlle de Scudéry's language suggests that readers of her time sought, if they did not find, a mirror image of themselves in their "portraits." Nothing is more important in writing a novel, she says, than to impress profoundly on the reader's mind "the Idea, or better yet, the Image of the Heroes." If this task is done correctly, it will seem that the reader knows the heroes, for an impression of familiarity is what really interests the public. Now in order to convey the sense of personal acquaintance, she continues, it is not enough merely to relate what happens to the characters; it is necessary to reveal their feelings through their discourse.

The mirror image results from a correspondence requiring an analogical imagination typical of sixteenth-century thought and language.[8] *L'Astrée* continues the past as it inaugurates the future. It succeeds in imposing verisimilitude by means of the time-honored mode of analogy. Shepherd corresponds to noble through a metaphorical and, in its systematization, an allegorical translation. The garb is different, but likeness is maintained through a variety of means. The discourse, too, may be familiar. This is certainly the case in *L'Astrée*, where the characters speak like personal acquaintances of the nobility because their conversations are straight out of a salon like the *chambre bleue*. In either verbal or illustrated portraits, personal characteristics may also be familiar to readers. Thus if the description of a shepherd or a

6. [Madeleine] de Scudéry, *Ibrahim, ou l'Illustre Bassa* (Paris, 1641), Preface (unpaginated).
7. See Emile Roy, *La Vie et les oeuvres de Charles Sorel* (Paris, 1891), pp. 117–18.
8. See Michel Foucault, *The Order of Things* (New York, 1973), pp. 46–77.

shepherdess includes enough distinguishing characteristics of a given person—physical or psychological traits, details of personal history—it will permit the identification to be made. Everyone who was anyone in 1624 rushed to get a copy of Jean Gombauld's *Endimion*, for example, because it was interpreted as an allegorical account of the author's infatuation with Marie de Médicis, the queen mother, who appears as Diana in the novel. The book's engravings make the identification explicit: Diana bears the features of the queen mother (fig. 1).

How eagerly d'Urfé's readers must have sought the originals behind the many portraits comprising the numerous cast of characters in *L'Astrée!* A young friend of d'Urfé's, the lawyer Olivier Patru, stopped off en route to Italy to see the novelist and to try to extract his secrets from him. Patru was supposed to get more information on his way back, a year later, but by that time d'Urfé was dead. The lawyer nonetheless drew up a set of "keys" to *L'Astrée* and published them in a collection of his own writings in 1681. They also appear in a bastardized 1733 edition of the novel titled *L'Astrée de M. d'Urfé, pastorale allégorique avec la clé.* D'Urfé himself gave much credence to the legend of the keys by writing to his friend Etienne Pasquier in 1607, shortly after the publication of the first volume of *L'Astrée,* that the novel was the "story of his youth" and of his "passions" or "follies." Pasquier in his reply praised d'Urfé for the appropriateness of his expression. D'Urfé had only followed the laws of *bienséance,* he said, in choosing pastoral figures to represent the lords and ladies of Forez ("Forest," hence a pastoral region).[9] Like his contemporaries, Pasquier saw in the story of d'Urfé's youth to which the author had alluded the real-life romance of Honoré and his sister-in-law and future wife, Diane de Châteaumorand. If in the early eighteenth century the chronicler Père Nicéron saw little interest in *L'Astrée*'s keys, he nevertheless gave the novel credit for being the first to lift the genre out of its "barbarism"; all the stories contained in it, he says, have a foundation in truth—in the guise of shepherds and shepherdesses, the author portrays his own and his friends' loves.[10]

The reflection in this literary mirror is a distorted one. Refracted through metaphor and allegory, it is a stylized equivalence. The noble ladies and gentlemen represented by their pastoral counterparts were used to identifying themselves by their dis-

9. Estienne Pasquier, *Choix de lettres,* ed. D. Thickett (Geneva, 1956), pp. 53–54.

10. Père Jean Pierre Nicéron, *Mémoires pour servir à l'histoire des hommes illustres,* vol. 6 (Paris, 1728), pp. 225–26.

1. Diana, by Crispin de Passe. From Jean Gombauld, *Endimion* (1624). By permission of the Houghton Library, Harvard University.

guise. They even adopted pseudonyms that functioned as abbreviated metaphors in the social intercourse of the salon. Thus thanks to the poet Malherbe, Catherine de Vivonne became known to the faithful of her *chambre bleue* as Arthénice, an anagram of her name. The rather strait-laced Mme des Loges was transformed into Uranie by the writer Guez de Balzac. If for Mlle de Scudéry, the Sapho of her own salon, the novelist must convey the "Idea" or the "Image" of the hero, it is because the conjunction of these two words in the aristocratic imagination of the time must have become habitual. Image can function as a Platonic Idea, incorporating a truth or reality of which its reflection then functions as an equivalent. Through long tradition, d'Urfé's arcadia had acquired for his readers the force of a higher truth. The many engraved mythological portraits in novels and other books of the time carried, as we shall see later, the same force of truth.[11] Henri IV as a modern Hercules, for instance, stands in the same relationship to his "portrait" as the aristocrat to the shepherd. Both real-life figures are equivalents of a reality or truth that is elsewhere. But if the image is the truth, where then is the reality? Is the image always the Idea, the original Platonic truth and reality, of which everyday reality is but the reflection? Or is the image merely a reflected image of the original, which in the case of *L'Astrée* would be the reality of the model, the real noble key to the portrait?

Such delight in apparent confusion, basic to the trompe l'oeil quality of baroque art, was natural in a society where life imitated art as much as art endeavored to imitate life. The story-within-a-story structure of *L'Astrée*, for example, may reflect forms of conversation in salons. Certainly the interspersed letters and verse closely resemble genres practiced in real life by salon habitués. Yet the process of imitation is reversed in one of the favorite salon games, the *jeu des romans*, in which, in imitation of the prevalent novel form, one person started a story and then broke it off, leaving it up to the next person to continue. The same reversal is evident in the customary aristocratic practice of copying love letters from novels when pressed for an inspired billet-doux.[12]

Life and art do of course stand in a reciprocal, really a dialectical relationship to each other, but that is not the question here. We must understand that the seventeenth-century nobility lived a

11. See Françoise Bardon, *Le Portrait mythologique à la cour de France sous Henri IV et Louis XIII: Mythologie et politique* (Paris, 1974).

12. See Maurice Magendie, *La Politesse mondaine et les théories de l'honnêteté en France, au XVIIe siècle, de 1600 à 1660* (Paris, 1925), 1:167–68.

confusion of the two, and for very good reasons. Salon life was built precisely on the model of art; the underlying effort of the salon habitués was to create an aesthetically acceptable enclave, to transform their life, with its annoyances and disappointments, into a work of art.[13] Thus for the nobles, life referred more and more to art rather than the reverse. Mme de Sevigné's comments on *L'Astrée* are typical. Rather than refer the novel to life, she refers life to the novel. On a visit to the banks of the Allier River she expects to see the shepherds of *L'Astrée*. When a neighboring priest drops by, she dubs him the "Adamas of the region."[14] What unacceptable conditions of life necessitated this flight into art?

By the end of the sixteenth century, after the disastrous Religious Wars, the French nobility was in such desperate straits that it had begun to petition the king for charity. In 1607 Henri IV actually complied with its request by adapting existing charitable institutions for the use of impoverished nobles.[15] Adding to the woes of the nobility was the fact that income from land had not kept pace with the accelerated economic developments of the sixteenth century. The commercial bourgeoisie had begun rapidly to outstrip the old landed nobility in wealth and power. The sale of offices had become an increasingly widespread means of raising money for the crown since the reign of François I. To the horror of the old nobles, hordes of arrivistes were buying their way into the nobility through the titles that these offices could confer, or through other means open to them: intermarriage with the nobility, purchase of land, "living nobly" for several generations. No longer legally a *roturier* (nonnoble), the newly ennobled bourgeois enjoyed tax exemption along with the members of the Second Estate. Although the nobility registered claims against this practice in the 1614 Estates General, it was only between 1670 and 1680 that the monarchy took a decisive step, when Colbert began a close examination of titles. The new *noblesse de robe* posed perhaps the most serious threat to the old nobility by their privileges, prestige, and power as judicial officers. Also, bourgeois financiers were accumulating wealth so quickly that their influence penetrated to the highest

13. Dorothy Backer discusses this phenomenon in relation specifically to the lives of seventeenth-century French women of the salons. See her *Precious Women* (New York, 1974).

14. Mme de Sévigné, *Lettres*, ed. M. Monmerqué, vol. 4 (Paris, 1862), pp. 453, 457.

15. Robert Mandrou, *Classes et luttes de classes au début du XVII⁰ siècle* (Messina, 1965), p. 39.

circles. It was to them that the monarchy looked to fill its depleted coffers. The hated tax collectors, moreover, were recruited from among the ranks of nonnobles. Between 1620 and 1640, nobles intervened several times in conflicts between peasants and royal fiscal agents. Here the interests of the seigneurs and their peasants seem to have coincided: both aimed to benefit from the disappearance of the tax collector. But whereas the seigneur was attempting to wrest the exclusive right to levy taxes from the royal agents to as to enjoy all the revenue himself, the peasant strove in vain to throw off a financial burden that in any case would fall on him alone. The alliance between noble and peasant was always precariously temporary; the struggle between noble and bourgeois was an ongoing contest for the meager resources of the peasantry. Only in the second half of the century, in the so-called feudal reaction, were nobles to obtain some income from those whom they had supposedly protected earlier. During the period of Colbert, the monarchy, caught between the necessity of supporting a nobility still essential to its interests and an increasing reliance on credit from bourgeois financiers, tried (ineffectively) to divert taxation from land to commerce and industry.[16]

The breakdown of traditional social stratification was furthered by Henri IV's installation in 1604 of the *paulette,* an annual tax legalizing the transmission of certain offices from generation to generation. One of the consequences of the *paulette* was to weaken further the status of the old nobility, for if social position could be inherited through cash payment, status no longer depended solely on birth. Given the legalized confusion between old and new nobility, how could the old nobles succeed in distinguishing themselves as such? And how could new nobles gain social recognition from those whom they challenged in order to emulate them? On the one hand, bourgeois with enough money to do so were purchasing legal nobility. On the other, the power of the old nobility had begun its slow decline. Its military importance had lessened considerably, through both evasion of service on its own part and penetration into the ranks by *roturiers.* The majority of officeholders were bourgeois or new nobles. Even vestimentary distinctions were breaking down. The parvenus were making so bold as

---

16. Ibid. See also Boris Porshnev, *Les Soulèvements populaires en France de 1623 à 1648* (Paris, 1963), pp. 123–27, 555–57.

to dress in aristocratic silk or velvet.[17] Attempts to enforce existing
regulations concerning vestimentary and protocol distinctions—
precedence at convocations, forms of salutation—did little to allay
the discomfort of the nobles because such attempts could have no
impact on the real situation of socioeconomic transformation.

In the face of economic displacement and loss of prestige, the
nobility's strategy was necessarily regressive. What it called for was
a return to the good old days. In the Estates General of 1614 it
requested that the number of offices be cut back to that existing
around a century earlier, under François 1.[18] In addition, it revived the old debate over birth and merit to its own advantage,
clumsily trying to overcome any contradictions this argument may
have involved. If, reasoned the noble, I have been displaced in
office by a *roturier,* this is because birth and merit are not rewarded. The argument raises difficult problems, for if the noble
would have liked to see offices distributed on the basis of merit,
how could he disregard the *roturier*'s claims to office precisely on
the basis of merit? In fact, the *roturier* was often more qualified
than the noble, especially for positions in the judiciary. Education
was not a high priority of the old nobility, and its members were
not necessarily better educated than the *roturiers* by the the seventeenth century. Its logical tactic was therefore to claim that birth
in and of itself constituted merit and that the noble combination
of birth and merit was diametrically opposed to the vulgar wealth
of the parvenu. True virtue would thus be allied with birth. After
all, the nobles, regardless of their merit, really wanted power and
privilege, their traditional prerogatives. Although the assertion
that birth and merit go together was by no means the only position taken by the nobility in explicit debates on the issue in the
sixteenth and seventeenth centuries,[19] it formed an essential component of an ideology that in its decline became increasingly satu-
rated with nostalgia.

17. Davis Bitton, *The French Nobility in Crisis, 1560–1640* (Stanford, 1969). For a
discussion of the question of military services, see pp. 26–41; for vestimentary and
protocol distinctions, see pp. 100–101. In his study of the new nobility in sixteenth-century France, George Huppert stresses the solidarity of this group,
which, according to him, did not wish to be identified with the *gentilshommes de race.*
By the seventeenth century, the situation had changed, and what had been a
distinct group (his "gentry") merged more and more with the nobility. Nevertheless, he asserts, social distinctions between the two continued to be made. See
George Huppert, *Les Bourgeois Gentilshommes* (Chicago, 1977), pp. 174–77.

18. Mandrou, *Classes et luttes de classes,* pp. 46–47.

19. See the discussion of this matter in Bitton, *French Nobility in Crisis,* pp. 77–
91. See also pp. 45–46.

The doctrine of innate social and moral distinctions belonged to a feudal hierarchical ideology in which the highest born was considered also the most virtuous. Both the centralization of the monarchy and the ascension of the bourgeoisie in seventeenth-century France were to result in the formation of a new ideology that would seriously threaten but not destroy the predominance of the older one. The hereditary configuration of virtues attributed to the noble included military prowess, courtly refinement and expertise in the art of love, benevolent protection of inferiors, chivalric behavior. The remarkable increase in the production of sentimental chivalric and heroic novels after the Religious Wars, at the beginning of the seventeenth century, attests to the nostalgic attraction that this ideology exerted at a time when its basis in socioeconomic reality had all but disappeared.

Cast in a pastoral genre that belonged to a previous age, *L'Astrée* offered its noble readers satisfactions that an outworn ideology could provide only with increasing difficulty. D'Urfé holds out the vision of a golden age in which the noble face shines through the transparent mask of the shepherd. There is no problem of social distinction here: d'Urfé repeatedly tells us that the high birth of his characters is immediately evident in their virtue, in their refinement of speech and manner. Note that the bourgeois is virtually absent from this paradise. The pastor figure merges with that of his flock. The role reversal between the seigneur and his peasant suggests a solidarity against the bourgeois, who could prove a threat to the feudal structure in the form, for example, of the tax collector. But we can have no doubts as to the real identity of d'Urfé's shepherd, for when the war against Polemas breaks out, the "shepherds" are exposed as true-blue members of the *noblesse d'epée* in taking up arms against the villain. In *L'Astrée* we find a compromise solution to the ideological debate on birth and virtue: the nobles are *poor* (shepherds) but virtuous; in their poverty they are easily identifiable by their virtue. Wealth and virtue are implicitly opposed to each other—the gentlefolk have voluntarily shed their worldliness to lead the simple life—and virtue and nobility are allied. The ambition of the noble in the real world is replaced by love in the world of Forez. The ubiquitous seventeenth-century French theme of *repos*, which d'Urfé uses here, has a distinct ideological value. Enforced idleness becomes voluntary retirement. Loss of social and economic privilege is transmuted into a world-weary flight from the world. The code of love in *L'Astrée* and in the salons where *L'Astrée* was used as a manual of

47

civility became ultimately self-repressive. As the centralized monarchy under Louis XIII and Louis XIV adopted fiscal policies detrimental to the nobility, the crown was obliged to repress challenges to its authority on the part of nobles. Ultimately the nobility was to see some advantage in a resigned acquiescence. It was this attitude that Louis XIV encouraged and reinforced in building up his vast reserves of courtiers at Versailles.

One reaction of the displaced nobility was, therefore, an attempt to strengthen its ideology by redoubled claims to its traditional myths. Thus the nostalgic image of the chivalrous knight is projected into the somewhat eclectic mythology of *L'Astrée,* where shepherd and soldier, courtier and military hero rub elbows in the idealized golden age of the nobility. Keys to the portraits give the mythology its sensationalism. They further encourage readers to take the metaphor seriously, to make of mythology a mirror, and to see themselves in the shepherds.

The seventeenth-century reader, then, saw a reflection in the metaphorical mirror of d'Urfé's pastoral. What we see instead is a projection, a literary image created not in reflection of any social reality but as a vehicle for the hopes, dreams, and fantasies of a class whose ideology was embarking on its long descent into obsolescence. *L'Astrée* produced a refinement rather than a reflection of aristocratic ideology. The relationship between literary work and ideology is not one of simple reflection but of historically conditioned complexity.[20] Verisimilitude here functions as a mediating force. It allows the reader to validate the work in terms of the reigning ideology and to validate the ideology in terms of the work.

Ideological Implications of *Le Berger extravagant*

Charles Sorel, born in 1602, belonged to the generation following that of d'Urfé. D'Urfé fought for the Catholic League; Sorel's father was in the League. Charles Sorel's grandfather was a magistrate in a small town in Picardy. His father went to Paris, bought

20. Much recent work on the relationship between literature and ideology has responded to that of Pierre Macherey, *Pour une théorie de la production littéraire* (Paris, 1974). Macherey's notion of literature as a distorted reflection of ideology has, in my opinion, been largely superseded by the efforts of, among others, Raymond Williams, Terry Eagleton, France Vernier, and Fredric Jameson. See Chapter 1 above, nn. 7, 9, 20.

himself a magistrate's study, and married a sister of Charles Bernard, a historiographer of the king. Sorel's sister married a magistrate. The author of *Le Berger extravagant*, then, was one of those whom d'Urfé banished from the world of *L'Astrée*. Within one generation, Sorel's upwardly mobile bourgeois family moved from the provinces to Paris, buying its way higher and higher into the ranks of the judiciary. By the time of Charles Sorel's youth the family was established, in possession of good property, of *rentes*, or an income from interest on loans to the government, and of a country house. The young author, following the practice of many writers at the time, attached himself successively to several aristocratic patrons, but was ultimately able to free himself of this constraint with an independent income. He could then buy his uncle's office of historiographer and return to life in the bosom of his family.

The Sorel family history illustrates the social mobility of *officiers* who within a few generations could rapidly ascend the echelons of the judiciary. In the upper strata—that, for example, of presidents of *parlement*—the long robe carried great prestige. Office-holding in and of itself, however, even if it meant ennoblement, did not guarantee the desired social recognition. Solid, long-established families of the robe could mingle easily with families of the sword, but families on the way up, like the Sorels, were often caught in a web of social ambiguities. The most cherished hope of such a family was not merely to feather its nest, as the Sorels succeeded so well in doing. It was to pass itself off as noble. The sale of offices flattered this dream, magnetizing bourgeois with the mystique of the nobility. Thus the Sorels attempted to delude themselves perhaps even more than others by believing that they were related to the old Picard family of Sorel d'Ugny, which supposedly included among its ancestors the early kings of England and Agnès Sorel. Charles Sorel retraces this fictionalized genealogy in his *Solitude et amour philosophique de Cléomède* (Paris, 1640). In reality, the Sorel d'Ugny family were simply neighbors of the author's family in Picardy.[21] But if Charles Sorel reveals his pretensions to nobility in the *Solitude*, he does not hesitate to satirize the nobility in his two best-known novels, *Francion* and *Le Berger extravagant*. Torn between conflicting social claims, Sorel provides an excellent example of the situation of those writers who came to dominate the literary scene in seventeenth-century France. Ra-

21. See Roy, *Charles Sorel*, pp. 1–11. On the social mobility of *officiers*, see Roland Mousnier, *La Vénalité des offices sous Henri IV et Louis XIII* (Rouen, [1945]), pp. 495–541.

cine, La Bruyère, Mme de La Fayette would find themselves in a historical predicament not appreciably different from his.

Before we counterpose *Le Berger extravagant* to *L'Astrée*, one of the chief targets of its satire, a warning is necessary: this is not a simple case of a bourgeois versus an aristocratic novel. Within *Le Berger extravagant* itself there is an ideological ambivalence typifying bourgeois artistic production under Louis XIII and Louis XIV. It is only by taking into account the novel's basic ambivalence that we will be able to follow the dialectical progression of verisimilitude from *L'Astrée* to *Le Berger extravagant*. For in *Le Berger extravagant*, Sorel was responding to a type of verisimilitude found in such novels as *L'Astrée*. His response is both positive and negative. The resulting verisimilitude in his comic novel incorporates even as it shuns the earlier variety we find in *L'Astrée*. This development is crucial to an understanding both of *vraisemblance* in French classicism and of the later history of realism in the modern novel.

Le Berger extravagant, unlike *L'Astrée*, is set in the contemporary "real" world. Louys, the orphaned son of a Parisian silk merchant, has completely succumbed to the mania of reading novels. His cousin and guardian, Adrian, had had hopes that with money left him by his father, Louys would buy an office and bring the luster of nobility to the family. But alas, instead of buying lawbooks Louys perversely buys only novels. They acquire so vivid a reality in his quixotic mind that he desires nothing more than to go off to Forez to find Astrée, Celadon, and the entire troop of d'Urfé's shepherds. Some gentlemen friends help to fulfill his dream by carting him off to Brie, which they easily deceive him into thinking is Forez. Louys plays out his fantasy to the extent of metamorphosing himself into the shepherd Lysis and the servant woman he loves, Catherine, into the shepherdess Charite. Are we to see in these names a reference to the pseudonyms adopted by the salon habitués? Undoubtedly, for Sorel lets us know in his "Remarks" on Book 1 (part of a lengthy learned commentary that he appended to his novel) that Lysis did not change Catherine into the full anagram of her name, which would have given Arthénice.[22]

22. Charles Sorel, *Le Berger extravagant* (Paris, 1627–28), facs. ed. (Geneva, 1972), 3:18 (554). The three volumes of the original are paginated separately; in the facsimile edition, which also reproduces the page numbers of the original, they are paginated consecutively. Accordingly, in all references to the facsimile edition, I will give first the page number of the original, followed by that of the facsimile edition in parentheses.

The allusion is of course to Mme de Rambouillet. In addition, Lysis announces that for over three years he has been part of a little group of young men and women who have been playing at *L'Astrée*, using names from the novel. *Le Berger extravagant* satirizes the portrait *and* the model, the pastoral representation and the real-life nobles who appear as shepherds in the novel, who play at being shepherds outside the novel, in real life. But they are not the only class satirized. Sorel devotes considerable space to a satire of Louys's very bourgeois guardian, Adrian. And what are we to make of the novel's ending? Lysis is finally cured of his literary insanity and, good bourgeois that he is, he adopts the very bourgeois solution of marriage in wedding Charite. His felicity cannot, however, be complete until he has bought an office exempting him from the *taille,* one of the most onerous taxes, as so many bourgeois actually attempted to do. So Louys can finally fulfill a real dream, as opposed to a literary fantasy, and transform himself into a country gentleman. Even Charite turns out to be better connected than a mere servant.

The double identity of Sorel's comic hero is one instance of ambivalence in the novel. As Lysis, he embodies both the portrait and the model of a shepherd from d'Urfé's Forez. Lysis, that is, serves to satirize both a noble literature and a way of life. In Louys, however, we see a "serious" progression from bourgeois to ennobled bourgeois. Of course we do not know how seriously Sorel may have taken the latter movement. What matters is that both a satire and a rehabilitation of the noble are present in this tale of a bourgeois who is ridiculous in his noble disguise as a shepherd, but who finds sanity in living nobly at the end.

In Louys/Lysis we see a double portrait that forms the essential structure of the novel. Sorel's contribution to the development of verisimilitude in *Le Berger extravagant* is that he calls into question the relationship of representation to represented. Both Louys and Lysis represent the Parisian bourgeois. Lysis, however, also represents Louys's representation of himself. What, therefore, was "true to life" in *L'Astrée*—that is, the transparency of the shepherd's mask through which a noble countenance could be perceived—is comedy in *Le Berger extravagant*, where the mask has become masquerade: through the mask of Lysis we see only the silly bourgeois Louys. *Le Berger extravagant* is both a satire and a parody: to denounce a mode of representation Sorel finds ludicrous, he must adopt the same mode himself.

With the question of representation at the center of Sorel's project, it is no wonder that discussions of portraits turn up obsessively throughout his novel. Portraits epitomize the very imitative virtue of conventional artistic representation which Sorel began to question.

The most famous portrait in *Le Berger extravagant* was illustrated by the Dutch engraver Crispin de Passe the Younger, for the original edition of Sorel's novel (fig. 2). (It was reengraved by Michel van Lochom for the 1646 edition.) In the text, Louys asks his friend Anselme to make him an engraved portrait of his lady love, echoing similar requests often heard in France at the time. Copperplate engraving, a technical innovation of the sixteenth century, had all but displaced woodcuts by the seventeenth. The fineness and precision of this new technique could produce likenesses so exact that people placed them in folders or wallets and carried them around in the way we do photographs today.[23] When Anselme finally gives Lysis the finished product, however, Lysis cannot recognize his beloved Charite at all.

What he sees is this: a face not flesh-colored but white as snow; two branches of coral at the mouth, a lily and a rose on each cheek, two suns with flaming arrows darting out of them at the place of the eyes, eyebrows black as ebony shaped like archers' bows, a forehead smooth as a mirror on which a cupid sits enthroned. Framing the face he finds not hair but golden chains, nets, fishhooks dangling their bait, and many captured hearts including one particularly large specimen directly below the left cheek. From the bosom rise two orbs. Poor Lysis fears that he has gotten a monster instead of his Charite until Anselme reminds him that he has only followed Lysis' description in making the portrait. Lysis then understands Anselme's "artistry" and even recognizes his own heart in the oversized one below Charite's cheek, so wisely placed, says he, near her ear so that it can make constant complaint to her of its pains. In what Anselme and Lysis call a "metaphorical portrait" of Charite, Anselme has merely made a literal visual transcription of Lysis' poetic description.[24]

Now what could such a metaphorical portrait have meant to Sorel's readers? How would they have reacted, first, to the bizarre engraving by Crispin de Passe, and second, to the outlandish ver-

---

23. Jeanne Duportal, *Etude sur les livres à figures édités en France de 1601 à 1660* (Paris, 1914), pp. 153–54. Part of what follows, from this paragraph to the end of the chapter, has appeared in my article "The Ideological Value of the Portrait in Seventeenth-Century France," *L'Esprit Créateur* 21 (Fall 1981):15–25.

24. Charles Sorel, *Le Berger extravagant* (Rouen, 1646), pp. 62, 66–69.

2. Charite, by Crispin de Passe. From Charles Sorel, *Le Berger extravagant* (1627–28). Courtesy of the Dartmouth College Library.

53

bal portrait? And what is the relationship between the visual and the verbal registers of representation?

The portrait of Charite responds to a long tradition of metaphorical or mythological portraits in France. This tradition, derived from the emblematic painting of the Renaissance, establishes an analogical relationship between the representation and the represented. If an emblematic painting signifies a general idea, a mythological portrait signifies an individuality. A mythological portrait of Henri IV as Hercules, for example, signifies not the strength of a giant, as might an emblem of Hercules, but Henri himself as a modern Hercules in his strength and power. At a time when the techniques of engraving were allowing for fine precision, the need to create exact likenesses in portraits became imperative, so that if the wider significance of the emblem (a story, an idea) was reduced to an individuality in mythological portraiture, the myth was also personalized. Where once the representation of a mythological character may have been understood to signify a particular monarch or prince without reproducing his actual features, from the time of Henri IV the prince is visually assimilated with his hero-model. Whether or not the portrait bears the features of the person it is supposed to represent, it refers to an absent text. Sometimes, especially in the case of nonpersonalized portraits, the text is essential to an understanding of the image. At other times the allegorical significance of the text may not be readily comprehensible without accompanying personalized illustrations. Such was the case with Gombauld's *Endimion*, where only the engravings of Marie de Médicis as Diana could really clarify the allegory of the novel. Text and image are always very closely associated in mythological portraits.[25]

Both the strictly allegorical portrait, which is not personalized, and the seventeenth-century mythological portrait are built on a structure of analogy, but the necessity for creating exact likeness in the seventeenth century comes to dominate the portrait more and more. Visually, this may mean a drastic reduction in mythological paraphernalia (Diana's costume reduced to a bow and arrow, for example) in order better to emphasize the individuality of the person.[26] A certain realism, then, was introduced into visual

25. Bardon, *Portrait mythologique*, pp. 15–16. The portrait of Charite may also be related to the tradition of the mock *blason*, as found, for example, in Elizabethan poetry. See Hallet Smith, *Elizabethan Poetry* (Cambridge, Mass., 1952). I am grateful for this reference to Bruce Erlich of the University of Nebraska–Lincoln.
26. Bardon, *Portrait mythologique*, p. 66.

metaphor in the seventeenth century. Through this analogical mode of representation a new mode was appearing. The allegorical portrait is a strictly analogical system of signs. Myth signifies history (a historical personage) through a system of correspondences between mythology and history. History, or real life, corresponds to a truth that is elsewhere, in another realm.

Engraving, rather than painting or sculpture, was the medium par excellence for mythological portraits in seventeenth-century France.[27] Engraved mythological portraits were found in broadsides distributed for propaganda purposes and as frontispieces and illustrations in books—histories, novels, royal entry books, and so on. Sorel's readers were no strangers to either the mythological portrait or the work of Crispin de Passe, who illustrated, among many other works, Borstel de Gaubertin's continuation of *L'Astrée* in 1626.[28] Sorel's readers could easily have seen Crispin's illustrations for Gombauld's *Endimion,* which were, as we have seen, serious metaphorical or mythological portraits.

A comparison of Crispin's satirical metaphoric portrait of Charite (fig. 2) with one of his serious metaphoric portraits of Diana for Gombauld's novel (fig. 1) will illuminate the relationship between the textual portrait of Charite and the textual portraits of d'Urfé's shepherds. Crispin's portrait of Charite is to his portrait of Diana as Sorel's portrait of Charite is to d'Urfé's portraits of shepherds.

The aesthetic of *ut pictura poesis* was literally construed and almost universally adapted or applied in sixteenth- and seventeenth-century art. In *Le Berger extravagant* we find more than one reference to poetry as "spoken painting" or to painting as "mute poetry."[29] The mythological portrait is an excellent exemplification of *ut pictura poesis.* Text and image are so interdependent that the meaning of the portraits, textual and visual respectively, often depends on the economy of their equilibrium. In the case of Charite's portrait, Crispin's rendering is completely incomprehensible without the text. We might be able to tell from looking at it that it represents a woman, but how could we possibly understand the weird assemblage of objects adorning Charite? It is a different matter with Crispin's Diana. Even if the engraver had not given her Marie de Médicis's features, the portrait of Diana could very

---

27. Ibid., pp. 129, 177–80.
28. Diane Canivet, *L'Illustration de la poésie et du roman français au XVII͞e siècle* (Paris, 1957), p. 94.
29. See, for example, *Berger extravagant* (1646 ed.), 1:70.

well have stood on its own—we would simply have had a mythological Diana. The signs in the Diana portrait have a unified set of referents. In the bow, arrows, sandals, and garb of the woman portrayed, we have no difficulty in finding the reference to the goddess Diana. The metaphorical meaning of the portrait is clear once we recognize Diana's face as that of the queen mother. In Charite's portrait, however, the signs point only to a hodgepodge of ill-assorted referents. Bows and arrows, suns and fishhooks indicate no clear reference. We can understand the meaning of each referent only through the text. Through parodic use of the structures found in the mythological portrait—analogical representation, close dependence on a text—Sorel discredits metaphor entirely. By having the visual portrait so completely dependent on the verbal one that it amounts to nonsense without it, he carries the mythological portrait to an absurd extreme. In fact, we can establish a scale of meaning for the mythological portrait which may help to put Sorel's project into perspective. In the allegorical portrait, where the analogy is not made explicit so that the reference is clear but not necessarily the meaning, the meaning is partially comprehensible. The text of Gombauld's *Endimion*, for example, can stand on its own as a mythological tale referring to Diana. The illustrations are needed to complete its allegorical meaning. In a mythological portrait—Crispin's Diana, for example—we have both reference (the goddess Diana) and meaning (Marie de Médicis is a modern Diana); the meaning is completely comprehensible. In Crispin's Charite, we have neither reference (a collection of diverse referents does not form a single reference) nor meaning; the meaning is incomprehensible.

Now d'Urfé's shepherds and shepherdesses follow right along in the tradition of the mythological portrait. True, the mythological paraphernalia is drastically reduced—d'Urfé felt that the only real concession he needed to make to local pastoral color was a golden staff or two. But here we see a good literary parallel to the development of realism in the engraved mythological portrait. The mythological sign in *L'Astrée* lets us see the noble through his rustic mask, and keys lend an authoritative dimension to the representation.

The implication of Sorel's portrait of Charite, however, is that a true portrait must do away entirely with metaphor. If Lysis had described Charite to Anselme exactly as she was, he would have gotten a comprehensible portrait. In other words, in the real or serious portrait of Charite which is the unexpressed obverse of the one in Sorel's text, referent and meaning would be one. The sign would be totally transparent. Representation would reflect the represented with no distortion whatsoever. Freed of the analogical mode, truth would shine pure and unvarnished through the sign.

A qualification must be appended to the scale of meaning for the mythological portrait which we have just established. The partial comprehensibility of the allegorical portrait and the complete comprehensibility of the mythological portrait depend first and foremost on an understanding of the referents. The referents were comprehensible only to the initiated, who had enough familiarity with mythology to be able to recognize and interpret its signs. A superficial familiarity with it may have been more common in seventeenth-century France than we may be inclined to think, since mythological imagery had for a long time been so widely used that it could have penetrated even to the lives of the very humble. Thus a royal entry turned an entire town into a carnivalesque fête, strewing mythological glitter everywhere in its path—portraits, triumphal arches, ballets, spectacles. In the tradition of the pastoral novel, to which *Le Berger extravagant* responds, mythology was associated with a conventional setting for aristocratic representations. The metaphor of the courtly shepherd in *L'Astrée* had a special appeal for those who were initiated into the courtly and pastoral traditions from Virgil and Ovid through the *Roman de la rose* and up to Ariosto, Tasso, Guarini, Castiglione, and that ever-popular favorite of the sixteenth century, *Amadis de Gaule*. Now Sorel comes along and says, No more metaphor! No more mythology! His transparent sign would have universal value. Anyone and everyone would be able to understand it, with no regard whatsoever for tradition. Truth would be in the here and now, accessible to all, not elsewhere in the clouds of mythology. We should not be surprised to find Sorel the author of a *Science universelle* in 1641. Like Descartes, he dreamed of a scientific truth that anyone could reach by thinking correctly. Like the French classicists, he confused truth with universality.

Charite and Lysis belong to the realm of the myth. Sorel would historicize them by returning them to their real roles of Catherine and Louys. For him the analogical mode of representation does not reflect accurately; it gives us the wild distortion we see in Charite's portrait. What Sorel claims, then, is that in rejecting the apparatus of myth he can give a real picture. His representation will be a clear reflection of what he represents.

Is this actually the case? We can gauge the accuracy of his claim with yet another portrait from *Le Berger extravagant*. This is a portrait of a carpenter rather than of a noble shepherd or shepherdess. Again we find an example of Sorel's parodic use of the same structures as those in the object of his parody. *Le Berger extravagant*, like *L'Astrée* and so many of the heroic or sentimental novels popular with the nobility, is constructed on the story-within-a-story principle. The carpenter's portrait occurs in the framed story of Carmelin, a poor orphan who had apprenticed himself to the carpenter. Parody demystifies: the poor are really poor in *Le Berger extravagant*. Sorel does not hesitate to equip his characters with all the concrete effects of their respective classes. Money, a vulgar subject that the noble d'Urfé would not have stooped to mention, plays its part in determining the course of these characters' lives.

Carmelin's carpenter is a "fat, pleasant-faced bourgeois" chosen as the neighborhood officer of the guards. Filled with pride in his new station, the carpenter orders a portrait of himself in his gold-trimmed scarlet uniform. He is quite satisfied with the finished product except for the colors, which are not bright enough for his taste. The painter tells him to rub the portrait with a wet cloth once the paint has dried in order to brighten it up—but only when he is ready to show it to important people. The occasion arises when the carpenter invites a small group of bourgeois to view his portrait. When he rubs the painting with a cloth, lo and behold, a "metamorphosis" occurs, says Carmelin, just like the ones Lysis is always talking about: the portrait completely changes its state (*estat*).

Sorel was undoubtedly punning on the double meaning of *estat*: both "state" (used here in the sense of the French *condition*, or rank) and "estate" (as in *Estats Généraux*, or Estates General). For in this metamorphosis the subject of the portrait changes in both *condition* and estate, as he moves down in rank from a member of the Second Estate to a member of the Third. The carpenter has in fact undergone two metamorphoses, since he had originally ordered a portrait of himself, a bourgeois, as a gentleman. In the original portrait, the uniform served to transform him into a member of the *noblesse d'epée*, for he had had all the trappings of the military nobleman: sword, plumed hat, boots, gauntlets, and so on. In the second metamorphosis, the plume gives way to a pair of horns, the boots to peasants' gaiters, the sword to a compass. Some carpenter's equipment lies on a table where previously there had lain gauntlets and a helmet. In the new portrait shining through the old, the carpenter is a cuckolded peasant.[30]

The carpenter's portrait repeats the overall structure of Sorel's novel. It is a double portrait just like that of Louys/Lysis. It expresses the subject's desire for self-representation just as Lysis expresses Louys's desire for self-representation. Lysis, moreover, is constantly requesting that someone write a novel about him, and by the end of *Le Berger extravagant* we might be fairly well convinced that we had been reading the response to his request if Sorel's Francion had not already announced his intention of writing a novel called *Le Berger extravagant*. How to represent is the fundamental question of *Le Berger extravagant* as it is of the carpenter episode. *L'Astrée*'s story-within-a-story structure integrated a conventional form of tales into a coherent, if overlong, novel. Mme de La Fayette's novel *La Princesse de Clèves* condenses essentially the same structure into a compact, highly readable narrative. In Sorel's novel the story-within-a-story structure gets out of hand. It degenerates into confusion: is the carpenter episode a story within the story of Carmelin within the story of Lysis, within the story of Louys? But if one of Lysis's friends is writing the novel, then within the story of Lysis? But what if, for assiduous readers of Sorel, Francion is writing the novel? The confusion is of course part of Sorel's satire. In his "Remarks" on Book 13 he complains that the story-within-a-story structure is so confusing that the reader ends up not knowing who is speaking anymore.[31]

As with the portrait of Charite, the implication is that the representation can stand in an unmediated relationship to the represented. If Louys had simply represented himself as Louys and the carpenter as a carpenter, they would have avoided ridicule and there would have been accurate representation. The sign should be completely transparent.

But in that case there would have been no *Berger extravagant* at all, no representation whatsoever, since representation is a mediation. If the aristocratic literary practitioner confused life and art, the early bourgeois literary practitioner confused modes of representation. We have seen that a certain realism was perfectly compatible with the mythological portrait. A portrait of Henri IV as Hercules could be allegorical *and* represent Henri with Henri's

30. See ibid., 2:127–30.

31. Sorel, *Berger extravagant* (facs. ed.), 2:94–95 (510). On *Le Berger extravagant*, see Jean Serroy, *Roman et réalité: Les Histoires comiques au XVII siècle* (Paris, 1981), pp. 294–319.

features. A conventional representation was, as we have seen with *L'Astrée*, a "realistic" representation for the nobility, for whom convention had acquired the force of truth.

What, then, does Sorel really do? What modes of representation does he use? In *Le Berger extravagant* Louys/Lysis represents Louys. But who is Louys? Representation does not stand in clear relationship to the represented not because of the double portrait, but because the object of representation is ambiguous. In the carpenter's portrait representation more nearly "reflects" the represented than in the case of Louys, because the double portrait clearly mocks the bourgeois carpenter's pretensions to nobility. Louys is represented in the novel both as a bourgeois Parisian and as Lysis, his noble representation of himself. Once the Lysis myth is exploded, however, we are left not with the Parisian merchant's son but with a country gentleman. Mythological representation would be appropriate for him. The parody is not complete because the object of the parody is unsettled. The entire Lysis episode has in fact advanced Louys in his social mobility since it has helped to win for him the amused affection of his aristocratic friends, who then help him to establish himself. Louys both discards noble disguise in giving up his incarnation as Lysis and adopts it in buying an ennobling office at the end. Sorel seems to be satirizing aristocratic literature and the noble way of life at the same time that he satirizes the would-be noble bourgeois for whom noble disguise is inappropriate. Here he reaches a literary impasse. Once Louys is ennobled, the parody is discredited on both counts. Louys loses his authenticity as a bourgeois; Lysis regains his power of mystification.

Now the problem here is that with *L'Astrée* we were dealing with an ideology that, if it no longer corresponded to the socioeconomic situation of the nobility, still remained more or less intact. Bourgeois ideology, on the other hand, was in the first phases of its slow formation at the time Sorel was writing his *Berger extravagant,* and it would not reach real coherence until the bourgeoisie obtained full power in the following century. In the early seventeenth century, the nobility knew how to represent itself and how to recognize itself in the representation. Bourgeois did not.

If we cannot speak of a unified bourgeois ideology at this time, it is because the French bourgeois had not yet coalesced into a bourgeoisie, but were in the process of becoming constituted as a class. By the end of the sixteenth century, the term "bourgeois" no longer had the literal medieval meaning of statutory resident of a *bourg*. Privileges granted to bourgeois from the twelfth century on varied greatly from town to town. It is therefore not possible to find a common legal definition of "bourgeois" applicable to all of France in the seventeenth century. Bourgeois now included merchants, masters of the corporative guilds, financiers, some *officiers, rentiers,* doctors, lawyers, and the like. The only common denominator among them was that they were all proprietors of one sort or another.[32]

The heterogeneity of the bourgeoisie opened it up to many contradictions. A measure of these contradictions may be observed in bourgeois reactions to popular uprisings. If in 1630 in Aix-en-Provence a small group of bourgeois led one of these uprisings and in 1640 in Moulins the bourgeois guard refused to march against the rebels, there are other instances in which bourgeois participated in the repression, or else, divided against themselves by opposing interests, took different sides, as was the case in Rouen in 1640. In a given local uprising, bourgeois could take a combination or a succession of positions. Bourgeois might be willing to stand with "the people" in protests against tax collectors, but they quickly deserted the cause when the anger was turned against the rich of their own number, threatening their property and interests. One source of a fateful rivalry among the bourgeois themselves was the gradual increase in number since the second half of the sixteenth century of intendants, or royal commissioners, sent out by the monarch to fill administrative functions in the provinces. Richelieu, who was eager to reduce the independent *officiers* to obedience, at first granted these intendants the status of *commissaires,* or temporary officials. In the last years of his ministry and Louis XIII's reign, the intendant became a permanent fixture. Increasingly, intendants displaced or overruled the established *officiers* of the region, who then reacted bitterly. At the beginning of the mid-century civil war known as the Fronde, the Paris *parlement* demanded the elimination of intendants, as the conflict between *officier* and intendant widened into one between *parlements* and crown.[33]

32. Pierre Goubert, *L'Ancien Régime* (Paris, 1969), 1:222. See his discussion of the various bourgeoisies, pp. 217–35. For a historical overview of the situation of French bourgeois in the ancien régime, see Joseph di Corcia, "Bourg, Bourgeois, Bourgeois de Paris from the Eleventh to the Eighteenth Century," *Journal of Modern History* 50 (June 1978):207–33.

33. See Mandrou, *Classes et luttes de classes,* pp. 49–53. Cf. Porshnev, *Soulèvements populaires,* pp. 143–47, 190–213. On the administrative role of the intendants under Louis XIII and Louis XIV, see Georges Pagès, *Les Institutions monarchiques sous Louis XIII and Louis XIV* (Paris, [1961]), pp. 78–105, 115–23.

The greatest source of division in the seventeenth-century French bourgeoisie was undoubtedly the rush toward ennoblement. One response to the economic crisis following the sixteenth-century period of expansion was abandonment of business and commerce by many bourgeois in favor of the safer routes to financial security: *rentes*, purchase of offices, and land. The institution of the *paulette* enormously increased the attraction and prestige of officeholding and helped to blur the distinction between old and new nobility. The fondest hope of the bourgeois was to desert the bourgeoisie in order to "live nobly." With a nice office, some *rentes* and land, the *anobli* desired nothing more than to be confused with a real nobleman. But the transformation was rarely complete in the first generation. The *anobli* still had to contend with the authentic noble in the countless everyday questions of precedence and protocol which harassed the disputants with disproportionate ferocity.

The sprawling, unwieldy system of taxation was another, related source of division among the bourgeois. Try as he might, the *anobli* rarely succeeded in shedding his condition of *roturier* gracefully. If he grumbled over the noble's exemption from the *taille*, when he himself became eligible for exemption he had to face loud protests from those who found it unfair that "false nobles" should enjoy the privilege. The striving for tax exemption and noble status set bourgeois against bourgeois, dividing this inchoate class politically, socially, and economically.[34] Bourgeois joined the nobility with which they were assimilating in protests against fellow bourgeois. The demands of the Third Estate in the 1614 Estates General included the revocation of all ennoblements since the reign of Henri II effected through "money and without valid reason."[35] The main reason for this demand was that ennoblement resulted in exemption from the *taille*, which meant an increased burden on the *roturiers* who still had to pay.[36] The ambitious *roturier* deeply resented the noble's privileges, which he scrambled to obtain for himself. Decline in income from land, sale of offices, a certain capitalization of wealth in commerce and industry, permitting investment in offices and *rentes*, the powerful attraction of noble status: all combined to produce that phenome-

---

34. Bitton, *French Nobility in Crisis*, p. 15. See also Porshnev, *Soulèvements populaires*, pp. 545–46.

35. See the extract from the *Cahier du Tiers Etat* for the 1614 Estates General in Mandrou, *Classes et luttes de classes*, pp. 90–91.

36. Ibid. See also Bitton, *French Nobility in Crisis*, p. 14.

non of seventeenth-century France which has so aptly been called the "feudalization of the bourgeoisie."[37]

The seventeenth-century nobility was on the defensive: it needed all its ideological strength to muster arguments in favor of a return to better times. The bourgeois had no unified program because they were as yet a disparate group, lacking the consciousness of a class. During most of the century the possibility of purchasing an office clouded their vision with the prospect of ennoblement. Charles Sorel himself came from the milieu of the *noblesse de robe*. In his literary production we see the contradictions of an unformed ideology, part of which betrays an ideological reaction against a nobility that still exerted a powerful attraction, another part the glimmer of a new social consciousness.

It is not surprising, then, that *Le Berger extravagant* on the one hand parodies and on the other takes seriously the mythological world of *L'Astrée* and the old nobility. The frame story of Louys's progress from distracted bourgeois to country gentleman is straightforward; the parody is in the framed story of Lysis, the mad shepherd. These stories, unlike those of *L'Astrée,* are imperfectly integrated into an artistic representation, because the novel hesitates between a parodic and a serious mode. Even the schema of frame and framed stories is somewhat arbitrary and misleading, for we have seen that Louys and Lysis become confused with each other: Lysis is Louys's representation of himself, and Louys becomes a sane Lysis at the end.

What Sorel discards from artistic representation of the type we find in *L'Astrée* and the mythological portrait is the analogical truth value of conventional mythology. Mythology in *Le Berger extravagant* is not a disguise for truth but a grotesque distortion of it. Thus when Lysis pesters a peasant to engage in courtly conversations with him, he appears as absurd as Don Quixote mistaking inns for castles. Charite's metaphorical apparatus is a monstrosity. Mythology cannot give a mirror image. One significant episode of the novel is a parody of the Narcissus myth in which the protagonist, Fontenay, finally breaks his mirror.[38] Every "metamorphosis" turns out to be a sham.

But if the parody of an old genre can result in the production of a new one, it is because parody necessarily follows old forms as

---

37. See Mandrou, *Classes et luttes de classes,* pp. 50, 61–62. Porshnev analyzes the political, social, and economic aspects of the "feudalization of the bourgeoisie" in his *Soulèvements populaires,* pp. 538–82.

38. *Berger extravagant* (1646 ed.), 2:42–52.

it questions them.[39] *Le Berger extravagant* conserves as it exaggerates, for example, the story-within-a-story structure. By not integrating the stories, by parodying their structure in an extension ad infinitum into utter chaos, Sorel points to the necessity of integration and concision in the service of clarity. This is the direction in which the novel would develop, with Mme de La Fayette's *Princesse de Clèves* marking a watershed a half-century later. Similarly, Sorel's parody of the mythological mirror points to the necessity of an unadorned mirror. The sign will be transparent, not analogical. Truth will no longer be accessible through mythology, but will be universally available as "history" (the ambiguity of French *histoire*, both "history" and "story," is significant in this context). History will no longer correspond to mythology: it can represent itself. Here are the seeds of a bourgeois, democratic ideology, in which truth descends from its mythological heaven into the realms of history and science, in which bourgeois values are universalized. For Sorel the old mirror could no longer give an accurate image; the portrait could not give an exact likeness. His Fontenay, we must realize, destroys only the mirror of Narcissus. *Le Berger extravagant* still lays implicit claim to a reflection that mythology can no longer provide. Sorel says, in effect, "I'm going to tell it like it is. My shepherds are real shepherds, my protagonist is a real-life character." Between the claim and the reality of the literary product, however, yawns an unbridgeable gap. Where is the reality that Sorel thought he could mirror? It is still permeated with the myth if not the mythology of the nobility; it is filled with the ambiguities of a nascent bourgeois ideology.

Sorel's claim to reflect accurately underlies that most bourgeois of genres, the modern novel. But the modern novel was not really to develop in France until the eighteenth century, and Sorel's attempt at verisimilitude had to wait some time before finding another vehicle. In the meantime, it was the ideology of the nobility, which a monarchy wanting to represent itself as absolute later utilized, that was to prevail.[40] *Vraisemblance* came to dominate the

---

39. Discussions of this process can be found in Jonathan Culler, *Structuralist Poetics* (Ithaca, N.Y., 1975); Northrop Frye, *Anatomy of Criticism* (Princeton, 1973); Tzvetan Todorov, *The Poetics of Prose*, trans. Richard Howard (Ithaca, N.Y., 1977).

40. Absolutism was constructed as an ideology by the monarchy at that historical moment when it became necessary to centralize administration in an attempt to protect the interests of the dominant class. Perry Anderson sees absolutism as "the new political carapace of a threatened nobility" in his *Lineages of the Absolutist State* (London, 1974), p. 18. Logically, then, absolutism borrowed much of the ideological apparatus of the nobility (see below, Chapter 3). This does not mean that the

aesthetic of French classicism only after the fundamental claim of accurate reflection had been made. Classical *vraisemblance* transformed truth as reflection of the individual and the particular into truth as reflection of the universal, not only according to an interpretation of Aristotelian theory, but also according to a new set of ideological demands. Truth as reflection persisted into French classicism and far beyond. By making *vraisemblance* the cornerstone of the aesthetic and then overlaying it with universal value, the classical writers, many of whom came from the *noblesse de robe*, maintained as they transformed an ideology that was no longer strictly speaking theirs.

Le Berger extravagant never caught on the way its noble predecessor did. *L'Astrée* outran it in popularity because d'Urfé's novel could flourish in the contradictions of seventeenth-century French society. Who were the readers of *Le Berger extravagant?* Thomas Corneille, for one, since, inspired by Sorel, he wrote a burlesque comedy of the same title, which was performed in 1653. There is no convincing evidence that it was among the more successful plays of the time.[41] The novel also figures in a ballet of 1644 titled *Le Libraire du Pont-Neuf* or *Ballet des romans*, in which, incidentally, *L'Astrée* also figures. The ballet's success, although considerable, was brief.[42] There is nothing in the history of *Le Berger extravagant* that can compare with the multitude of adaptations, imitations, and commentaries inspired by *L'Astrée*.[43] *L'Astrée* initially found a large audience in the nobility, who were only too happy to find their mirror image in it. Later on bourgeois, too, enjoyed it. It must have become one of their cultural requisites for "living nobly." But neither nobles nor bourgeois could appreciate *Le Berger extravagant,* for neither found a flattering portrait in it. Bourgeois certainly did not want to find their reflection in Louys; they preferred a nobler image. In 1627 or 1628, not long after the *paulette* had conferred re-

---

so-called absolutist state served only the interests of the nobility. Louis XIV spurred the development of merchant capital with Colbert's mercantilism. Paradoxically, absolutism could serve noble and bourgeois interests simultaneously (see Anderson, *Lineages*, pp. 40–41). Recent studies on absolutist ideology have been based on the assumption that it emanated only from the monarchy, to serve the monarch's political interests alone. See Jean-Marie Apostolidès, *Le Roi-machine: Spectacle et politique au temps de Louis XIV* (Paris, 1981), and Louis Marin, *Le Portrait du roi* (Paris, 1981).

41. See Thomas Corneille, *Le Berger extravagant,* ed. Francis Bar (Geneva, 1960), pp. 20–21.

42. See Victor Fournel, *Les Contemporains de Molière* (Geneva, 1967), 2:243–59.

43. See Maurice Magendie, *Du Nouveau sur L'Astrée* (Paris, 1927), pp. 424–62.

spectability on the purchase of offices, bourgeois were not in the mood to look at their own pretensions to nobility. The ideology projected into *L'Astrée* could take d'Urfé's novel far, because if the nobles it represented were being displaced, they were being displaced by bourgeois imitators. The hiatus in the development of the bourgeoisie as a class and of capitalism in seventeenth-century France was filled by a period of enchantment with nobility. When the spell was broken during the eighteenth century, bourgeois ideology and the modern novel could resume the course of their development. Sorel would have had his day.

Interestingly enough, most readers and critics today consider that the modern novel, from the eighteenth century on, meets Sorel's demands. The commonly held notion of the nineteenth-century realistic novel, for example, is that it "reflects social reality." Yet in that faraway herald of realism, *Le Berger extravagant*, accurate reflection was only a claim. In fact Sorel's novel was no more realistic, perhaps less so, than *L'Astrée*, which did hold a workable mirror up to its public. What happened is that when a different type of viewer held up the same mirror, he did not see his own image. Sorel could not find *his* ideological reflection in d'Urfé's portraits, so he found *L'Astrée* unrealistic (or, as he would have said, *romanesque*, novelish). But between Sorel's affirmation of accurate reflection and his actual literary practice we have found a wide discrepancy. What we have uncovered in *Le Berger extravagant* is not the real socioeconomic contradictions of the early seventeenth-century French bourgeois, but an unsuccessful attempt to conciliate their conflicting ideological demands. We may yet ask: When the right viewer—that is, the bourgeoisie fully constituted as the class in power—comes along and finds its unadorned mirror in the modern novel, what then? Does it not find an accurate reflection of itself? Like d'Urfé's public, it sees what it wants to see.

To view realism as reflection is to confuse a claim with actual literary practice. It is to assume that representation and represented can stand in an unmediated relationship to each other. It is to forget what we have seen in both *L'Astrée* and *Le Berger extravagant:* ideology works in the service of verisimilitude as verisimilitude can work in the service of ideology. *L'Astrée* suceeded as a work of art because its mode of representation was perfectly suited to the nobility's and the "false nobility's" ideological projection of themselves. *Le Berger extravagant* failed because it attempted only halfheartedly to contest the dominant ideology, and it could not satisfactorily resolve the contradictions of the ideology in formation. Verisimilitude is a functional, not an eternal value. If we still tend to view realism as reflection, is it not because we are now in the position of d'Urfé's noble public, viewing ourselves, still mystified by our own ideology?

3

Of Portraits

Portraits, portraits, all over France there were portraits. By the mid-seventeenth century, painted portraits adorned the galleries and chambers of the great *hôtels;* engraved portraits graced the pages of printed books or collections. Above all the verbal portrait had its heyday at this time. Nobles produced and consumed these portraits with passion. The idea in the 1650s was to "get into" Mlle de Scudéry's ultrafashionable novel *Le Grand Cyrus,* a collection of thinly disguised portraits of the contemporary nobility held together by a sprawling, multivolume narrative set in ancient Persia, much as one wanted to get into the author's salon, where habitués "did" verbal portraits of one another. Mlle de Montpensier, the "Grand Mademoiselle," Louis XIII's niece, spent the year 1657–58 dabbling in portraiture. She called on a select circle of her friends to collaborate with her, and the result was an anonymously published limited edition of *Divers portraits* (1659). The "precious" polite society of the time, raised on *L'Astrée,* loved nothing more than to exercise its wit on portraits in the highly polished, often esoteric, metaphorical language that it employed to perfection (if not to absurdity, as Molière attempted to show in his *Précieuses ridicules*). The *précieux* and *précieuses* diligently gathered their labors into *recueils,* or collections, of prose and verse, such as the *Recueil de Sercy* (1653–60) and the *Recueil La Suze* (1663 on).

Verbal portraits were too popular to be confined to salon games and novels. Memorialists of the period, such as the Cardinal de

Retz, inserted them easily into their narratives. One of the most impressive histories to appear during the century, François Eudes de Mézeray's monumental *Histoire de France depuis Pharamond*, was organized around full-page engravings of every French king and queen, with a rhymed quatrain by Jean Baudoin under each. Such portraits, combining engraved image and verse, were, on a less lavish scale, a commonplace of seventeenth-century French books. Portraits of authors for frontispieces often as not took this form. So great was the vogue for portraits that it had not yet begun to wane before satires of it made their appearance in such diverse places as Antoine Furetière's *Roman bourgeois* (1661) and Charles Sorel's humorous utopia, *Description de l'isle de portraiture* (1659).

The painted portrait had traditionally served illustrious families as a record of its members for posterity. In the seventeenth century, both painted and verbal portraits gained value as art forms. If the literary portrait seemed but a conceit, an extended metaphor with painting as its vehicle, its underlying message was quite serious: the verbal portrait would represent its subject with the same accuracy as its pictorial counterpart. In the portrait, verisimilitude unfolds its paradoxical nature of truth as *semblance*. The portrait must record, or represent accurately; it must also imitate, and in its imitation lies its art or "artifice," as the seventeenth-century critics would have said.[1] The Aristotelian concept of mimesis takes on an inscrutable quality in seventeenth-century art forms. Imitation (of an action for Aristotle, of a model for the portraitist) succeeds in approximating its object only through artfulness. That is to say, imitation achieves congruence with its object only through the distancing medium of artifice. Sixteenth- and seventeenth-century treatises on poetics attempted to codify this paradox. The principle of *ut pictura poesis*, that painting should imitate the rules of poetry as poetry should imitate those of painting, was based on the concept of art as a faithful representation of "nature." But the reciprocal imitation involved also an artful imitation of art, that is, either of the art of poetry or of the art of painting. It appears that the verisimilitude of this

---

1. On imitation and *vraisemblance*, see A. Kibédi Varga, "La Vraisemblance—problèmes de terminologie, problèmes de poétique," in *Critique et création littéraires en France au XVIIe siècle*, Colloques Internationaux du Centre National de la Recherche Scientifique no. 557 (Paris, 1977), pp. 325–36; Jacques Thuillier, "La Notion d'imitation dans la pensée artistique du XVIIe siècle," in ibid., pp. 361–74. See also Timothy J. Reiss, "Power, Poetry, and the Resemblance of Nature," in John D. Lyons and Stephen G. Nichols, Jr., eds., *Mimesis: From Mirror to Method, Augustine to Descartes* (Hanover, N.H., 1982), pp. 215–47.

period emphasized rather the seeming than the truth, as the prevalence of trompe l'oeil and illusionism indicates. The art of imitation is thus the baroque transmutation of mimesis. And yet, must we discount as merely part of the game the seventeenth-century poetic theorists' and practitioners' pretensions to accurate representation?

Both the mania for portraits and the paradox of verisimilitude underlying their poetics are related to the ideological function of this genre for its producers and consumers. The aesthetic value of the portrait is linked to its function. Function and value, in turn, are inseparable from the conditions of production that form the material cultural setting of the portrait. We will follow the changing ideological function of visual and verbal portraits from the reign of Louis XIII through the first half of Louis XIV's personal reign. During this time the portrait became an ideological focal point, first for the struggle between the monarchy and the nobility which culminated in the Fronde, and later, during the so-called classical period, for that between nobles and bourgeois.

Under Richelieu, the portrait filled a new function in its contribution to the royal legend of absolutism. Richelieu used traditional elements of noble and royal iconography to glorify the growing strength of the French monarchy. These elements were gradually transformed in the development of absolutist ideology. The attempt to build an autonomous ideology of absolutism with materials that had been shared by both nobles and royalty revealed some of the stresses and strains that the monarchy was experiencing in its efforts to reduce the power of the nobility.[2] Nobles reacted with a new exclusivity in a spate of abstruse verbal portraits around the time of the Fronde, the civil war in which they played such a prominent role. This war marks a turning point in the fortunes of the portrait. At its close, the nobles' power was diminished, and as courtiers of Louis XIV they played a very different role. Their chief rivals for power and prestige were now the rich bourgeois or the new nobles. The verbal portrait that characterized much of French classical literature was stamped with this rivalry. While courtiers danced attendance on Louis XIV at Versailles, money infused the portrait with a new ideological value.

2. On Richelieu's efforts to subdue the nobles and the *grands*, see William F. Church, *Richelieu and Reason of State* (Princeton, 1972), pp. 173–236.

The Tradition of the Portrait Book

At the beginning of the seventeenth century, Marie de Médicis conceived the shrewd idea of erecting an equestrian statue of her husband, Henri IV. Her fellow countrymen Jean de Bologne and Pietro Tacca built this monument between 1615 and 1635 on the Ile de la Cité in Paris. It was the first such royal effigy, built for posterity and on view for all, in a public place. The statue was only the most dramatic piece in a royal iconography that had flourished ever since the beginning of Henri's reign and whose aim was to celebrate the victories over civil disorder and over Spain as well as the king's recent conversion. A monarch whose authority had been established in the controversial atmosphere of abjuration was exalted in a flurry of engravings; after the assassination he was immortalized in commemorative statues and in busts made from the death mask. Later on, Richelieu accorded top priority to portraiture and architecture in his program of royal glorification. And he did not neglect himself when he ordered his projects. Philippe de Champaigne painted at least four full-length portraits of him for 150 livres each (not a large sum by the standards of the day), and there were many more by other painters.[3]

In the sixteenth century, drawings had been the most popular form of portrait. Daniel Dumoustier, master of a great family of portraitists, was somewhat cynical about his subjects' reactions to their likenesses. "They're so stupid," he is reputed to have said, "that they think they look the way I draw them, and they pay me all the more." The painted portrait, eclipsed by drawings during the reign of Henry IV, emerged as a medium of central importance with the arrival of François Pourbus from Flanders. Marie de Médicis's painter set the style for the state portrait with his figures in ceremonial attire placed against an imposing backdrop of architecture or drapery.[4] A little later, two members of another famous family of artists, Charles and Henri Beaubrun, made a veritable pictorial tour of royalty in their portraits of Anne of Austria, Queen Marie-Thérèse, the Grand Condé, the Grande

3. René Crozet, *La Vie artistique en France au XVIIe siècle* (Paris, 1954), pp. 54–57, 90.
4. François Gebelin, *L'Epoque Henri IV et Louis XIII* (Paris, 1969), pp. 59–61. Cf. Gédéon Tallemant des Réaux, *Historiettes*, ed. Antoine Adam (Paris, 1960–61), 1:660.

Mademoiselle, and the infant dauphin, Louis XIV's son, among others. "Les Beaubrun," as the cousins were known, were lionized in polite society, where they excelled in the latest *jeux d'esprit.* Every great château had its portrait gallery. Mlle de Montpensier in her *Mémoires* describes in some detail which pictures she chose for her gallery at St-Fargeau.[5] And royalty often tried its hand at the various arts. Gaston d'Orléans is said to have worked with Jacques Callot during a stay in the engraver's town of Nancy, and he hired Pierre Mignard to teach drawing to his daughter, the Grande Mademoiselle.[6]

In the 1620s, 1630s, and 1640s, France saw a great outpouring of deluxe editions of books illustrated with engraved portraits. These portrait books, as I shall call them, had diverse titles. Some were labeled "histories," some "portraits" or "true portraits"; others "panegyrics" or "famous [*illustres*] men" (or women). In addition to certain formal properties to be considered presently, what all the portrait books had in common was their official or semiofficial nature as products of Richelieu's newly created propaganda machinery. His organization of the press and of cultural-intellectual life in the service of the monarchy was the necessary complement to his efforts at centralization. At the same time that he was sending to the provinces royal commissioners or intendants to displace the more independent local officials, he was systematically constructing the image of a monarchy strong enough to neutralize the influence of the *grands.*

Although historians have found it difficult to determine just how large an audience these books may have reached, it is certain that specific groups did have access to them: the royal entourage, the nobility, including the *noblesse de robe,* and some of the wealthier members of the bourgeoisie.[7] Among these groups were the very people who were to produce literary portraits of their own a few decades later. Producers and consumers of art formed a highly restricted circle in seventeenth-century France. Their rela-

5. Mlle de Montpensier, *Mémoires,* ed. A. Chéruel, vol. 2 (Paris, 1868), pp. 283–84.

6. On the Beaubruns, see Louis Dimier, *Histoire de la peinture française du retour de Vouet à la mort de Lebrun (1627 à 1690)* (Paris, 1926–27), 2:68; Crozet, *Vie artistique,* p. 78. On royalty's enthusiasm for portraits and the arts, see Crozet, pp. 70, 78, and Dimier, p. 43.

7. See Jeanne Duportal, *Etude sur les livres à figures édités en France de 1601 à 1660* (Paris, 1914), pp. 66–67, 83. She also says that illustrated books were used for pedagogical purposes at all levels of society (pp. 342–43).

tionship constitutes one of the fundamental conditions of production of the mid-century portrait.

In general, those whom Richelieu commissioned to produce portrait books held royal offices. They were, therefore, beneficiaries of the cardinal's massive program to expand his own influence and that of the crown through the creation and sale of offices. With a weak monarch and restive, powerful nobles, Richelieu took it upon himself to play the part of first patron of the arts.[8] Here he faced some competition from noble patrons: throughout his ministry the monarchy and the nobility shared the same iconography, the same mythological forms of representation in plastic and verbal portraits.[9] A writer did not have to serve only one patron at a time, although a patron's protection did tend to imply "exclusive rights" to his work.[10] All the more reason for Richelieu to press a propaganda campaign. With his protection, a corps of writers, engravers, and painters set out to build up a library of praise for the king. The producers of portrait books typically bore the title of *conseiller du roi* or *historiographe*. Sometimes they worked in collaboration with *peintres et graveurs ordinaires du Roi*, as in the case of Vulson de la Colombière's collection of engraved reproductions of the famous men whose portraits covered the walls of Richelieu's palace (*Les Portraits des hommes illustres françois qui sont peints dans la gallerie du palais Cardinal de Richelieu*, 1650). Sometimes the enterprise was directed by a royal engraver, such as Jean Valdor, *calcographe* (engraver) *du Roi*, who supervised one of the most ambitious of these projects, *Les Triomphes de Louis Le Juste*.

Richelieu's protégés were by and large men of modest background, bourgeois who had gained the favor of the court. Their titles could confer a low-ranking nobility and pensions whose

8. Orest Ranum, *Artisans of Glory: Writers and Historical Thought in Seventeenth-Century France* (Chapel Hill, N.C., 1980), pp. 152–53. I am very grateful to Professor Ranum for the use of his book in manuscript form before its publication and for helpful discussions on certain points. In my treatment of official cultural production under Richelieu, I emphasize the minister's deliberate efforts to produce effective royal propaganda. William F. Church has studied writers who supported Richelieu's policies without necessarily having been recruited specifically to produce propaganda for him. See his *Richelieu and Reason of State*, pp. 236–82, 415–71. On Richelieu's attempts to control public opinion in the press and through his institutional creation, the Académie Française, see Church, pp. 340–49.

9. See Françoise Bardon, *Le Portrait mythologique à la cour de France sous Henri IV et Louis XIII* (Paris, 1974), p. 284.

10. See Ranum, *Artisans of Glory*, p. 150.

amounts and regularity of payment varied unpredictably. Theoretically their offices allowed them some participation in the affairs of state; practically, their political involvement was probably
limited to the title and acceptance at court. As to their qualifications, the painters and engravers had manifestly acquired a certain technical command of their craft. Richelieu's historians or
historiographes were not necessarily, however, well versed in history
or experienced as writers. Loyalty to the crown seems to have
been the only important requirement for their post.[11]

The career of Jean Puget de La Serre (c. 1593–1665), a court
historian who thrived during Richelieu's administration, was perhaps more celebrated than those of his colleagues, owing to the
sheer mediocrity of his talents, but it was nonetheless typical. Tallemant des Réaux, one of the greatest, best-informed gossips of
the seventeenth century, tells us that La Serre used to frequent
the members of Richelieu's newly founded French Academy.
When it came time to mount his carriage, he would say to them,
"Get in, get in, it's the wheel of Fortune."[12] La Serre had certainly
had his turn on the goddess' wheel. The grandson of Jean Puget,
an apothecary from Toulouse, La Serre, like his uncle Etienne
before him (who later became a somewhat unscrupulous crown
treasurer), came to Paris without a sou and took up residence in
an attic. All you needed to succeed as a writer, he maintained, was
a nice title and a pretty engraving. One of his relatives called him
the Muses' tailor because he outfitted them so well. After his
Parisian stint, La Serre went off to Lorraine, where he seems to
have acquired some noble patrons. Thus launched, he next turns
up in the capacity of official historian following the queen mother
on her trip to Brussels. At the death of Marie de Médicis, Richelieu recalled him to Paris and gave him lodgings in the Palais
Cardinal, the carriage he was to boast of, and a pension of 2,000
écus. This generation of Pugets fared well. La Serre's notorious
cousin Montauron became so rich after buying a *charge* in Guyenne that he could permit himself the insolent luxury of addressing the *grands seigneurs* by the familiar *tu* form. One of these
nobles is said to have turned one day to La Serre with the com-

---

11. Ibid., pp. 58–102. On pp. 58–59 Ranum gives an excellent analysis of
names as gauges of the hierarchy in titles. On p. 63 he discusses pensions and
other rights of officeholders; discussion of payment will be found on pp. 96–100.
For political rights, see pp. 58–63, 98–99. On the requirement of loyalty, see
p. 110.
12. Tallemant, *Historiettes*, 2:543.

ment "By God, Monsieur, we are nothing but common scoundrels compared to you. Do me the honor of employing me in your service and I will abandon all my claims at the Court."[13]

If a Châtillon could say such a thing to a Puget (the "La Serre" comes from a piece of property purchased by the family), things had come to a pretty pass. People such as La Serre of course lacked the prestige of the *noblesse d'épée*, but they rapidly acquired the outward trappings of authority which the authentic seigneurs, with their declining income from land, could less and less well afford. The bitterness underlying Châtillon's sarcasm is all the more comprehensible considering that Richelieu regularly gave out pensions to such newly ennobled parvenus as La Serre or to foreigners such as the royal engravers Jean Valdor and Jacques de Bie.

The producers of portrait books during the time of Richelieu were thus paid officials, an anonymous, long-forgotten team of workers commissioned to serve and to promote a royal ideology elaborated under the cardinal's aegis. The products were striking neither in their originality nor in their aesthetic merit. Nevertheless, they form the tangible evidence of a crucial phase in the history of the aesthetic notion of verisimilitude, for they endow the traditional iconography and mythology of the hero with a new ideological function.

Jacques Amyot's Plutarch, *Les Vies des hommes illustres grecs et romains,* provided a formal model for the portrait book. The 1584 engraved edition (there were no woodcuts in the original 1559 edition) reveals an emerging pattern of construction that was to remain in use for decades to come. Each of Amyot's "lives" is preceded by a small woodcut profile head in a frame of laurel leaves. The illustrations are modest, occupying only about a quarter page (fig. 3). On the title page we are told that they have been made with a scrupulous attention to accuracy. The illustrations are said to be "living effigies . . . , carefully taken from ancient medals." The authenticity of the verbal portrait is thus reinforced by the complementary visual portrait based on an artifact of alleged historical authenticity.

One of the earliest of the official luxury portrait books, André Thévet's *Vrais pourtraits et vies des hommes illustres grecz, latins, et payens . . .* (1584), repeats and develops the pattern of construction

13. For La Serre and his family, see ibid., pp. 530–44. The final quotation of the paragraph is from p. 538.

LA VIE DE LYCVRGVS

LICVRGVS.

SOMMAIRE.

1 Opinions diuerses touchant le temps auquel a vescu Lycurgus, sa genealogie, Deces de son pere, Lycurgus refuse le royaume des Lacedæmoniens, Est tuteur de Charilaus, Lycurgus se bannist pour euiter au soupçon de la royauté affectée.

2 Voyage de Lycurgus en Candie, Il persuade à Thales d'aller à Sparte, voyage de Lycurgus en Asie où il recueillit & assembla la poësie d'Homere en vn corps, son voyage en Egypte & Affrique.

3 Du retour de Lycurgus en Lacedæmone, il consulte Apollo en Delphes pour l'institution de ses loix, institution d'vn Senat composé de vingt & huict Senateurs, de l'oracle Retra, du lieu du conseil, de l'autorité du peuple Spartiate appellé au conseil, puissance du peuple au conseil reiglée.

4 Institution des Ephores, Lycurgus fait de nouueau partir les terres, & fait descrier toute sorte de monnoye, fait forger monnoye de fer, Bannit tous les mestiers superflus, gobelet Laconique, Ordonnance touchant les conuies, Alcander creue l'œil à Lycurgus en vne mutinerie, punition d'Alcander, teple à Minerue Ophiletide, ceremonies de Sparte pour estre receu en copagnie des conuies, brouet noir.

5 Loix de Lycurgus non escriptes, des contracts, loix contre la superfluité, ordonnance de ne faire souuent la guerre contre mesmes ennemis.

6 Ordonnance touchant l'exercice des filles, punition contre ceux qui ne se vouloient marier, ceremonies touchant les mariages en Sparte, enfans communs en Sparte, nuls adulteres en Sparte.

7 De la naissance & nourriture des enfans, du gouuernemēt des enfans estans en l'âge de sept ans, de celuy en l'aage de douze & de vingt ans, larrecin familier aux Spartiates, des demandes Laconiques, de l'amour qu'ils s'entreportoient, du parler des Spartiates.

8 De l'estude des Spartiates à bien chanter & composer chansons, des sacrifices que faisoit le Roy auant vne bataille, exercices des Spartiates moins penibles en guerre qu'en paix, chāson de Castor, le Roy des Spartiates marche le premier en bataille, ordonnance de marcher en bataille des Spartiates, Spartiates misericordieux en victoire.

9 Du gouuernement des Spartiates estans paruenuz en aage d'homme, du grand loisir & oisiueté que Lycurgus introduisit en sa ville, proces bannis de Sparte.

10 Des premiers Senateurs de Sparte, de ceux qui estoient substituez aux decedez, ceremonie en l'election d'vn Senateur.

11 Ceremonies pour les sepulcures, temps du dueil limité, deffenses de sortir hors le territoire sans congé, de l'ordonnance dite Cryptia contre les Ilotes.

12 De la subtile inuention de Lycurgus pour faire entretenir ses loix, serment donné par les Spartiates à Lycurgus, Lycurgus se fait mourir pour tenir ses citoyens obligez à ses loix.

13 L'or & l'argent commença à se couler dedans Sparte du temps du Roy Agis, Lisander infracteur des loix de Lycurgus, Sparte commande à toute la Grece, Temple & sacrifices instituez en l'honneur de Lycurgus, Lycurgides, cendres de Lycurgus espandues en la mer & pourquoy.

3. Lycurgus. From Jacques Amyot, *Les Vies des hommes illustres grecs et romains* (1584). By permission of the Houghton Library, Harvard University.

in Amyot's *Vies*. Thévet's title specifies the origin of the portraits and lives contained in his book: "taken from paintings, books, ancient and modern medals." His portraits are "true," therefore, because they are exact representations of earlier representations, a proof of supposed accuracy in the engraving of portraits that continued to be advanced far into the seventeenth century. The relative proportions of image and text change dramatically in Thévet's *Pourtraits*. Whereas in Amyot the small woodcuts serve primarily as embellishments of the text, Thévet announces with pride that he is the first to popularize copperplate engraving in Paris,[14] and allots a half page for each plate in this large folio (fig. 4). The advantages of the newer technique of copperplate engraving, which permitted much finer detail than the cruder woodcut process, are obvious here. The half-page portraits have an imposing intensity that gives them an importance equal to that of the text. As in the ubiquitous Renaissance emblem, the text prolongs the image, and the image signifies the text. The portraits also reveal their affinities with the medals from which they were said to be taken: like the reverse side of a medal bearing the companion emblem to the portrait on the obverse, the text serves as an expository amplification of the image preceding it.[15]

We should not be surprised to learn that Jacques Amyot and André Thévet were royal officials. Like other writers of historical genres in the sixteenth century, they were learned men. In their capacity as court writers, they put their learning to a celebratory purpose.[16] In their respective prefaces, both Thévet, *premier cosmographe du Roy*, and Amyot, *Conseiller du Roy*, make pronouncements on the nature and uses of history, which form the most basic topoi of the portrait books.

History and the portrait are as closely associated as poetry and painting.[17] For the translator of Plutarch, history is "a depiction

14. André Thévet, "Au Benevole lecteur," in *Les Vrais pourtraits et vies des hommes illustres grecz, latins et payens* . . . (Paris, 1584), unpaginated.

15. See Bardon, *Portrait mythologique*, pp. 15–16, 65.

16. On the background of sixteenth-century French historians, see George Huppert, *The Idea of Perfect History* (Urbana, Ill., 1970), pp. 6–7. On historical research in sixteenth-century France, see Donald R. Kelley, *Foundations of Modern Historical Scholarship: Language, Law, and History in the French Renaissance* (New York, 1970).

17. For an analysis of the rhetorical relationship between history and the portrait in the reign of Louis XIV, see Louis Marin, *Le Portrait du roi* (Paris, 1981). There is no historical dimension to this analysis. In focusing exclusively on history and the portrait as rhetorical strategies of the representation of absolutism in the reign of Louis XIV, Marin neglects the entire tradition of the portrait book and pictorial history.

IEAN GVTTEMBERG, INVENTEVR
de l'Imprimerie   Chapitre 97.

Ntre les plus belles & loüables inuentions il nous faut librement confeſſer que l'Imprimerie a eſté & eſt auiourd'huy la meilleure & plus à eſtimer : par le moyen de laquelle deux perſonnes roulans la preſſe imprimeront en vn iour plus grande quantité de liures, que n'euſſent ſceu auparauant eſcrire pluſieurs perſonnes en vn an. On tient que ceſt art a eſté inuenté à Mayence, ville d'Allemagne, en l'an mil quatre cens quarante deux par Iean Guttemberg, ou, ſelon les autres,

Premiers inuenteurs de l'art d'imprimer.

4. Gutenberg. From André Thévet, *Vrais Pourtraits et vies des hommes illustres grecz, latins, et payens . . .* (1584). By permission of the Houghton Library, Harvard University.

that places before our eyes, no more or less than in a painting, things worthy of memory."[18] Thévet's "image" functions as history, for it is "a resemblance, example, and effigy, which represents the person of whom it is the portrait, seemingly restores to life in a representation before our very eyes a long dead or absent person."[19] Both history and the portrait serve, therefore, in the tradition of classical antiquity, as examples of virtue and greatness.[20] Amyot sees in history examples that "move and teach." Thévet finds that portraits and images have "the power and internal gift of making us cherish virtue and detest evil." History for Amyot is faithful to Horace's *utile dulci;* images of the dead or absent, according to Thévet, bring us a "marvelous utility and joy." Furthermore, Thévet grants a universal pedagogical value to the image in that it can teach the illiterate. This property explains why painting, by his account, has commonly been called "mute history, and the book of idiots." Is this an echo of the famous comment that Plutarch attributed to Simonides on painting as mute poetry, poetry as spoken painting, a favorite Renaissance topos for partisans of the *ut pictura poesis* doctrine? In any event, the topos recurs regularly in the later portrait books, which offer variants of Thévet's formula.

History and the portrait, Amyot and Thévet agree, are glorifications of the great. Interestingly enough, Thévet qualifies this position with remarks concerning the need to glorify the virtuous and the erudite as much as the highly born. Such statements disappeared in the later portrait books, where the writer effaced himself before the greatness of the subject that he had been commissioned to represent. *Gloire* is at the heart of Thévet's doctrine. Illustrious deeds, he maintains, should be "engraved on the copperplate of memory." History, we read in Amyot, is a "thesaurus of human life, which preserves the memorable words and deeds of men from the death of oblivion."

Amyot's *Vies* were dedicated to Henri II; Thévet's *Pourtraits* were dedicated to Henri III. Both appeared during a period of bitter civil and religious strife. In 1558 Pierre Paschal was appointed royal historiographer, the first such appointment re-

18. Jacques Amyot, "Aux Lecteurs," in *Les Vies des hommes illustres grecs et romains. Comparees l'une avec l'autre par Plutarque de Chaeronee* (Paris, 1584), unpaginated.
19. Thévet, "Au Benevole Lecteur." Further quotations from Thévet and Amyot are from the prefaces to their works, cited in nn. 14 and 18.
20. On the poetics of history and the exemplum, see Karlheinz Stierle, "L'Histoire comme exemple, l'exemple comme histoire: Contribution à la pragmatique et à la poétique des textes narratifs," *Poétique* 10 (1972):176–98.

corded in the seventeenth-century lists. Paschal's first announced project was a "lives of illustrious men."[21] Did the crown feel an especially pressing need to sponsor such works as Amyot's and Paschal's just on the eve of the Religious Wars? We may never have enough documentation to answer this question satisfactorily, but the fact that all three authors held court-appointed positions indicates that their books must have had a certain ideological value for a monarchy faced with extreme disunity in the land. The Protestant Théodore de Bèze also wrote a *Vrais pourtraits* (Geneva, 1581, a translation of his *Icones,* published in Geneva the preceding year), but his was of "*hommes illustres en piété et doctrine.*" Was Thévet's portrait book meant in part as a response? We know that Catholic reformers after the Council of Trent were eager to promote the use of illustrations in their own books and to suppress them in Protestant works.[22] Whatever may have been the value of Thévet's portraits in religious polemic, the secular ideological function of both Thévet's portraits and Amyot's *Vies* is closely tied to the Renaissance concept and practice of analogy. In royal iconography, the depiction of a prince as a Roman emperor signified both the emperor as a model and the prince as a modern example.[23] The modern prince was thus the equal or the superior of his predecessor. In the traditional "mirrors of princes," the heroes of antiquity served the modern ruler as so many examples to emulate.[24] Amyot and Thévet continue and renew this tradition. As we commemorate these ancient heroes, they seem to be saying to the monarchs to whom they dedicate their efforts, so shall you be commemorated. One term of the analogy, the modern ruler, is not explicitly present in Amyot and Thévet, but it is more than implied by the eloquence of the dedications.

Thévet speaks of painting as a kind of divine imitation; Amyot says that history always tells the truth. These rhetorical statements are part of a coherent system of representation founded on the belief that history is as truthful as painting, painting as truthful as history, because both represent heroes of the past and restore the dead to life. Truth is analogical: the truth of the past is present example, and therefore the present will be example to the future. To imply that Henri II is at least the equal of any hero in Plu-

21. Ranum, *Artisans of Glory,* p. 71.
22. Duportal, *Livres à figures,* pp. 229–30.
23. Bardon, *Portrait mythologique,* p. 14.
24. See Ranum's discussion of the "mirror of princes" genre, *Artisans of Glory,* pp. 44–48.

tarch's *Lives* is thus part of a significant rhetoric of praise. As the ancient heroes are represented as examples to Henri, so Henri will be an example to the future.

The analogical system of representation by Plutarchan "parallels" is the formal foundation of La Serre's paean to Richelieu, *Le Portrait de Scipion l'Africain* (Bordeaux, 1641), the very type of portrait book produced in the cardinal's administration. It is rigorously constructed according to a correspondence or "parallel" between Scipio and the French minister. The plan of the book is announced in the subtitle: "l'image de la gloire et de la vertu représentée au naturel dans celle de Monseigneur le cardinal, duc de Richelieu." Richelieu's portrait is to be a representation of Scipio's, or of the "image of glory and virtue." In other words, the correspondence between Richelieu and Scipio is established through the middle term of "glory and virtue" shared by both. Accordingly, the first part of the book is devoted to the portrait of Scipio, the second to the "parallels" between Scipio and Richelieu. Lest we forget the moral value of Scipio's portrait, La Serre accompanies his narration with marginalia containing useful aphorisms drawn from the Roman hero's life. In the second part, the "Parallels," several paragraphs relating Richelieu's achievements alternate with corresponding ones about Scipio. La Serre's history, like that of his sixteenth-century predecessors, is in the tradition of classical antiquity, where "lives" are so many exempla and history is inseparable from morality.

The engravings so explicitly transpose the correspondence to the visual medium as to render the text superfluous. The emblematic relationship between text and image of the earlier books has been transformed here: text and image now merely reproduce each other. The implicit analogy between ancient and modern which we found in Thévet and Amyot has become obvious and redundant in the work of La Serre. The pressing ideological need for the portrait to "resemble" the person portrayed has reduced the wider-ranging moral meaning of emblematic portraits to a narrow, pointed praise of the subject, thus impoverishing the representation.[25] The engraving by Michel Lasne for La Serre's frontispiece (fig. 5) depicts a winged Fame in the Temple of Honor bearing aloft an open book; the left-hand page carries this inscription: "Le Portraict de Scipion l'Affricain ou l'image de la

25. For the concept of "impoverishment," see Bardon, *Portrait mythologique*, pp. 53–54.

TEMPLVM
LE PORTRAICT DE SCIPION LAFFRICAIN OV LIMAGE DE LA GLOIRE ET DE LA VERTV
REPRESENTE DANS CELLE DE MONSEIG LE CARDINAL DVC DE RICHELIEV

5. Scipio, by Michel Lasne. Frontispiece. Jean Puget de La Serre, *Le Portrait de Scipion l'Africain* (1641). By permission of the Houghton Library, Harvard University.

gloire et de la vertu"; on the right-hand page: "Représenté dans celle de Monseigr. le Cardinal duc de Richelieu." Below this inscription a statue of Scipio bears a portrait of Richelieu framed in laurel leaves, repeating the wreath around Scipio's head. Facing the dedication page is a full-length portrait of Richelieu with a laudatory quartrain beneath it (fig. 6). Two additional engravings precede the section titled "Parallèles," which follows the "Portrait de Scipion l'Africain." The first of these engravings, by Nicolas Carré (fig. 7), shows a statue of Virtue in her temple, holding two symmetrical portraits: on the left, Scipio in an oval frame bearing the legend "Hoc opus naturae"; on the right, Richelieu also in an oval frame bearing the legend "Hoc opus intelligentiae." Above this scene Fame again extends her open book with "Parallèles de Scipion l'Africain" inscribed on the left, "Monseigr. le Cardinal, Duc de Richelieu" on the right. The second engraving preceding the "Parallèles" (and following the Preface) offers a double full-length portrait of Scipio and Richelieu by Jean Picard (fig. 8).

La Serre was justly ridiculed by his contemporaries as a hack writer. As he changed subjects he hardly bothered to change his material, altering but little the construction and formula of each book. Thus his *Alexandre ou les parallèles de Monseigneur le duc d'Anguien avec ce fameux monarque* (Paris, 1645) repeats the form of his *Scipion* with respect to both text and engravings. The engravings of the *Scipion* and other works by La Serre are of special interest, however, because they are so frequently in the portrait-within-a-portrait mode, an already existent device that became widespread in the seventeenth century.[26] Engravings lent themselves particularly well to this technique, since they were often made not from live models but from painted portraits. Thus, as in the work of Nanteuil, the frame was incorporated into the engraved version and was made an essential part of it.[27] The actual portrait within a portrait is another matter, nonetheless, for in it we see a figure (often allegorical) holding the portrait of another figure, sometimes a dead person, emphasizing the commemorative aspect of the portrait, but sometimes a living one. In either case, the *gloire* of the figure portrayed was assured by its very depiction in a portrait, a form traditionally reserved for the noble

26. See Francis H. Dowley, "French Portraits of Ladies as Minerva," *Gazette des beaux-arts*, May–June 1955, pp. 266–70. Dowley's discussion of painted and literary portraits in this article contains very useful information.

27. See T. H. Thomas, *French Portrait Engraving of the Seventeenth and Eighteenth Centuries* (London, 1910), pp. 15–16.

6. Richelieu. From Jean Puget de la Serre, *Le Portrait de Scipion l'Africain* (1641). By permission of the Houghton Library, Harvard University.

7. Temple of Virtue, by Nicolas Carré. From Jean Puget de La Serre, *Le Portrait de Scipion l'Africain* (1641). By permission of the Houghton Library, Harvard University.

Ioan. Picart fecit.

Tu vois deux Scipions tu vois deux Richelieux
Dont la rare vertu n'eut jamais de Seconde

Mais Si l'yn a cueilly tous les lauriers du monde
L'autre en doit moißoner les palmes dans les Cieux.
la Serre.

8. Scipio and Richelieu, by Jean Picard. From Jean Puget de La Serre, *Le Portrait de Scipion l'Africain* (1641). By permission of the Houghton Library, Harvard University

86

and the great. Thus in Michel Lasne's engraving for La Serre's book, Scipio, raised to glory himself in his representation as a statue, bears the portrait of the living Richelieu.

A variant of this device is the mirror image,[28] as found, for example, in La Serre's *Portrait de la reyne* (Paris, 1644). The engraving facing the title page depicts Virtue in a three-quarter view holding up a mirror to Anne of Austria in profile (fig. 9). In a block initial on the first page, a woman shows a portrait of Anne to the queen, again with the queen in profile and the inner portrait in a three-quarter view (fig. 10). One critic has remarked that the increasing use of the three-quarter view in seventeenth-century mythological portraits indicated a greater realism in the depiction.[29] This observation does not explain, however, the persistence of the profile and its use in conjunction with the three-quarter view. According to Meyer Schapiro, frontal and profile views in group portraits function as a semiotic system, in which individual elements have meaning only in relation to the other features in their context. Thus, whereas in one system the frontal view could signify "living" and the profile "dead," in another these meanings could be reversed, or else they could denote a completely different opposition, such as good and evil, sacred and profane. In Western art, the three-quarter view seems to have developed from a tradition in which the sacred and the eternal were depicted frontally; the profile, by contrast, was reserved for historical figures.[30] This distinction holds true for La Serre's *Portrait de la reyne*, in which the real or historical Anne is shown in profile, while the glorified Anne in the inner portrait and the figure of Virtue are shown in three-quarter view. Whence the metaphor: Anne is to Virtue as the real Anne is to the portrait; or Anne is the incarnation or portrait of Virtue. La Serre's texts, like the engravings, are also conceived as portraits within portraits. Within the portrait of Scipio we find the portrait of Richelieu; within Alexander that of the future Grand Condé. The *Portrait de la reyne* is actually a portrait of Virtue, with each chapter devoted to another of its manifestations: piety, justice, goodness, and so on. Again, the inner portrait, that of the modern hero or heroine, makes explicit the analogy that remained implicit in the earlier sixteenth-century works.

The ideological function of the portrait within a portrait is

28. See Dowley, "French Portraits," p. 267.
29. Bardon, *Portrait mythologique*, p. 66.
30. Meyer Schapiro, *Words into Pictures* (The Hague, 1973).

La vertu luy tient le miroir
Mais Ellemesme en est la glace
Puis quelle seule nous fait voir
Tous les traits qui font sur sa face
P. de la Serre.

9. Virtue and Anne of Austria. From Jean Puget de La Serre, *Le Portrait de la reyne* (1644). By permission of the Houghton Library, Harvard University.

10. Anne and her portrait. From Jean Puget de La Serre, *Le Portrait de la reyne* (1644). By permission of the Houghton Library, Harvard University.

clear. Tallemant relates that La Serre planned an engraving of himself in the following manner: his own portrait at the top of the plate, below it a library stocked with La Serre's works; still lower a Minerva holding Time enchained and showing him another portrait of La Serre while forbidding him to touch it.[31] Thus did Richelieu's hireling dream of immortalizing himself for a posterity that was not to be his.

Even under the heavy hand of a La Serre, this type of representation has a disturbing, trompe l'oeil kind of ambiguity. Which is more real or historical, the portrait or the inner portrait, Scipio or Richelieu? The same Anne is shown in the three-quarter allegorical view and in the historical profile. La Serre somewhat crudely

31. Tallemant, *Historiettes*, 2:544.

observes the symmetry of *ut pictura poesis:* the image tells a story within a story as the text draws a portrait within a portrait. But both text and image provoke the same confusion: which is the historical and which the allegorical? This ambiguity is inherent in a concept of history as primarily a series of exempla and in the standard representations of moderns in mythological garb. But whereas in earlier Renaissance representations the explicit (ancient hero) and the implicit (modern ruler) were merely related through the analogy, in the seventeenth century they merge: the modern ruler becomes the ancient hero, and an "exact" portrayal—that is, one in accord with the ideological demands of the time—will portray him as such. The portrait allegorizes history as it historicizes allegory.

About the same time that La Serre was composing portraits whose verisimilitude was inseparable from their glorifying function, another type of "true portrait" appeared. Jacques de Bie's *Vrais portraits des rois de France* (1634), dedicated to Louis XIII, is like Thévet's *Vrais pourtraits* in that its "truth" lies in the portraits' supposed resemblance to their archaeological models: monuments, seals, medals, and the like.[32] But this gallery of heroes depicts neither classical antiquity nor mythological figures; it is a royal genealogy. Richelieu became convinced that history would serve his needs better than the more facile genre of panegyrics which La Serre also practiced along with portraits.[33] The cardinal endeavored to build an official history to record the achievements of French kings.[34] The question of the origins of the French people and of the Franks had been a subject of much discussion for some time, but under Louis XIII and Richelieu increasing stress was laid on the great antiquity of the French monarchy at the expense of the prestige of the nobility.[35] Scipion Dupleix, in

32. The full title reads: *Les Vrais portraits des rois de France: tirez de ce qui nous reste de leurs Monumens, Sceaux, Medailles ou autres Effigies, conservées dans les plus rares et plus curieux Cabinets du Royaume* (Paris, 1634).

33. L. Delavaud, *Quelques collaborateurs de Richelieu,* in *Rapports et notices sur l'édition des Mémoires du Cardinal de Richelieu,* ed. Jules Lair, le Baron de Courcel (Paris, 1907–14), 2:254. La Serre wrote, for example, the *Panégyriques des hommes illustres de notre siècle* (Paris, 1655).

34. William F. Church, "France," in *National Consciousness, History, and Political Culture in Early Modern Europe,* ed. Orest Ranum (Baltimore, 1975), p. 52.

35. See Michel Tyvaert, "L'Image du roi: Légitimité et moralité royales dans les histoires de France au XVIIe siècle," *Revue d'histoire moderne et contemporaine* 21 (October–December 1974):523–26; Emile Roy, *La Vie et les oeuvres de Charles Sorel* (Paris, 1891), p. 340.

his *Histoire de Louis le Juste* (1635), named as one of Louis XIII's three major achievements the fact that he had made royal authority "absolutely sovereign" by bringing "the greatest of the great as well as the humblest into obedience." Dupleix reminds the king that he had previously presented him with a general history of all French kings preceding him (the *Histoire générale de la France*, 1621–28).[36] The implication seems to be that the present work is a logical continuation of the former. That is, once the historian had conformed to the crown's propagandistic designs in establishing the superiority of royal over noble genealogy, he could then commence a history of the present reign. Other historians interwove the two projects of glorification in one work where the histories of past and present kings functioned as mutually reinforcing metaphors for the grandeur of the reigning monarch.

In Jacques de Bie's portrait gallery, Louis XIII comes last, a position that is both logical and significant: the modern ruler is the incarnation of his forebears, whom he will surpass in his glory. The implied comparison is not with heroes of classical antiquity, but with French kings, a much more exclusive metaphor than the analogies derived from ancient mythology, which were applicable to nobles and monarchs alike. A small number of images served for a variety of occasions; the signs used in mythological representation were polyvalent.[37] Even Dupleix in his dedication compares Louis XIII to Alexander, Scipio, Caesar, and other ancient heroes as well as to Charlemagne and Henri IV. But only the monarch can appropriately be compared to his ancestors. In royal genealogy absolutist ideology found its most suitable metaphor.

This is not to say that the genealogical metaphor actually replaced the heroic or mythological during the period of Richelieu.[38] The repertory of representational possibilities was too large for any single procedure to take over. But as the heroes of classical antiquity functioned differently in Puget's books than in their sixteenth-century precedents, so royal genealogy in turn acquired a

---

36. Scipion Dupleix, *Histoire de Louis le Juste, XIII du nom, Roy de France et de Navarre* (Paris, 1635), "Au Roy" (unpaginated).

37. See Bardon, *Portrait mythologique*, pp. 276–77.

38. For a different analysis of the relationship between these two metaphors during the period of Richelieu, see Ranum, *Artisans of Glory*, pp. 114–28. The practice of writing genealogical histories spread among the French nobility at the end of the sixteenth century and in the seventeenth. Family histories were even older. See Natalie Z. Davis, "Ghosts, Kin, and Progeny: Some Features of Family Life in Early Modern France," *Daedalus* 106 (Spring 1977):96–98.

new ideological value in Richelieu's time. When the function and value of representational material changes, there follows a change in the nature of the representation.

In his preface, Jacques de Bie, like Thévet before him, informs the reader of the method that enabled him to achieve such exact likenesses of the kings. Assuming that the archaeological model was itself a faithful replica, Bie was shocked to discover, he says, how little resemblance some modern portraits bore to the artifacts that he claimed to uncover. He would make faithful portraits or none at all. And in the absence of seals, medals, or monuments to serve as models for the portrait of a particular monarch, he simply left a framed blank in its place. Bie requests that anyone possessing the requisite materials for his missing portraits forward them to him. Mézeray, in his *Histoire de France depuis Pharamond*, followed Bie's lead in leaving blank space when necessary.[39]

The effectiveness of the royal genealogy as exemplum depended on belief in its authenticity. Historical accuracy was the measure of authority. When, however, the reign of an individual monarch was advanced as an exemplum, the historicity of the representation yielded to pomp and circumstance. Such was the emphasis in the *Triomphes de Louis le Juste* (1649), an immense collaborative effort, directed by the royal engraver Jean Valdor, which contained 154 engravings, including maps of cities, sieges, and battles, and heroic poems, emblems, and odes in praise of Louis XIII. It has been called the most important illustrated historical work to appear between 1600 and 1660.[40] The dedicatory epistles to the queen regent and to the young Louis XIV make it abundantly clear that the book was conceived along the lines of a "mirror of princes" in which the late king would serve as an exemplar.

Valdor's extravaganza called forth all the mythological paraphernalia suitable to the depiction of Louis XIII in his "triumph." An ode, paralleling Louis XIII and Hercules, is accompanied by an engraving of Hercules, with a bust of the young Louis XIV functioning as an inner portrait (fig. 11). Strewn about Hercules are the traditional symbols of his wisdom (an owl), power (a

39. We should take Bie's statements with a grain of salt. It seems that his "method" was to make up most of his medals. Mézeray was later led into error by following him. See Josèphe Jacquiot, "La Littérature et les médailles," *Cahiers de l'Association Internationale des Études Françaises*, May 1972, p. 203n.

40. Jean Valdor, *Les Triomphes de Louis le Iuste, XIII du nom, Roy de France et de Navarre* (Paris, 1649). I refer to unpaginated sections of the book. On this work, see Duportal, *Livres à Figures*, pp. 285–86.

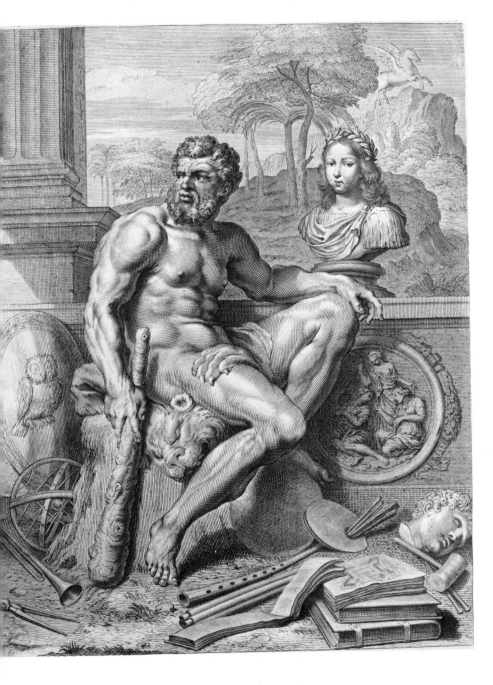

11. Hercules. From Jean Valdor, *Les Triomphes de Louis le Juste* (1649). By permission of the Houghton Library, Harvard University.

globe), artistic accomplishments (a palette), and other virtues. In the ode, the representation of Louis XIII as Hercules is developed by the parallel between the monster-slayer of old and the modern victor in battle.[41] Accuracy in the *Triomphes de Louis le Juste* is applied not to the poetic and visual depiction of the late king but to the graphic illustration of his exploits in the form of city maps, battle plans, drawings of sieges. Mythological representation, then, was not abandoned in favor of greater accuracy during the formative period of the ideology of absolutism; it was simply assigned to a more appropriate place.

The use of royal genealogy as exempla could be broadened to include pillars of the monarchy other than the king himself. In his *Portraits des hommes illustres françois qui sont peints dans la gallerie du palais Cardinal de Richelieu*,[42] Vulson de la Colombière, in collaboration with two royal painters and engravers, produced a kind of genealogy or "lives" of state heroes and heroines, which was designed to function for Chancellor Séguier as Bie designed his *Vrais portraits* to function for Louis XIII. Deriving added value from the fact that the originals adorned the walls of Richelieu's palace, Vulson's twenty-six portraits include, among others, Simon de Montfort, Bertrand du Guesclin, Joan of Arc, Gaston de Foix, Marie de Médicis, Henri IV, Richelieu, Anne of Austria, and Gaston d'Orléans. Each portrait is accompanied by a summary of the subject's life. These portraits implicitly serve as exempla to Séguier, whose portrait (fig. 12) faces the dedication to him, as Séguier then serves as the exemplary state hero to posterity. The example, like that of the royal genealogy, is French (with the exception, of course, of the foreign queens), not mythological. The older allegorical mode of representation is relegated to the elaborately decorated frame of each portrait, where emblems alternate with scenes from the subject's life.

The portraits in these genealogies conform in at least one important respect to theories of representation that were slowly being

---

41. How vivid were the topoi we find in Valdor's *Triomphes* to the audiences of Racine's *Phèdre* some decades later? Was the analogical mode of representation still so alive that Theseus the monster-slayer would have been associated with a modern monarch? In that part of the *Triomphes* devoted to the "Exposition des Devises qui sont pour la Reyne Regente," one of Anne's emblems is a labyrinth through which she guides the young king. Phèdre's famous labyrinth speech (II, v) must have taken on quite a topical meaning if it was received with the same imagination as that which animates Valdor's book.

42. Vulson de la Colombière, *Les Portraits des hommes illustres françois qui sont peints dans la gallerie du palais Cardinal de Richelieu* (Paris, 1650).

12. Chancellor Séguier. From Vulson de la Colombière, *Portraits des hommes illustres françois qui sont peints dans la gallerie du palais Cardinal de Richelieu* (1650). By permission of the Houghton Library, Harvard University.

elaborated in the new academies: Richelieu's Académie Française and the more recent Académie Royale de Peinture et de Sculpture, founded in 1648. André Félibien's *Conférences,* or minutes to the meetings of the Académie Royale de Peinture, are prefaced by an outline of the rules that painting, like music and poetry, should follow. The artist must possess "perfect knowledge" of the object of representation, says Félibien. Although one must imitate nature, the highest form of painting is allegorical. *Vraisemblance* is necessary to all representation, and consists both of Aristotelian probability (what Félibien calls "possiblity") and *costume,* or decorum. *Costume* is "an exact observation of everything appropriate to the persons represented." It is part of the "*bienséance* [propriety] that must be observed concerning age, sex, country, profession, custom, passion, and manner of dress peculiar to each nation." In its ability to adhere to the rule of *costume,* the genealogical portrait held an immeasurable advantage over its mythological counterpart. The portrayal of Louis XIII as a descendant of French kings was, after all, more appropriate to him by Félibien's standards than his portrayal as Hercules. And yet the academicians could not let go of allegory.[43] It was too venerable a tradition, too well established in the arsenal of royal iconography to receive anything but a place of honor in the academic annals. Thus mythological representations persist, even dominate French classicism, when theory seems to repudiate them. And all the contradictions attendant on the coexistence of *costume* in theory and mythology in practice persist along with them.

Verbal Portraits and the Fronde

In January 1649, right in the middle of the Fronde, the first two volumes of a very different type of portrait book appeared. From the first to the last volumes, published in 1653, Mlle de Scudéry's novel (to which her brother Georges affixed his name) *Artamène ou le Grand Cyrus* remained an unqualified success. As the volumes appeared, the publisher, Augustin Courbé, ran out of stock so quickly that he had to boost his printing orders for the

---

43. See [André Félibien], "Preface," *Conférences de l'Académie royale de peinture et de sculpture pendant l'année 1667* (Paris, 1669), unpaginated. Bernard Magné explains this paradox by the rise of what he terms a "national ideology." See his *Crise de la littérature française sous Louis XIV: Humanisme et nationalisme* (Paris, 1976), pp. 578–651.

latest volumes and to reprint the first three in 1650. In 1654, with the entire work just off the press, he was obliged to produce a third edition of the first two volumes, and in 1655 he brought out a complete fourth edition.[44]

Madeleine de Scudéry, who as a nonagenarian was still reading *L'Astrée,* which she had adored as a girl, learned her lesson well.[45] In *Le Grand Cyrus,* as in d'Urfé's novel, the beau monde appeared in exotic disguise. All the principal habitués of Mme de Rambouillet's salon and the Hôtel de Condé form the cast of ancient Persian characters. Everyone wanted to figure in this modish gallery. A portrait in *Le Grand Cyrus* was, after all, a status symbol. "You wouldn't believe how happy the ladies are to be put into her novel," says Tallemant, "more exactly, to have people see their portraits there." And how many women have had the ambition to appear in her portraits! he adds. Mlle de Scudéry's roman à clef set the style even in the rue Saint-Honoré, where a feather dealer announced his wares with the sign "Le Grand Cyrus."[46] Madeleine's portraits had a greater piquancy than d'Urfé's, owing to the troubled times. Condé, as Artamène, or Cyrus, the hero of the novel, was also one of the heroes of the Fronde, having gained wide sympathy during his imprisonment. His sister, Mme de Longueville, to whom the novel is dedicated and who appears in it as Mandane, was one of the leading intriguers of the Fronde. The entire novel is like a literary equivalent of the collective or group portrait, a genre that goes back at least to the Renaissance. The characters in these paintings, generally of biblical episodes and prevalent in Rome under Sixtus IV, appear with the features of well-known real-life people. Certain paintings in the Sistine Chapel depict biblical episodes reminiscent of contemporary events, and contain portraits of the participants in those events. Viewers of the time would have recognized not only the biblical figures but the contemporary personages as it were beneath the mask. If the frescoes in the Sistine Chapel could be read as a "Who's Who of 1482,"[47] *Le Grand Cyrus* could be read as a "Who's Who of the Fronde."

The crown's fiscal policies had for several decades prepared the way for the Fronde. A tax revolt in the Paris Parlement initiated

44. Georges Mongrédien, *Madeleine de Scudéry et son salon* (Paris, 1946), p. 47.
45. Ibid., pp. 13–14.
46. Tallemant, *Historiettes,* 2:689, 690, 693.
47. The phrase is John Pope-Hennessey's, in his *Portrait in the Renaissance* (New York, 1966), pp. 16–17. See his discussion of collective portraits, pp. 5–23.

its first phase, the so-called Parlementary Fronde. In the second phase, or Princes' Fronde, various disaffected members of royalty and nobility took the opportunity to satisfy private ambitions in acts of rebellion and lawlessness. One historian has seen this mid-century web of political and amorous intrigue less as a revolt against Richelieu's successor, Mazarin, than as a "posthumous revenge on Richelieu," a conflict of princes versus royal authority.[48] Scholarly opinion is divided over the question of just how much Richelieu's intendants may have encroached on the authority of those *grands* who acted as provincial governors. Condé, the governor of Burgundy and Berry, and Longueville, the governor of Normandy, were leaders of the noble frondeurs, but Vendôme in Brittany, for example, was a Mazarinist. Both the *noblesse d'épée* and the *noblesse de robe* were dissatisfied by the crown's manipulation of the *paulette*, or annual tax on officials, the former because venality posed a constant threat to their status, the latter because suspensions or threatened suspensions of the tax were a menace to their very existence. The expectations of the *noblesse d'épée* had been disappointed after the death of Louis XIII in 1643. Everyone had then expected Anne of Austria, certainly no friend of the former minister, to take her revenge and restore the privileges that Richelieu had withdrawn from the *grands*. Much general astonishment greeted her appointment of Mazarin, a foreigner who had been naturalized only four years before the regency, as Richelieu's replacement. Financial discontent, extreme resentment on the part of the princes and the *noblesse d'épée*, jockeying for prestige and power on the parts both of the *noblesse d'épée* and the *noblesse de robe:* all these factors figured as causes of the Fronde.[49]

After the four years of intrigue, fighting, and devastation that had begun in 1648, all the disparate rebellious groups emerged as losers in a war that resulted in a strengthened monarchy. It has been argued that even the crown was not unequivocally victorious, since the legalism of Parlement and certain reforms that it had

48. Pierre-Georges Lorris, *La Fronde* (Paris, 1961), p. 12.
49. Ibid., pp. 12–17. See also the following analyses of the Fronde: Ernst H. Kossmann, *La Fronde* (Leiden, 1954); A. Lloyd Moote, *The Revolt of the Judges: The Parlement of Paris and the Fronde, 1643–1652* (Princeton, 1971); Boris Porshnev, *Les Soulèvements populaires en France de 1623 à 1648* (Paris, 1963), pp. 505–82. Moote sees the discontent of the *parlementaires* and the *officiers*, particularly over matters such as the *paulette*, as essential motivating factors of the Fronde. Porshnev (p. 80) has questioned to what extent the provincial governors, as commanders of regional armies, had been weakened by the crown's policies before the Fronde.

won during the Fronde posed a lasting counterweight to royal authority. It is certain, however, that for the remainder of Louis XIV's reign, the authority of the crown was increased at the expense of the nobles. In the wake of the Fronde, Condé was off sulking with his Spanish troops, the archintriguer Retz in exile. Mazarin's return spelled crushing defeat for all frondeurs. Louis XIV, in a *lit de justice* of October 22, 1652, asserted his will over Parlement by forbidding its interference in affairs of state and reinforced the already existing split between *noblesse de robe* and *noblesse d'épée* by forbidding judges to enter the service of a noble or to join a noble party. This edict was merely a legalization of the powerlessness that the *grands* had experienced during the conflict, when, for example, Condé had not been able to control the Palais de Justice. Condé had been humiliated by the formation of a rebel administration in which nobles were obliged to share governance with judges. The collapse of the Fronde destroyed the prestige of the noble rebels.[50]

How titillating it must have been to the frondeurs and their sympathizers to see themselves glorified as heroes and heroines of ancient Persia in Mlle de Scudéry's *Grand Cyrus!* But for their Persian disguise, all of Condé's great battles are there, in accurate detail taken from contemporary accounts.[51] Mme de Longueville in her exile must have enjoyed reading of her brother's exploits and her own charms in the volumes of *Le Grand Cyrus* which the author had the thoughtfulness to send her. As a token of her gratitude she gave the Scudérys her portrait and a diamond necklace that may have been worth as much as 200 écus.[52] If the Scudérys easily won the hearts of the frondeurs with Madeleine's novel, they fared less well with the monarchy. With an arrogance typical of his class, Georges had informed d'Hozier, the king's genealogist, that he planned to write a history of the Scudéry family. When his governorship at Marseille was revoked, it is not unlikely that such incidents, along with his known loyalty to Mme de Longueville, played their part in the king's disfavor.[53] In her post-Fronde novel, *Clélie* (1654–61), Mlle de Scudéry was careful to include a flattering portrait of Mazarin. The characters of this

---

50. See Moote, *Revolt of the Judges,* pp. 352–54, 368.

51. Mongrédien, *Madeleine de Scudéry,* pp. 60–61.

52. Tallemant, *Historiettes,* 2:691. See also Victor Cousin, *La Société française au XVIIᵉ siècle, d'après Le Grand Cyrus de Mlle de Scudéry* (Paris, 1858), 1:45–67.

53. See Mongrédien, *Madeleine de Scudéry,* pp. 32, 39–40.

new roman à clef were no longer the flamboyant frondeurs but instead the more subdued guests of Madeleine's "Samedis," the erudite members of her famous salon.

The portraits in *Le Grand Cyrus* spoke to their audience with an eloquence that Richelieu's portrait books could never attain. For the message that Madeleine conveyed to her readers was simply this: You, not the monarch, are the real heroes of the day. And this is exactly what she says in her dedication to Mme de Longueville. With your mixture of Bourbon and Montmorency blood, she tells the rambunctious duchess, your family history consists of thrones, scepters, and crowns. Moreover, the maternal, Montmorency, or noble side of your family has produced as many heroes as the Bourbon or royal side; for this illustrious family is in fact older than the monarchy. I will make of you an example for posterity, she further informs her frondeuse friend, just as Xenophon did for his heroes.[54]

As the monarchy in Richelieu's portrait books had taken over the exemplary function previously allotted to the heroes of classical antiquity, so now this function devolves upon the princes and the nobles. The monarchy appropriated traditional mythological and genealogical representation for its own use; the nobility in turn reappropriated both for itself. It recreated its own mythology and its own genealogy to exemplify its greatness. I will make my Cyrus just as much an example as Xenophon made his, declares Mlle de Scudéry,[55] and indeed her casting of Condé as king is perfectly suited to her intention. The portrait as example lends further historical value to a narrative already written in the guise of history.

The portraits of *Le Grand Cyrus* derive also from another, related classical tradition, that of the literary portrait, a schematic arrangement of the exterior and interior aspects of the model. It had acquired the status of a literary genre from its use in Suetonius and other writers of classical antiquity through the Middle Ages and into the Renaissance. The Renaissance literary portrait was usually found in histories; since history, however, was itself considered an art form, this in no way detracted from its "literary" value.[56] The literary portrait provided a pause in the narra-

---

54. [Madeleine de] Scudéry, *Artamène ou le Grand Cyrus* (Paris, 1654), vol. 1, dedication to Mme la Duchesse de Longueville (unpaginated).

55. Ibid., "Au lecteur" (unpaginated).

56. Blanchard W. Bates, *Literary Portraiture in the Historical Narrative of the French Renaissance* (New York, 1945), pp. 1–30.

tive. It was rigorously stylized, self-consciously adhering to formal, generic rules.

Georges seems to have been less eager than Madeleine to render both the example and the embellishment easily decipherable. When, in the process of correcting his sister's proofs, he found a recognizable character, he would quickly modify something in the physical description, changing, for instance, blond to brunette.[57] Thus the portraits in the finished novel retain the stylistic features of the literary portrait with its division into physical and psychological description; yet it is more through the psychological or "moral" depiction that they function as keys to the people that they actually portray. Portrait rejoins exemplum, for the link between the ancient and the modern heroes of this tale is "moral," not physical.

If we read *Le Grand Cyrus* as its first public did, and as earlier publics "read" the collective portraits of the Sistine Chapel, the rhetoric of Mlle de Scudéry's prefatory remarks on her novel's verisimilitude acquires a new meaning. "The hero you are about to see," she says, "is not an imaginary one, a mere daydream who never existed. He is a real hero, one of the greatest of those whose memory History has preserved." The portrait of Condé is, as it were, a portrait within that of Cyrus. Both are real or historical heroes, and so to the initiates Mlle de Scudéry can claim a double authenticity for her characters. "You can see," she goes on to say, "that even though a fable is not a history and that all you need do to compose a story is to respect verisimilitude [the *vray-semblable*], not truth itself [the *vray*], nevertheless in writing my fiction I have not departed so much from [the ancient historians] as they from one another. . . . Thus sometimes I follow one, sometimes another, according as to how they best fit my purpose; and sometimes, following their example, I have said things that not one of them has said. For after all I am writing a story, not a history."[58] Surprisingly, this double talk makes sense. Mlle de Scudéry protests that she has written "true" fiction because of her careful documentation. She has also taken liberties with her documentation, which is all right, because she has written fiction, not history. In fact, both statements are true: according to the standards of the day, *Le Grand Cyrus* richly fulfills the ambiguity of the word *histoire*, for it is both a story and a history. The story of Cyrus is

57. Tallemant, *Historiettes*, 2:690.
58. Scudéry, *Grand Cyrus*, "Au lecteur."

fictionalized history, as the story of Condé is historicized fiction, that is, a fictional narrative in both an ancient and a contemporary historical setting. In their function as exempla the portraits historicize fiction; in their function as literary embellishments they fictionalize history.

Mlle de Scudéry wrote *Le Grand Cyrus* in the ardent optimism of the Fronde. As exempla, her portraits glorify and historicize the real characters of the book at a time when it seemed that history was going to belong to them. As literary portraits, they embellish and fictionalize this cast of characters. But perhaps because Georges's revisions of the literary portraits attenuated the accuracy of physical detail, the portraits turn out to resemble their models more through their function as exempla, or as "moral" depictions, than through their function as literary portraits. Georges's revisions could only reinforce the historical value of the portraits as celebrations of frondeur heroism.

Some of the same people whose portraits were done by Madeleine reappear in Mlle de Montpensier's *Divers portraits*. The Grande Mademoiselle and her friends decided, as Mlle de Scudéry had done, to "paint" a real cast of characters, but in this case they themselves were the characters. If in the portraits of *Le Grand Cyrus* the function of exemplum predominates, Mademoiselle's portraits tend much more to function as literary portraits.

Mlle de Montpensier was a malcontent. Undoubtedly the richest heiress in France, she could find no husband with whom to enjoy her wealth. After the Fronde, her weak-willed and unprincipled father, Gaston d'Orléans, made her life wretched by trying to cheat her out of her money. In her younger years she seems to have been bewitched by Gaston, who during the Fronde could never decide whether he wanted to participate heroically in the fray or to retire to quiet anonymity. Heroism was, however, just what his daughter needed at the time of the conflict. Her marriage prospects had begun to dim. The dream of marrying her younger cousin, Louis XIV—"*mon petit mari*," as she and the queen mother teasingly used to call him—was never much more than a fantasy. And her crush on another cousin, the Grand Condé, had to be tempered by the sober fact that he was already married, albeit to an ugly woman. So when in March 1652 her father hesitated to go to Orléans in order to prevent royal troops from entering his appanage, Mademoiselle eagerly offered herself in his place. Although the escapade did little to advance the cause

of the frondeurs, it was a moment of glory for Mademoiselle.[59]
Later on that year she gained further dubious glory by opening
the Porte Saint-Antoine to let Condé's troops into Paris, which
they occupied immediately before their final defeat.[60]

The Grande Mademoiselle spent the post-Fronde years in
mournful exile, the boredom of which was relieved by some building and interior decoration. After she was restored to favor in
1657, she turned her talents to immortalizing in portraits the lost
prestige of the *grands*. Her *Divers portraits* (1659) was a highly
exclusive endeavor: its fifty-nine pieces were destined for none
other than the participants in the project. Only sixty copies were
printed, according to Huet; the figure cited by Segrais is thirty. As
early as 1659, Sercy and Barbin published two editions of another
collection, the *Recueil de portraits et éloges*. These astute booksellers
probably decided to take advantage of the current literary fashion
and imitate the arcane *Divers portraits* for a wider public. The fact
that only 21 of the 105 pieces in the *Recueil* had appeared in
Mademoiselle's volume seems to indicate that it was by "leaks" or
by the inevitable circulation of portraits in salons that the contents
of the *Divers portraits* were partially divulged to outsiders. Sercy
reprinted the *Recueil* in 1663 under a new title, *La Galerie des
peintures*. In this edition, no more pieces from the *Divers portraits*
were added to the twenty-one that had figured in the *Recueil*. So
Mademoiselle's secrets were largely safe.[61]

It is understandable that in the *Divers portraits* the literary portrait prevails over the historicizing exemplum, for this cast of
characters, with Mademoiselle at their head, no longer had any
historical role to play. The living casualties of the Fronde were
castoffs. Nobles and members of royalty alike would be given no

59. For a highly readable biography of Mlle de Montpensier, see Francis Steegmuller, *The Grand Mademoiselle* (New York, 1956). See also Cardinal de Retz,
Mémoires, ed. Maurice Allem and Edith Thomas (Paris, 1956), pp. 643–45, for an
account of the Orléans episode.

60. See Lorris, *La Fronde*, pp. 361–66.

61. On the various imitations and editions of the *Divers portraits*, see Denise
Mayer, "Recueils de portraits littéraires attribués à la Grande Mademoiselle," *Bulletin du Bibliophile*, 1970, pp. 136–74. The standard but inadequate anthology of all
these editions is Edouard de Barthélemy, ed., *Galerie des portraits de Mademoiselle de
Montpensier* (Paris, 1860). I have used the edition of the *Divers portraits* of 1659
reprinted in Mlle de Montpensier, *Mémoires* (Maestricht, 1776), 8:89–413. Some of
the portraits in the Sercy and Barbin collections belong to the same social circle as
those in the *Divers portraits*, and they are similar in spirit and style. For references
to these portraits I have used the Barthélemy anthology, cited as *Galerie*.

further opportunities to play at what for some of them proved to be "petticoat wars"; the age of Louis XIV had arrived.[62]

Mademoiselle's portraits accordingly place less emphasis on the correspondence between historical figures and contemporaries than they do on correspondence between the verbal and the painted portrait. *Ut pictura poesis* has been turned into a conceit, and the entire collection forms many variants on that metaphor. The metaphor itself has the facility of a play on words, for the verb *peindre* ("to paint," "to portray") meant also "to write," in the calligraphic sense (she writes well, she has a nice hand), and there are instances of both uses in the *Divers portraits*.[63] The "preciousness" of Mademoiselle's portraits derives from the working out of this basic conceit in the extreme stylization of each portrait. Her collection includes various kinds of portrait: group portraits, allegorical or pastoral portraits (shades of *L'Astrée* are everywhere), religious, mirror, and even satirical portraits. In general, the exterior/interior division is respected, but sometimes the former is omitted, in which case the portrait becomes a *caractère.*"[64] When both traditional parts are present, the external or physical description takes over the role of the engraving in Richelieu's portrait books. The text, or psychological description, does not in any way enlarge, prolong, or generalize the image, or physical description, as it would have done in emblematic representation. Rather it repeats the same person from the internal perspective, as it did in the portrait books. Usually the subject of the portrait is identified with his or her real name even if a pastoral or mythological name is also given. When the subject is unidentified, the portrait becomes an enigma. The game here is of course to identify the subject, but even the portraits with identified subjects present themselves as games. The purpose in the case of a portrait with an identified subject was to see how well one could execute it, that is, with how much art one could imitate the model.

---

62. Cf. Sandra Dijkstra, "La Grande Mademoiselle and the Written Portrait: Feminine Narcissism, Aristocratic Pride, or Literary Innovation?" *Pacific Coast Philology* 13 (October 1978):22, 24.

63. For an example of *peindre* in the sense of "to write," see *Divers portraits*, p. 138.

64. The seventeenth-century English "character" seems to have been related to the French "portrait," but it emphasized the interior aspect. See David Nichol Smith, ed., *Characters from the Histories and Memoirs of the Seventeenth Century* (Oxford, 1929), esp. pp. ix–lii.

What distinguished one portrait from another was the manner in which it was painted, its artifice. Mademoiselle and her friends must have delighted in the battles of wits that resulted in the maxims and metaphors that fill the pages of the *Divers portraits*. How they must have striven to outdo one another in metamorphosing defect into virtue! Mme de Brégis was adept at this game. Here is what she says about Queen Christina of Sweden: "[Her eyes] are blue, that beautiful sky-blue azure. They are large, beautifully formed, and more brilliant than light itself. They make everyone they focus on their subject, and if they see less well than others, nature gave them that little defect only to give others the time to look at them before being seen, which privilege respect would otherwise have forbidden." Of the queen mother she wrote: "If she seems a little less generous than is appropriate for such a princess, it is only because of her greatness of soul, which prevents her from seeing riches as good."[65] This is exactly the type of portrait that Molière made fun of in *Le Misanthrope* (II, iv, 711– 30), that is, the very type of "precious" portrait whose value lay in its artistry rather than in its truth.

Yet oddly enough, Mademoiselle and her friends claimed to be striving for a certain realism in their work. They aimed to portray both vices and virtues, they maintained, in order to produce a closer likeness of the model. ". . . I have been very pleased to take the time to do your portrait," says Mademoiselle to Mme de Choisy, "in which I will speak to you without flattery. I will include all I know of the good and bad in you with as much frankness and sincerity as I used in my own portrait."[66] Mademoiselle, not "nature," sets the standards of accuracy here. The "precious" aesthetic centers on the particular; the classical aesthetic soon to take over prescribed the depiction of things according to "nature," for it centered on the general or the universal. A commonplace in the *Divers portraits* is a coy disclaimer of accurate representation on the grounds that the model's perfection will not admit of replication. The portrait's value as a parlor game derived precisely from the particularity of its reference, for only the initiates could either appreciate the artifice in the imitation of a known model or guess the model from the artfulness of the imitation.

65. For the comments on Queen Christina, see *Divers portraits*, p. 163. The second citation is from the *Galerie*, p. 13.
66. *Divers portraits*, p. 334.

How do we reconcile a representation real enough to include defects along with virtues with an artfulness and virtuosity that transform defects into virtues? Representation in the *Divers portraits*, in other words, seems to bring together an art of imitation and a concept of art as imitation.

Claims to realistic representation in the *Divers portraits* have in fact a basis other than supposed fidelity to the real model: they are rooted in the opposition portrait/flattery: a good portrait resembles, a poor portrait flatters. The anonymous author of the portrait of M.D.L.C. (Mme de La Calprenède) laments that the muses have been languishing of late. Now "apprentices" have taken over portraiture. Their work is characterized by the arrogance of their claims. They "attribute to themselves everything fine, whether in wit or in lofty sentiments. The lowliest little schoolboy asserts that he is nobler, more magnanimous, a truer friend, and more enlightened than he appears; and the lowliest little woman assures us that she cherishes her friends with unshakable loyalty, that she hates slander and coquetry more than death itself, and that she hasn't a mean or jealous impulse in her." The writer offers the portrait of M.D.L.C. as "Isabelle," by contrast, "with a promise to flatter her as little as I can."[67] Note that flattery is inseparable from rank. The flatterers, of a lower rank than true portraitists, resemble the paid professionals that Richelieu hired to produce his portrait books.

Lignière's devastating poem in his "Portrait d'Amarante" makes perfectly clear who the flatterers were:

> How ungrateful are the poets;
> How indifferent are their souls;
> They have yet to depict the heavenly charms
> Of the incomparable Amarante.
> These authors do nothing for nothing,
> And if they had to scribble stanzas
> For all the Fouquets, for the great Servien,
> Or for other heroes of high finance.
> They wouldn't lose a minute.
> Obviously their inspiration
> Suffers a little suffocation
> When it flows not for a Midas,
> A Croesus or another fine Maecenas

---

67. Ibid., pp. 292–94.

> Who buys them all their shoes and stockings.
> Still I know a lot of poets
> Whose souls are of the noblest;
> They are people of high condition.
> Not poetasters by profession,
> With pen for hire and words for sale.
> Their sentiments are great and noble.
> My comments don't refer to them,
> For them I love, and them I prize.[68]

Flatterers, says another portraitist, are the types who write panegyrics. They are the *beaux esprits* who beautify "people that nature
wanted deformed," says yet another.[69] What does this character-
ization indicate concerning the models of such portraits? Evidently they were as distasteful as the flatterers to the portraitists
surrounding Mademoiselle. In order to appreciate these implied
attacks on a monarchy that accorded no place to the Montpensier
circle, we must recall that the subjects whom the portraitists disdained included some of the king's most powerful ministers.

For the Grande Mademoiselle, her friends and epigones, the
portrait resembles *because* it embellishes. The self-conscious literary portrait differs from panegyric in that its subjects are sup-

---

68. *Galerie*, p. 160. Here is the original of my highly inadequate translation:
> Que les poëtes sont ingrats
> Et qu'ils ont l'âme indifférente,
> De n'avoir point encor peint les divins appas
> De l'incomparable Amarante;
> Ces auteurs ne font rien pour rien,
> Et s'il falloit faire des stances
> Pour Messieurs les Fouquet et pour le grand Servien
> Ou pour d'autres héros qui sont dans les finances,
> Ces beaux auteurs le feroient bien.
> On remarque assez que leur veine
> Ne coule qu'avec grande peine
> Quand ce n'est point pour un Midas,
> Pour un Crésus ou pour quelque Mécène,
> Dont ils ont des souliers, des habits et des bas.
> Toutefois je connois quantité de poëtes
> Dont les âmes sont fort bien faites,
> Qui sont gens de condition,
> Non auteurs de profession,
> N'en faisant point métier ni marchandise,
> Et dont les sentiments sont grands et généreux;
> Ce que j'ai dit n'est point pour eux,
> Car je les aime et je les prise.

69. Ibid., pp. 199, 184.

posed to be worthy of embellishment and the high rank of its practitioners should preclude the need to flatter. How these people in their enforced post-Fronde idleness must have resented being displaced by the monarch's ministers and the hordes of court officials on the royal payroll! How pathetic are their attempts to eternalize themselves in portraits! As their power declined, so was the exemplum emptied of value. In its rare appearances in the portraits emanating from Mademoiselle's coterie, it is based solely on birth. Thus in the unsigned portrait of Mme de la Boulaye (Mlle de la Marck), the marquise is praised for the number of sovereigns she can count in her family tree. It is her high birth, says the author, "that gives you such extraordinary merit that you can be held up not only as an example but as a marvel of our century."[70] Alas, in their attempts to rout the flatterers, the new portraitists have run the risk of imitating them. Many of their portraits are nothing but embellished flattery. And without the redeeming historical value of the exemplum, the portraits run the further risk of falling into mere narcissism. Yet to fight their rivals on a literary battlefield they had to adopt their weapons.

A subtle process of ideological transformation underlies these portraits. They are an instance of what one critic has called "text-distortion," in a reference to Freud's study of dreams. As the psychoanalyst arrives at the meaning of a dream by reconstructing the process of its production, so the critic of ideology can arrive at the meaning of a given cultural product by a similar reconstruction.[71] The meaning of a dream resides in the individual's distortion of unconscious material; the meaning of a cultural product resides in a class's distortion of nonconscious material. No matter how much the protestations of realism in Mademoiselle's portraits may sound at times like empty claims, the consistent opposition portrait/flattery confers on them the authority of statements. The dynamic of the opposition operates so as to reduce on the one hand the previous efforts at portraiture by the professionals to mere flattery, on the other hand to elevate their own efforts to the category of accurate representation. The result is that a claim acquires the status of perceived fact. One object of ideological work, the social parallel to Freud's dream-work, is to transform claims embodying wishes, hopes, fears, and other types of affect

70. Ibid., p. 159.
71. Terry Eagleton, *Criticism and Ideology* (London, 1978), pp. 90–95. Eagleton limits his discussion of distortion to the literary text. My extension of the concept to include cultural production in general is consistent with his idea.

on the part of a given class into fact. Again and again we will uncover this transformation in the elaboration of a representational system distantly related to another known as "realism."

The discrepancy between claim and fact in these portraits derives from the historical situation of the writers, who are also their own protagonists. They project an image of themselves which is in sharp contradiction to their known historical role. That image informs Pierre Bourguignon's *portrait historié* (1671) of Mademoiselle (currently at Versailles) (fig. 13). Mademoiselle herself may not have dictated the choice of iconographic material, but the finished painting recalls the tone of the *Divers portraits* in certain important respects. It is a portrait within a portrait. Mademoiselle, represented as Minerva, holds an oval-framed portrait of her father. Because the subject of the inner portrait had been dead since 1660, he could be eternalized in a memorial portrait. But the inner portrait has another function in relation to the representation of Mademoiselle, for it imposes a continuity between the dead hero and the living heroine. Both are worthy of being *historiés* (embellished) in the tradition of mythological heroes; both belong to history. History and myth are linked through the glorification of a royal line in the mythological atmosphere of the goddess Minerva. Yet this latter-day Minerva confined her artistic patronage to the mediocre production of the *Divers portraits* and to a few provincial efforts at building and decoration. Her military activity was limited to her ineffectual adventures in the Fronde. And was descent from the line of her ambivalent, cowardly father really something to celebrate for all eternity? In the same spirit, Gaston d'Orléans's bastard son, whom Mademoiselle chose to befriend as her protégé, says in his portrait, ". . . I am persuaded that you have to be Caesar or nothing."[72] Apt alternatives! For this young man, who acquired his rank as the chevalier de Charny—not a high one, at that—thanks only to Mademoiselle's good offices, was a nobody. Willfully ignored by his father and denied any active participation in court life, he left no distinguishing traces other than his inclusion in the *Divers portraits*.

The discrepancy between claim and fact is less immediately evident in the case of another living casualty of the Fronde, the notorious Cardinal de Retz. Unlike the Grande Mademoiselle,

72. *Divers portraits,* p. 393. On Bourguignon's portrait, see Dowley, "French Portraits," pp. 272–75, and Françoise Bardon, "Fonctionnement d'un portrait mythologique: La Grande Mademoiselle en Minerve par Pierre Bourguignon," *Colóquio* 26, 2d ser. (February 1976):4–17.

13. The Grande Mademoiselle, by Pierre Bourguignon (1671). Photo: Musées Nationaux, Paris.

Retz had been able to exert some influence on the course of the Fronde's events by his intriguing in the highest circles of the land, which he chronicled in his *Mémoires*. Paul de Gondi, who spent a good deal of his life scheming to be named Cardinal de Retz and archbishop of Paris, also found the time for politicking with members of the Paris Parlement, the nobility, and the royalty. He was a special confidant of Gaston d'Orléans. He seems to have had midnight rendezvous with everyone who counted, including the queen regent, Anne of Austria. He ruffled and unruffled the feathers of almost all the principals of the Fronde with consummate ease, but never quite made it back into the good graces of the monarchy after the end of the troubles.

Now in the same way that the opposition portrait/flattery runs through the *Divers portraits* like a refrain, the opposition true history/vulgar history underlies Retz's claims of authenticity for his memoirs. The series of seventeen portraits which he inserted into his narrative to amuse the unnamed woman for whom he wrote the *Mémoires* contrasts markedly with those both of the *Divers portraits* and of the flatterers. Retz does not hesitate to include his subjects' defects, and indeed in his cynical portrayals defects generally outweigh virtues. His portrait of the queen mother, like that done by Mme de Brégis, is built on a conceit, but here the purpose of the conceit is to destroy rather than to create illusion:

> More than anyone I've ever seen, the queen had that kind of intelligence which was necessary for her not to appear stupid to those who didn't know her. She had more sourness than haughtiness, more haughtiness than greatness, more surface than depth, more ineptitude in money matters than generosity, more generosity than self-interest, more self-interest than disinterest, more attachment than passion, more callousness than pride, more memory of wrongs than of services, more piety in intention than in fact, more stubbornness than firmness, and more incompetence than any of the above.[73]

How far we have come from La Serre's *Portrait de la reyne!* For Retz this cynicism was a source of pride insofar as it seemed to be a measure of direct access on his part to important people. The assumption is that only someone as well placed as the cardinal could write such a truthful account. "There is as much difference

73. Retz, *Mémoires*, p. 154. Further references to the *Mémoires* will be placed in parentheses in the text. On the relationship of Retz's *Mémoires* to history and to the novel, see Monique A. Bilezikian, "La Triple Ecriture dans les *Mémoires* du Cardinal de Retz," *Symposium* 34 (Summer 1980):91–106.

between a narrative based on memoirs, no matter how good they may be, and an account of facts you yourself have witnessed," he says elsewhere, "as there is between a portrait done from hearsay and a portrait done from the original" (p. 657).

What do such portraits retain of the double function as exemplum and embellishment? Insofar as they do provide a pause in the narrative and are explicitly intended to provide pleasure for the reader, they do embellish the text, but the embellishment is at best bittersweet. As exempla, they conform to the tradition inversely, for they tend to serve as examples of how *not* to be. Unlike Mlle de Scudéry's romanticized version, Retz's account of the Fronde contains few heroes. One of the rare instances of the old-style exemplum occurs, significantly, in a hortatory context. When in 1652 Retz went to Compiègne to urge the king to return to Paris and put an end to the troubles, he held up to him the examples of Louis's ancestors Henri IV (as well as Retz's own, the Cardinal de Gondi) and Saint Louis (pp. 719–21). The implication is not, as in the portrait books of Richelieu and the sixteenth century, that the present monarch has surpassed his ancestors and can himself be held up as a model for posterity, but rather that if he does not try to equal them, he will remain their inferior. Retz was nothing if not arrogant.

Retz's "portrait and parallel" of Richelieu and Mazarin is equally removed from the earlier Plutarchan mode of "parallel lives" which La Serre imitated in his *Portrait de Scipion l'Africain*. In Retz's portrait of the queen mother every virtue was qualified by a vice; in his portrait of Richelieu the reverse is true. Every vice listed by the memorialist turns into a virtue, for "all of his vices were such that great fortune easily renders illustrious, because they were such that only great virtues could be their instruments." By contrast, if Mazarin had any good qualities, they resulted from a fundamentally vicious nature: "He had wit, wiliness, sprightliness, manners; but his nastiness always showed through. . . ." In La Serre's parallel between Scipio and Richelieu, the Roman and the Frenchman had both served as models; in Retz's parallel neither minister is a model. We could consider the Richelieu of Retz's portrayal as the lesser of two evils but for one important factor. "Cardinal Richelieu," says Retz in the opening line of the portrait, "had birth." Of Mazarin, by comparison: "His birth was low, his childhood shameful" (pp. 69–70).

The parallel is structured not, as of old, on correspondence, but on decline. Gone are the good old days when an otherwise pernicious minister at least had birth; now we are left with nothing. Gone, too, are the days of the great monarchs, Henri IV, Saint Louis, and the rest; now we must bear the ignominy of a king forced to abandon his capital in its hour of need.

In this lamentable situation Retz found an abiding source of comfort and pride in his own high birth. It is the sole basis of his claims of truth in the *Mémoires*, for only by virtue of his birth was he privy to the innermost secrets of state during the Fronde. In a conversation he records with the great military hero Turenne, both men agree that everything we read in most historical lives is false, because truth can be written only by those who have lived it, not by outsiders (p. 37). Only actual participants can appreciate contradictions involved in great events that may seem incredible to others; Retz has learned through his own experience, however, that "everything that is incredible is not necessarily false" (p. 601).

"Vulgar historians," says Retz, insolently believe that they must explain every single event even though they cannot possibly possess knowledge of the inner workings of history (p. 480). Only the initiates understand just how much can never be known by anyone and are consequently "superior to the ridiculous vanity of those impertinent authors who, born in the barnyard and never having gotten past the antechamber, have the gall to think they know everything that went on in the king's *cabinet*." Retz once happened to find on a desk in Condé's study a few books by "these servile and venal souls." "The wretches," Condé said to him, "have made you and me into what they would have been had they been in our places" (p. 485). Although Retz does not name the culprit historians, it is obvious that they are the paid ("venal") portraitists who aroused such resentment in the Montpensier circle.

Retz seems to have begun composing his memoirs in 1662,[74] a crucial year in the organization of royal propaganda under Louis XIV. In a letter of November 18, 1662, by Jean Chapelain to Colbert, the academician told the minister essentially what Retz says about historians in the *Mémoires*. To be a good historian, in Chapelain's opinion, one must understand the mainsprings of each event. But Chapelain's conclusions are very different from those of the memorialist. How, he asks Colbert, can we allow such historians to do their work? For if they were in on all state secrets, as they would have to be if they were to write decent history,

---

74. Retz, *Mémoires*, Introduction, p. xiv.

national security would be violated. Chapelain is of course referring to paid historians and other officials to be hired for the purpose of glorifying Louis XIV. Better to celebrate the king, counsels Chapelain, through panegyrics that can be embellished by fiction and are thus closer to poetry than to history.[75]

The policy that Chapelain recommended and Colbert followed was a tightening of Richelieu's. The French "history" that flowed from the pens of court officials under Louis XIII and Louis XIV would hardly qualify as history by modern standards. Accordingly, when we seek credible contemporary accounts of historical events in seventeenth-century France, we turn to Retz or to Saint-Simon rather than to La Serre or Racine (later appointed court historiographer). The official nature of court histories raises a curious question concerning genre: is the fundamental distinction between memoirs and history in seventeenth-century France that between personal and impersonal accounts, as is commonly held, or rather that between an unofficial, independent account and an official or paid one? Memoirs turned out to be "truer" than the so-called histories of the time. Often memoirs that appeared posthumously, as Retz's did, escaped royal censorship and could provide a critical perspective on royal policy.

Yet this is not precisely the sense of Retz's claims of truth for his memoirs. He professes to have knowledge superior to that of the La Serres of the world owing to his rank. As a nobleman, he can record his most private interviews with the great, but he is above taking money for his labors. What Retz leaves unsaid is that the "vulgar historians" prospered under a regime of censorship and terror that ultimately drove Retz himself into a very uncomfortable exile. And while Retz was discontentedly roaming about foreign lands, such incompetents as Benjamin Priolo were at home receiving tidy sums from Colbert to write what passed for history.[76] But from first to last the caustic cardinal was a monarchist. No matter how vehemently he opposed Anne's continued protection of Mazarin and Louis's departure from Paris, he never questioned the legitimacy of the monarchy, and in that he was a child of his times. Even the swashbuckling Condé always remembered that he was first and foremost a Bourbon. Retz's protestations of truth are therefore one-sided. He insists only on the privileges of nobility, not on the disintegration of this class, which had set in long before

75. Philippe Tamizey de Larroque, ed., *Lettres de Jean Chapelain*, vol. 2 (Paris, 1883), pp. 273–76.
76. See Ranum, *Artisans of Glory*, pp. 164–68.

the eruption of the Fronde. In order to perpetuate the myth of
noble greatness, Retz had to resort to the structure of decline.
Gens de néant, he calls the vulgar historians (p. 485), implying
that he and his peers are people of substance. The famous memorialist of Louis XIV's later years, Saint-Simon, would employ
a similar opposition between being and nothingness to bemoan
the displacement of the true nobility by the riffraff of Louis
XIV's court.[77]

The opposition true history/vulgar history in Retz's *Mémoires*
reflects a deeper opposition between time past, when kings were
heroes and noblemen their loyal supporters, and time present,
when kings are cowards and pay the lowly to flatter them. The
memoirs are permeated by a nostalgia for a largely fictionalized
past that serves as their justification and their rationale. In this
respect they herald the coming cultural era of Louis XIV's personal reign, which Chapelain announced differently in his letter
to Colbert. Our traditional image of French classicism (another
product of ideological work) is that of a glorious unfurling of arts
and letters. In fact, nostalgia for a vanished past pervades all of
French classicism, for this is the legacy it was to receive from a
class that had played out its last heroic act in the Fronde.

New Functions of the Portrait under Louis XIV

Retz stands out as a champion of the old social order. As a
leading frondeur, he took up with passion the defense of his own
class interests. He looked back to a time when birth and merit
were unhesitatingly linked, when privilege and prestige were the
natural prerogatives of the nobility. The nobles of the robe, a
seemingly progressive element in the Fronde, had a different set
of interests to defend. In their jealous attempt to guard the *paulette* against the monarchy's efforts to suspend it, in their resistance to the crown's moves toward imposition of new taxes, the
parlementaires struggled to preserve the wealth and property that
the old nobility so often begrudged them. Any alliance between
robe and sword during the troubles was as temporary and precarious as most of those between progressive and reactionary
forces. The monarchy steered a natural course in its subsequent

---

77. See Jules Brody, "Saint-Simon, peintre de la vie en declin," *Marseille* 109 (2d
trimester 1977):185–92.

attempts to isolate the two camps and to play one off against the other, a policy it followed until the French Revolution. In the meantime, the split between robe and sword which had become evident during the Princes' Fronde was slowly developing into a social conflict based on wealth rather than on privilege. The formation of a new moneyed elite composed of both nobles and bourgeois resulted eventually in a progressive struggle against an ancien régime as obsolete as the old nobility that it traditionally protected. What Retz left unsaid in order to present a one-sided "truth" from the noble perspective was said by some of the other participants, chiefly satirists, in this nascent historic struggle. And so we come to the previously taboo subject of money.

Nobles found the mention of it distasteful. Honoré d'Urfé, for example, could not possibly have let it intrude into the golden age of his aristocratic shepherds in *L'Astrée*. It would certainly have been out of place in Mlle de Scudéry's oriental tale of noble valor, *Le Grand Cyrus*. Retz disposed of the matter quickly and with disgust every time it came up. He did not and would not, he insisted repeatedly, ever take bribes from the Spanish. In exile he was forced to accept money from his friends, but did so only, according to his account, with the deepest reluctance. The new rich bourgeois, the archenemies of his class, he dismissed as "venal."

But the harsh reality was that many nobles were getting poorer and poorer. Bussy-Rabutin, for one, did not hesitate to say so. Roger de Rabutin, comte de Bussy, possessed undeniably noble credentials, but he was painfully short of cash. In 1657 he was so destitute that he wrote to his famous cousin Mme de Sévigné for a loan. He seems never to have forgiven her for her refusal. His *Histoire amoureuse des Gaules,* in which he relates the whole incident, contains an extremely unflattering portrait of her.

The *Histoire amoureuse des Gaules* is something of a milestone in the history of literary portraits, for it demonstrates that abuse of a genre in seventeenth-century France could result in imprisonment. The first edition of Bussy's novel—really a collection of short stories—was probably the one that appeared in Liège in 1665 with a key. By the fifth edition, one of seven that appeared in 1665–66 with the authentic title, the key had disappeared and the real names of Bussy's characters were placed in the text.[78]

---

78. Roger de Rabutin, comte de Bussy, *Histoire amoureuse des Gaules,* ed. Francis Cleirens (Paris, 1961), pp. xxxv–xxxvi.

The queen mother was scandalized by Bussy's uninhibited portrayals of leading court figures in a roman à clef so transparent that it quickly became a roman sans clef. Condé and Turenne, among others, were dissatisfied enough with their portraits to complain to the king. The former frondeurs had become indispensable to the military policies of the monarchy, and Louis decided to take them seriously. On April 16, 1665, Bussy was arrested and locked up in the Bastille. The following September he was released, only to be exiled to his estates in Burgundy. Bussy's repentant efforts to flatter his enemies in his *Histoire de Louis le Grand* and *Histoire du Prince de Condé* did not succeed in regaining royal favor for their author. Like Georges de Scudéry, he nursed his wounds by assembling materials for an *Histoire généalogique* of his own family.[79]

The *Histoire amoureuse* is in part the story of high-class prostitution. If Retz's posture was largely defensive, Bussy is on the offensive, against both his own class and its enemies, the new rich bourgeois. The cynicism of Retz's portraits was mixed with admiration and pride. His depiction of foibles in both nobility and royalty revealed how much he was in the know. The cynicism of Bussy's portraits is bred of disenchantment and despair. The portrait of Mme d'Olonne is the case history of a noble prostitute, a woman who accepts money from her lovers as proof of their affection. For the impoverished nobility, love has become a commodity. Everywhere in the *Histoire amoureuse des Gaules*, the noble code of love in its seventeenth-century "precious" form has been violated. Men no longer swear eternal fidelity and languish at the feet of their implacable ladies; the ladies now make advances to the men. The blushes and swoons of *L'Astrée* and *Le Grand Cyrus* have been replaced by hard cash. Thus when one of her lovers pays her, Mme d'Olonne confesses to him that she never really believed he loved her until that moment. "It is not," she tells him, "that I haven't observed some behavior on your part which made me suspicious, but I am so repelled by posturing; signs and languor are in my opinion such shoddy merchandise and such feeble signs of love that if you hadn't adopted nobler conduct [*une condu-*

---

79. [Roger de] Rabutin, [comte de] Bussy, *Histoire amoureuse des Gaules*, ed. Georges Mongrédien (Paris, 1930), 1:xiii–xvii. Further references to the *Histoire amoureuse* are to this edition. The entire episode of the imprisonment following the appearance of Bussy's *Histoire amoureuse des Gaules* is related in Emile Gérard-Gailly, *Bussy-Rabutin: Sa vie, ses oeuvres, et ses amies* (Paris, 1909), pp. 78–98. Finally in 1691, a year and a half before Bussy's death, the king did award him a pension of 4,000 livres. See Gérard-Gailly, p. 126.

ite plus honnête] with me all your efforts would have been for nothing."[80] The ironic use here of *honnête*, an adjective reserved for a nobility expected to behave nobly, conveys the debasement of true, noble value by exchange value in its money form.

Bussy may have viewed the increasing number of robe–sword and bourgeois–noble marriages as but institutionalized instances of the prostitution that he describes. The rapid acquisition of wealth by financiers and families of the *noblesse de robe* since the time of Richelieu had resulted in more of these matches, which were advantageous to both sides, since they brought status to the bourgeois or robe family and money to the nobility.[81] Bussy, although he does not explicitly discuss such marriages in the *Histoire amoureuse*, disapproves of both parties to an informal misalliance. One of Mme d'Olonne's noble lovers reproaches her in these terms for her liaison with the financier Jacques Paget: "Aren't you ashamed to put me in the position of being threatened by a miserable bougeois, who is to be feared only for the audacity you give him?"[82] Mme d'Olonne and Paget are equally guilty in Bussy's eyes, because both transgress the traditional laws of their respective classes, thereby altering the equilibrium of a class structure that Bussy would like to see as permanent.

Although Bussy's portraits respect such formal generic rules as the exterior/interior division, they break with tradition in that they are no longer heroic idealizations of the nobility. In this they resemble Retz's, but they lack his self-congratulatory tone. The *Histoire amoureuse* is nevertheless written from a strictly noble perspective. Although the key turned out to be superfluous since the models were so easily recognizable, Bussy's novel was addressed to initiates who alone could possess the firsthand knowledge required to appreciate the characterizations it contained. And if Bussy attacks his class, it is only in order to save it from the new rich bourgeois.

His enemies included some very powerful people. Court histori-

---

80. Bussy-Rabutin, *Histoire amoureuse*, p. 13.

81. See Carolyn Lougee, *Le Paradis des Femmes: Women, Salons, and Social Stratification in Seventeenth-Century France* (Princeton, 1976), pp. 113–70, esp. pp. 157–58. Lougee would view Bussy's position as antifeminist and reactionary. She argues (pp. 41–59) that the salon, where women played an important public role, promoted social fusion through the acceptance of misalliances. She identifies one group of people opposed to the spread of noble culture to nonnobles as those who wanted to eliminate the false nobles and to revitalize the old aristocracy of birth (p. 105). Bussy belonged to this group.

82. Bussy, *Histoire amoureuse*, 1:9.

ographers and other official propagandists were generally recruited from the bourgeoisie. Those bourgeois who rose most
rapidly in status, however, were in legal and financial circles.
When they succeeded in buying certain offices conferring nobility, or hereditary *charges*, they could qualify for the *noblesse de robe*.
Financiers who lent money to the state were able to amass fortunes in amazingly short periods of time. Parvenus were a contin-
ual annoyance to such nobles as Bussy. As for the socially mobile
bourgeois, they were caught in a maze of contradictions. Even as
new nobles, they were not necessarily able to cross the class barrier in their everyday life. In the face of rejection by the social set
they courted, they could but return its hostility. Once they obtained their desired status, often after generations of "living nobly," they in their turn might despise the bourgeois. The old
nobility watched with dismay the growing prestige and influence
of new wealth. Bourgeois and new nobles, while striving for the
top of the old social order, were challenging the very meaning of
that place.

For Bussy, the bourgeois is the villain who has forced the nobility into prostitution. The "reality" of Bussy's portraits derives less
from a realistic depiction of actual noble life than from a polemical reference to the past. Like Retz's *Mémoires*, Bussy's bitter satire
is predicated on the assumption of decline. Things are not as they
should be because nobles no longer enjoy their historical prestige
and power. The past determines the present, for it is only with
reference to a once-intact class structure that Bussy can deplore its
present violation.

In Retz's *Mémoires* the portrait still retained something of its
embellishing function, which allowed the author to stylize his wit,
to condense his cynicism into a conceit. Like an engraving with an
accompanying rhymed quatrain, the portrait in Retz's *Mémoires* is
set off from the narrative, drawing attention to itself as a genre.
Bussy's portraits read more like factual descriptions, continuous
in tone with the general narrative. In some cases their language
contrasts strikingly with that of portraits in earlier novels. Mlle de
Scudéry would never have dreamed of saying that her beautiful
heroine Mandane, the fictionalized Mme de Longueville, was, in
Bussy's words, "unclean," or that she "smelled bad."[83] But it is not
any intrusion of "reality" into Bussy's portraits that distinguishes
them from Mlle de Scudéry's or even from those in the *Divers*

83. Ibid., p. 81.

portraits, which did include satirical portraits. It is rather the presence of the previously unmentionable, money, which creates a new function, that of moralizing, for the literary portrait. This function was already latent in Retz's portraits, for the discrepancy between past and present on which they were based implied that the past was to serve as a standard for the present. Retz does not distance himself enough from his subjects to speak as a *moraliste;* in their function as revelations, glimpses into the intimate character of the great, his portraits are closer to the "secret histories" that became fashionable later in the century. Bussy, however, disengages himself from his subjects in his criticism of their attraction to money. As a potential *moraliste,* he generalizes his criticisms to the extent that they seem applicable to almost any of his characters.

It was Bussy's class loyalty that prevented him from being a genuine *moraliste.* The *Histoire amoureuse* is still precise in its reference to a restricted circle of nobles. The portraits in Antoine Furetière's *Roman bourgeois* (1666) resemble more closely the work of a *moraliste* in their claim to general applicability. Furetière was a Parisian lawyer best remembered for his still authoritative *Dictionnaire.* In his comic novel, the literary portrait of the 1650s and 1660s undergoes a decisive transformation: it turns bourgeois.

The function of the mythological portrait was to glorify the model. Its value lay in the "art" with which the portrait "resembled" the model, that is, in how appropriately and beautifully the artist succeeded in portraying the model. Even if only a pretext, the model was the ordering principle of the portrait. Furetière was to reverse the order of priorities. An excellent portrait, he maintains in his preface to the *Roman bourgeois,* will elicit our admiration even if we have none for the model. Similarly, fictional stories with made-up characters can be more impressive than true ones with real heroes. A mime imitating a hunchback can make a real hunchback more painfully aware of his plight than would the sight of another real hunchback. Satire and comedy, Furetière tells his readers, must be moral correctives. To this end comic stories and characters must be so applicable to our mores that they make us believe that we recognize everyday people in them.[84]

The portrait is more "real" than the model, because the model has lost its specificity. It is no longer an individual but a type. The

---

84. Antoine Furetière, *Le Roman bourgeois,* ed. Georges Mongrédien (Paris, 1955[?]), p. xxviii. On *Le Roman bourgeois,* see Jean Serroy, *Roman et réalité: Les Histoires comiques au XVII͏ᵉ siècle* (Paris, 1981), pp. 585–656.

value of Furetière's portrait lies not in its resemblance to a model, but in the general truth it can express through its portrayal of a condition, that is, in the "truth" of its moralizing. The mythological portrait functioned effectively for a noble (or royal) audience that could understand the specificity of its reference. The "realistic" portrait functions effectively for a bourgeois audience with no hero other than itself. In his preface Furetière claims autonomy for his portraits. In detaching them from specific models he denies that his novel is a roman à clef. Don't look for any key, he warns the reader, "because the lock is no good. Beware, as there are portraits here of several kinds of fool, lest you find your own. For practically no one is privileged enough to be exempt and not to find some feature of his own, morally speaking."[85]

This is but a joke. *Le Roman bourgeois* is blatantly a roman à clef. If the real identity of some of its characters is not so transparent as that of Charroselles (Charles Sorel), the references are nonetheless there. The homely bluestocking Polymathie, for example, is almost certainly Mlle de Scudéry.[86] Her appearance in the novel would be particularly appropriate, since *Le Roman bourgeois* presents itself as a satire of such novels as *Le Grand Cyrus*. Furetière claims to break with the mythicopastoral tradition not only by elimination of a key but in other ways as well: by not beginning *in medias res,* by not depicting exclusively noble characters but rather people of all conditions.[87] Yet his claim to have created recognizable characters strangely echoes a similar claim by Mlle de Scudéry. In the preface to her novel *Ibrahim* (1641), she says that novelists must create heroes so recognizable that they could be acquaintances of the readers. Parody incorporates its object as it transcends it. Furetière's bourgeois portraits are cast in the noble mold. At once portraits requiring a key and realistic portraits of general types, they respond to the ideological demands of bourgeois still unsure of their relationship to the nobility.

Supposedly in the interest of greater realism than that afforded by Scudéry's novels, Furetière would drop the exterior part of the literary portrait. He will not describe the beauty of his blue-eyed, blond heroine, Javotte, for fear of rendering her unrecognizable. So many heroes and heroines, he says in a patent allusion to Mlle de Scudéry, are beautiful on paper and ugly in the flesh. I would

---

85. Furetière, *Roman bourgeois,* pp. xxviii–xxix.
86. See Antoine Adam, *Histoire de la littérature française au XVIIe siècle* (Paris, 1958), 4:196.
87. Furetière, *Roman bourgeois,* pp. 1–2.

have included an engraved portrait of Javotte, continues Furetière, if the publisher had been willing to go to the expense. It
would certainly have made as much sense as all those engravings
of battles, temples, and ships, which serve only to raise the price
of books.[88] The realism of Furetière's portraits is understandable
only against the background of noble portraits. He presents his
portraits both as truer to life than Scudéry's and as cheaper, for
the noble was traditionally *libéral*, a spendthrift.

Bourgeois frugality is not necessarily a virtue for Furetière.
Here his satirical moralizing rejoins Bussy's criticisms, only now
from the bourgeois perspective. Money is the vital principle of
Furetière's world. His bourgeois characters do not indulge in
amorous adventure, *galanterie,* like the aristocrats. Their sex lives
are strictly subordinated to the demands of marriage, and marriage is above all a financial transaction. The *Roman bourgeois* includes a "price list of appropriate matches," showing the exact
monetary value of eligible partners from various social levels.
There is also another price list, of different parts of books, in
which portraits are rated among the highest.

Furetière's moralizing is aimed at a class concerned primarily if
not exclusively with money. The mythological portrait of the nobility did not wear a price tag. Distributed widely throughout
fictional or historical celebrations of the great, it was evidence of
aristocratic generosity. If Furetière's portraits have the ring of
universality, it is the universality of money as a universal value
form. Everything has its price. Furetière's universality is a dialectical response to the older, noble mode of representation. It conserves the roman à clef form while transforming the reference
from particular into general. Bouregois realism is understandable
dialectically only against the background of noble *vraisemblance.*
Here again, between the claim and the fact of such realism is the
process of ideological work. Furetière's claim is to speak for a
universal "us"; in reality, he speaks to a class on its way to establishing an identity as specific as that of the old nobility. Universality is the hallmark of the bourgeoisie.

Later realistic novels of the eighteenth and nineteenth centuries
would drop the key entirely to become self-enclosed fictional
worlds. With the loss of a key, portraits as a genre disappear,
though not without traces, from the novel. As the exterior division of the literary portrait gradually gave way to a greater moral-

88. Ibid., pp. 5–6.

izing function depending more on elaboration of the interior division, so in realistic novels, the sentimental, heir to the moral, is the path to the universal. Text replaces image, the abstract replaces the concrete, as particular is transformed into universal.

These ulterior developments of the portrait take us far beyond our confines of the 1650s and the 1660s in France. What we call classicism was to intervene before realism emerged as an artistic mode in France. La Bruyère was the classical portraitist and *moraliste* par excellence. His *Caractères* mark the final modification of the seventeenth-century portrait before its incorporation in the realistic novel. A glance at his work will let us measure the distance that we have traveled with the portrait since we set out in the sixteenth century.

The first three editions of the *Caractères* appeared in 1688, and five more, with additions, followed before La Bruyère's death in 1696. As soon as the work appeared, it provoked the anger of almost every group mentioned in it: courtiers, financiers, clergy, and more. The society journal *Mercure galant* reported in 1693 that when the *Caractères* first went on sale, the book became a *succès de scandale* at court. The early editions, however, did not contain attacks on nearly so many people as did the later ones of 1689 and 1693. In 1693 a great number of lists of attributions flooded Paris. La Bruyère stoutly defended himself against the accusation of any defamatory intention on his part. He did not deny that he might have had live models in mind when he drew his portraits, but insisted that he hid their identity effectively from his readers. Fleury, his successor in the French Academy, to which La Bruyère was admitted in 1693, said that the author "overloaded" his descriptions—that is, used several models at a time—in order that the portraits might not "resemble" too closely.[89]

La Bruyère had good reason to protect himself. He certainly did not want to be carted off to prison like his friend Bussy, who supported La Bruyère's unsuccessful candidacy for election to the French Academy in 1691. The author did not have many important connections at court in case of need, for he was a bourgeois who resigned his ennobling treasurer's office after taking on the duties of tutor in the Grand Condé's household. A study of La Bruyère's successive corrections and revisions of the first edition

---

89. Gustave Servois, "Notice biographique," in La Bruyère, *Oeuvres* (Paris, 1865): 1:xcvii–xcix.

indicates that he took special pains to avoid incurring the displeasure of the king.[90]

In general, La Bruyère drops the exterior division of the literary portrait. Thus his title is not simply a repetition of Theophrastus', whose work initially inspired the Frenchman, but a definition of the genre: these are not really portraits; they are "characters" or interior descriptions. As a *moraliste*, La Bruyère was concerned specifically with analysis of "character"—morals, manners, customs, sentiment. His characters tend more and more toward abstraction. Many stand alone as commentaries on behavior without any personalized reference whatsoever, and so are more properly speaking maxims. Thus "Love that grows little by little and by degrees is too much like friendship to be a violent passion."[91] The maxims, liberally sprinkled throughout the *Caractères*, reinforce the distancing effect created by La Bruyère's seemingly omniscient, depersonalized remarks on various segments of his society. How removed are his *Caractères* from the old mythological portrait! Of mythology there remains practically nothing. Although La Bruyère did borrow substantively from Theophrastus, he evokes the atmosphere of classical antiquity chiefly through the intermittent use of ancient names. Otherwise he respects Félibien's principle of *costume* in his descriptions of thoroughly French contemporaries.

Both La Bruyère and his critics were right. The *moraliste* does attack the *grands*, the financiers, the courtiers, and others. But any proposed key has become irrelevant. The references are to types and conditions, not to individuals. Moreover, La Bruyère is not unequivocal in his attitudes toward these groups. His attack on the *grands* is counterbalanced by his rage against the financiers who have been displacing them. With a recent family history that included a good number of parvenus, La Bruyère sounds a suspicious note in his invective against the new rich. As one who bought an ennobling office, who lived in the intimate shadow of the *grands* in a royal household, his natural wish would have been to dissociate himself from his own class.[92] This was exactly the

90. Ibid., pp. c–cii. Servois's "Notice" contains complete biographical details of La Bruyère.

91. La Bruyère, *Oeuvres complètes*, ed. Julien Benda (Paris, 1951), p. 134. Further quotations from the *Caractères* are from this edition, and the references are given in parentheses in the text.

92. For a discussion of La Bruyère's ambivalence in relationship to his social position, see my "Classical Disproportion: La Bruyère's *Caractères*," in *From Humanism to Classicism*, ed. Jules Brody, *L'Esprit Créateur* 15 (Spring–Summer 1975):189–210.

posture of bourgeois on the rise in La Bruyère's day. The sale of offices was theoretically a profitable business for the monarchy, because bourgeois customers were only too eager to buy their way into the nobility.

La Bruyère seems to have attained a certain negative universality in his apparently indiscriminate criticisms of nearly all the social groups within his purview. Closer inspection of the *Caractères* reveals that his negativism is in fact an ambivalence occurring within precise class limits. Of the *grands*, La Bruyère says: "[They] think that they alone are perfect and are hard pressed to admit that other men have integrity, cleverness, sensitivity; they claim these rich talents as their due because of their birth. . . . They have large lands and a long line of ancestors: so much cannot be disputed" (*Des Grands*, 19). If La Bruyère refuses to equate greatness with birth, he is ready to equate lack of birth with evil. New money is for him the disrupting agent of an old social order which he despises as one excluded from its upper ranks, and which he admires as one aspiring to solidarity with the elite. The constant opposition rich/poor in the *Caractères* refers to two precise social groups: the new rich financiers and the impoverished nobility. Poverty is the poverty of "merit" or birth (the two are often identical for La Bruyère), wealth the riches of ruthless parvenus: "In every condition, the poor man is very nearly the upright man, and the rich one is not far removed from knavery. Savoir faire and cleverness do not always lead to enormous wealth" (*Des Biens de fortune*, 44).

Behind the facade of universality ("in every condition") is a very specific reference. Reference to social class replaces the reference to an individual within a class, as in the earlier mythological portrait and in the roman à clef. Furetière universalized the roman à clef by claiming that his key unlocked types; La Bruyère neutralized the key to the point where his book would not offend the court but would intrigue a public grown eager for the scandal that it might afford. Furetière's portraits had a moralizing function, but within a bourgeois perspective. Openly bourgeois novels, such as his and also Scarron's *Roman comique*, did not make much of an impact on the bourgeoisie of the time, a class in formation, unwilling and unable to come to terms with its identity. The function of La Bruyère's characters is to reveal a truth valid for all classes, to attain a universality purified of any class affiliation.[93] Many

93. Cf. Dijkstra, "Grande Mademoiselle," p. 23.

French classical authors, like La Bruyère, came from a bourgeois or robe background. Often pensioned by the monarchy, they nevertheless responded also to the needs of a nascent class divided in its loyalties and aspirations between a disparate bourgeoisie and a nobility in decline. The universality of French classicism is masked negativity. It denies class conflict by transcending it in a universalization of humanity. From concrete particularity in mythological representation the portrait has found its way to abstract universality in classicism.

Does it seem that the vicissitudes of the French portrait from the sixteenth century to the 1650s and 1660s, on into classicism, follow a linear scheme? If so, a word of caution: although a progressive transformation did occur, the contradictions of a society harboring the incipient class conflict that was to explode later in the French Revolution do not admit of linear description. Thus before all the volumes of Honoré d'Urfé's mythologized pastoral novel *L'Astrée* had been published, Charles Sorel produced a "realistic" novel with his *Francion* (1623). And Saint-Simon's *Mémoires*, chronicling the postclassical period, contain portraits closer to those of Retz than to those of La Bruyère, who was more nearly his contemporary. Portrait books were produced with some regularity until the French Revolution. Charles Perrault's *Hommes illustres qui ont paru en France pendant ce siècle*, which appeared at the end of the seventeenth century, continued the Plutarchan tradition. The article on the painted portrait in the *Encyclopédie* pokes fun at mythological portraits in a way reminiscent of seventeenth-century satirists. The unique function of the portrait, according to the *Encyclopédie*, is to "resemble." Any mythological trappings will merely detract from the resemblance. "Can you easily recognize your wife . . . in the pagan image of a madwoman escaped from Mount Olympus breezing through the heavens on a cloud? . . . But people who have their portraits painted like such disguises; they ask for masks and are surprised when they're not recognized."[94]

The portrait was a linchpin of the *ut pictura poesis* representational system. Like other elements of this system, some of which it often incorporates, the portrait underwent transformation in ac-

---

94. "Portrait (Peinture)," in *Encyclopédie, ou Dictionnaire raisonné des sciences, des arts, et des métiers* (Neuchâtel, 1765) (facs. ed. Stuttgart, 1966), 13:155.

cordance with changing ideological demands. Not all elements were transformed at the same time; contradictory functions of the same element were often necessary to its value for the system. When the function of an element changed, its value for the system was modified. When internal change reached such proportions as to alter the entire system, quantity turned to quality, replacing one system by another. But that final transformation is beyond the confines of our story.

The sixteenth-century mythological portrait served the iconographic needs of royalty and nobility alike, but the verbal portrait—"lives" in the Plutarchan mode—was increasingly put to political use by a monarchy desirous of asserting its hegemony over the Protestants and the nobility. Richelieu's propaganda campaign made use of sixteenth-century iconographic and historical elements in order to project the image of an absolute sovereign. Much of this material was taken over during and after the Fronde by nobles eager to reclaim their declining suzerainty. The noble portrait is suffused with nostalgia for a time, somewhat mythical, when nobles shared both representational status and power with the monarchy. We should not be surprised to see this nostalgia paradoxically invade the bourgeois portrait too, because the bourgeoisie's aspirations to unity with the nobility form one of the conditions of artistic production of the newer portrait.

This has not been an exhaustive description of the ideological-representational transformation of the portrait in the *ut pictura poesis* system. I have tried to select certain key elements along with certain key transformational processes. Such basic aesthetic values of the system as *vraisemblance* and imitation effectively served the needs of the ruling classes (the monarchy and the nobility) until such time as a newly powerful class (the bourgeoisie) began to appropriate them for its own use. Competition for exclusive rights to these values among monarchy, nobility, and bourgeoisie accelerated change in the system.

Historically, there have been two principal modes of conceiving of "verisimilitude" and "realism": the eternal and the relative. Either representation itself always has and forever will refer in some way, no matter how remote, to a reality that it necessarily represents; or else it is relative to the artistic, social-economic, historical context of the representation in question. Both modes rest on the same fallacy: that behind representation is a separate reality. Re-presentation is an ideological, therefore a real process.

It is not separable from reality but part and parcel of it. Ideological work transforms a real representational claim into a representation of fact. Art persuades that claim is fact. I have tried to show how art and ideology dialectically formed and transformed each other in the successive metamorphoses of the portrait in the *ut pictura poesis* system. The ultimate metamorphosis of *ut pictura poesis* into a system of realism is a tale yet to be told.

4

History and Fable

In the days of Louis XIII and Louis XIV, "fiction" (*fable*) and "novel" (*roman*) were not nice words. They frequently carried the odor of "lies," and, perhaps more faintly, even of something slightly pornographic or at best scandalously titillating. Often as not contrasted with "history," they could be used to underline the serious writer's intentions. I am offering you truth, such a writer argued, not the stuff of novels. The literate person's proclaimed attitude toward novels was roughly that of today's intellectual toward television: a vulgar phenomenon that must be tolerated for the benefit of the weak-minded (in seventeenth-century France this meant, chiefly, women). Yet as the century wore on, novels came to represent a proportionally larger bulk of book production. At the same time, after the mid-century flourishing of François Eudes de Mézeray, there was not a single important historian of France. By the end of the century, literary and historical truth had acquired new value.

Change in the value of this truth occurred along with fundamental generic change. The *roman*, or heroic romance (for convenience, I often translate both *roman* and *nouvelle* very loosely by the English "novel") was, despite the distinction made by its critics, generically related to history. With a decline in production of official histories of France, a new generic relationship developed between historical and fictional narrative. The *roman* gave way to a literally new genre, the *nouvelle*, a prototype of the modern novel. Its closest relative was not history, but *nouvelles*, or newsletters, one corruption of historical writing among others that filled the vacuum left by the disappearance of history. Formerly, truth (*vérité*) had been perceived as the hallmark of *histoire* and *vraisemblance* as that of the *roman*. Now, increasingly, writers of fiction as well as of historical narrative claimed to be conveying *vérité*.

The great divide in this evolution of history and fiction was the decade of the 1660s, that is, the decade that marks the beginning of Louis XIV's personal reign. History ceased to serve the purposes of absolutism for the Sun King, and so he sought other modes of glorification. Without its royal patron, history became pseudohistory and took on a very different function. History and fiction stood in a significantly different relationship to each other even by the 1670s than they had before the young monarch's assumption of personal rule in 1661. To trace the course of this change is to uncover the functional development of fiction, history, and truth in the age of absolutism.

Histoire and *Roman* before 1661.

Since at least the sixteenth century historical writing in France had been graced with honor and distinction. Many of the better-known practicing historians were court appointees. Most royal historiographers also held ennobling titles as officers of the crown: *conseiller du roi, secrétaire du roi, maître des requêtes,* and the like.[1] Historiographers were paid for their services, but it is unlikely that they were in it for the money, which was often meager and only irregularly forthcoming. The attraction was more probably the status and prestige that accompanied their positions as officers, bringing them close to the source of power—even if the offices themselves may not always have carried any real exercise of authority. Above all, royal officers enjoyed among the most highly coveted privileges in the kingdom. Here are some of the privileges Charles IX granted to the *notaires* and *secrétaires du roi,* whose principal function was to write French history, in his edict of Moulins, January 1566: they were exempt from the much-hated *gabelle,* or tax on salt, an important cause of uprisings in the seventeenth century; they were exempt from the entry tax on wine (certain products traveling from one province to another were subject to a tariff); they were allowed both entry and prece-

1. Orest Ranum, *Artisans of Glory* (Chapel Hill, N.C., 1980), p. 59.

dence—the latter a bitterly disputed right—into sovereign courts and *parlements;* they were permitted exemptions from property taxes, one of the most eagerly sought exemptions in the *ancien régime.* For their wages historians were expected to work from the "necessary memoirs," with which they would be provided.[2]

And so the sixteenth century passed on to the seventeenth a tradition of privilege for the royal historiographer, who, along with many other officers of the crown, was not typically from the ranks of the old miltary nobility. In the legalistic, humanistic circles of the sixteenth century, historians tended to come from a robe background.[3] Learned men, they had the solid erudition of the bourgeoisie, for the sword nobility traditionally rejected both the pursuit of learning and professional affiliation as writers.[4] Was the military nobility's distaste for erudition and professionalism to grow more pronounced as it saw more bourgeois encroaching on its privileges, stealing its favor and status at court? The shaping of the well-known seventeenth-century aristocratic ideal of the *honnête homme,* a cultivated but unintellectual nonprofessional, indicates that this may have been a tendency;[5] but it is certain that the old nobility felt increasingly threatened by the multiplication of royal offices among the bourgeois in the seventeenth century. Royal historiographers have a special place in this story, for they were to have an effect on novelists in the century of Louis XIII and Louis XIV. And the most influential of the novelists in the first part of the century were nobles addressing themselves to nobles.

History enjoyed distinction not only as a métier but also as a form of writing. Since classical antiquity, historical writing had borne a moral value. It was a "mirror of princes," an instructional manual in the art of ruling, an example for all, a "mistress of life." Usually written for and about the great, it intended to immortalize their deeds for posterity. To do so with appropriate dignity, it still clung to the ancient classical ideal of *fides historiae,* or fidelity

2. Abraham Tessereau, *Histoire chronologique de la Grande Chancelerie de France* (Paris, 1676), pp. 135–37.

3. See Donald R. Kelley, *Foundations of Modern Historical Scholarship* (New York, 1970), pp. 242–43; and Ranum, *Artisans of Glory,* pp. 58–59. See also George Huppert, *The Idea of Perfect History* (Urbana, Ill., 1970), pp. 6–7.

4. See, for example, John Lough, *Writer and Public in France from the Middle Ages to the Present Day* (Oxford, 1978), pp. 123–26.

5. On the *honnête homme,* see Domna C. Stanton, *The Aristocrat as Art: A Study of the Honnête Homme and the Dandy in Seventeenth- and Nineteenth-Century French Literature* (New York, 1980), esp. pp. 14–30, 45–53.

to the facts.[6] Seventeenth-century history consisted of different but related genres or subgenres, "literary" in that they were derived by and large from the rhetoric of classical antiquity.

History is to be distinguished generically from both memoirs and chronicles. Memoirs were usually written by an active if not leading participant in the events they described. Chronicles were typically concerned with the present rather than the past, and they tended to be ordered chronologically. Until the end of the fifteenth century, France had practically no written history other than the *Grandes chroniques de France*.[7] These chronicles were reprinted and continued well into the sixteenth century; they formed the basis for more recent histories.[8] It was not until the flowering of humanistic history, beginning early in the reign of François I with the work of the Italian Paolo Emilio (known in France as Paul-Emile), that historical genres in France came into their own. They may be roughly categorized thus: universal history, a philosophical or moral genre inherited from the Middle Ages;[9] particular history, or the history of one prince or monarch; general history, by far the most preferred kind, known usually as "*l'histoire de France*" and comprising a history of the French nation from the reign of the first king, Pharamond, to the present.[10]

In addition to these fundamental subgenres, usually signaled by the presence of the word *histoire* in the title, there was a variety of minor historical subgenres. *Vies,* or a compilation of lives of illustrious people, became a favored genre in France, particularly after the publication of Amyot's translation of Plutarch's *Lives* in 1559. Charles Sorel, in his *Bibliothèque françoise*—an excellent source of generic distinctions as they were made in seventeenth-century France—says that *éloges,* or eulogies, were like abbreviated "lives." Eulogy and panegyric, however, seem generally to have been practiced and perceived as distinct historical genres in their own right. Sorel goes on to compare eulogies to miniature portraits, but he ends up—understandably—confusing portraits and eulogies.[11] These categories are only approximations; six-

6. Kelley, *Foundations,* p. 22.

7. See Gustave Dulong, *L'Abbé de Saint-Réal: Etude sur les rapports de l'histoire et du roman au XVIIe siècle* (Paris, 1921), pp. 2–5.

8. Philippe Ariès, *Le Temps de l'histoire* (Monaco, 1954), p. 160.

9. Wilfred H. Evans, *L'Historien Mézeray et la conception de l'histoire en France au XVIIe siècle* (Paris, 1930), pp. 10, 30.

10. There is a very useful discussion of the *histoire de France* genre in Ariès, *Temps de l'histoire,* pp. 155–94.

11. Charles Sorel, *Bibliothèque françoise,* 2d ed. (Paris, 1667), p. 156.

teenth- and seventeenth-century writers respected conventional forms, but there was much individual variation in their use and practice.[12] In this case, Sorel's confusion is illuminating. As an example of eulogy, he mentions Thévet's *Eloges des hommes illustres,* which was in reality titled *Les Vrais pourtraits et vies des hommes illustres grecz, latins, et payens,* and consisted of a series of lives, each accompanied by an engraved portrait. Sorel cites other well-known portrait books, or collections of lives with accompanying engraved portraits, such as those by Paolo Giovio, one of the earliest masters of the genre, and Vulson de la Colombière. He includes Mlle de Montpensier's collection of written portraits, the *Divers portraits,* in his category of eulogy. And in this connection he also mentions perhaps the most famous—or infamous—producer of portrait books in Richelieu's time, Jean Puget de La Serre.[13]

The portrait does seem to have been practiced as a discrete genre, for a genre could occur within a genre—portraits were regularly found in novels, for instance—but the portrait was inseparable from the very fabric of historical writing. Even in general histories, a portrait of each king was a necessary component. The most famous seventeenth-century general history, Mézeray's *Histoire de France depuis Faramond jusqu'à maintenant,* was also a portrait book, with supposedly authentic engraved portraits of each king and queen. Even a very different kind of history, which does not fall within these categories because it was not "literary" (it was subject to no formal conventions), made use of the portrait. This was "antiquarian" or "erudite" history, history as practiced by scholars who sought above all documents and texts.[14] Real historical research, cultivated for its own sake, to satisfy curiosity about the past, went its separate way in the sixteenth and seventeenth centuries. Unadorned by humanistic use of classical rhetoric, it aimed not to celebrate and to glorify, but to unearth, to authenticate, to verify. Such *érudits* as Claude Fauchet, Papyre Masson, and André Duchesne were removed from the humanistic tradition of Paolo Emilio, which formed the mainstream of sixteenth- and seventeenth-century history. Emilio's was the history

12. Cf. Ranum's discussion of forms and genres of the *Ars Historica* in *Artisans of Glory,* pp. 17–21.

13. Sorel, *Bibliothèque françoise,* pp. 156–57.

14. See Ariès, *Temps de l'histoire,* pp. 195–216. Ariès' discussion of the relationship between the portrait and history focuses on the antiquarian tradition in history. Not all the historians he discusses, however, were strictly antiquarians: Thévet is a case in point.

that sacrificed precision to embellishment, that sought the effect of rhetoric at the expense of accuracy.[15] Both humanist and antiquarian history went by the name of *histoire* in seventeenth-century France, but not until the eighteenth century were the two traditions to unite.[16] Before that time a historian did not have to be a scholar, and historical writing was primarily a literary activity. All of history itself was but a "true story"—*histoire véritable,* as opposed to *histoire feinte.*

Relations between true and fictional stories were uneasy in the earlier seventeenth century. The principal aim of history was utility, yet in order to captivate a public rapidly succumbing to the fashionable new mania for novels, history was obliged to borrow some of the "pleasure" that the novel advertised as its chief attraction. As early as the sixteenth century, certain authors had engaged in a conscious effort to win the reading public over to history.[17] The royal historiographer Pierre Matthieu defended his use of ornamentation by citing the current neglect of "good books" in favor of "vulgar ones," implying that readers of the latter needed some cheap adornment to attract them. Readers take such pleasure in these vulgar books, said the historian, that they "lose all knowledge of languages, . . . and from the day they leave school they make a great show of having retained nothing." Matthieu informed the readers of his *Histoire de France* that it would help them to repair their ruined memories and to retain "an infinite number of beautiful things without tears." They would thereby lose their taste for "little books that in the main offer no knowledge to form the intellect, or piety to satisfy Religion, or truth upon which to found knowledge." The books he was referring to, of course, were "fables and amorous novels [*romans d'amour*] invented by a love of chatter."[18] A typical intellectual's diatribe against the ignorance of the nobility! Who, after all, read history? Research into this matter, although impeded by insufficient documentation, indicates that the greatest number of its readers came from a robe background. Those nobles who did dip into history may well have been motivated by a desire to keep up with their bourgeois rivals for royal offices.[19]

15. See Evans, *l'Historien Mézeray,* pp. 11–17.
16. See Huppert, *Idea of Perfect History,* p. 5.
17. Evans, L'Historien Mézeray, pp. 13–14.
18. Pierre Matthieu, *Histoire de France* (Paris, 1609[?]), "Avertissement sur tout le livre," unpaginated.
19. Henri-Jean Martin, *Livre, pouvoirs, et société à Paris au XVII' siècle (1598–1701)* (Geneva, 1969), pp. 512–25, 655.

Humanist history offered all the features of easy reading. In this tradition, style was just as important as substance. *Harangues,* or speeches often as not dreamed up by the historian, interrupted the action at a crucial moment, such as right before a major battle. While held in suspense, the reader could take delight in the oratorical skill of the speaker. With justification by precedent in classical antiquity, historians employed a variety of such devices to embroider their material. Exempla, sententiae, and reflections on politics helped to form the "moral" dimension; character analysis and portraits added psychological interest. Above all, a clever historian such as Mézeray was a good storyteller. In the right hands, an account of historical events could read like the most absorbing of novels.

How could history proclaim its *fides historiae* while so unabashedly making use of fictional devices for embellishment? This was the question that made the relationship of history to the novel so problematic. The major criticism of French history in the seventeenth century was that, like the novel, it was full of lies. "What can be said of those who promise us history and give us fables instead?" was a typical complaint.[20] Truth was supposed to be the "soul of history," according to a favorite topos of the time. The Protestant historian Jean de Serres modestly graced his oft-reprinted *Inventaire général de l'histoire de France* (Paris, 1597) with a deified, allegorical Truth represented in a title-page engraving and commented on at length in a dedicatory epistle to the king. Yet such critics as Charles Sorel pointed accusingly at history for betraying its ideal through falsehood.[21] La Mothe le Vayer perhaps best typified the general confusion on this issue. In one and the same treatise he cautioned against passing off lies as historical truth and acknowledged that history as an oratorical art should make use of the poetic eloquence that Quintilian had recommended.[22]

The difficulty here is in the notion of truth. For in fact humanist history as it developed in seventeenth-century France was to make two very different claims of truth, which were only intermittently—and dimly—perceived by contemporaries as contradictory. On the one hand, history had to report true facts (*la vérité*),

20. [Charles Sorel], *Le Tombeau des romans* (Paris, 1626), p. 5. This work is generally attributed either to Sorel or to Fancan.

21. [Charles Sorel], *De la connoissance des bons livres* (Paris, 1671), p. 72.

22. François de La Mothe le Vayer, *Discours de l'histoire* (Paris, 1638), dedicatory epistle to Richelieu (unpaginated) and p. 42.

"things as they are," leaving "things as they should be" to fictional narrative, according to another favorite commonplace, Aristotelian in derivation. Truth, however, is harsh and immoral. The good are often punished, the wicked rewarded. The moral dimension of history provided a corrective to truth, not exactly in rewriting history, but in adding reflections, in converting fact into example, so that truth became a lesson. In this way, truth (*la vérité*) was modified by another kind of truth, verisimilitude, or *vraisemblance*. Well-written history, said the critic René de Lusinge, echoing Thucydides, should be the mirror of antiquity. It should allow us to see, as in a painting, the virtues and vices, the good and evil of ancient times. And as we read the classical historians we will see ourselves, for "nature is always one," and through exempla we can uncover the resemblances between past and present. "We are moved by the same springs. . . . It's almost the same fable represented in the same Theatre. . . ."[23] So humanist history, not yet concerned with scholarly research after the manner of the *érudits,* ran the permanent risk of lapsing into "fable." Despite insistent apologetics, it was not to extricate itself from the "fabulous" for a long time, because verisimilitude was essential to its functioning as historical truth.

The sixteenth- and seventeenth-century historian was subject to the demands of his royal or noble patron. He had both to record and to glorify, to transmit past and present to posterity in a halo of praise. Whether or not the historian believed in the truth of his utterances is irrelevant. We shall never know if Mézeray was completely gulled by his predecessor Jacques de Bie into believing in the supposed authenticity of the portraits and medals he assembled for his *Histoire de France depuis Faramond,* or if he chuckled inwardly over his artful deceit.[24] History was written for the practical purpose of immortalizing the rulers. Historians in the humanist tradition quite naturally made use of the conventions of a historical literature of praise derived from classical antiquity. In the period of developing absolutism, history took on a more overt propagandistic value. The flourishing of panegyric and portrait books under Richelieu indicates that the minister took very seriously the ideological potential of traditional history. The image of the king as example was part and parcel of the truth about the

23. René de Lusinge, *La Manière de lire l'histoire* (Paris, 1614), p. 2.
24. See Chapter 3 above, p. 12 and n. 39.

king. Correspondences found so frequently in emblem literature between a reigning monarch and a mythological figure of classical antiquity turn up in portrait books and in histories, where they, too, are incorporated into the truth conveyed about the monarch. The moral aspect of history was part of its truth; *vraisemblance* was a part of *vérité*.

Fissures in this system were inevitable. Historians wanted to claim that they were writing *la vérité:* authenticated, objective, impartial truth. For the royal historiographer, objective truth was a sign of authority because historical authenticity implied a knowledge of state secrets. Charles Sorel and René de Lusinge, both court appointees, insinuated that their status gave them superiority over other historians—clergy, nobles, some members of the Third Estate—because as royal officials they were closer to the source of truth than unofficial writers.[25] For the robe intellectual, the pen became a badge of power. As the monarchy increasingly pensioned writers, intellectual activity acquired a prestige that rivaled that of the military. Here was yet another arena of conflict for the long and the short robe; *robins* and royalty alike were conscious that the pen could accomplish almost as much for the monarchy as the sword. So it is not surprising to find literary topoi of pen and sword poised in mutual confrontation. "The pen shoud celebrate the deeds of the sword," said La Mothe le Vayer, "and if the Muses do not intervene, all of Mars' conquests, all the successes won by the highest Virtue and the cleverest Politics will soon be consigned to oblivion."[26]

Eyewitness testimony merited the greater credibility. Most seventeenth-century historians and critics insisted on the importance of firsthand accounts. Each claimed unique status as eyewitness, because nothing so enhanced the prestige of the historian as to be thought a participant in affairs of state. Such noble memorialists as the Cardinal de Retz proclaimed their superiority over mere historiographers in this respect.[27] Marin Le Roy de Gomberville, a *conseiller, notaire,* and *secrétaire du roi,* took up the theme of Sorel and Lusinge. According to him, monks, gentlemen, doctors, and lawyers were not able to write good history because they had no

25. See Charles Sorel, *Histoire de la monarchie françoise* (Paris, 1632), pp. 26–27; and Lusinge, *Manière de lire l'histoire*, pp. 57–58.
26. La Mothe le Vayer, "Du peu de certitude qu'il y a dans l'histoire," in *Oeuvres,* new ed. (Dresden, 1757), p. 464.
27. See Chapter 3 above, p. 113.

experience in affairs of state; they did not participate in councils, in "great undertakings."[28] The implication is that he, a court official, enjoyed such participation.

Truth, then, depended on the status of the writer. Even this criterion was not exempt from qualification. The insider could not reveal too much, for then he would be giving away state secrets. Pierre Matthieu, although he obviously considered himself fit to write history, nevertheless warned that not everyone should be allowed to "gather incense in Arabia" or to "discourse on the councils of the ruler. . . ." "It's perilous," he cautioned, "to set sail on the oceans of state secrets."[29] Here are the seeds of an important debate, which was to have epoch-making consequences in the reign of Louis XVI: how much should the historian know? Under Louis XIII, a clever historiographer such as Matthieu steered a precarious middle course between inside and outside. He claimed to know some, but not all, things at firsthand. Only thus could he make plausible his primary claim of impartiality, for the participating eyewitness, so Matthieu argued, was subject to both prejudice and obsequiousness.[30]

Historical truth is thus a historical claim, made in a historical situation. French court historiographers of the early seventeenth century were mainly men of a relatively new class enjoying and endeavoring to preserve a new prestige. Over against the old military nobility, these *robins* asserted that their power lay in their ability to write true history. They alone would get the inside story, while at the same time retaining their objectivity. In their own self-interest they would write what they were hired to write, a glorification of the monarch, occasionally conserving enough independence to distinguish *vraisemblance* from *vérité*.

Pierre Matthieu, astute historian that he was, seemed conscious of the need to maintain an equilibrium between the conflicting demands of *vérité* and *vraisemblance*. He informed the reader of his *Histoire de France* that the history was decorated with the "useful" oratorical adornments of classical antiquity. But you can skip them, he advised. They can easily be removed without affecting the substance of the whole.[31] Interestingly enough, Mlle de

28. Marin Le Roy [de Gomberville], *Discours des vertus et des vices de l'Histoire, et de la manière de la bien escrire* (Paris, 1620), pp. 159–60.
29. Matthieu, *Histoire de France*, "Avertissement."
30. See ibid.
31. Ibid.

Scudéry, in the preface to her novel *Almahide* (1660), gave her reader very similar advice. Since she is a "great teacher," she says, she has included in her novel descriptions of some houses in the Granada of two centuries ago, which she chose for her historical setting. But if you are not interested in these "ornaments of the main Fable," she added, you can skip them in order to "follow the thread of the story [suivre le fil de l'Histoire]".[32] Fable and history rejoin each other through *vraisemblance*. The novelist and the historian respectively opposed their fable and their history to the ornamentation that served both as the vehicle of verisimilitude. But whereas historians claimed to be writing truth while at the same time using verisimilitude, novelists feigned truth and claimed verisimilitude.

Honoré d'Urfé had set the tone for novels in the period before the 1660s with his enormously influential *Astrée* (1607–27). The setting for his multivolume tale, fifth-century Gaul, was supposedly historical, but by standards that were to develop following its publication, local color was minimal. Nevertheless, *L'Astrée* inaugurated an important tradition of historical novels whose history was two-tiered: the fictionalized past corresponded to the real present; each character of the historical story corresponded to a real figure of present history.[33] The secret of these correspondences was unlocked through keys to the characters, often published separately by persons who claimed to possess the correct interpretation. The roman à clef was in effect a rewriting of history, an imitation history. What was La Calprenède's *Faramond, ou L'Histoire de France* if not a trompe l'oeil "Histoire de France" in the manner of Mézeray's? In his preface, La Calprenède sought to promote the illusion by deliberately confusing true and fictional narrative. He admitted that the purpose of *Faramond* and of his other historical novels, *Cassandre* and *Cléopâtre*, was "diversion," but he denied that this fact warranted their classification as *romans*. He would distinguish them from the old *romans de chevalerie*, such as the popular *Amadis de Gaule*, which offered neither truth (*vérité*) nor verisimilitude (*vray-semblance*). Maybe you should view my works as histories, he tells his reader, embellished with "inventions" and "ornaments." Nothing in my novels violates the truth

32. [Madeleine de] Scudéry, *Almahide, ou L'Esclave reine* (Paris, 1660), "Au Lecteur," unpaginated.
33. See Ariès' discussion of these "deliberate anachronisms" in his *Temps de l'histoire*, pp. 253–56.

of history, he continued, but (a sly modification) some things may go "beyond" it. Don't look for keys, he admonishes, knowing full well his reader would do just that, because there are few heroes nowadays who resemble the ones in *Faramond*.[34]

Mlle de Scudéry's enormously successful *Grand Cyrus* was an epic romance of the Fronde: beneath the masks of her ancient Persian protagonists were the faces of France's most illustrious frondeurs and frondeuses. Her Cyrus may have been fictionalized, but the real presence of his modern avatar, Condé, "actualized" him, as she suggests in her preface. Scudéry went even further to create the illusion of truth for her audience. She asserted that her history was well documented, and she enumerated the ancient historians she used as sources. She declared that she was no less accurate than her historical sources, yet that she respected verisimilitude. "For after all," she stated, "I am writing a story, not a history."[35]

Like Honoré d'Urfé, Mlle de Scudéry and La Calprenède knew their public well. Their fictional-historical characters were of interest primarily to those who thought they had the keys to find the contemporary references. Their readership was the highly restricted society of the salon. Who else but the social élite had the leisure to wade through ten or fifteen volumes of a *roman* in the heroic manner, in which the inevitable reunion of hero and heroine was delayed by thousands of pages of abductions, battles, misunderstandings, letters, madrigals, and subplots? Charles Sorel's analysis of this reading public is basically accurate: ". . . Women and Girls, Men of the Court and of the World, either people of the sword, or people whose idleness allows them to take pleasure in the vanities of the World."[36] The idleness of the "people of the sword" was in part enforced. Increasingly displaced in the exercise of political power by officials of bourgeois origins, they had also suffered a decline in financial status since the economic crisis of the sixteenth century. In terms of political and economic power, it was undoubtedly the *grands seigneurs* that paid the highest price for the centralization of the monarchy and the development of absolutism. One of Richelieu's most urgent tasks was to rid the kingdom of the last vestiges of feudal author-

34. [Gautier de Costes de] La Calprenède, *Faramond, ou L'Histoire de France*, vol. 1 (Paris, 1664), "Au Lecteur" (unpaginated).

35. [Madeleine de] Scudéry, *Artamène, ou Le Grand Cyrus* (Paris, 1654), vol. 1, "Au Lecteur" (unpaginated). See Chapter 3 above, p. 101.

36. Sorel, *De la connoissance des bons livres*, p. 136.

ity, and the nobles' desperate bid for power in the civil strife of
the Fronde marked a decisive step toward their practical demise
as figures of political importance. The *roman héroïque* revived the
noble of olden times, the knight with functioning sword, ready
to receive his just deserts for doing chivalric duty. The *roman*
traveled a limited circuit. Written by nobles or intimates of
nobles, it appropriated history for those who were beginning to
be excluded by it. Keys created an atmosphere of exclusive complicity, for only insiders could claim to possess them. Thus
nobles, who were fast becoming outsiders in the world of practical power, constructed a mock history by and for insiders. Nothing so pleased a reader as to find his or her own prettified
portrait in one of these novels. The illusion of history responded
to a real need on the part of those who persisted in viewing
themselves as participants in a history that was in the process of
passing them by.

If historians were unsure as to just how much of the attractions
of a novel they could borrow without entirely sacrificing their
ideal of truth, novelists sought the disguise of history as legitima-
tion. Royal historiographers were paid to immortalize the king;
nobles looked to themselves to immortalize themselves in novels.
Historiographers were pensioned; novelists were not—all the
more reason to promote the glory of their class, as against a class
finding glory in the employ of the monarchy. True, the novelist,
like any other writer, could not publish without a royal privilege
giving one bookseller authorized monopoly over the work for a
specified time. And some novelists did receive gifts from the king.
So novelists were ultimately as dependent on royal favor as historians; yet they did not reap the rewards in prestige and status that
were conferred on a pensioned official. The historiographer's
standing at court was ambiguous: to the extent that he held office
and had access to memoirs and other information, he was an
insider; to the extent that he was excluded from the innermost
secrets of state, he was an outsider. But with respect to the old
nobility, he was painfully conscious of being an outsider. Monetary rewards and prerogatives of protocol notwithstanding, nobility was the historiographer's dearest aspiration, as it was that of
everyone else at the time. Only the oldest robe families could
hope to be confused with the sword nobility. The average historiographer knew very well the distance that separated him from the
noblesse d'épée. If novels were the pastime of nobles, why then
historians would make their histories read like novels.

Novelists and historians of the earlier seventeenth century were, then, engaged in a muted social conflict provoked by the economic crisis of the sixteenth century, the sale of offices, and the centralization of the monarchy. Fiction and history provided them with a literary arena in which to play out their ideological conflicts.

The novelist could imitate history as the historian could borrow from the novel, because both forms of writing had come to share certain formal features. "Portraits" or brief descriptions of a character's physical exterior and psychological interior, *harangues* or speeches, moral reflections, descriptions, and a plot of epic dimensions could often be found in both. In addition, the baroque aesthetic of artifice and trompe l'oeil sanctioned the novelist's imitation of history. As both a historiographer and renegade writer of comic or antinovels, Charles Sorel, always ready with testy comments on novels, deplored this tendency. Novels are counterfeit histories, he charged, and even the best novel in the world will be only a pale copy of the real thing.[37] For Mlle de Scudéry, on the other hand, such artifice formed the core of literary theory and practice. In the preface to *Ibrahim*, one of her most complete theoretical statements, she called verisimilitude the fundamental rule of composition. To give greater verisimilitude to this novel, she chose a historical setting with historical characters. She "observed the customs, laws, religions, and inclinations" of the peoples in her novels. Her historical verisimilitude is artifice itself: "And if this charming deceiver [*la vraisemblance*] does not dupe the mind in Novels, such literature will disgust rather than divert." Lies and truth must be so artfully mixed, says the novelist, echoing Aristotle and Horace, as to be almost indistinguishable. In this way, disillusionment will not destroy the reader's pleasure, as it would if the lies were obvious.[38] In other words, naked fiction—pure lies—will not do; fiction must be masked as the truth of history in order to be pleasurable. Mlle de Scudéry claims to respect verisimilitude—that is, to use a plausible historical setting—in order to lend an air of authenticity to her fiction. But verisimilitude deceives as it authenticates. To claim verisimilitude in theory is to feign truth in practice; to write a novel is to rewrite history.

37. Ibid, pp. 160–63.
38. [Madeleine de] Scudéry, *Ibrahim, ou l'Illustre Bassa* (Paris, 1641), Preface (unpaginated).

History and Fiction in the Reign of Louis XIV

In the reign of the Sun King, literary truth changed in value. The *vraisemblance* that had cross-fertilized *romans* and *histoires*, contributing to the generic confusion between the two, came to be disdained in favor of the *vrai*. This change was closely linked to an important generic evolution. The multivolume heroic novel all but disappeared, and the word *roman* no longer figured prominently in titles of fictional works.[39] History (particuarly the *histoire de France* genre) went into eclipse. The replacement of the old *roman* by newer forms of fictional narrative and the virtual departure of history after Mézeray were accompanied by the progressive disengagement of truth from the constraints of verisimilitude.

Everyone agreed that it was very difficult, if not impossible, to find a good historian of France. The reasons behind this pessimism changed significantly from the time of Louis XIII's historiographers and officials to that of the critics in his son's reign.[40] The latter came to despair of ever finding that truth which was supposed to be the soul of history. They came to suspect the impartiality of a history penned by hirelings of the monarchy. How can one expect to find truthful history, Father Rapin sighed, since most historians are pensioned by courts?[41] Father Le Moyne was even more emphatic. "You have to be a Poet to be a Historian," he stated, "but not a Historian of the legend makers' and Chroniclers' school, nor of that of newspaper and gazette mongers, nor even that of Messrs. the Historiographers, those everlasting Compilers who think they've earned their pension when they've slipped in some snatches of Froissart, Nicolas Gilles, or Du Haillan and dressed them up in new clothes. I mean a Historian such as Sallust, Livy, or Tacitus, who were free Poets, unconstrained by numbers and measures. . . ."[42] If Le Moyne fulminates against

39. See Marie-Thérèse Hipp, *Mythes et réalités: Enquête sur le roman et les mémoires (1660–1700)* (Paris, 1976), pp. 46–47; R. C. Williams, *Bibliography of the Seventeenth-Century Novel in France* (New York, 1931), pp. 109–261; Frédéric Deloffre, *La Nouvelle en France à l'âge classique* (Paris, 1968), p. 33; Roger Francillon, "Fiction et réalité dans le roman français de la fin du XVIIᵉ siècle," *Saggi e ricerche di letteratura francese* 17, n.s. (1978): 99–130.

40. See, for example, Matthieu's "Avertissement"; Sorel, *Histoire de la monarchie françoise*, pp. 3–5; Le Roy, Discours, pp. 11–12; Père René Rapin, *Instructions pour l'histoire* (Paris, 1677), p. 149; Père Pierre Le Moyne, *De l'histoire* (Paris, 1670), pp. 320–21.

41. Rapin, *Instructions pour l'histoire*, pp. 34–35.

42. Le Moyne, *De l'histoire*, pp. 7–8.

gazeteers as much as he does against historiographers, it is because the only gazeteers to receive royal privileges and pensions in his time were those few, such as Théophraste Renaudot, with his *Gazette de France,* who were mouthpieces of the court. Is this jealousy talking? Perhaps. Le Moyne's impatience was nevertheless a typical reaction of the learned Jesuit fathers who took it upon themselves to judge contemporary belles lettres. History as written by insiders was a literature of praise, as the insiders themselves were often aware. In the latter part of the seventeenth century, "truth" came more and more to mean the objectivity of the outside view.

The outside view was in fact profoudly incompatible with humanist history as written by court historiographers. Although the humanist tradition survived well into the eighteenth century and even its most ardent critics were loath to reject it entirely, in the later seventeenth century such history came to be equated with a distortion of truth. Rapin said of Paolo Giovio that as a pensioned writer of the emperor Charles V, he was "partial [*intéressé*], unjust, sly, a great flatterer. The portraits he did of the most notable figures in his History are pieces he detached for *Lives* [*Vies des hommes illustres*] in order to earn some money. He wrote according as he was paid."[43] Writing the truth, in Rapin's opinion, required strength. You need more than just will, he thought, you must also have ability. You have to seek truth in "the purity of its source, by burrowing in the most obscure offices, by consulting statesmen's memoranda. . . ."[44] So along with the condemnation of humanist rhetoric came a new respect for research and erudition. Father Gabriel Daniel, author of the first important *Histoire de France* (1696) since Mézeray's, criticized the latter's scholarship, declaring that a historian should be knowledgeable about the antiquities of the countries he writes about and should always cite his sources. Most historians of France, he said, such as Paolo Emilio, Du Haillan, Jean de Serres, Nicolas Gilles, and Mézeray, did not conform to these standards. Daniel advised simplicity of style, that is, great moderation in the use of the traditional oratorical flourishes: *harangues,* sententiae, portraits, and the like.[45] Rapin, too, was all for pruning the reflections and sententiae, which, acording to him, either altered or confused truth. Rapin advised a judicious use of portraits. It is novels, he complained, that have ruined our taste;

43. Rapin, *Instructions pour l'histoire*, p. 130.
44. Ibid., pp. 34–35.
45. Père Gabriel Daniel, *Histoire de France,* vol. 1 (Paris, 1755), Preface (to 1713 ed.), pp. lxxxii–lxxxviii, cxvi–cxvii.

we use far too many portraits that are in no manner likenesses.[46] Le Moyne, for his part, wanted to separate history from oratory. History should not be classified under grammar or rhetoric, he opined, for "how can you reconcile Truth, the soul of History and the goal of the Historian, with verisimilitude, the form of Oration and the aim of the Orator . . . ?"[47]

Le Moyne's problem of reconciling truth and verisimilitude, a cause for malaise for the earlier court historiographers and critics, was to prove increasingly vexing for literary theoreticians and practitioners in the latter part of the century. Following Aristotle's distinction between history and poetry, critics wanted to assign truth to history, the realm of things as they are, and verisimilitude to fiction, the realm of things as they should be. Almost everyone who wrote on the subject agreed with the abbé de Saint-Réal that history is not *vraisemblable* because the most improbable things can happen in real life.[48] But the humanist tradition was too strong for many to renounce their penchant for verisimilitude in historical writing. They rationalized its use in various ways. Like their predecessors, they considered *vraisemblance* a function of "eloquence," the rhetoric needed to embellish history.[49] More important, verisimilitude in some manner reinforced truth. "The slightest falsehood spoils everything," said Rapin, "and makes truth a mere fable. Even the truest things should not be related if they seem unbelievable or extraordinary, unless you give them an air of truth or at least the coloring of verisimilitude."[50] In his *Sentiments sur les lettres et sur l'histoire* (1683), the theoretician Du Plaisir took a firmer stand in separating truth and verisimilitude. "Verisimilitude," he said, "consists of saying only what is morally believable. . . . Truth is not always probable [*vraisemblable*], and yet the author of a true story [*une histoire vraie*] is not always obliged to modify his material to make it believable. He is not responsible for its verisimilitude, because he has only to report things as they have happened . . . , but the author of fiction [*histoire fabuleuse*] himself creates his heroes' actions and he does not want to leave himself open to contradiction. . . ."[51] Le Moyne, who was nothing

---

46. Rapin, *Instructions pour l'histoire*, pp. 86–88; 92–94.
47. Le Moyne, *De l'histoire*, pp. 83–85.
48. See César Vichard de Saint-Réal, 'De l'usage de l'histoire," in *Oeuvres*, new ed. (Amsterdam, 1740), 1:3–12.
49. See, for example, Rapin, *Instructions pour l'histoire*, pp. 104–5.
50. Ibid., p. 32.
51. Du Plaisir, *Sentiments sur les lettres et sur l'histoire avec des scrupules sur le style*, ed. Philippe Hourcade (Geneva, 1975), pp. 46–47.

if not self-contradictory on this issue, came closer to putting his finger on the dilemma of verisimilitude. Despite his assertion that history is not an oratorical art, he attempted to justify the use of *harangues* in both history and fiction. They provide verisimilitude, he said, and their use by historians is not a usurpation of poetic material. Historians and poets both use verisimilitude, but historical verisimilitude supports truth to the exclusion of falsity, whereas poetic verisimilitude supports falsity to the exclusion of truth. The latter is "disguised falsity, dressed up, which is all to the honor of poetry."[52]

Le Moyne's was one of the most penetrating comments on the function of verisimilitude. Both true and fictional narrative needed the moral support of verisimilitude. In history, it padded truth so as to present an acceptable image of the great; in fiction, it helped to strengthen the illusion of truth by imitating history. For both, it provided decorum in the tradition of classical antiquity: reflections, *sententiae*, *harangues*, and so on—all the paraphernalia of morality which justified the utility of history but added to it the embellishments of fiction, and modified the pleasure of fiction in the direction of historical utility. The paradoxical nature of verisimilitude is such that it can support either fact or fable.

Whereas earlier in the century both historians and novelists claimed verisimilitude for their works, in this later period *vraisemblance* was viewed more as an embarrassment, a throwback to olden times. Now novelists claimed to present truth, while historians and theoreticians accused them of violating it. Everyone claimed to be writing in the name of a truth obviously superior in value to mere verisimilitude.

Early in the seventeenth century most novels had dealt with love and were called *romans*. The heroic novel of the roman à clef type reached its zenith in the 1650s with the works of Mlle de Scudéry. Starting in the 1660s a new type of fictional narrative called the *nouvelle* started to account for a much larger proportion of fictional production, replacing the older *roman*. Other fictional narratives related to the *nouvelle* were called *anecdotes, annales, journal, histoire, historiette*. These narratives were generally reduced to one volume; indeed, the *nouvelle* was also known as a *petit roman*.[53] The

52. Le Moyne, *De l'histoire*, p. 243.

53. See Deloffre, *Nouvelle en France*, pp. 33, 42–44; and Williams' chronological list of novels in his *Bibliography*, pp. 109–261. Bernard Magné links the production of shorter fictional narratives to a rise in the price of paper and a general crisis in the book trade (1630–69). See his *Crise de la littérature française sous Louis XIV: Humanisme et nationalisme* (Paris, 1976), pp. 72–75, 105.

anachronistic two-tiered history of the roman à clef was not a feature of the *nouvelle*. Such novelists as d'Urfé, Mlle de Scudéry, and La Calprenède had appropriated history in order to rewrite themselves into it, in order to project a heroic image of themselves by superimposing a glorious past on the faded present. The appropriation of history in the newer fictional narratives was more complete: the *nouvelle* was presented directly as a history. Either fictional characters appeared as historical figures in a historical setting, or else actual historical figures were fictionalized; in both cases fiction was disguised as history without the mediation of keys. The truth of the narrative no longer depended on a system of correpsondences between past and present, but rather on an approximation of real history by means of its revision.

The excitement of the roman à clef was essentially narcissistic: readers looked for themselves or for their friends in the fancy dress of ancient Persians or gentle shepherds. Written by and for an in-group, these novels satisfied the insecure snobbism of a threatened elite. The excitement of the new historical fiction was different: it afforded a more mixed audience access to history not provided by history itself. It offered a glimpse into the private lives of the great which no official history could ever relate. Its authors numbered people of diverse backgrounds—adventurers and adventuresses, nobles of sword and robe, bourgeois: Mlle de Villedieu, Catherine Bernard, Mlle de la Force, Donneau de Vizé were representative types. The new fiction gave to outsiders a special view from the outside. For with Louis XIV's assumption of personal power, everyone, nobles and bourgeois alike, was on the outside. The humiliation of the nobles in the aftermath of the Fronde was completed by Louis's deliberate development of an idle colony of noble courtiers at Versailles. Only the king's very rarefied managerial staff of councillors and statesmen, headed by Colbert, had real access to state secrets. The novelist as pseudohistorian did not claim to possess inside information, but rather that source material—texts, documents, memoirs—accessible to the outsider could provide a much more reliable view of the inside than could any insider. Both novelist and reader were now outsiders, and the narcissistic pleasure of the roman à clef was replaced by the voyeuristic pleasure of the *nouvelle*. The latter type of historical fiction separated observed from observer by creating a new complicity between author and reader: both were now spectators of history.

Nowhere is this more evident than in the especially successful genre of "secret history." Taking Procopius as their model, practitioners of the genre aimed at total mystification. Even a more than superficial glance at the abbé de Saint-Réal's *Dom Carlos* (1672), subtitled *Nouvelle historique,* would not necessarily tell us if we were reading a history of the young Spanish prince or a novel about him. The learned abbot, who was from a robe background and who had studied with the Jesuits, cited his sources and interspersed his narrative with references to the lacunae in previous accounts which he was allegedly filling. He did actually have access to important documentation during the time that he worked in the royal library under the direction of Antoine Varillas.

Saint-Réal may well also have come under Varillas's literary influence. Although the latter's works were published after Saint-Réal's, they seem to have circulated in manuscript before publication and to have been in great demand by eager readers.[54] Now Varillas, who was also from a robe family, obtained a *charge* as historian to Gaston d'Orléans, Louis XIII's weak-willed brother. He kept it only four years.[55] No wonder! If his published statements on historical writing are any indicator of his real opinions on the matter, he could not have made a very good court historiographer. In the preface to his *Anecdotes de Florence* (1685), a kind of manifesto of secret history writing, he suggested that the historian's use of verisimilitude produced watered-down truth. The historian, in Varillas's view, was required to make his truth *vraisemblable,* but the secret historian could dispense with this rule in his pursuit of pure, unadulterated truth: "The writer of Anecdotes takes as his object the whole truth and examines it impassively, be it probable [*vrai-semblable*] or not. . . ." But the secret historian paid a price for his freedom, Varillas added, because his selfless quest for truth could lead to his downfall. One historian he knew of was even threatened with a thrashing for not sticking to officially sanctioned documentation. Varillas declared that he himself had seen several manuscripts in the Royal Library which would never be published because "they paint a slightly too realistic portrait of several illustrious people with whom History until now has found no fault, or at least has wanted not to find any fault."[56]

Varillas recommended revision of the old portrait because the

---

54. Dulong, *L'Abbé de Saint-Réal,* p. 94. On Saint-Réal, see Andrée Mansau, *Saint-Réal et l'humanisme cosmopolite* (Paris, 1976).

55. Dulong, *L'Abbé de Saint-Réal,* p. 91.

56. Antoine Varillas, *Les Anecdotes de Florence, ou L'Histoire secrète de la maison de Médicis* (The Hague, 1685), Preface, pp. 7ff.

type of history he rejected was conveyed through the vehicles of portraits and portrait books. Written to impress as well as to conserve, official history wedded visual and verbal appeal. "There are excellent painters," said Varillas, "who do portraits according to all the rules of the art, but their portraits are not exact likenesses." Something is always added—a certain air, some color—to make the original more attractive. Varillas charged that all historians were guilty of this fault. His own project, he said, was to write about Pope Leo X. Now three historians, including the famous portrait book writer Paolo Giovio, wrote about the pope, but their attempts resulted in three separate accounts of him, each of which differed radically from the others. Varillas implied that each of these official writers was partial according to his particular relationship with the pope. The anecdote writer of Varillas's conception would proceed differently. "Whereas the others painted Pope Leo in ceremonial dress, the [secret historian] will represent him *en déshabillé*." The new variety of historian would unearth secrets that had escaped his predecessors. Varillas himself would use all available sources (he even mentioned documents he claimed to have found in the Royal Library) to extract the pope's "character."[57]

Portraits in the old style—that is, in the productions of court historiographers—were, it is true, always "in ceremonial dress," both visually and verbally. So were the fictional portraits in the roman à clef, where both the exterior and the interior of a contemporary were dressed up in historical finery, as, for instance, the archintriguer Mme de Longueville, who was transformed into the beautiful princess Mandane for Mlle de Scudéry's *Grand Cyrus*. Portraits, like other devices of the earlier novels—speeches, framed stories, and so on—did not entirely disappear in the new fiction, but were rather modified in accordance with changing narrative demands. The portrait was more integrated into the narrative flow of the text and tended, precisely as Varillas suggested, to focus more on the interior. The historical figure's character was now of primary interest. La Bruyere's *Caractères* (1688) attest to the significance of the shift from portrait to *caractère*.

Like the historians and critics of their day, writers of fiction in the later seventeenth century opposed well-documented, impartial history to the official history of court historiographers. If the elusive truth sought by such erudite Jesuits as Rapin and Daniel

---

57. Ibid., unpaginated.

was supposed to be objective, the pseudohistorical truth of the secret historian was scandalous. The *caractère* is almost the symmetrical opposite of the portrait, for instead of enhancing the original, it uncovers the seamy side. The one dignifies, the other exposes; the one dresses in robes of state, the other undresses. Verisimilitude as decorum was an aristocratic value that maintained dignity and censored the unseemly. The secret historian—who nevertheless still protested respect for morality in revealing the horrors of vice—all but threw such verisimilitude out the window. In the hands of writers no longer limited to the narrow confines of salon society, fiction was on its way to *embourgeoisement*.

In liberating narrative from verisimilitude, writers of *nouvelles* and secret histories removed their work from both the old *romans* and official history. Although Jean de Segrais in a well-known passage of his *Nouvelles françoises* (1656) placed the *nouvelle* closer to history than to the *roman* on the grounds that the latter was obliged to respect decorum (*la bienséance*) at the expense of truth,[58] the decorum of history would never have allowed for the modernized portraits of the *nouvelle*. Standards of decorum had to be observed in both history and *roman;* in both, truth required the discretion of verisimilitude. *Romanistes* and historians alike could not be too careful, as the episode of Bussy-Rabutin's imprisonment had proved.[59] Bussy departed from the tradition of the earlier novelists in that he did not choose a setting far removed in time for the portraits in his *Histoire amoureuse des Gaules* (1665). Writers of *nouvelles,* too, preferred recent to ancient history, one of their favorite periods being the sixteenth century. All the more reason for their revealing portraits to have had a shock value for the public. Never in official history or in a roman à clef could you have found portraits quite like this one by Mlle de la Force of Marguerite de Valois: "Marguerite, queen of Navarre . . . , was much more beautiful and likable than [Claude de France]; but she was also much less prudent. She was born with such an extraordinary penchant for amorous intrigue that, if you believe the Authors of her time, nothing was beneath her lubricity."[60]

58. Jean Regnault de Segrais, *Les Nouvelles françoises, ou Les Divertissemens de la princesse Aurélie* (The Hague, 1741), 1:146.

59. See Chapter 3 above, pp. 116–17.

60. [Charlotte Caumont de la Force], *Anecdote galante, ou Histoire secrette de Catherine de Bourbon, duchesse de Bar, et soeur de Henry le Grand. Avec les intrigues de la cour durant les regnes de Henry III et de Henry IV* (Nancy, 1703), p. 3. Similar portraits could be found in memoirs of the time, most of which—understandably—received posthumous publication considerably later on.

Public taste now veered very definitely toward the ersatz history of gossip and scandal that such portraits provided. Preference for the new as against the old type of portrait is reflected in the progressive transformation of fictional subject matter from the first to the second half of the seventeenth century. Nicolas Boileau, one of the century's most famous belletrists, said that he waited until Mlle de Scudéry had disappeared from the world to publish his devastating critique of her novels in his *Dialogue des héros de roman*. The satire in his dialogue turns on Scudéry's fictionalization of historical characters through imagined romance. For the exigent Boileau, Cyrus the Great in love was but a mockery of the man.[61] For nobles of the salon society in which Mlle de Scudéry's novels circulated, on the contrary, love dignified both the historical character and his or her modern counterpart. For nobles who played at love in salons, it was only fitting that their favorite pastime be given heroic dimensions in the roman à clef. Besides, no one took the *galanterie* of Cyrus the Great seriously; he was, after all, only a cover for the Prince of Condé. In the roman à clef, the past was refracted through the present: the loves of ancient Persia belonged to seventeenth-century France. Love played quite another role in the new fictionalized history. No longer a vehicle for deliberate anachronism, the amorous intrigues of secret history belonged unequivocally to the historical characters to whom they were assigned. These characters came not from the dim past but from an all too near present. In the 1680s and 1690s especially, love brought the history of the new fiction uncomfortably close. A glance at book titles of the time is like a register of scandal sheets. In 1687, a *Loves of the Cardinal de Richelieu* appeared. "*Amours*" or "amorous histories" of many reigning monarchs cropped up. Louis XIV himself was a preferred hero of such books. The very titles were a challenge to decorum: *Scarron* [Mme de Maintenon's first husband] *as he appeared to Mme de Maintenon and his reproaches to her for her love affair with Louis the Great* (1694); *Secret History of the Loves of Henri IV, King of Castille, Nicknamed the Impotent* (1695).[62]

61. See Nicholas Boileau-Despréaux, "Dialogue des héros de roman," in *Oeuvres* (Paris, 1966), pp. 453–60. Boileau seems to have had other reasons than his alleged consideration for Mlle de Scudéry for waiting to publish the "Dialogue," which appeared without his knowledge in 1688 and 1693. It was published with his consent in a posthumous edition of his complete works in 1713. See pp. 1089–90, n. to p. 443.
62. See Williams, *Bibliography*, pp. 218–61, for these and similar titles that appeared after 1680.

Needless to say, such books were not published with a royal privilege. Once he was found, the printer of the book about Mme de Maintenon was treated to a public hanging.[63] To escape this fate, many authors arranged for publication abroad. A more dangerous dodge of censorship was surreptitious publication within France; books published in this manner appeared without the printer's name or with a spurious imprint. Many works also appeared anonymously, usually without imprint. Of the titles mentioned above, two list as place of publication Cologne, one The Hague. Nor did the guilty fiction that managed to get by royal restrictions escape heavy criticism once it was off the press. Turn-of-the-century critics such as Pierre Bayle and the abbé de Belle-garde reserved harsh words for the novels of their day. After a thirty-four-year battle against novels carried on by the influential Jesuit periodical *Journal de Trévoux*, they were finally prohibited in France in 1737.[64]

Outcries against the supposed immorality of novels date from at least the period of the romans à clef. The newer fiction clearly presented both a moral and a political threat. Secret histories and true romances of royalty undermined the foundations of history. By pretending to peer into the hearts and boudoirs of the great, they suggested that history's leaders were just like everyone else, if not worse.[65] Generic distinctions of the earlier seventeenth century had maintained the hierarchical social distinctions of the ancien régime. History written in the main by bourgeois celebrated primarily the monarchy; the roman à clef served as an ideological prop to a collapsing nobility. Even then there were writers who overstepped generic boundaries, thereby challenging accepted notions of truth. Gomberville as early as 1620 had chided writers of particular histories and of *histoires de France* for including details of their subjects' personal lives—generally amorous in nature—which would have been more appropriate for a "life."[66] With the disappearance in the later seventeenth century of both the old *romans* and official history, the new fiction tended to replace both. Written and read by bourgeois and nobles alike, secret histories and *nouvelles* filled an ideological gap created by the distance

63. Martin, *Livre, pouvoirs, et société*, p. 758.
64. See Deloffre, *Nouvelle en France*, pp. 57–58.
65. Saint-Réal said as much in his *De l'Usage de l'histoire* (1671). See René Demoris, *Le Roman à la première personne* (Paris, 1975), p. 81.
66. Le Roy, *Discours*, pp. 96–99, 174–75.

Louis XIV chose to put between himself and his subjects. Without good history to satisfy curiosity about their rulers, the public turned eagerly to pseudohistory. Excluded from history by the strategies of absolutism, secret historians subverted history, and the modern novel appeared on the horizon as a subversive genre.

The Disappearance of History

The 1660s mark a turning point in the evolution of historical and fictional genres in the ancien régime. It was during this decade, when Louis XIV assumed personal rule, that official history faded from the literary scene. Louis's appointment in 1677 of Racine and Boileau as court historiographers was consistent with the devaluation of history. Both writers were poets, not historians, and neither one produced any French history comparable in importance to the work of the earlier historiographers. In the void created by the absence of any major *histoire de France,* both fictional and historical genres were modified. Under what conditions did these changes occur? What political and ideological factors may have motivated the disappearance of history?

Royal policy concerning the writing of history underwent crucial modifications from the time of Richelieu to that of Colbert. Richelieu was as shrewd in his manipulation of history as he was in his control of the arts and the press. He wisely seized the available and obvious means of ideological support for his threefold political program: subordination of the *grands,* reduction of the Protestants, the successful emergence of France from the labyrinth of the Thirty Years' War. His aim was to create the image of a strong monarch at home and abroad—and, not so incidentally, of a strong steward in the person of himself. Portrait books, panegyrics, eulogies, particular and general histories: Richelieu marshaled all of history for his ends. Portrait books, panegyrics, and eulogies diffused an imposing picture of Richelieu and helped to transform the diffident, rather pathetic son of Marie de Médicis into the august Louis le Juste in public imagination. General and particular histories strengthened the tradition of glorifying both the monarchy and some of its leading figures. In addition, Richelieu conceived the grand project of a history of his time, for which purpose he elicited the collaboration of many historians, secretaries, clerks, and the like. It was a project never destined to come to fruition; instead we have the minister's *Mémoires,* which represent an intermediary stage, a kind of sketch for the unfinished history.[67]

Richelieu was always adept at using his resources. If cultural patronage was the order of the day, he would outdo the *grands* and become first patron of the land. And so he attempted to organize a network of literary creatures after the fashion of his creatures of state, Bullion, Bouthillier, Chavigny, Sublet de Noyers. Founding the Académie Francaise was but an institutionalization of his cultural policy.[68] The cardinal had to keep a watchful eye on his creatures. His most successful historiographer, Scipion Dupleix, followed what was common practice in submitting sheets of his histories to Richelieu for approval before sending them off to the printer.[69]

For his efforts, Dupleix, along with the other chosen members of Richelieu's cultural network, received a pension. Colbert, however, switched the form of payment for scholars and men of letters to that of a gratification, or gift, in 1663, thereby breaking a century-old tradition of awarding stipends to men of letters. Historiographers were now no longer necessarily listed as such in official documents; they were cited as the recipients of gifts. A gratification implied a lesser monetary commitment on the part of the monarchy than did a pension. The latter generally signified remuneration in regular installments (in theory if not in practice) for a permanent office (*charge*), function, or honor. A gratification was not necessarily renewable. Colbert continued to employ Richelieu's system of cultural patronage, as Mazarin had done before him. But in asking such people as Pierre Costar and Jean Chapelain for extensive evaluations and assessments of the nation's human resources in arts and letters, Louis's minister depersonalized and bureaucratized the old system of *fidélités,* in which the relationship between protector and protégé was individual and immediate.[70]

Another equally consequential shift in royal policy toward history took place under Colbert. This was a profound change in the very program of historical writing. On November 18, 1662, the

---

67. See L. Delavaud, *Quelques collaborateurs de Richelieu,* in *Rapports et notices sur l'édition des Mémoires du Cardinal de Richelieu,* ed. Jules Lair, le Baron de Courcel (Paris, 1907–14), 2:45–308. See also Marc Fumaroli, "Les Mémoires du XVIIe siècle au carrefour des genres en prose," *XVIIe Siècle* 94–95 (1971):25–26.

68. See Ranum, *Artisans of Glory,* pp. 148–57.

69. Evans, *L'Historien Mézeray,* p. 21.

70. Ranum, *Artisans of Glory,* pp. 162–63, 193–95.

poet and critic Jean Chapelain responded by letter to a request
from Colbert for his advice on the use of history in the service of
the monarchy. Chapelain was all for the production of medals
and of verse to immortalize the king, but he expressed serious
reservations about history. Even an epic poem, in his opinion,
would present certain difficuties. Poetry, he says, upholding Aristotle's oft-cited distinction, differs from history in that it permits
the inclusion of fiction. But in an epic poem with the monarchy as
its theme one could not make up impressive events, which might
be denounced as untrue by knowledgeable people. Better to celebrate the king in panegyric, Chapelain advises, because fiction is
more acceptable there. Now he comes to his central point: any
history worthy of the name must explain the "motives of things"
and be accompanied by "prudent reflections." Both of these requirements present disadvantages: to fulfill the former during the
lifetime of the monarch one would run the risk of revealing important state secrets.[71] Chapelain does not specifically discuss the
latter requirement, but his reservations clearly relate to a celebrated debate at the time over the inclusion of moral judgments
in history. Richelieu was against the practice, Chapelain for it,[72]
and both for much the same reasons. History could not be left to
the public without supervision. Richelieu would correct it by selection: if the historian added no judgments, the events themselves
would have to be extremely well chosen. Chapelain would correct
it by addition. Elsewhere he states that most readers of history
need someone to "digest things" for them in order for it to be
useful; if the historian adds no judgments for the benefit of the
public, then "naked History wil be nothing but the vilest Novel."[73]
Although they took opposite sides in the debate, both Richelieu
and Chapelain held a similar view of truth in history: it should not
exceed the bounds of decorum. For the monarchy, historical truth
could not violate verisimilitude. The "prudent reflections" of
Chapelain's counsel in his letter of November 1662 obviously
posed a problem similar to that of the "motives of things." How
much of either could the historian include without touching on
sensitive matters best left unmentioned?

Chapelain's letter of 1662 to Colbert also contained what by this

71. Jean Chapelain, *Lettres de Jean Chapelain*, ed. Philippe Tamizey de Larroque
(Paris, 1880–83), 2:272–75.
72. Delavaud, *Rapports et notices*, pp. 163–64; Ranum, *Artisans of Glory*, pp. 184–
85.
73. Chapelain, *Lettres*, 1:36.

time had become a commonplace enumeration of the good historian's necessary qualifications: a thorough knowledge of the monarch and the monarchy; familiarity with political theory and military practice; a command of chronology and geography, as well as a knowledge of the customs of various nations; access to original versions of official communications and treaties. How can we ever find someone so qualified? Chapelain asks, varying the theme of Le Moyne and Rapin. For Chapelain was not interested in the objective truth that the Jesuit fathers despaired of achieving. Colbert's consultant deplored the very idea of letting such truth escape the royal walls. Only you yourself, he concludes in his letter to Colbert, are capable of writing history.[74] And indeed it seems that the minister had the same thought, for he produced several chapters of a history of Louis XIV around this time.[75]

Panegyric, eulogy, and medals—these were the core of Chapelain's program for celebrating the reign of the Sun King. He also recommended such architectural monuments as pyramids, triumphal arches, and equestrian statues, along with adornments: tapestries, frescoes, engravings, and the like. Such things, he owned, lay outside the area of his expertise.[76] His chief message to Colbert was to eschew history—presumably particular and general histories—in favor of more direct means of praise.

Chapelain's advice seems to have been extremely influential. One of the main functions of the Académie des Inscriptions et Belles-Lettres, which Colbert founded in 1663, was to supervise the production of medals for the monarchy. And Louis XIV was certainly assiduous in building architectual monuments to himself, as the château at Versailles attests. The 1660s inaugurated an era of expertise. From the Académie des Sciences, founded by Colbert in 1666, came much of the know-how that powered the spec-

74. Ibid., 2:275–76.
75. See Pierre Clément, ed., *Lettres, instructions, et mémoires de Colbert* (Paris, 1868), 5:lix.
76. Chapelain, *Lettres*, 2:277. My view of this matter differs from that of Orest Ranum. Ranum states that the history officially sponsored by Colbert and the crown was "more restrained than those panegyrical histories spawned by the Academicians" (p. 263). The importance of this distinction is questionable, since such academic histories were sanctioned by the crown. Ranum sees the appointment of Racine and Boileau as historiographers as part of a plan conceived by Louis XIV to dampen praise of himself and to "restore simplicity to the writing of history" (p. 296). If Louis was less interested in promoting praise of himself than in promoting greater sobriety and objectivity in the writing of history, why did he sponsor production of the monuments of praise recommended by Chapelain? It seems more likely that the monarch decided to devote more attention to those forms of praise that he could most effectively control.

tacular machinery of the royal gardens and fêtes. The young king drew on the intellectual and technological resources of his newly founded academies to construct his own distinctive apparatus of glory. True to the order of the day, the academician began to take the place of the historiographer.

It is not easy to account for the changes in royal policy on historical writing from the administration of Richelieu to that of Colbert, but several factors are evident. By 1661 Richelieu's political goals had in some measure been met. The civil disorders of the Fronde had weakened the power of the *parlementaires* and the *grands*. In the post-Fronde years, the nobles of neither sword nor robe were serious rivals of the monarchy as cultural patrons. The disgrace of Fouquet, who was well on his way to becoming a major patron, left Colbert virtually unchallenged in the field. Moreover, Louis XIII had won a crucial victory over the Protestants at La Rochelle in 1628. And the Peace of Westphalia in 1648, ending the Thirty Years' War, had marked the close of at least one phase of France's struggles abroad, bringing the country some gains in the conflict with Spain and the Hapsburgs.

Thus by the opening years of Louis XIV's personal reign, the ideological purposes of official history were no longer what they had been under Richelieu. The cardinal had exploited a traditional literary vein in building up royal history. His was largely a formative effort. If he himself did not create the ideology of absolutism, he was instrumental in creating its cultural-ideological apparatus. His literature of praise was a literature of combat. The image of an absolutely powerful monarchy had to be projected against threats from both home and abroad. By 1661 the threats from abroad were no longer imminent, Louis dealt summarily with those from home, and the apparatus was formed. Colbert's sponsorship of Benjamin Priolo's history was the seventeenth-century monarchy's last major—and notably unimpressive—attempt to use historical writing as a polemical tool against the *grands*.[77] From now on the effort would be not to form but to maintain. In the quarter-century preceding Louis's Revocation of the Edict of Nantes, the monarchy successfully maintained its ideology in the accomplishments of what we now call French classicism.

Chapelain may have perceived general and particular histories as superfluous in the coming of age of absolutism under Louis XIV. For the Sun King, panegyric and eulogy could perfectly well

77. See Ranum, *Artisans of Glory*, pp. 157–68.

meet the literary requirements of glorification. More important, these genres would avoid the pitfalls of history to which the poet alluded in his letter to Colbert. History had the disadvantage of being less amenable to supervision, as the case of Mézeray had proved.

François Eudes de Mézeray was perhaps not the wisest choice as court historiographer. A *libertin* of definite frondeur leanings, he nevertheless wrote an *histoire de France* so appealing that young Louis XIV's tutor used to read it to his pupil at bedtime.[78] Publication of the three-volume *Histoire de France depuis Faramond* from 1643 to 1651 spanned the troubled years of Mazarin and the Fronde. It has been called a "truly national history," because, unlike other general histories, it dealt with France's economic and social conditions, the affairs of French cities and provinces, administrative abuses, problems of peasants and merchants, religious issues.[79] Mézeray found a loyal protector in Chancellor Séguier, even won over Mazarin, and finally received from Colbert the highest pension (4,000 livres) awarded any man of letters in 1664.[80] His *Histoire* was in the humanist tradition, but was somewhat eccentric in its slightly antiquated, sixteenth-century style.[81] Although for a perceptive reader the history contained some pointed social criticism, Mézeray was not really to get into trouble until the publication of his three-volume *Abrégé chronologigue, ou extrait de l'histoire de France* in 1667–68.

Unfortunately for the historian, Colbert happened to come upon his own son, a student at the time, reading Mézeray's *Abrégé*. This happenstance gave the minister an opportunity for a firsthand look at some of Mézeray's not so favorable comments on taxes and the sale of offices. Understandably distressed, Colbert forthwith dispatched one of his officials, Charles Perrault, with a sharp message for the historian: Louis XIV hadn't paid him 4,000 livres to write such things. Fearful for his pension, Mézeray set to work revising the *Abrégé* in accordance with Colbert's instructions. Perrault was assigned the task of censoring the corrected sheets. The revised edition appeared in 1672, but Mézeray lost half of his pension anyway. Later it was withdrawn completely.[82] As if this

78. John B. Wolf, *Louis XIV* (New York, 1974), p. 24.
79. Evans, *L'Historien Mézeray*, p. 22.
80. Ranum, *Artisans of Glory*, pp. 208–11, 225–28.
81. Evans, *L'Historien Mézeray*, pp. 155–56.
82. Ibid., pp. 75–76.

were not enough punishment, Colbert also ruined Mézeray's standing in the Académie Française, to which the historian had been elected in 1648. He cruelly arranged for supervision of work on the academy's *Dictionnaire* to be taken away from the guilty Mézeray.[83]

With a little learning and some royal memoirs, a historian could get out of control. Mézeray's case illustrates the difficulties of managing history for the crown. Richelieu had worked hard to keep his staff in line. Why stuggle so, if panegyrists and eulogists could do the job? History was patently less suitable to the purposes of glorification than other forms that did not require the same kind of censorship and control.[84] There were, then, very definite practical reasons for the eclipse of history in the latter part of the seventeenth century. An analysis of royal accounts of gratifications awarded to French and foreign savants and men of letters from 1664 to 1685 reveals that the disappearance of court historiographers formed part of a pattern of changing ideological needs and outlets in the reign of Louis XIV.[85]

In order to determine who replaced court historiographers as ideological servants of the crown, I have used three modes of analyzing the accounts, according to the following questions: (1) Which individuals received the highest sums annually in gratifications? (2) What proportion of the total annual amount in gratifications was allocated to historians? (3) What categories of scholars and men of letters were awarded gratifications, and how many individuals were represented in each category from year to year?

The answers to these three questions show striking changes from 1664 to 1685. Before his downfall Mézeray received the highest sum in 1664, 1665, and 1666 (4,000 livres), with the historian Godefroy close behind him (3,600 livres); the highest sum (6,000 livres) in 1667 went to the Dutch scientist Christian Huygens for his invention of a pendulum clock. Mézeray did not figure on the lists for his unlucky years of 1667 and 1668, when Huygens continued to be awarded the highest sum, 6,000 livres. When the historian reappeared in 1669, his 4,000-livres gift was

83. Ranum, *Artisans of Glory*, p. 229.
84. Cf. Magné, *Crise de la littérature française*, p. 332.
85. I have used the accounts as published in Jules Guiffrey, *Comptes des bâtiments du roi sous le règne de Louis XIV* (Paris, 1881–1901), 5 vols. On gratifications during the reign of Louis XIV, see Georges Couton, "Effort publicitaire et organisation de la recherche: Les gratifications aux gens de lettres sous Louis XIV," *Le XVIIᵉ siècle et la recherche*, Actes du 6ᵉᵐᵉ Colloque de Marseille, Centre Méridional de Rencontres sur le XVIIᵉ Siècle, January 1976, pp. 41–55.

still less than Huygens' by 2,000 livres; this was the situation in 1670 also. By the following year, Mézeray's gratification was reduced to 2,000, while Huygens was continued at 6,000. Mézeray again received 2,000 in 1672, the last year he figured in the accounts. When during the 1670s the historian Godefroy sporadically appeared in the accounts, he figured high but was generally outdone by Huygens and the Italian astronomer Cassini. In 1680 the historian Clairambault shared the honor of the highest award with Boileau and Racine, the *érudit* d'Hérouval, the belletrist Gallois, and four scientists. Cassini, Huygens, and the mathematician Carcavi led in 1681. In 1682, Loir, the engraver of *jetons* for the Académie Française and the Académie des Sciences, got the highest amount, followed by an astronomer. Loir was again the highest paid on the list in 1683. In 1684 and 1685, Cassini received the highest amount.

Because increased military expenditures forced Louis to cut back on spending in letters and science, the total amount allotted to all gratifications in these areas in 1685 was considerably lower—some 31,000 livres—than the total amount for 1664. Annual totals allocated to historians also declined sharply during this period. Even when we take into account possible inaccuracies in the lists and the difficulty of knowing what a particular individual was compensated for when no explicit qualification was cited with the name, the figures are highly significant. In 1664, some 21 percent of the annual total was allotted to historians. In 1665, the figure was 17 percent; in 1668, 11 percent. In 1672, 23 percent of the total went to historians; in 1675, 8 percent; and in 1679, 15 percent. By the 1680s the situation had changed drastically. In 1682, historians were allocated some 5 percent of the total; in 1683, nothing at all; and in 1685, 3 percent. (See Table 1.)

Very interesting figures emerge from the third mode of analysis. (See Table 2.) Here I have broken down the gratifications into the following categories: letters, science, *érudits*, miscellaneous. Historians, except for a few erudite ones, are included in the first category. Technologists such as geographers and engravers are counted as scientists. If a name appears without a qualification, even if the individual's main occupation is known, I generally classify the item under "miscellaneous" except in very obvious cases. Specializations were not so restrictive in the seventeenth century as they are today, and very often one person could serve the crown in a variety of capacities, as evidenced by the category

Table 1. Annual expenditures for gratifications to all recipients and to historians, selected years, 1664–85 (in livres)

	1664	1665	1668	1672	1675
All recipients	77,500	82,800	90,300	100,500	55,450
Historians	16,400	13,900	9,900	22,995	4,200
Percentage to historians	21%	17%	11%	23%	8%

	1679	1682	1683	1685
All recipients	53,200	63,023	32,552	46,400
Historians	7,800	3,400	-0-	1,200
Percentage to historians	15%	5%	-0-	3%

"science and letters" applying to 1664.[86] In 1664, 41 of 57 recipients were in letters. For 1668, the figure is 23 of a total of 59. In the 1660s, recipients in letters consistently surpassed scientists in number, sometimes by a considerable amount. But by the 1670s, scientists began to outdo the belletrists. By the 1680s, the shift was decisive. Scientists decidedly outnumbered the belletrists, and in 1683 not a single belletrist was awarded a gratification.

Until the early 1680s, historians continued to be well represented in the category of letters on these rosters. But they were mainly *érudits*, working on manuscripts and documents, or else official historiographers who produced no noteworthy volumes.[87] During these sterile years for history, the ranks of a new ideological army were forming. The splendor of the Sun King shone not in *histoires de France*, but in the châteaux, gardens, fountains, and machinery of lavish spectacles that were to eternalize his reign. Louis wisely chose to glorify himself in the silent impersonality of stone and marble rather than in the human voice of history. Scientists, mathematicians, architects, and other technological specialists could best be expected to carry out the specifications of orders for monuments appropriate to his magnificence. The

86. When several person are mentioned together on one item, I count them as one person. I count each *item* as one person, even if the same name reappears on another item. I include theologians under "letters." *Erudits* include scholars working on documents, archives, medals, etc., and those trained in languages. I count sums given to heirs of a deceased person as belonging to the category of the deceased's occupation.

87. Cf. Joseph Klaits, *Printed Propaganda under Louis XIV: Absolute Monarchy and Public Opinion* (Princeton, 1976), pp. 192–93.

Table 2. Numbers of gratifications awarded in selected years, 1664–85, by category

	1664	1668	1672	1675	1679	1682	1683	1685
Letters	41	23	27	10	13	14		9
Science	4	21	23	17	12	22	25	14
Letters and Science	2							
Erudits	10	12	6	3	6	8	1	4
Miscellaneous		3		1	1	3	2	
Total	57	59	56	31	32	47	28	27

founding of the Académie des Sciences in 1666 institutionalized that sector of learning—science and technology—which was soon to get the lion's share of gratifications. While Cartesianism was making fitful headway in its namesake's native land, a new rationality had put in a stealthy appearance. In the latter part of the century, an outpouring of dictionaries and critical writing in all domains, including biblical exegesis, testified to a major attempt at the rational ordering of knowledge which was at the heart of Descartes's method.[88] Louis marshaled the forces of science and technology to support the massive edifice of absolutism. But the new rationality ironically undermined as it supported. In its very formation, it laid the foundations for an ideology of opposition. In sponsoring science and technology, Louis unwittingly bequeathed to his survivors the tools of the *Encyclopédie*.

Pseudohistorical Genres and the *Nouvelle*

The institutional and ideological changes of the 1660s opened the way to a generic realignment of fictional and historical narrative. The emergence of a new fictional genre—the *nouvelle*—was conditioned by the rise to prominence of a set of pseudohistorical genres that flourished in the place of history. As the old *roman* is generically described by its relationship to *histoire*, the *nouvelle*, forerunner of the modern novel, can be described in relation to the pseudohistory that sprouted in the interstices of absolutism.

With the decline of the royal historiographer, what did the future hold for a would-be historian? If commissions were not forthcoming from the crown, where did he turn for support? By the first decades of Louis XIV's personal reign, noble patrons no longer offered a writer the type of direct sponsorship they had

88. See Martin, *Livre, pouvoirs, et société*, pp. 847–48, 874–83.

formerly made available. The writer could expect to receive a position as secretary or tutor in a noble household, but such work would not always satisfy his literary ambitions. So he also tried to make connections at court or with an academy. More and more, however, as the royal coffers were running dry, the writer turned to the public. From about 1665 on, changes in publishing regulations worked in the author's favor. Previously a royal privilege, giving one bookseller virtual monopoly over a book, was issued for a maximum of about ten years. Booksellers generally purchased manuscripts in one lump sum; there were no royalties. Now Parisian booksellers were granted extensions of their privileges. This practice gave the author an advantage over his publisher in negotiating the sale of a manuscript. No longer could the bookseller get away with a low price by arguing that the short duration of his privilege gave him no opportunity to make a good profit. The book acquired new value as a commodity, while the author began to exercise proprietary rights, asking higher prices, and even demanding a share of the profits.[89]

Whereas previously a writer worked for the glory of a royal or noble patron, now increasingly money was the object. Earlier in the century, the image of the indigent poet was a literary commonplace; by the 1660s that of the avaricious author began to take its place. In 1685, Parisian booksellers defended their high prices with a statement on changing financial practices in the literary world. Formerly, they declared, authors paid money to booksellers to help defray printing costs; their money came from royal pensions and gratifications. If they didn't have any money, at least they didn't demand any. Now that the practice was just the opposite, the booksellers charged, literary art was degraded to a means of earning a living.[90]

The best way for a writer to make money, however, was to go into journalism. Journalists blessed with a royal privilege had the surest incomes, for they were independent of booksellers and could count on a fixed financial return from subscriptions.[91] There were three main official periodicals in seventeenth-century France. In 1631, the physician Théophraste Renaudot started the most celebrated of these journals, the *Gazette*, later the *Gazette de France*. The *Journal des sçavans*, which began publication in 1666, the year of the founding of the Académie des Sciences, was the

89. Ibid., pp. 913–14.
90. Ibid., pp. 914–15.
91. Ibid., p. 920.

official organ of scholars and scientists. In 1672, Donneau de Vizé started publication of the *Mercure galant*. Both Renaudot and Donneau held posts as *historiographes du roi*. Mézeray was on Renaudot's staff.[92]

The cases of Renaudot and Donneau suggest an alliance between history and journalism, two forms of writing that were not unrelated in their time. Not all those interested in history, however, were so fortunate as the two editors in garnering royal protection for their journalistic talents. Donneau enjoyed some nice privileges as royal historiographer, but as editor of the *Mercure* he did considerably better than most historians, earning a pension of 6,000 livres, which was raised to 15,000 in 1697.[93] The historians Antoine Varillas and the abbé de Saint-Réal never received more than 1.200 livres a year for their work with manuscripts in the Royal Library. Their gratifications ceased in 1671, and Saint-Réal was unsuccessful in his bid for the preceptorship of the future Victor Amadeus II in Torino.[94] Rubbed from the slate of official historians, deprived of the comforts of patronage, the two scholars turned to composing secret histories, or *nouvelles*.

Both journalists and secret historians, then, wrote *nouvelles,* for the word included a variety of genres, much in the same way as did *histoire.*[95] The journalists' *nouvelles* were news items, although Donneau's *Mercure,* aimed primarily at an aristocratic public drawn from the society of the salons, also offered brief fictional narratives. People in the time of this nascent journalism, however, tended to view news as a kind of instant history. Renaudot's efforts to delimit the activities of history and journalism imply a

---

92. Claude Bellanger, Jacques Godechot, Pierre Guiral, and Fernand Terrou, *Histoire générale de la presse française* (Paris, 1964), 1:83–94, 137.

93. Ibid., pp. 137–39.

94. See Dulong, *L'Abbé de Saint-Réal*, pp. 90–115.

95. For the ambiguity in meaning of *nouvelles*, see the discussion of papers by Varga and Godenne in *Cahiers de l'Association Internationale des Etudes Françaises* 18 (March 1966):249–53. See also Deloffre, *Nouvelle en France*, pp. 17–18. The connection between journalism and the development of the English novel in the seventeenth and eighteenth centuries has been studied by Lennard J. Davis, "A Social History of Fact and Fiction: Authorial Disavowal in the Early English Novel," in *Literature and Society*, selected papers from the English Institute, 1978, n.s. no. 3, ed. Edward W. Said (Baltimore, 1980), pp. 120–48. Davis makes many of the same points that I do in this chapter, suggesting that prose narrative in early modern France and England followed a parallel development. In particular, Davis points to an "ontological insecurity in the categories of fact and fiction" in England before the eighteenth century (p. 125). What he calls the "news/novel discourse" embodied this insecurity. The ambiguity of the *nouvelle* is the French equivalent of Davis' news/novel discourse.

confusion of the two, which was reinforced by Renaudot's appointment as historiographer in 1644. In the second year of the *Gazette*'s publication, Renaudot gave out the following clarification of its function: "History is the account of things that have happened, the *Gazette* that only of their advance reports. The former is obliged always to tell the truth, the latter only to ward off falsehood."[96] The editor's statement bespeaks ready compliance with the propagandistic limitations imposed on this paper by royal censorship. The *Gazette* was never more than the vehicle for officially sanctioned news of the court and the nobility.[97] Yet in the preface that Renaudot wrote for the first year's issues when he bound them together in a volume, his tone had been more uncompromising: "In one thing alone I will yield to no one: the quest for truth."[98] Here surely speaks a historiographer for whom truth is truth for the monarchy; Renaudot makes the same claims for journalism that historians made for history. Indeed, Charles Sorel classified Jean Richer's *Mercure françois,* an annual that ceased publication in 1648, as a "history, or rather a historical Book."[99]

The official periodical press was only one source for news at the time. An even more instant history was diffused through an enormous pamphlet literature. With a tradition dating from the earliest days of printing, this literature reached a public much more vast than that of any book of fiction, religion, or history. Known figures for book printings vary from 300 to 800 copies. But often 1,000 copies of pamphlets or brochures were printed at a time (printings of the *Gazette* may have reached 1,500 copies).[100] Pamphlets came in a variety of genres. The government used them to issue information on administrative and judicial acts, such as those concerning the creation and sale of offices. Engaging its own printers to ensure control over typography, the monarchy sent out a prearranged number of its informational pamphlets to magistrates and other interested functionaries. Royal printers seem to have made a considerable profit from such assignments. Peddlers hawked the pamphlets on the streets for exorbitant prices.[101]

96. As quoted in Bellanger et al., *Histoire générale de la presse,* 1:89.
97. See Klaits, *Printed Propaganda,* pp. 59–65.
98. As quoted in Bellanger, et al., *Histoire générale de la presse,* 1:89.
99. Sorel, *Bibliothèque françoise,* p. 358.
100. Marie-Noële Grand-Mesnil, *Mazarin, la Fronde, et la presse, 1647–1649* (Paris, 1967), p. 32.
101. Martin, *Livre, pouvoirs, et société,* pp. 258–61. On seventeenth-century pamphlet literature see also Hélène Duccini, "Regard sur la littérature pamphlétaire en France au XVII^c siècle," *Revue historique* 528 (October–December 1978):313–37.

Other varieties of pamphlets could be of either official or unofficial origin. The provenance of pamphlets is often hard to trace because they were usually unsigned, even when they defended royal policy, and they frequently do not bear a printer's address or mark of privilege or permission. Many unofficial pamphlets, of course, used false imprints or originated abroad.[102] *Occasionnels* appeared on the occasion of a specific real or imaginary event: a king's accession to the throne, a royal entry or funeral, a battle, the passage of a meteor. Printed *occasionnels* in France date from the fifteenth century. *Occasionnels* relating news of the king's life started to turn up under Louis XI and Charles VIII. Along with such related genres as *libelles*, or satires, *occasionnels* flourished during the Religious Wars. The anti-Mazarin pamphlets known as *Mazarinades*, thousands of which were distributed during the Fronde, were a variety of *occasionnel*. Promonarchy *occasionnels* could take the form of panegyric in short verse or in epic poetry, or of sermons in honor of the king composed by a celebrated priest.[103]

Pamphlet news, which was destined for rapid and widespread consumption, often had an aura of sensation about it. Some titles read like tabloid headlines: *Lamentable Speeches of three young children who were executed in the city of Tours for having stabbed their 70-year old Father with a knife, on the 17th of April, 1611. With the regrets of lamentations of their Sister; Execrable cruelty of three thieves dressed as hermits, who killed and robbed all Passengers and Travelers in the environs of Nantes in Brittany, Together with the murder and rape of a Young Lady from Poitiers, wife of a rich Seigneur of said city, committed by said thieves dressed as Hermits* (1625); *True Account of the monstrous and frightful dragon killed in a mountain of the Auvergne by Jean de la Brière, Native of Cervière in Forez* (1632).[104]

These pamphlets straddle the genres of the *occasionnel* and the *canard*. *Canards* reported marvels and miraculous events, diabolical manifestations, catastrophes, phenomena of nature, criminal cases. Specifications of time, place, and other particulars were intended to attest to the accuracy of the account. Such adjectives as "true" and "veritable" were inserted for the same effect. Events

---

102. Martin, *Livre, pouvoirs, et société*, pp. 268–69.
103. Bellanger, et al., *Histoire générale de la presse*, 1:29, 35; Grand-Mesnil, *Mazarin, La Fronde, et la presse*, p. 45; Martin, *Livre, pouvoirs, et société*, pp. 261–62.
104. A. Claudin, ed., *Diverses pièces curieuses et extraordinaires*, 3 vols. (Lyon, 1875). Pamphlets are separately paginated. The first cited is from vol. 1: the second and third are from vol. 2.

related in the *canard* were typically pretexts for moral or religious messages; they signified the workings of divine Providence or the infernal punishments elicited by human acts.[105] Here are some sample titles of *canards: True Stories of what happened to two bourgeois from the town of Charleville who were strangled and carried off by the devil in said town (1637); New, marvelous, and dreadful story of a young man from Aix-en-Provence carried off by the Devil and strung up on an almond tree for having impiously blasphemed the Holy Name of God and scorned the Holy Mass, two of his companions remaining without harm. As it happened the 12th of January of the present year 1614; Discourse on and interpretation of the marvelous apparition of three suns over the city of Marseille, as it occurred in the present year 1637, and the causes thereof; Dreadful, true Story, which took place in the town of Soliers in Provence, of a man who, having failed to fulfill his Holy Vows, had his private parts cut off by the Devil, who also slit the throat of a little girl aged two or thereabouts (1619).*[106]

Occasionnels, libelles, and *canards* were all used as weapons of the ideological warfare waged in pamphlet literature from the time of the Religious Wars. Pamphlet controversy raged during the reign of Louis XIII and throughout the period of the Fronde. *Canards* were well suited to religious polemic because their hidden moral message often had a proselytizing thrust. The title of this *canard* from the years of continuing religious conflict under Louis XIII makes clear its tendentious, combative purpose: *Great Sorrow of the supposedly reformed religion* [nearly always referred to thus in anti-Protestant pamphlets] *over the trial and horrible death of a minister from Nîmes who in his pulpit had his neck twisted by a huge thunderclap, then was lifted into the air and made invisible, to the great astonishment of his congregation, while preaching the opposite of the true, Apostolic, Roman Catholic Faith.*[107] For political purposes, the preferred form of combat pamphlet literature was the personal attack. In the early years of Louis XIII's reign, ministers and favorites came in for a bombardment of *libelles.*[108] By the middle of Louis XIV's reign, the Sun King himself was the target. Thus the official type of *occasionnel* relating episodes in the king's life was parodied in the unofficial satirical pamphlets. Seventeenth-century politics was above all the politics of personality, as we know from the many accounts of

105. Bellanger, et al., *Histoire générale de la presse,* 1:44–62.
106. Claudin, *Diverses pièces.* The first three titles are from vol. 1, the last from vol. 2.
107. Ibid., vol. 1.
108. Martin, *Livre, pouvoirs, et société,* p. 270.

intrigues in high places found in memoirs of the time. The slanderous reports of Louis's sex life which figured in pamphlets during his reign were chiefly political in intent. An attack on the man was an attack on the ruler.[109]

Techniques of personal attack were perfected in the *Mazarinades,* which had as their goal the destruction of Mazarin. *Mazarinades* could be presented as news, or *nouvelles,* sometimes parodying the monthly "extra" issue of the *Gazette.* At the beginning of the Fronde, Renaudot had followed Queen Anne and her two sons to their retreat in Saint-Germain, leaving Paris without an official newspaper. A frondeur paper called the *Courrier français* and also a *Journal du Parlement* quickly sprang up in the beleaguered city, but the real source of "alternative news" lay in the *Mazarinades.*[110] Such titles as the following did not deceive anyone as to their message, but they did indicate that one of the functions of the *Mazarinade* was to provide uncensored news: *Extraordinary News containing everything that has happened at Court since the defeat of the Mazarins* (Paris, 1652); *News brought to King Louis XIII in the Elysian Fields, and his conversation with the Heroes and principal Lords of his Court concerning the fatal war set off by Mazarin in France. And the description of the main things that have happened since the abduction of the King, which is the entire History of the Times* (Paris, 1649). In another *Mazarinade,* titled *Nouvelles,* and also presented as a dialogue of the dead, the frondeur Châtillon contests Renaudot's accuracy. Châtillon accuses the "snub-nosed Renaudot," "that rascal Gazeteer," of having given incorrect information about the siege of Charenton.[111]

Owing to the absence of the queen regent and the general disarray of the land during the Fronde, an avalanche of pamphlet literature was able to descend on the public relatively unimpeded by censorship. In the mid-sixteenth century, Protestant pamphlet literature had inspired a series of royal edicts initiating censorship of the press in France.[112] The monarchy, in its attempt to crush opponents, thereby took the negative step of trying to eliminate oppositional literature. After 1624, Richelieu organized a pamphlet campaign of his own and trained a skilled staff of propa-

---

109. Klaits, *Printed Propaganda,* p. 22.
110. See Grand-Mesnil, *Mazarin, La Fronde; et la presse,* pp. 50–73.
111. "Nouvelles burlesques portees par le duc de Chastillon à l'Empereur des Tenebres, aux affreuses cavernes de sa domination" (n.p., 1649), pp. 3–4 (Houghton Library Collection, Harvard University).
112. Bellanger, et al., *Histoire générale de la presse,* 1:65.

ganda writers to produce the image of himself that he wished to spread abroad.[113] Richelieu's policy of controlling opinion through the press was twofold: "to censor and to sponsor," as one historian has aptly formulated it.[114]

Unofficial pamphlet literature responded doubly to the monarchy's twofold policy. It evaded censorship through a variety of subterfuges, and it sponsored "alternative news." Official journalism in its dimension of instant history propagated history for the crown, an abbreviated form of the historiographer's history. The unofficial press contested instant history with its own version, a counterhistory. For this function it found an established precedent in the almanac.

Related to the popular literature published in the *Bibliothèque bleue* collection and yet distinct from it, almanacs had an even wider circulation than pamphlets: some were printed in editions of as many as 150,000 to 200,000 copies. The almanacs combined astrological lore with accounts of all kinds of historical events, ranging in importance from the death of a king to the accidental collapse and consequent reconstruction of a Parisian bridge. The history in its pages was one of strange and marvelous happenings. Like the *canard*, the almanac claimed exact truth for even its most extravagant reports. But primarily the almanac told its own version of the ever-present *histoire de France*, popular versions of which were printed in the *Bibliothèque bleue* collection. History in the almanac, like that of the pamphlets, was anecdotal and fictionalized; it was the "story of history." Only in eighteenth-century almanacs did tables of contents begin to indicate an effort to separate fact from fiction in their contents, history being consigned to such rubrics as "Relation" and "Anecdote," fiction left to the category of *histoire* (in the sense of "story").[115]

Why did the monarchy from Charles IX to Louis XIII feel the need to issue special edicts regulating the publication of almanacs? Almanacs certainly had a less threatening aspect than did most

113. Martin, *Livre pouvoirs, et société*, pp. 272–73.

114. Klaits, *Printed Propaganda*, p. 39. On the historical roots of seventeenth-century censorship, see Alfred Soman, "Press, Pulpit, and Censorship in France before Richelieu," *Proceedings of the American Philosophical Society* 120 (December 1976):439–63. Soman dates the beginning of methodical propaganda in France from the period of Richelieu (p. 463). According to Soman, an effective system of book censorship in France was established only in the mid-seventeenth century (p. 457). I am grateful to Elizabeth L. Eisenstein of the University of Michigan for this reference.

115. For the almanac, see Geneviève Bollème, *Les Almanachs populaires aux XVIIe et XVIIIe siècles: Essai d'histoire sociale* (Paris, 1969), esp. pp. 12–40, 89–94, 110–24.

books, pamphlets, and periodicals, which required the control of censorship. One view is that the astrological predictions in almanacs were a mode of intervention in history,[116] but the very wide extension of almanacs gives us yet another clue. There is evidence that all classes of French people read almanacs, from peasants to nobles. By the eighteenth century, when it became the fashion to own an almanac, everyone had one, including the king. The almanacs offered a recurrent piece of advice: Read! One of the oldest added to its list of propitious times to stock up on wheat, wine, or wood, or to buy thread, horses, fields, or clothes, this directive: "Buy books any time" An almanac of 1673 instructed its readers: "Hope for the best and read often." Was this counsel addressed chiefly to peasants? Were the almanacs destined to be literacy manuals for the large proportion of France's population who could not read? In villages where nearly everyone was illiterate, one person would read aloud from almanacs, spreading the message.[117]

There are no definite answers to these questions concerning literacy. But one thing we do know is that it was in the interests of the seventeenth-century French monarchy to keep its subjects uneducated. Pupils in the *collèges* of the time were drawn from various ranks of society, including artisans and peasants. Moreover, the Jesuit *collèges* offered their services free of charge. The education provided by the *collèges* and many smaller schools was too widespread to suit some people. Richelieu, in his *Testament politique,* was adamant in his opposition to the extension of education. It could lead, in his view, to revolt: letters would ruin commerce and agriculture, deplete the military, and disturb the peace.[118] The cardinal would have liked to reduce the number of *collèges* to two per city, assigning control of one to the Jesuits, of the other to the universities, so that neither group should obtain a monopoly and thereby threaten the authority of the state.[119]

Seen in this context, the almanacs' advice is hardly innocuous. In a society whose leaders feared that education might foster rebellion, urging the general public to read carried the ring of a battle cry. Like the unofficial press, almanacs bore a subversive

116. Ibid., pp. 26–27.
117. Ibid., pp. 12–15.
118. Lough, *Writer and Public,* p. 74. It is interesting to note with Lough, pp. 167–68, that the prejudice against popular education extended into the eighteenth century, with such figures of the Enlightenment as Voltaire opposing it.
119. Victor L. Tapié, *La France de Louis XIII et de Richelieu* (Paris, 1967), pp. 165–66.

message. But subversive as they may have been, almanacs and pamphlets were aboveground. They were visible, and the monarchy could resort to proven means of controlling them. Less easy to combat, because much less visible, was a kind of underground news network run by people known as *nouvellistes.*

Nouvellisme is one of the more bizarre phenomena of the ancien régime. By the reign of Louis XIV it had become a ubiquitous yet elusive force. With Renaudot's government mouthpiece alone regularly supplying news items, supplemented by *occasionnels, canards,* and other pamphlets that often as not were polemical, where was one to turn for information? Nobles thirsted to know the essential of their survival: who was the up-and-coming favorite at court, which royal or noble mistress was the preferred, which minister was about to be disgraced, what were the latest military maneuvers. The clergy needed to know which important livings were going to be available. Financiers' speculations depended on the latest news of the Bourse. Was the fashion in ladies' headgear about to change? Merchants needed to know. It was the *nouvellistes*'s business to supply this information, for the *Gazette* did not print such items. So *nouvellistes* were everywhere, ferreting out their precious knowledge, circulating it to a widespread clientele in Paris, in the provinces, and even abroad.[120]

Who were the *nouvellistes? Luftmenschen* from the margins of society, they had a certain reckless courage and some learning. Former law clerks, renegade priests, students, dismissed military officers populated the hive of news gatherers. There were less learned folk, too: wives or widows of *nouvellistes,* even laundresses. The organization of this vast verbal industry was such that it implicated everyone, from the highest ranking to the most obscure members of French society.

The idea seems to have originated in personal correspondence. Mme de Sévigné's perfected epistolary art is a sophisticated example of *nouvellisme. Nouvelles à la main,* or manuscript newsletters, evaded the restrictions of printed matter and found a natural shield in the routine of the postal circuit. From humble beginnings an efficient clandestine operation developed. By the seventeenth century, news bureaus had taken charge of supplying an ever more curious public. Located in a miserable attic room, a

120. For information on the *nouvellistes,* see the two studies by Frantz Funck-Brentano: *Figaro et ses devanciers* (Paris, 1909) and *Les Nouvellistes* (Paris, 1905).

café, or a cabaret, each bureau was headed by an editor in chief, the *chef de nouvelles.* He was assisted by an "editorial secretary" who transcribed the news and hired scribes and copyists. The secretary was also obliged to be a watchdog, for news leaks and contraband were the most notorious black-market activities of the black-market traffic in news. In addition, the secretary supervised subscriptions, which supported the entire staff. The clientele was a well-heeled one, consisting primarily of France's social elite, and they were prepared to pay the high prices demanded of them. Still, copyists could barely eke out a living from their task.

Nouvellistes à la bouche, or talking *nouvellistes,* supplied news for the *nouvelles à la main,* which came also to be known as *gazettes secrètes.* Little knots of babblers—*pelotons*—could be spied dotting the public gardens and promenades of Paris. Swarms of people eager for news, along with paid reporters for the *gazettes secrètes,* descended on them. Nobles and wealthy families sent their servants out to bring back news; these servants also often worked for a *nouvelliste. Pelotons* may have been organized according to specialization, since the talkers seem to have been divided into four main categories: the *nouvellistes galants* reported on amorous intrigues; the *nouvellistes de Parnasse* had literary and theatrical news; the *nouvellistes enjoués* were responsible for amusement; and the *nouvellistes d'Etat* dealt with political matters. Reporters for news bureaus could not just rely on the *pelotons,* however. They also had to frequent society, to station themselves in the Galerie du Palais, a labyrinth of shops and booksellers next to the Palais de Justice, to hang around theaters, to coax information from lackeys and porters—in short, they had to be everywhere.

Little by little, the system took on the character of a vast espionage outfit. The reporter turned informer when he supplied foreign ministers with state secrets or worked for the police. Frequently he was a double agent, working both for the government and for an editor, or for himself. Richelieu, who knew full well just how important it was to keep up with the *gazette secrètes,* had his informers. Louis XIV read *nouvelles à la main.* In the eighteenth century, the monarchy distributed its own *nouvelles à la main* in counterattack. The *cabinet noir* run by Froncé, head of the postal service, sent out a biweekly *gazetin,* or *gazette secrète,* which was a systematic revision of the newsletters it opened and read.[121]

The *nouvelles à la main* had an immense circulation in France

121. Klaits, *Printed Propaganda,* pp. 50–51.

and abroad. With thousands of readers, they had awesome potential for influence over public opinion. Penalties for *nouvellisme* were correspondingly severe. Royal edicts against *nouvelles à la main* date back to the time of the Religious Wars, when the *nouvelles* consisted mainly of defamatory satires. In the seventeenth century, a *nouvelliste* ran the risk of corporal punishment, fines, imprisonment, the galleys, or even death.[122] For his illicit journalism one Elie Blanchard got off lightly in 1663. He was condemned to a thrashing on the Pont-Neuf, and for the occasion he was required to wear two placards, one in front, one in back, each bearing the ignominious legend "Gazetier à la main."[123]

Despite the prospects of such punishment, *gazetiers* flourished throughout the latter part of the ancien régime. No sooner was one nest routed than another took its place. *Nouvellistes* thrived during the most oppressive times, for that was precisely when their services were most in demand. Was Théophraste Renaudot's *Gazette* an early attempt to control this plague by official sponsorship of news? In his preface to the bound volumes of 1631, Renaudot said that the *Gazette* would be especially useful in "preventing rumors spread by those who write to their friends . . . and satisfy their curiosity by laboriously transmitting news that is for the most part made up or founded on hearsay."[124] Whatever may have been the monarchy's purpose in according Renaudot a privilege, the editor's accusations have some basis in fact. With the reliability of informants so often in question, news and gossip were virtually indistinguishable. To keep the number of their subscribers competitively high, editors of *gazettes secrètes* added to their reports sensational items that they made up to please their clientele. Readers were well aware of the ploy, and even placed bets on the authenticity of the stories. To satisfy public taste for sensation, scandal made its surreptitious way into printed gazettes also. Destined for insertion into such papers as the *Mercure galant,* strips of paper evocatively called *lardons* were printed abroad with "secret news" and smuggled into France. *Lardons* pullulated in the 1680s, when their goal was to rally Europe to war against Louis XIV.[125]

122. See Eugène Hatin, *Histoire politique et littéraire de la presse en France* (Paris, 1859), pp. 54–59; and Funck-Brentano, *Nouvellistes,* pp. 8–10.

123. Hatin, *Histoire politique,* p. 58.

124. Théophraste Renaudot, *Recueil des Gazettes de l'année 1631* [*Gazette de France*] (Paris: Bureau d'Adresse, 1632), p. 5.

125. Bellanger et al., *Histoire générale de la presse,* 1:147–48.

As in unofficial pamphlets, scandal in the *nouvelles à la main* was at once personal and political. A *nouvelliste d'Etat* would produce more politically oriented scandal. Thus in 1716 one *gazetier* had the following item about the young Louis XV: "We have a sulky, opinionated little king. Mme de Ventador found it impossible to make him give a favorable audience to the King of Sicily's ambassador. When he made his entrance, he hid behind the curtains of his bed and refused to appear, heeding no one. It's not easy to make a good king of a young king."[126] The *nouvelliste galant* concentrated on scandal of a more amorous nature, yet, like the *nouvelliste d'Etat*, he aimed at exposing secrets both personal and political in their implications. Here is a typical excerpt from the early eighteenth century: "The Duke of Maine's death has resulted in the revelation of a piece of news that we expect will soon receive official confirmation: the secret marriage of the Prince of Dombes and Mlle de Charolais. Their clandestine affair has not been deprived of heaven's blessing, since six living offspring of the union have been counted."[127]

Official confirmation of the last item never came through. Such was the problem with *nouvelles à la main*: you could never be sure of their authenticity. In 1663, a satire on *nouvelles à la main* appeared. Its author was none other than the future editor of the *Mercure galant,* Donneau de Vizé. Did his satire help to win him the honor? Whatever the story behind his appointment and the fat rewards he received from it, Donneau's criticisms of *nouvellistes* must have pleased the crown. His chief complaint was precisely that *nouvelles à la main* were not reliable; they were not *true.*

Now we have seen that opponents of fiction leveled the very same accusation of untruth against the novel. And as one listens to Donneau, it often seems that the satirist has gotten confused in his object. Is he talking about *nouvelles* or *romans*? He says that *nouvellistes* are guilty of reporting things that they couldn't possibly know, such as the thoughts and intentions of ministers. *Nouvellistes* repeat their every word, he protests, as if they had informants in the ministers' chambers night and day, writing down each syllable.[128] Earlier in the century, Charles Sorel had objected

---

126. Edouard de Barthélemy, ed., *Gazette de la Régence* (January 1715–June 1718) (Paris, 1887), p. 105.

127. Item of May 24, 1736, in *Nouvelles de la cour et de la ville* [ed. Edouard de Barthélemy] (Paris, 1879), p. 104.

128. [Donneau de Vizé], *Nouvelles nouvelles* (Paris, 1663), 2:265.

to narrative techniques of the novel on virtually the same grounds: narrators of framed stories often displayed a knowledge far beyond their capacities.[129] Donneau's confusion of novels and *nouvelles* is deliberate, for he suggests an obvious equation: *nouvelles* are just as untrue as fiction.

To this end he employs the narrative technique of the romans à clef, which Sorel, too, had adopted in his satirical antiroman, *Le Berger extravagant*: the story within a story. The frame story of Donneau's satire, *Nouvelles nouvelles*, seems to approach the truth of everyday reality. It concerns two friends, Arimant and Cléonte, who entertain three *nouvelliste* friends of theirs with the folly of *nouvellisme*. In the course of the merriment, a valet brings one of the *nouvellistes* a letter from Spain, addressed to "Monsieur Ariste, Historiographe de France." Arimant whispers to Cléonte that every writer or would-be writer now has the imperetinence to assume the title of historiographer. The letter contains news of a young man who left his native Algiers to go to Madrid for the purpose of converting to Catholicism, but was deceived by his mother into returning home. Is this fact or fiction? The writer has warned his reader that his letter will sound like a novel. When the letter has been read aloud, another of the *nouvellistes* makes up an alternative version of its contents. The third then explodes at them for their habit of palming off their "reveries" as truth. "By the pernicious embellishment of your art," he thunders, "you are so clever at confusing truth and error that it's impossible to know anything. This is how you deceive posterity and give out lies as truth."[130]

An ingenious satire. Is the story of the letter true of false? Does it offer that mixture of truth and falsehood which Mlle de Scudéry recommended as a good recipe for novels? Is it a piece of news or a framed story like others in the second and third volumes of Donneau's *Nouvelles*, which are told by the protagonists of the frame story? Is the frame story itself a news item or an invented tale? Is Donneau as reliable as theoretically befitted the historiographer he became in reality or is he merely a storyteller? In short, are his *nouvelles* news items or stories?

Donneau's public appreciated trompe l'oeil, and it suited the

129. Charles Sorel, *Le Berger extravagant* (Paris, 1627–28) (facs. ed. Geneva, 1972), 2:94–95 (510). For an explanation of the pagination in this edition, see Chapter 2 above, n. 22.

130. Donneau de Vizé, *Nouvelles nouvelles*, 2:286–99.

purpose of his satire. Just as the public could tell the difference between an *histoire de France* and a *roman* that called itself *histoire,* as La Calprenède's did, so could they tell the difference between news and that new variety of fiction which became so successful after 1660, the *nouvelle.* Each presupposed the other as a distinct but related genre. So when Isaac Claude's *Comte de Soissons,* for example, appeared in 1687 with the subtitle *Nouvelle galante,* no one took it for real news. Everyone recognized it for what it was: a fictional pastiche of an item in the repertoire of a *nouvelliste galant.* And what were *histoires secrètes* if not fictionalized reproductions of the *gazette secrètes?* The *histoires secrètes* and *nouvelles galantes* were like expanded news items. As unofficial *occassionnels* parodied the official form with gossip about lives of royalty and nobility, so *nouvelles galantes* and *histoires secrètes* parodied the gossip of *nouvelles à la main* by weaving bits and pieces of dubious "news" into a coherent, book-length narrative. As the old *romans* such as La Calprenède's *Faramond* offered history in trompe l'oeil, so the *nouvelles* were *nouvelles à la main* in trompe l'oeil. Seventeenth-century French fiction was a trompe l'oeil "truth."

Between the *roman* and the *nouvelle* lay a discredited and destitute nobility, a rapidly forming bourgeoisie eager to take its place in power and prestige, and a monarch that desired "absolute" rule over both. The roman à clef had aspired to the status of the history it parodied. The *nouvelle* was truly new, as new as the latest news item.[131] It aimed not to repeat and outdo history, as did the *roman,* but to undermine it, after the fashion of the *nouvelles à la main.* Like the latter, like all unofficial versions of official news and history, it presented the unauthorized and the scandalous. Gone now are the state portraits of the *roman;* in their place are the *galanteries* of a satirical *caractère.* History in trompe l'oeil emulated as it imitated. Trompe l'oeil newsletters imitate subversion.

In subversion the *nouvelle* found its own truth, and it bequeathed the process to the modern novel. For of course it is the *nouvelle,* not the *roman,* that most closely resembles the modern novel. Although its length varied, the seventeenth-century *nouvelle* was generally a one-volume prose narrative with a dominant main plot. Only in the following centuries would the *nouvelle* change so

---

131. Cf. Davis, "Social History," p. 126, and Magné, *Crise de la littérature française,* pp. 111–12. Magné notes the semantic field of *nouvelle:* "new," "news item," "novella." His analysis, fundamentally different from mine, does not include an examination of the *nouvellistes.*

as to take on its modern meaning of short story.[132] Truth in the seventeenth-century *nouvelle* was no longer of and for the nobility, as in the *roman*, but *against* an oppressive regime. The writer, noble or bourgeois, now worked for money. For the aristocratic *romaniste* of old, it would have been unthinkably vulgar to do so. But the *nouvelle* was vulgar. It discarded the decorum and verisimilitude essential to noble genres in favor of a new truth. This truth was where censorship was not. It was behind the scenes, underneath the robes of state. It was the unknowable. The novelist removes the facade, and such was the task of the secret historian. Le Sage's *Diable boiteux* (1707) epitomizes the process: thanks to the demon Asmodée, the roofs of Madrid's houses disappear, and the secret histories of their inhabitants are revealed.

The *nouvelle* filled a vacuum left by the disappearance of both history and the *roman*. It had to do for both. It invented a story in place of the history it contested because no historian was going to get the real story. Its truth was the fact of its contestation and the fiction of its invention. It was the truth of history dialectically unfolding against the noble history of the novel, against official history, toward a democratic future with an accessible history, toward a bourgeois novel. Like the *nouvelle à la main*, like history itself, the *nouvelle* had to be a mixture of fact and fiction. History had embroidered fact with fiction to the monarch's specifications; *nouvelles à la main* could not disentangle the two so easily, and so reported their own version of fact and fiction. The *nouvelle* followed their lead, as the *roman* had followed that of history.

Literary genres in the seventeenth century were not divided according to fact and fiction, as they would come to be in the era of the philosophes, when history reappeared in its modern amalgam of the humanist and erudite strains. Objective or scientific truth as we conceive it today was the pivot of an ideology in formation. It found its appropriate vehicle not in history but in Cartesianism. Only in the eighteenth century would the ideology crystallize in the militant phase of opposition to the ancien régime. In the seventeenth century, generic truth functioned as a mask for ideological truth. The truth of the *histoire de France* lay in the endless repetition of France's successive monarchs, stretching to eternity with the addition of each new king. Its ideological

132. For a different view of the evolution of the *nouvelle*, see René Godenne, "L'Association nouvelle–'petit roman' entre 1650 et 1750," *C.A.I.E.F.* 18 (March 1966):67–78.

truth was a truth for the monarchy as against the forces that threatened it, whether Protestants, *grands*, or Hapsburgs. The roman à clef found its truth in the patina of history artfully applied to salon society. This Janus-like mask concealed the truth of a bitter rivalry: the nobles' attempt to reclaim history as their own.

The official press published a truth that conserved the ceremonial robes of the state portrait. Unofficial pamphlet literature and *nouvelles à la main* were the first groping attempts to expose the ideological truth concealed behind the generic. But, except for the brief period of the *Mazarinades*, such efforts were unorganized, incoherent, and sporadic. Even the *Mazarinades* represented not the interests of a unified class, but the hodgepodge complaints and demands of disaffected nobles, unruly *parlementaires*, and restive bourgeois.

Trompe l'oeil was the suitable vehicle for an ideological truth in search of a mask. But the *nouvelle* imitated a genre that was not really a genre and that *had no positive truth*. *Nouvelles à la main* did not imitate; they countered and contested. They sought the truth, and truth seeking was their very primitive attempt at ideological truth. They filled in the blanks of fact with the fiction of gossip. The truth of the *nouvelle* was the real story, the secret, untold history. *Véritable* and *secrète* are almost synonymous when they modify *histoire* in titles of these fictional works.[133] Their ideological truth was a blank. During the height of the *nouvelles*' success, in the last few decades of the seventeenth century, their truth was simply a negation of official truth as broadcast in periodicals, pamphlets, and other court literature.[134] *Nouvelles*, like *nouvelles à la main*, sought to expose whatever truth lay behind the facade of the generic. The function of their ideological truth was negative and subversive.

The *nouvelle* told a story that was counterhistory, a pastiche of alternative news. One day the story would achieve independence

133. In Magné's view, the *nouvelle* moved away from *vraisemblance* toward *vérité* between 1680 and 1715, when it began to turn to history as a model. In his discussion of the *roman* and the *nouvelle*, Magné seems to discount the role played by history in the production of the former, adopting the traditional view that the *roman* was modeled on the epic. See Magné, *Crise de la littérature française*, pp. 93–145.

134. Cf. Robert Darnton, *The Literary Underground of the Old Regime* (Cambridge, Mass., 1982), pp. 34–35, 142–47. These fascinating studies suggest that underground writing and publishing in the eighteenth century were a continuation and expansion of seventeenth-century activities. Darnton tends to view the work of the eighteenth-century hacks of Grub Street as revolutionary, but he does not indicate that it ever passed beyond contestation.

from official history and would assume responsibility for its condition as fiction. Nobles had emulated royalty in the trompe l'oeil history of the *roman*. Bourgeois literature in its very beginnings adopted the preexisting mold of trompe l'oeil, for bourgeois in their turn wanted to emulate nobles. When the bourgeois became unified as a class and pen triumphed over sword, they no longer needed the imitative virtues of trompe l'oeil. The *nouvelle* became a novel.

5

An Unlikely Princess

By the end of the 1660s, the new literary fashion was well established. No one bothered to wade through the many cumbersome volumes of a roman à clef anymore. Instead, the French reading public was enthusiastically consuming the latest fictional fare: the streamlined one- or two-volume *nouvelle*. Like last year's style in dress, the old *romans* began to appear antique almost as soon as they were discarded. Critics poked fun at them; novelists professed scorn for the old techniques. Yet the *nouvelle* was as much a continuation of the *roman* as it was a reaction against it. In the language of the day, it was a *petit roman*, *petit* both in its small, easy-to-carry (often duodecimo) format and in its literary form of an abbreviated *roman*. For in fact it frequently contained the same narrative structures and devices as the *roman*, with the necessary formal modifications and condensations.

The significance of the *nouvelle* is twofold. It was the result of a generic development that critically transformed the *ut pictura poesis* system. The *nouvelle* also initiated a decisive phase in the formation of the modern novel. The genesis of the *nouvelle* was influenced by interrelated material and ideological conditions specific to the reign of Louis XIV: the now booming clandestine book trade and a search for new truth in the age of absolutism. The secrecy of illicit publishing combined with a new passion for scandal to produce the underground or unofficial *nouvelle*, that is, one published without benefit of a royal privilege. Those *nouvelles* that I call "official," or those bearing a royal privilege, were a tamer species of the unofficial variety and shared with it the same basic generic properties. The most famous of the official *nouvelles* was Mme de La Fayette's *Princesse de Clèves* (1678). Among the many *nouvelles* published in the seventeenth century,[1] it is the only one still read today. The book is commonly labeled as one of the first modern novels and praised for its psychological penetration and polished style. In the seventeenth century, however, it was not easy to differentiate *La Priucesse de Clèves* from the profusion of its generic relatives.

Official and unofficial *nouvelles* alike grew up in an ambience of the clandestine. The function of the genre was to tell the untold story of history, to leak pseudosecrets of state. We cannot be surprised, then, to find so many *nouvelles* published without a royal privilege. Because the generic properties of the *nouvelle* are intimately bound up with its mode of production, we will first take a look at the mechanisms of clandestine book publishing and then proceed to an examination of the generic features of the unofficial *nouvelle*. Viewed in this context, the history of the *ut pictura poesis* system during the reign of the Sun King gains in complexity, for its evolution was such as to make possible the emergence of the prototypical modern novel, *La Princesse de Clèves*. By exploring the relationship between what is commonly regarded as Mme de La Fayette's masterpiece of classical sobriety and the underground shockers of her time, we will come to understand the embryonic subversion of *La Princesse de Clèves*. It was this subversion, so characteristic of the modern novel, that in a more developed form finally destroyed the *ut pictura poesis* representational system.[2]

In the 1720s, just about a decade before novels were prohibited in France, the crusty Nicolas Lenglet-Dufresnoy wrote in *De l'usage des romans:* "Ban novels all you like, thunder out against them, hurl down every lightning bolt in the Universe to extermi-

---

1. The three basic checklists for seventeenth-century *nouvelles* are: René Godenne, *Histoire de la nouvelle française aux XVII^c et XVIII^c siècles* (Geneva, 1970), pp. 247–74; Maurice Lever, *La Fiction narrative en prose au XVII^c siècle* (Paris, 1976); and Ralph Coplestone Williams, *Bibliography of the Seventeenth-Century Novel in France* (New York, 1931). Throughout this chapter I will use the English term "novel" to designate what seventeenth-century readers called both *nouvelle* and *roman*. For even after the vogue of the *nouvelle* had set in, *roman* continued to be used for both the new and the older forms. I will be discussing mainly the book-length *nouvelle*, although the term was also used for shorter tales that appeared in collections, such as Jean de Segrais's *Nouvelles françoises* (1656) or Donneau de Vizé's *Nouvelles nouvelles* (1663).

2. I will discuss the more developed form of this subversion in Chapter 6.

nate them—everyone will keep coming back to them, and the more you attempt to decry them, the more people will persist in publishing, reading, and enjoying them. Say nothing and they will disappear on their own."[3] With cavalier disingenuousness, Lenglet refers to the ban on novels but draws no attention to the official or unofficial status of the fiction he discusses. Yet he had to have been aware just how crucial was the difference to his appreciations, for *De l'usage des romans* itself, with its many irreverent asides on religious matters, not to mention its casual treatment of scandalous literature, appeared pseudonymously under one of the many transparently false imprints from abroad: "At the close-cropped Widow's place, at Naked Truth." When Lenglet realized that the public was attributing his work to the correct author, he prudently wrote a refutation, *L'Histoire justifiée contre les romans* (1735). Nevertheless, he was imprisoned several times. The critic knew very well that forbidden fruit always has the greatest appeal.

At the beginning of the new literary wave, Lenglet-Dufresnoy's predecessor Charles Sorel suggested that scandal was a generic property of the *nouvelle*. Now that overlong *romans* have worn us out, he said, writers have come up with "little detached Stories called *Nouvelles* or *Historiettes*." They are all very fine and well, he continued; they are easier to understand than those huge *romans* where you have to keep track of so many different "adventures" all mixed up together. But there is a danger: the *nouvelles* are often not "prudent" or "discreet"; they are, on the contrary, "foolish and impertinent," depicting "every passion and vice." The action is apparently everyday, but it "soon slides into a terrible libertinism where there is finally no virtue or honor."[4]

Now the scandal alluded to by Sorel and Lenglet-Dufresnoy, among other critics, varied according to the official or unofficial status of the *nouvelle*. A public fed up with the bland diet of officially approved histories and news and, in the post-Fronde period, no longer lured by the closed, aristocratic mythology of the *roman*, sought more exciting tidbits elsewhere—not the censored, official "facts," but the "true story" behind the political scene.[5] It follows that the more shocking the *nouvelle*—which typically delved into the hidden lives of history's great figures—the more powerful its appeal. Contemporary critics' stress on the scandalmongering of the *nouvelle* indicates that the unofficial vari-

3. [Nicolas Lenglet-Dufresnoy], *De l'usage des romans* (Amsterdam, 1734), 1:26.
4. [Charles Sorel], *De la connoissance des bons livres* (Paris, 1671), pp. 165–66.
5. See above, Chapter 4.

ety enjoyed widespread success. It further suggests that the seventeenth-century public read both varieties, or, put another way, that both varieties were aimed at the same public. Just as a noble family might at the same time subscribe both to the *Mercure galant* and to one of the underground newsletters, read the *Mercure* while dispatching a servant to the talking *nouvelliste* stationed at the nearest street corner for the latest gossip, so might a fashionable *précieuse* order from the publisher Barbin the latest novel, such as Mme de La Fayette's *Princesse de Clèves*, while awaiting a package of contraband *nouvelles* from Holland. People undoubtedly did not care to discuss openly the provenance of their reading matter, much less write about it for posterity. Perhaps that is one reason that recent critical discussion of seventeenth-century fiction deals rarely if at all with this topic. Novels were considered either of so little market value, so unworthy, or so dangerous to mention that they were rarely broken down by title in inventories of private libraries after their owners' death, but were instead noted simply as a packet of *histoires*.[6]

The distinction is of crucial importance for this reason: as the contemporary critics so astutely perceived, scandal has an explanatory value for any generic discussion of the *nouvelle*. The *nouvelle*, like history, came in several genres: secret history (*histoire secrète*), historical novel (*nouvelle historique*), amorous novel (*nouvelle galante*), *nouvelle galante et historique*, anecdote, and so on. The lines between these genres are often blurred, because they are all interrelated. The *nouvelle galante*, for example, did not necessarily deal with the love lives of historical figures, but when it did it could be classified just as easily as a *nouvelle historique* or a *nouvelle galante et historique*. I will be discussing only those genres that made use of historical figures, for by the 1670s they comprised the bulk of *nouvelles*. Excepting, therefore, purely fictional stories, whatever the genre that may have been specified in the title, it was limited by the narrator's implicit claim to give the untold version of the official story, the inside view denied to all the outsiders (practically everyone) in Louis XIV's reign. Official publications never of course dared to go as far in their exposés as the unofficial, and by 1678, the date of publication of *La Princesse de Clèves*, they must have been following rather than leading fashion. I am not concerned here with which variety actually came first in chronological order—a question that, given the uncertain condi-

6. Henri-Jean Martin, *Livre, pouvoirs, et société à Paris au XVIIe siècle (1598–1701)* (Geneva, 1969), pp. 926, 939.

tions of writing and publishing at the time, it seems to be impossible to settle—but rather with a generic mold determined in this case largely by changing ideological conditions and changing conditions in the book market. Publishers made their big money in the clandestine trade. And *nouvelles* were a hot item for this trade. Well-placed courtiers such as Madame de La Fayette were never too far removed from the literary underworld. Even if they did not stoop to read its products themselves, they certainly heard of them in the salons they frequented. Beneath the official lurked the unofficial, providing grist for the literary mill. The laxity of the unofficial required as its obverse the restraint of the official or the so-called classical. As we rethink the value of this term in the following analysis of official and unofficial *nouvelles*, the princess whom seventeenth-century readers found *invraisemblable* should acquire new meaning.

Clandestine Book Publishing and the *Nouvelle*

The era of Louis XIV was not an easy one for the publishing industry. New corporative regulations and censorship laws caught the trade in a tightening vise. Clandestine publishing dangled promises of rewards to those willing to brave the dangers of evading the law. The *nouvelle* held special attractions for black marketeers. The traffic in underground *nouvelles* gave stiff competition to the licensed publishers, who did their best to keep up. If changing literary tastes are in part the result of changes in the market, as I hope to show, then a brief account of the development of French publishing conditions in the seventeenth century is in order.

With the edict of June 1618 establishing the French book corporation, book production in France declared independence from its medieval subservience to the university and could flourish as an infant capitalist enterprise enjoying certain tax exemptions not granted to other trades. The industry was also subject to increasingly severe restrictions. By 1661 the censorship of all but religious books had been removed from the jurisdiction of the doctors of theology at the University of Paris and placed in the hands of the chancellor, who had the right to appoint the royal censors.[7]

7. My main sources for this discussion of censorship and the book trade are Martin, *Livre, pouvoirs, et société;* Harriet D. Macpherson, *Censorship under Louis XIV, 1661–1715* (New York, 1929); and David T. Pottinger, *The French Book Trade in the Ancien Régime, 1500–1791* (Cambridge, Mass., 1958).

Censors were not the only restrictions on book production. In October 1643, at the time of the Thirty Years' War and the rise of Mazarin as virtual head of state after the deaths of Louis XIII and Richelieu, a decree was passed ordering three syndics of the book guild to make a thorough inspection of the trade and then to report back to the chancellor. Several weeks later, another law carefully set out the limits of the university quarter in Paris, established by the edict of 1618 as the only permissible one, except for the Palais de Justice area, within which printing and bookselling in the capital could take place. By the very conditions of its existence, the book corporation, like any other in the ancien régime, functioned according to a trade-off: it benefited from the protections officially granted it while it both benefited and suffered from what appeared to be its self-imposed regulations. Publication required a permit to print before the granting of a privilege conveying the censor's approval. The privilege gave a theoretical monopoly to the bookseller or printer for a specified number of years (usually not more than twenty), but it also drastically limited choice of material and opened the way to heavy competition in counterfeit editions. Even a royal privilege, therefore, was not a guarantee of protection, especially since a book could be condemned *after* publication.

Additional restrictions involved limitations on the numbers of guild members and print shops. In 1666, Colbert's council forbade the reception of new master printers until further notice, and shortly thereafter thirteen print shops that had little work were closed. This situation obtained until a new code was issued in 1686, which applied first only to Paris but which was later extended to provincial cities. One of the provisions of the 1686 code stipulated that no more printers were to be received until their number was reduced below thirty-six, after which time thirty-six was to be the maximum allowed number. Printers themselves had demanded the restriction, because it reduced competition and thereby increased prices.

Given such conditions, it is not difficult to appreciate the appeal of clandestine publishing. For those willing to run the risk of the death penalty within France, the rewards in profits counterbalanced the dangers. Provincial presses, especially those of Lyon and Rouen, were responsible for most of the clandestine publishing in France, but even Parisian journeymen practiced the smuggling of small presses into hideouts where they could ply their illicit trade. Competition between the favored Parisian publishers and their less-favored provincial colleagues, however, strongly motivated the latter to engage in counterfeit production. This practice in turn led to what Henri-Jean Martin has called a "counterfeit war" between Parisian and provincial publishers, which raged with special intensity between 1660 and 1665. Printing or publishing abroad, chiefly in Holland, was the other option for profit seekers in clandestine work. The great Dutch publishing house run by the Elsevier family did a large illegal trade under false imprints. French provincial publishers also often had their illegal printing done abroad. Martin estimates that by the end of the seventeenth century, Belgian, Dutch, and French provincial publishers derived their profits mainly from forbidden or counterfeit works.

If little mention has thus far been made of authors, it is because the person who stood to gain the highest profits was the publisher. In the seventeenth century, there were in reality three categories of French publishers, who lived very uneasily together: (1) the printer-bookseller, or *grand libraire,* who did all his own printing and who made the most money of the three; (2) the *petit libraire,* who associated with others in this category to have an edition printed and who then affixed his name to his share of the edition, which he offered for sale in his shop as if he alone had printed it; (3) the simple bookseller (*étalant*), who merely sold books printed by others.[8] Publishers of the first two categories paid an author a lump sum for the manuscript and reserved all the profits for themselves. Under Louis XIV, conditions slowly began to change. If an author could not depend solely for his or her livelihood on income from published works until at the earliest the eighteenth century, nevertheless by the time of the Sun King sales of *romans* had led to a competition for manuscripts, and printing and publishing had gained an independent place in business enterprise. Certain of the more successful authors, such as Chapelain, Molière, and Boursault, received considerable sums for their work. Around 1690, the average price of a novel was 300 livres, not a trifling amount. Moreover, some publishers began to give their authors a share in the profits.

The *nouvelle* presented definite advantages first and foremost to the publisher. The Elseviers had earned their prestigious reputation chiefly by their production of the small duodecimo edition—

---

8. Gervais E. Reed, *Claude Barbin, libraire de Paris sous le règne de Louis XIV* (Geneva, 1974), p. 61.

the "pocket book" of its day. The Dutch family's success in promoting this format encouraged French printers to imitate them in producing handy books at low prices.[9] Under Louis XIV the number of books in small format multiplied rapidly. The duodecimo became the usual size for *romans* and *nouvelles*. The larger folio, quarto, or octavo editions came to be reserved for learned publications. Had the reading public grown, or were publishers endeavoring to widen the market by producing volumes at lower prices? It has been estimated that during the ancien régime the size of editions increased from 200 or 300 copies to 1,500 or more.[10] Evidence on these matters, however, is scarce and not easy to interpret. Undoubtedly the powerful Elseviers would not have put 42 percent of their titles into duodecimos had they not foreseen good profits to be made from them.[11]

The small, unobtrusive *nouvelle* could easily be stashed into false-bottom suitcases and smuggled over borders. It held instant appeal for gossip-hungry readers in its seditious and libelous aspects. When it dealt with the sexual adventures of male and female ecclesiastics, it even acquired an alluring heretical glow.[12] Since the French censorship laws of the sixteenth and seventeenth centuries—the era of the Religious Wars, the Fronde, and the rise of Jansenism—were directed almost exclusively at cases of heresy, sedition, and libel, the *nouvelle* was an inherently dangerous item. But censorship could be put to good use by a smart publisher. Since the advertising of books was prohibited in France, a forbidden or banned book advertised itself. For the publisher who wanted to remain within the letter of the law and yet earn a good living, what better way than to entice the public with only a hint of scandal in an otherwise sedate history or *nouvelle galante*?

For the author who had another source of income—if not land, then a patron or, increasingly, a profession—the *nouvelle* may have promised some good extra money, especially if it was clandestinely published. It must be supposed that in an age when authors' rights were virtually unknown, publishers bore a great responsibility for fashion and the laws of demand. A writer eager for pocket money, like today's best-selling author, had to keep a

9. Donald W. Davies, *The World of the Elseviers, 1580–1712* (The Hague, 1954), pp. 146–47.

10. Pottinger, *French Book trade*, pp. 347, 202.

11. The figure is quoted in Davies, *World of the Elseviers*, p. 146.

12. For titles, see Léonce Janmart de Brouillant, *La Liberté de la presse en France aux XVIIe et XVIIIe siècles: Histoire de Pierre du Marteau, imprimeur à Cologne* (Paris, 1888), pp. 120–22.

watchful eye on the market. But whatever their motives, authors of *nouvelles* had to be wary. The machinery of censorship was in place, ready to be mobilized at any time. It has long been thought that the main reason that so many seventeenth-century French writers were loath to sign their works was the influence of the nobles' disdain for professionalism. This may well have been simply an ideological rationalization for fear. The boundary between legal and illegal works was precariously thin. Who knew if a book granted a privilege might be banned? Even authors of official works often preferred to publish pseudonymously, or, as in the case of *La Princesse de Clèves*, anonymously. Frequently publishers managed to obtain a manuscript copy of a work without the author's permission, or else a clever author would surreptitiously slip a copy to a publisher, waiting for publication to claim rights. Is this in effect what Mme de La Fayette did for her *Princesse de Montpensier* in 1662? In her letters to Gilles Ménage, she complains that a servant stole and circulated a manuscript copy, yet once Ménage had it anonymously published, she was eager to have thirty copies for herself.[13]

Even when they published anonymously or pseudonymously, novelists were taking serious risks. The rewards were at best less certain than the dangers. Is this why there were so few novelists among the *grands seigneurs* and *grandes dames* of the seventeenth century? According to currently available data, most seventeenth-century novelists came from the petty nobility or from families of small officeholders with enough income to permit their offspring careers in law or teaching.[14] Many novelists during the reign of Louis XIV possessed a strong streak of adventurism. They knew that their novel would be a fly-by-night affair, with at most two or three printings in Paris. If their works were more frequently printed abroad, especially in Holland, where the French Protestant refugee colony grew dramatically during the period preceding and following the Revocation of the Edict of Nantes, they did not necessarily profit thereby. Generically, the *nouvelle*, like the *nouvelle à la main* and the *gazette secrète*, was "new," a "novelty." Its charm faded as quickly as the latest gossip. Publishers did not

13. See letters 93 and 94 (1662) in *Lettres de Marie-Madeleine Pioche de La Vergne, comtesse de La Fayette, et de Gilles Ménage*, ed. Harry Ashton (Liverpool, 1924), pp. 107–8.

14. See Martin, *Livre, pouvoirs, et société*, p. 911; Pottinger, *French Book Trade*, p. 93.

stand to gain from a single item, but rather from a high turnover in a constant supply. The more money a novelist hoped to make, the more novels he or she would have to churn out.

The case of one of the most prolific and successful underground novelists of the day illustrates both the pleasures and the pitfalls of this type of writing, as well as its great readership appeal. Gatien de Courtilz, or Courtilz de Sandras (1644–1712), as he called himself, was a noble short of cash whose sojourn in the Bastille and banishment from Paris did not put a stop to his literary activities. From Holland he published a type of *gazette secrète*, the *Mercure historique et politique*, the first issue of which appeared in November 1686. Later he launched another scandal sheet that he called the *Elite des nouvelles de toutes les cours de l'Europe*. In order to keep himself financially afloat, Courtilz had to be constantly on the go, diversifying his talents in various literary enterprises. Around 1689, he wrote his wife that he hoped to make some money from a fictionalized biography, the *Vie du Vicomte de Turenne*.[15]

When he was out of prison, the police kept close tabs on him. Of course, he never signed his works with his own name, but that did not keep the authorities off his trail. A police report of 1702 sketches a view of Courtilz "earning money every day by selling pernicious books in Paris. . . . He has his wife, his brother, and his sister-in-law selling them to the booksellers of the Palais [de Justice] and the quai des Augustins, and in all the best Parisian homes. He also uses peddlers at his service to distribute them in the city. Often he goes to Holland to have his works printed. He can send them secretly through the mails into Paris." An anonymous letter of 1701 from Rotterdam to the police chief d'Argenson shows us how closely interrelated were the activities of the novelist and pamphleteer. The letter writer states that Courtilz' latest scandalous book, the *Annales de la cour et de Paris*, is similar in style to other works by the same author, such as the highly successful *Mémoires du comte de Rochefort* of 1687. This person, the informer continues, passes himself off as someone privy to all the state secrets, but in reality "he's a puny individual with no property or fortune, who apparently writes all of this only to sell it to Dutch publishers. But he has to have some contacts with

15. Benjamin M. Woodbridge, *Gatien de Courtilz, sieur du Verger: Etude sur un précurseur du roman réaliste en France* (Baltimore, 1925), pp. 6–7.

the good-for-nothing idlers of Paris, who tell him the latest fact and fiction circulating among the *nouvellistes*. One would hope that someone in some journal or other would discredit the works of this man, who has infatuated an infinite number of readers."[16]

Fiction and History in the Unofficial *Nouvelle*

The charm of the *nouvelle* was the lure of the forbidden. Its triple meaning evoked impropriety. As a novel, it presented a story that was pseudohistory; its "newness" consisted in the sensationalism of the latest news item. Although authors of *nouvelles* allegedly rejected the rhetoric of *romans,* they created a rhetoric of their own in seeking to authenticate their "facts." Because the *nouvelle* purported to reveal the underside of history, the novelist sought devices to guarantee the veracity of the account. If it was not a discovered manuscript, then it was an eyewitness report, and the narrative took the form of memoirs. Readers craved these ploys, as is apparent from their complaints concerning what they perceived to be one of the structural defects of the old *romans:* how could the narrator overhear recorded soliloquies of certain characters, or know what was going on in their minds? Such complaints continued, nevertheless, to be directed against some of the *nouvelles* also.

The rhetoric of the *nouvelle* challenged history and tradition. Its own facts were as much a contestation of as a supplement to officially sanctioned facts. The world of the *nouvelle* was topsy-turvy: the masters of history were its slaves, as greatness was debased and humbleness exalted. These efforts to reorder history had a democratic air, but even fictional class distinctions were not so easily effaced. Yet the *nouvelle* betrayed an undeniably democratizing tendency in its break with the traditions of the *roman.* Whereas the *roman à clef* was addressed to that limited public of insiders who possessed the keys to its portraits, the *nouvelle,* which did not require a key, was ostensibly addressed to anyone. If noble readers of the *roman* felt privileged to identify with fictional characters so exclusive as to be locked into a world of their own,

16. The police's information on Courtilz is quoted in ibid., pp. 11–13. Courtilz seems to have needed money so badly that he was willing to sell his pen indiscriminately. At one point the French government hired him to write in favor of Colbertism. See Lionel Rothkrug, *Opposition to Louis XIV: The Political and Social Origins of the French Enlightenment* (Princeton, 1965), p. 386.

readers of the *nouvelle* were called upon to identify with characters whose different stations in life merely dramatized their common humanity. Portraits in the *nouvelle* facilitate the identification of readers with fictional characters by abandoning mythological disguise. The new portraits drop the conventional mediations of art so that human nature can stand unadorned for all to see and to share.

The rhetoric of the *nouvelle* exposes fact and reveals truth. It is therefore more fully developed in those samples of the genre that enjoyed freedom from the constraints of official publishing. Accordingly, we will turn to them for an inventory of the pseudohistorical rhetoric that was to be used with such art by the author of *La Princesse de Clèves*.

If the word *nouvelle* does not appear in the titles of Courtilz de Sandras's books (which is probably why René Godenne does not list many of them), they do follow closely the formulas of the genre. Courtilz in effect wrote secret histories, in which, through memoirs or manuscripts that he claimed to possess or through his own professed observation, he reported the behind-the-scenes activities of France's high and mighty. In 1684 he came out with his own version of Louis XIV's love life, in the style of Bussy's *Histoire amoureuse des Gaules,* which, as a *succès de scandale,* had given rise to numerous imitations and counterfeit editions.[17] Titled *Les Conquestes amoureuses du grand Alcandre dans les Pays-Bas,* it also recalled an immensely successful earlier work about the *galanteries* of Henri IV called *L'Histoire des amours du grand Alcandre,* which had managed to slip into print in France during the disorders of the Fronde. The name Alcandre, a synonym for Hercules, had come to be used for both Henri IV and Louis XIV in underground literature about their love lives.[18] In his foreword to the *Conquestes,* Courtilz makes it clear that the work is to be read as a secret history. These memoirs may look like a novel, he says, but they are absolutely accurate. He claims to have derived his information either from his own observation or from authoritative sources. He cautions the reader to suspend judgment concerning certain "very secret" circumstances and to consult a reliable person before concluding that the book's contents were made up by the author. For instance, a reader might question how he came to know what went on during the birth of Mme de Montespan's

17. Woodbridge, *Gatien de Courtilz,* p. 24.
18. See Janmart de Brouillant, *Liberté de la presse,* pp. 159ff.

baby, a scene he describes in the book, since only two women and the "grand Alcandre" himself were in the room at the time. "Consider," he replies, "that one of the women could have spoken to me and that I wouldn't say what I do if I didn't know what I was talking about. If you accuse me of indiscretion for revealing what was told to me, I will reply that I was not asked and did not promise to keep it a secret."[19]

Despite the author's enticements, *Les Conquestes du grand Alcandre* turns out to be pretty tame stuff. Louis is not unfavorably portrayed, and the truly scandalous tales concern not him but his courtiers and mistresses. It was only in later works that Courtilz came to exploit fully the scandalous potential of the *Conquestes,* that is, love and sexual adventure among the great. In this respect, the opening sentence of *Les Conquestes* is perhaps the most significant passage in the entire novel: "The occupations of Alcandre the Great, who had made himself the terror of all his enemies as well as the object of admiration of all rulers, did not prevent him from making love now and then."[20] Implicit in this statement is the profoundly subversive—because potentially democratic—proposition that explains the value of love in the secret history: in the boudoir, all of history's great, including the monarch himself, are just like anyone else.

This is the principle on which the action turns in one of Courtilz' more outrageous novels, *Le Grand Alcandre frustré* (1696). For seventeenth-century readers, the charm of this story probably lay in the very simplicity of its plot: the torments of Louis XIV thwarted in love. Throughout the book, the king engages in a series of unsuccessful attempts, often comical in their awkwardness, to seduce an unnamed Comtesse de L. Louis's every action illustrates the democratic topos, which Courtilz expressed thus in an imitation of *L'Histoire amoureuse des Gaules*, on which he collaborated with Bussy: "Alcandre the great, elevated as he was above all others, was of a character no different from the common man."[21] Yet Louis is not made to look utterly foolish in *Le Grand Alcandre frustré.* The straitlaced countess actually begins to fall in love with him, and her struggles with "love and virtue," as indicated in the

19. [Gatien Courtilz de Sandras], *Les Conquestes amoureuses du grand Alcandre dans les Pays-Bas. Avec les intrigues de sa cour* (Cologne, 1684), Avant-propos (unpaginated).

20. Ibid., p. 7.

21. [Bussy-Rabutin, Courtilz de Sandras], *La France galante, ou Histoires amoureuses de la cour* (Cologne, 1689), p. 4.

subtitle of the novel, form the central conflict of the story.[22] It is
the *king* she loves in Louis more than the individual man. She
admires "his handsome face, his carriage, and his noble manners,
evident in his every act." She observes that "he does everything
like a king, and this characteristic was the most likely to win over a
lady proud by nature" (p. 50). Like the frondeurs whom he resembled in spirit, Courtilz was a royalist. The subversive, democratic thrust of his works lies in the direction of demystification:
like Brantôme before him, he depicts the seamier side of court
life. If he suggests that class distinctions mask an identical human nature, he salvages the king as an institution, as supreme
authority of the land. The political interest of the *nouvelles* published unofficially during Louis XIV's reign consists not in serious
criticism but rather in naughtiness.

Courtilz nevertheless carried his naughtiness rather far, and it is
easy to see how readers accustomed to his wicked insinuations
were happy to find their tastes further indulged after the death of
the Sun King in the more "libertine" fare of the Regency and the
later eighteenth century. *Le Grand Alcandre frustré* combines the
lightly pornographic and the politically daring in repeated scenes
of Louis's sexual frustrations. Entering the countess' apartment at
Fontainebleau, the king has the pleasure of viewing her asleep,
her maids conveniently absent. When he cannot resist the opportunity to kiss her bared breasts, she awakes and cries, "Leave me,
you abominable monster, remove yourself forever from my pres-

22. *Le Grand Alcandre frustré ou les Derniers efforts de l'amour et de la vertu*, by
M. P. C. (Cologne, 1696; reprint ed., San Remo, 1874). Woodbridge (*Gatien de
Courtilz*, p. 89) does not think that the work should be attributed to Courtilz, but
he adduces no evidence to support his statement. More recently, Jean Lombard,
using internal evidence, denies the attribution to Courtilz. See Jean Lombard,
Courtilz de Sandras et la crise du roman à la fin du grand siècle (Paris, 1980), pp. 212–
16. I am following the standard bibliographies in attributing the book to Courtilz,
although the question of authorship, in my opinion, is not particularly important
here. Further references to this edition of *Le Grand Alcandre frustré* are inserted in
parentheses in the text. *Le Grand Alcandre frustré* is a good illustration of what one
critic has seen as a function of the *nouvelle historique*. René Demoris says that the
genre permitted readers to identify in fantasy with mysteries of state through an
identification with the physical body of the king, since this body was supposedly
identical with the symbolic body of the king, or the state. See René Demoris, "Le
Corps royal et l'imaginaire au XVIIᵉ siècle: *Le Portrait du Roy* par Félibien," *Revue
des sciences humaines* 172 (December 1978):18–19. Jean-Marie Apostolidès develops
the notion of the dual royal body in his *Roi-machine* (Paris, 1981). In the second
part of Louis's reign, Apostolidès says (p. 140), the real body lost its power to stand
for the imaginary, into which the bourgeoisie could then insinuate itself. Cf.
Demoris, "Corps royal," pp. 28–30. The growing split between the real and imaginary bodies noted by Apostolidès is evident in Courtilz' work.

ence. Or else have me put to death immediately, since in speaking to you in this fashion I am guilty of lèse-majesté" (pp. 41–42). But punishment for lèse-majesté is not common in unofficial *nouvelles*. It is indeed the king, not his subjects, who appears as a "criminal" in this type of fiction. Thus when the countess later thinks back on her "shocking words" to the king, she reflects that he "meekly swallowed" them. And the king writes her a self-incriminating note: "However much I might want to speak to you, I dare not attempt it. Your last speech to me was so terrible that I will never dare present myself before you unless I have written permission signed by you bearing absolution of my crime" (pp. 48–49). Later, in one of the seduction scenes, when the countess reminds Louis of a promise he made her not to violate her honor, he protests: "Can a slave keep his promises? I am no longer in possession of myself; I am all yours, Countess. I feel impelled by an irresistible force; I am no longer master of my movements" (p. 59). These are not merely the usual clichés of *galanterie*. In this context, what I call the master/slave topos acquires a special significance. Fictional love effects a role reversal, humbling the great, elevating the humble. Master ceases to reign over subject, who reigns in his stead.

Now the nominal master in *Le Grand Alcandre frustré* is of course the real historical figure, Louis XIV, while the real master of the tale is the imaginary Comtesse de L. I call her "imaginary" although such a passage as the following might lead us to wonder if the key to the countess were not Mme de Maintenon: "Instead of a mistress, the king found a governess, who gave him lessons in wisdom, honor, justice, probity, and all the virtues" (p. 13). No one has been able to identify the countess, and the narrator does not furnish us with enough hints to warrant looking for a key. So we must conclude either that she was entirely fictional or that Courtilz parodied the roman à clef by teasing his public into thinking that they were reading one. In any event, the distribution of characters effectively conforms to the first of two basic patterns that the *nouvelles* follow: (1) fictional and historical characters intermingle; (2) all the characters are historical. In both cases, of course, there is much fictional embroidering of the historical characters, but in the first case the fictional is used as a foil for the historical. It is the fictional, and not the historical, character who is the embodiment of virtue. The virtuous fictional character turns out to be the real master of the tale, while the nominal master, the historical figure, turns out to be the real slave.

Thus in Catherine Bedacier's short story "Les Amours du pape Gregoire VII et de la Comtesse Mathilde," the fictional ingenue Theodorine refuses to serve as a cover for her aunt, Countess Mathilda of Tuscany, in the latter's love affair with Hildebrand (Pope Gregory VII). Theodorine virtuously repels Hildebrand's advances to her and turns a deaf ear to his Tartuffe-like declaration of love: "I am the pope, but I am a man. . . ." Later, in the master role, she admonishes him: "Holy Father, I would like to forget your follies, and never to consider you other than as the sacred Pastor of Christians." He replies: "I'd rather that you consider me your slave."[23]

The relationship of fictional and historical characters points to set formulas of construction in the *nouvelle*. As an alternative or counterhistory, the *nouvelle* interwove fiction and history in basic patterns that functioned to demystify history. As a secret history, it revealed the hidden if not fictionalized vices of the great; in so doing, it replaced the exempla of official histories with fictional characters who served as exempla against a background of "historical" vice. Thus the fictional character came to usurp the traditional function of that character in history books who acted as the embodiment of moral value for posterity.

All the *nouvelles* that made use of historical figures were in some measure secret histories: secret because they revealed the hidden "truth"—usually sexual in content—about those figures, but also because love functioned as the secret, thus as the real motive behind certain historical events for which historians might or might not have offered adequate explanation. When the secret functions as motive, the secret history is more blatantly a revised or counterhistory. The secret history both contests the veracity of official history and renders accessible the censored and inaccessible. In an age when individuals—monarchs, princes, mistresses, prime ministers, and the like—were viewed as the forces of history, and when politics was above all a matter of personality or personal alliances, the secret history was an incipiently democratic project: it explained the mysteries of state by something that everyone could understand—love.

Secret historians commonly advised their readers not to look for information on the subject at hand which could easily be found in

23. [Catherine Bedacier], "Les Amours du pape Gregoire VII et de la Comtesse Mathilde," in *Histoire des amours de Gregoire VII, du Cardinal de Richelieu, de la Princesse de Condé, et de la Marquise d'Urfé*, by Mademoiselle D . . . (Cologne, 1700), pp. 37, 49.

official histories. Such was their way of trivializing history and of strengthening their claim to be giving out the real lowdown. Isaac Claude, for example, in his *Amours de Madame d'Elbeuf* (otherwise titled *Le Comte de Soissons*), warns the reader that he will not be going into details on the rivalry between the Comte de Soissons and the Prince de Condé because "history has made this well known." Claude's story concerns instead the unknown rivalry between the count and Richelieu for the love of Mme d'Elbeuf. According to Claude's fanciful version of the period of Richelieu, it was this rivalry that led the prime minister to try to marry off his niece, Mme de Combalet, the future Duchesse d'Aiguillon, to Soissons.[24] Now in reality Richelieu did attempt to foster the alliance, but probably not for the reasons that support Claude's story. Similarly, Courtilz in *Le Grand Alcandre frustré* has Louis fall ill—which he certainly did—but not for love of the elusive Comtesse de L.[25]

Fiction and history in the *nouvelles* are closely intertwined because their fiction fills the interstices of history. The unknowable, the censored, the unsatisfactorily explained are what the secret historian takes as the starting point for fiction. Documentation therefore is not just a fictional device in the *nouvelle*, but is essential to the project of the genre. The old *roman* could make do with a verisimilitude that imitated history in a usually flimsy historical setting. The *nouvelle* had to guarantee its authenticity in order to look like real history. The first-person-singular narrator of most of the framed stories in *romans* created an atmosphere of authenticity, for presumably the speaker was conveying firsthand information. The frame story, as, for example, in *L'Astrée*, did not require the first-person singular because it was presented either as a story or as a historical tale. Scudéry's fictional histories were only imitations of history, and although the famous "Sapho" did use and cite historical sources, she did not absolutely need them to guarantee the authenticity of her tales. She was aiming not for authenticity but for the double entendre of the roman à clef, appealing to insiders who could play at identifying her nobles in ancient historical disguise. The *romaniste* consciously wrote a history of limited accessibility; the secret historian unconsciously

24. [Isaac Claude], *Les Amours de Madame d'Elbeuf: Nouvelle historique* (Amsterdam, 1739), pp. 22–25. The first edition of this work was probably the one published by Pierre Le Jeune (Cologne, 1687).
25. *Le Grand Alcandre frustré*, pp. 64–65.

strove to make history accessible to everyone. The secret historian had to be more careful than the *romaniste* in choice of narrator. The first-person singular was appropriate only if the narrator was relating his or her own eyewitness account in the form of memoirs or was transcribing the "discovered manuscript" of another person. The much more vulnerable omniscient narrator had to claim to be writing history based on only the most reliable sources.

Framed stories, which often spilled out into the endless stories within stories of such novels as *L'Astrée*, were a narrative luxury for the secret historian. The framed story of the *roman* had a suspiciously fictive air, as if the *romaniste* were telling a story simply for the pleasure of telling a story, which was in fact most often the case. Authors of *nouvelles* did not abandon the narrative structures of *romans;* on the contrary, the *roman* was their most immediate model for prose fiction. Also, taste did not change overnight. The "precious" frills of *romans*—letters, *billets,* verses, and so on—continued to appear in *nouvelles* past the turn of the century. But the secret historian who strained for the authenticity of a document tended to make a more serious attempt to integrate the framed story into the main plot so that it would be less obviously a piece of gratuitous fiction. At the beginning of the craze for *nouvelles*, Charles Sorel considered the form of the *nouvelle* that of a framed story detached from a *roman*.[26] As the *nouvelle* came into its own, paradoxically, it came more and more to look like a shortened *roman*, a *petit roman*. The novels of such late-seventeenth-century writers as Charlotte Caumont de la Force and Mme d'Aulnoy often come complete with framed stories, letters, and verses. The *nouvelle* was nevertheless not simply a *petit roman*. The combination of *roman* and *nouvelle,* of which the *nouvelle* was inevitably composed, resulted in a new form, distinct from and yet related to the old. It was a combination inherent in all genres of secret history: *nouvelle historique, nouvelle galante,* and the rest. The main subject of the *roman* was love, and it was de rigueur that its historical characters be portrayed as being in love. The *nouvelle* uses love to motivate—therefore to contest or revise—history. The framed story is a significant vestige of the *roman*. In its new context, it reinforces the importance of love, which, like so many variations on a theme, turns up in frame and framed stories alike, inspiring

26. Sorel, *De la connoissance des bons livres,* p. 165. Interestingly, Lenglet-Dufresnoy, some fifty years later, said the same thing. See his *De l'usage des romans,* pp. 202–3.

without distinction both historical and fictional characters. The "democratic" principle of the *nouvelle* applies just as much to the historical and the fictional as it does to the humble and the great.

Mlle de la Force acknowledges in the preface to her secret history of Catherine de Bourbon that critics may object to the episodes that she has added to the main story. She protests that most of them are essential to her history, and that the others are "naturally" related to it. In narrative structure, *L'Histoire secrette de Catherine de Bourbon* is not unrelated to *L'Astrée.* There are stories within stories, and even stories within stories within stories. Letters and notes inserted into both frame and framed stories are not uncommon. Mlle de la Force even uses the basic plot of the star-crossed lovers in much the same structural manner as the *romanistes;* that is, framed stories function as so many devices to postpone resolution of the main plot "agreeably." Most of the framed stories, however, concern historical figures related in some way to the main characters, such as Henri III or Henri IV and Gabrielle d'Estrées, and are thus secret histories within secret histories. Generally they are told by eyewitnesses or relatives of eye witnesses, thus guaranteeing their "authenticity."

As a guarantee of the authenticity of the book as a whole, Mlle de la Force appends a scrupulous list of her sources to the preface. They are books, she pointedly remarks, which are "in everyone's hands," implying that her documentation can be easily checked by anyone. The only problem with her list is that, in addition to works by such serious historians as Mézeray, it includes a book on the loves of "Alcandre the Great" and [Vanel's?] *Galanteries des rois de France.* As further evidence for the authenticity of her tale, Mlle de la Force states in her preface that if Catherine and her lover, the Comte de Soissons, may not seem as virtuous as the reader would wish, it is because the author has followed history faithfully. No one should object to her portrayals, she says, since her work is a "true history" (*une histoire véritable*) and not a *roman.*[27] Indeed, critics of the day were wont to remark that heroes and especially heroines of the old *romans* were too virtuous to be believable.

Mlle de la Force's secret history clarifies the relationship between the modified portrait inherited from *romans* and *histoires* and the democratic topos. In what came to be a formulaic intro-

27. [Charlotte Caumont de la Force], *Anecdote galante, Histoire secrette de Catherine de Bourbon, duchesse de Bar, et soeur de Henry le Grand. Avec les intrigues de la cour durant les regnes de Henry III et de Henry IV* (Nancy, 1703), Preface (unpaginated).

duction to many of the *nouvelles,* authors gave a brief historical background, usually an overview of the life of the particular court in question. The material of the background included a collection of portraits of the chief princes, princesses, and courtiers. Now these portraits, as we have seen,[28] no longer conform exactly to the pattern of those in *romans.* They tend to drop the exterior division, the physical description, and thus to fall into the genre of *caractère* or psychological description. And they no longer require a key to be fully appreciated, although readers accustomed to keys may have sought them nonetheless. The series of portraits at the beginning of *L'Histoire secrette de Catherine de Bourbon* demystifies as it identifies. Brutally frank in her descriptions, Mlle de la Force follows the usual path of the secret historian in exposing the seamier side of royal history. Her portraits also serve as a kind of roll call of Henri III's court, identifying each figure for the benefit of knowledgeable and unknowledgeable reader alike. Portraits in the roman à clef functioned for the reader like an initiation rite: if you could identify the contemporary noble key to the ancient historical figure, you were a bona fide insider. Portraits in the *nouvelles* identify the vices of recent historical figures for all to see. In Mlle de la Force's novel, the Duc de Bellegarde, loyal as ever to Gabrielle d'Estrées even after her elevation to grandeur as Henri IV's mistress, writes her that a faithful lover is worth as much as the crown. Take away Henri's titles, he says, "and you will see that he is no more or less than another man."[29] As love in the *nouvelle* has a democratic value—great and humble alike experience it—so too the modified portrait has a democratic value: through open identification, it strives to make history's great accessible to anyone and everyone.

How much the new portraits differed from their ancestors in the *romans* and *histoires* is evident in critical discussions of the time. Du Plaisir, who also wrote a *nouvelle* titled *La Duchesse d'Estramene* (1682), devotes some space to considerations of portraits in his *Sentiments sur les lettres et sur l'histoire* (1683). In connection with the genre of the dedicatory epistle, he warns authors to avoid comparisons in composing portraits of their dedicatees. If the subject of the portrait has good reason to feel self-satisfied, that person will resent being placed on an equal footing with someone else. "The King can claim that he is not comparable, and he could

28. See above, Chapter 4.
29. Caumont de la Force, *Anecdote galante,* p. 464.

disapprove of someone saying of him: 'He's as handsome as Achilles, valiant as Alexander, prudent as Caesar.' " The subject might like to serve as a comparison for others (and so as an exemplum) but would not like to be compared to them.[30] Du Plaisir thus firmly rejects the mythological portrait, which in history, paintings, engravings, and later in *romans* had glorified a royal or noble personage through the mediation of metaphor. In the *nouvelle*, where the object is not glorification but demystification, the mythological portrait disappears. This type of portrait ennobled the subject as it distanced the reader or viewer. When the trappings of mythology are discarded, reader and subject approach each other more immediately. The glorified portraits of the *roman* inspired admiration; portraits in the *nouvelle* elicit identification. The prodigious adventures related in the *roman*, says Du Plaisir, do not touch us because they are so extraordinary. In the *nouvelle*, "familiar and natural portrayals suit everyone; you see youself in them and apply them to yourself." Moreover, the exterior/interior division of the traditional portrait was not conducive to such identification. Tastes in physical appearance vary, the critic tells us; they are not "universally pleasing." "The qualities of the soul . . . please everyone." For Du Plaisir, a general word or two will suffice for the exterior, but it is the *caractère* that, in its wider applicability, requires greater attention.[31]

Seventeenth-century critics liked generic rules, and they liked to derive such rules from classical antiquity. They tried, without much success, to apply rules for epic poetry to the novel. In the principle of identification they hit upon a way to reconcile Aristotle with the democratizing rhetoric that crept into cultural production during the reign of Louis XIV. The reader was supposed to identify with the hero not through pity and terror alone, but through the portrayal of feelings, character, and actions that were to represent those of everyone's everyday life.

The opinions of other critics of the *nouvelle* make it plain that the famous "nature" that writers and artists were constantly summoned to imitate depended on the principle of identification. The more writers and artists rejected the artful mediations of imitation, the more democratically they applied the principle. Note how the Abbé de Bellegarde democratizes Aristotle, for whom the tragic hero was ideally a noble historical figure. In novels (he

---

30. Du Plaisir, *Sentiments sur les lettres et sur l'histoire avec des scrupules sur le style,* ed. Philippe Hourcade (Geneva, 1975, facs. of 1683 ed.), p. 41.
31. Ibid., pp. 50, 54.

means *nouvelles*), says Bellegarde, as in tragedy, terror and pity are the mainsprings of all passions. "You put yourself . . . in the place of those you see menaced by some danger . . . because these kinds of accidents can happen to anyone; and they move us all the more as they are ordinary effects of nature." Heroes of the old *romans*, on the other hand, were too outré in personality, their adventures were too out of the ordinary to touch us. What happened to them wasn't "natural." "The Heroes of modern Novels," says Bellegarde, are better characterized. "They are given passions—virtues and vices—which smell of humanity. Thus we all see ourselves in their portrayals."[32] "Nature" for these critics is a reaction against the "artifice" of old, that is, the conventional modes of representation whose primary function was glorification: mythological portraits, keys, high adventure, and so on. To shed these mediations was to democratize representation, to say that great and humble alike share in a human nature recognizable by all.

It follows that the rhetoric that the *roman* had borrowed from history was no longer appropriate to the would-be simplicity of the *nouvelle*. Moral reflections, maxims, *sententiae*, and the like were part of the artifice of the *roman;* they functioned as signs that the *roman* was an imitation of a history. For the more modern taste, such rhetoric was another unnecessary mediation between art and nature. Bellegarde counsels against the use of these rhetorical devices. They are better suited to "discourse for the purpose of instruction than for *Nouvelles historiques,* whose main goal is to please."[33] Du Plaisir had earlier expressed a similar sentiment. According to him, *nouvelles* supply utility through pleasure. Moral reflections are superfluous in the *nouvelle,* where character portrayals themselves provide the moral instruction. Writers of *nouvelles* should prefer to the high-blown rhetoric of *romans* the more natural air of everyday language. In fictional conversations, Du Plaisir allows, the writer can use incorrect constructions so as better to simulate ordinary speech.[34] A "plain-speaking" topos recurs in many works of various genres in the late seventeenth century, and is evidence of the increasingly widespread reaction against conventional modes of representation. In the preface to her secret history of Catherine de Bourbon, for example, Mlle de

32. Abbé Morvan de Bellegarde, *Lettres curieuses de littérature et de morale* (The Hague, 1702), letter 2, pp. 56–58.
33. Ibid., p. 63.
34. Du Plaisir, *Sentiments sur les lettres,* pp. 61–62, 64.

la Force ironically apologizes for her unadorned, free style, explaining that she wrote the book in only six weeks.[35]

By the early eighteenth century, when Lenglet-Dufresnoy wrote his *De l'usage des romans,* prose fiction had traveled a long way toward democratization. This critic, too, was opposed to instruction through reflections and allegory in the *nouvelle.* He saw them as holdovers from the sixteenth century. They will just make a novel boring, he said, and "will transmit poor principles to two thousand persons who will read it." If Lenglet-Dufresnoy is a reliable guide to the trends of the day, the size of an edition had definitely expanded. Furthermore, he conveys the impression that readers of novels formed a more varied group than previously. Novels provide a different kind of instruction from that of history, says Lenglet-Dufresnoy. You can look to them not for erudition but rather for hints on how to behave in polite society. In novels you find "polite, civil, agreeable people, very different from those you've seen in *collèges.* You see wise, reasonable men, unlike those often found in the Academies where you study. They are people who, with none of the pompous, sanctimonious character acquired through a convent education, can combine modesty and virtue with all the charm and affability of the Court." The critic seems to be thinking of a large group of well-educated bourgeois eager to learn something of the refinements of the nobility by sharing in their traditional reading matter. For Lenglet-Dufresnoy, as well as for the other critics we have been discussing, the portrait in this democratized fiction had become *embourgeoisé.* Now that it no longer glorified a high-ranking personage, its value as an exemplum had become abstract and universal. The instruction that Lenglet-Dufresnoy desired was filtered through "graceful Portraits of virtue, honor and probity." He considered that Mlle de la Force and Mme de La Fayette, among other novelists, had successfully portrayed the attractions of virtue.[36]

Portraits in the *nouvelle* had several functions. Especially in a historical novel portraits often identified the dramatis personae. A portrait frequently exposed the secret vices or characteristics of a well-known figure. On the other hand, it could also play the role of modified exemplum, in which the portrait as embodiment of virtue served as a moral lesson. In reality, the second two func-

35. See Caumont de la Force, *Anecdote galante,* Preface.
36. Lenglet-Dufresnoy, *De l'usage des romans,* pp. 208–10, 214–19.

tions are like the obverse and reverse of the same coin, for the more "natural" character was the one with a mixture of virtue and vice. These two functions are based on the principle of the reader's identification with the protagonist, while all three have a democratic value in that all three render the portrait accessible to the reader. If we were to follow Lenglet-Dufresnoy, we would make a further distinction here. Earlier critics had distinguished fiction from history by saying that everything in the latter had to be true, and thus that vice had to be portrayed when necessary, whereas in the former, *vraisemblance*—decorum and decency—had to be maintained. Lenglet-Dufresnoy varies this tradition in assigning the portrayal of vice to history and that of virtue to novels. How attitudes toward history had changed since the days of Louis XIII's historiographers! It did not always happen that in a historical novel peopled by both historical and fictional characters, the former were wicked and the latter virtuous, but, as we have seen, this was one pattern of the *nouvelle*. What is interesting during the period of the *nouvelles* is that while novelists made use of the portrait to fictionalize and contest history, they inevitably began to separate fiction from fact in the process of historical revision. At the same time, when critics were not complaining about the confusion of fiction and history, they were devising new arguments to distinguish the two.

Du Plaisir grumbled that "you can't distinguish truth from fiction anymore."[37] Mme de La Fayette's good friend Pierre-Daniel Huet, in his treatise on the origin of novels, traced their derivation as a genre from history and asserted that the novelist was but a degenerate historian. He saw fiction as a substitute for history, as lies to take the place of a missing truth. Fiction, according to him, was an "imitation" or "image" of truth.[38] Lenglet-Dufresnoy varied the formula in applying it to secret histories. Historians, he said, never answer certain questions asked by "those with no knowledge of the secret Mysteries of state." Novelists, however, do. Historians may disagree on facts, but there are no uncertainties in novels. "Nothing is equivocal or doubtful: I am shown the motives and secret movements behind a plot. Everything is given to me, down to the most private letters and the most personal feelings, which in most events the public never sees." Historians

37. Du Plaisir, *Sentiments sur les lettres*, p. 124.
38. [Marie Madeleine (Pioche de la Vergne), comtesse de La Fayette], *Zayde: Histoire espagnole*, by Monsieur de Segrais, with a treatise on the origins of the *romans* by Monsieur Huet (Paris, 1670), pp. 67–69, 80.

never give women their due, never show their importance in history, this critic noted. But novels regularly do. Lenglet-Dufresnoy had to acknowledge, however, that his concept of fiction rendered it necessarily less realistic than history. Just because the novel reached a widespread public, "from the Cardinal, Archbishop and Bishop down to the humblest Shepherdess," he felt that it had to respect decorum (*vraisemblance*) more than did history. Huet, he says, condemned the novel *Daphnis and Chloé* because it was written "too much according to nature and to history."[39] By the 1720s, nature was thus associated with fact, history, and realism. Although Lenglet-Dufresnoy seems to condemn its appearance in the novel, earlier critics welcomed nature as an improvement over the artifice of the *roman*. To imitate nature was for them in effect to place restrictions on the representation of nature, because imitation required all the conventional mediations of art. Secret histories are the first glimmerings of realism in the novel. They point the way from a tentative rejection of artifice to a striving for the realistic appearance of fact.

Some three and a half decades before Lenglet-Dufresnoy wrote *De l'usage des romans*, Pierre Bayle carped at secret historians for deceiving the public with their ersatz facts. How much of this criticism was ironic is unclear. The celebrated Protestant refugee himself used Holland as his base of operations to produce abundant literature of a suspicious nature. He admitted that he found the *nouvelles galantes* he saw pouring out of Liège and Cologne "entertaining." Whether or not they were "useful" is another question, he said.[40] Elsewhere he spelled out their defects more clearly: "This mixture of fact and fiction is spreading through an infinite number of new books, depriving young people of taste, and making us not dare to believe what is fundamentally believable."[41] The only way to tell fact from fiction in these books, said Bayle, is to consult other books.

> This is a disadvantage that grows greater every day through the liberty people are taking to publish the secret loves, secret history, etc., of such-and-such a famous lord in history. Booksellers and au-

39. Lenglet-Dufresnoy, *De l'usage des romans*, pp. 67, 73–75, 83–107.

40. [Pierre Bayle], *Nouvelles de la République des Lettres*, September 1686, pp. 1081–82. For speculations on the relationship between Protestantism and clandestine publishing, see Elizabeth Eisenstein, *The Printing Press as an Agent of Change* (Cambridge, Eng., 1979), 1:416–19.

41. Pierre Bayle, "Jardins," in *Dictionnaire historique et critque* (Paris, 1820–[24]), 8:332.

thors do all they can to make us believe that these secret histories are taken from manuscript accounts. They know very well that love intrigues and other adventures are much more pleasing when you think they're real than when you are persuaded they're just made up. This is why writers are avoiding a novelish air as much as possible in the new novels. But in doing so they are spreading thousands of shadows over true history; and I think that finally the powers that be will have to be forced to order the new novelists to choose: they write either pure history or pure fiction. At least let them use brackets to separate truth from falsehood.[42]

Secret historians both confused and separated fact and fiction, history and the novel. In aiming to produce the illusion of real history, they also said—implicitly or explicitly—what history was not. The critics' hesitation over whether to stress the confusion or the distinction reflects this dialectical process. Paradoxically, the unofficial *nouvelle*, which could portray nature much more realistically than the official, came to look more fictional as its revelations grew more shocking. The only way out of this impasse would be for writers to follow Bayle's advice and liberate fiction entirely from history so that it could proclaim its own truth. The process by which this liberation came about was not fully completed until the nineteenth century. In the meantime, it fell to the unofficial *nouvelle,* freed as it was from the fetters of censorship, to furnish a vehicle for incipient realism in French fiction. Pierre Bayle was perspicacious enough to realize this. In a discussion of old and new novels, where it is clear that he is contrasting the official literature, published in France, with the unofficial variety published abroad, he says that writers of *petits romans* seem to have gotten closer to nature than authors of the multivolume variety. "And in effect," he continues, in the *nouvelle* "things happen in a somewhat more human way. Nevertheless, hundreds of things that go on between people who love each other are never mentioned there. So it seems that Nature has been obliged to take refuge in the novels of Holland, for they say that novels that are consistent with Natural History are sold there."[43]

Now one of the *petits romans* that Bayle chooses to cite as an example of the lack of realism in official novels is none other than Mme de La Fayette's *Princesse de Clèves.* Sometimes, the critic re-

42. 'Nidhard," in ibid., 2:152. Cf. *Nouvelles de la République des Lettres,* October 1684, pp. 864–65.

43. Pierre Bayle, *Nouvelles lettres de l'autheur de la Critique générale de l'Histoire du Calvinisme,* in *Oeuvres diverses,* vol. 2 (The Hague, 1727), p. 304.

marks, characters in *petits romans* can be just as outré as those in the old *romans*. "What could be more fantastic than the Duc de Nemours or the Princesse de Clèves?" he asks. Nemours knows that the princess loves him, is one of the most dashing men at court, and yet doesn't dare to breathe a word of his love to Mme de Clèves. "The world doesn't produce such people; they are purely the Work of a Novelist. Show me a Lady in France who could be the original of the Princesse de Clèves. If such a one existed, I promise I'd go to see her, even if I had to do four hundred leagues on foot." He finds Brantôme's depiction of the historical Duc de Nemours (which Mme de La Fayette used) much closer to reality.[44]

An Official *Nouvelle: La Princesse de Clèves*

La Princesse de Clèves was published anonymously in 1678 by Claude Barbin. A *petit libraire*, Barbin specialized in catering to the tastes of polite society. In 1659, together with Charles de Sercy, he put out an imitation of Mlle de Montpensier's *Divers portraits*, the *Recueil de portraits et éloges*, which included a portrait by Mme de La Fayette of Mme de Sévigné, her friend and relative by marriage. Later, when the rage for travel accounts swept the fashionable world, he published a good amount of voyage literature. And when his public turned to fairy tales, these stories proliferated on his shelves. Around 1661, an inventory taken after the death of Barbin's first wife revealed that the duodecimo was the best represented format in his stock. He was certainly keeping up with the times. Like so many *nouvelles*, *La Princesse de Clèves* came out in duodecimo. These small books must have delighted ladies and gentlemen, who could easily carry them around and finish reading them as quickly as possible so as to be ready to emit an informed opinion in the next literary discussion. Isaac Claude, in his *Amours de Madame d'Elbeuf*, shows us the Comte de Soissons waiting at court for a meeting with Mme d'Elbeuf. To while away the time, he pulls out a book from his pocket.[45] In an inventory taken after Barbin's death in 1698,

---

44. Ibid., pp. 304–5. My discussion of the evolution of the novel in seventeenth-century France is substantially different from that in Georges May, *Le Dilemme du roman au XVIIIe siècle* (New Haven, 1963). May does not deal with conditions of production, so that, in my opinion, his conclusions have an ahistorical character.
    45. *Amours de Mme d'Elbeuf*, p. 75.

books in small format—octavos, duodecimos, and even smaller—
were still the best represented.[46]

Barbin never made a fortune, yet he did do moderately well for
a number of years. Writers and literary people gathered regularly
in his well-appointed shop on the steps of the Sainte-Chapelle.
Barbin published much of Molière and Boileau, as well as novels
by the irrepressible Mlle Desjardins (Mme de Villedieu) and works
by Guez de Balzac, Saint-Réal, Racine, La Fontaine, La Rochefou-
cauld, and so on. In his last years, especially after the Revocation
of the Edict of Nantes, Barbin suffered a decline. His most outstanding new publication during the years 1680–98 was the so-
called Barbin Collection of 1692, an anthology of three centuries
of French poetry, probably collected by Fontenelle. The *Receuil
des plus belles pièces des poètes français depuis Villon jusqu'à M. de
Benserade* was used in classrooms and by literary people through
the mid-eighteenth century. Three years after he published the
Barbin Collection, the bookseller was obliged to sell his stock to a
certain Jean-Henri Mauvais, Sieur de la Tour, and by 1698, the
year of his death, he was nearly bankrupt. On the day he died he
was still selling his property.

The last decades of the seventeenth century were not good ones
for official French publishing. After Colbert's death in 1683,
Louis wasted the treasury's money more lavishly than ever. The
accelerated Protestant exodus before and after the Revocation of
the Edict of Nantes boosted the clandestine book trade by furnish-
ing an ample supply of producers and customers abroad. The
edict of 1666 limiting the number of new masters to be received
and that of 1686 limiting the number of Parisian shops to thirty-
six severely impaired the book business. With the reduced competition and rising costs of labor that resulted, competition from
provincial and foreign presses grew ever more threatening. One
of the oldest, most respectable houses in Paris, Cramoisy, went
under during the crisis. Barbin chose to respond by avoiding any
material that would spark controversy and holding closely to royal
policy on religious and political matters. Around the time of the
Revocation of the Edict of Nantes, he published works by the
former Jesuit Louis Maimbourg, the purpose of which was to
convince Calvinists of their error and bring them back to the fold.
He commissioned Antonine Varillas to do a history of European

---

46. My information on Barbin comes from Gervais E. Reed's *Claude Barbin.* For
the inventories, see pp. 9–10, 52.

heresies. He tried to popularize pious books by publishing vulga-
rized biographies of such religious figures as François de Sales. In
1685 he collaborated with two other *libraires* on a new folio edition—expurgated this time—of Mézeray's *Histoire de France*. But
how could such works compete with the secret histories and more
savory items coming off the clandestine presses?

Under publishing conditions during Louis XIV's reign, French
booksellers probably saw duodecimo novels as good risks. Barbin
continued to put them out, with some exceptions, at the rate of
about one a year during his critical years. The duodecimo could
be produced cheaply; besides, most of Barbin's books were
printed on paper of mediocre quality with little in the way of
typographical ornamentation.[47] Clandestine publishing revealed
the *nouvelle*'s potential as a shocker with wide audience appeal.
Publishers of official books tried to exploit the potential of the
secret history without stepping over the censor's line—a difficult
but possibly rewarding enterprise. The action of the official *nouvelle* was usually set in recent times, typically the sixteenth century. Such a setting had the advantage of being more realistic,
because closer to home, than the ancient decor of most *romans*.
In using characters whose descendants were very much alive and
could even be called on as witnesses or informants for the events
described in the novel, the official *nouvelle* just barely skirted the
danger, on which unofficial literature thrived, of dealing with
contemporary figures. (Of course unofficial *nouvelles* were also
often set in the sixteenth century or earlier.) Lenglet-Dufresnoy
ironically deprecated "those who have the indiscreet itch to try
their hand at similar subjects [secret loves] during the lifetime of
the Princes of whom they speak." If the princes had been dead
long enough so that their descendants would not be implicated,
he approved of such stories.[48] The official *nouvelle* teases the
reader. It has the appearance without the substance of an unofficial secret history. It promises more than it delivers. It hovers on
the border between harmless gossip and scandal.

Some of these official novels, such as Jean de Préchac's *Princesse
d'Angleterre* (1677) and Boisguillebert's *Marie Stuart, reine d'Escosse*
(1675), concern English royalty. Others, such as Préchac's *Yolande*

---

47. Ibid., pp. 72–74. For a list of Barbin's publications, see pp. 83–118.
48. Lenglet-Dufresnoy, *De l'usage des romans*, pp. 152–53. Cf. Barbara R. Woshinsky, *La Princesse de Clèves: The Tension of Elegance* (The Hague, 1973), p. 58,
and Pierre Malandain, "Ecriture de l'histoire dans 'La Princesse de Clèves,'"
Littérature 36 (December 1979): 20.

de Sicile (1678), are set in Spain. The censors may have felt more relaxed about tales concerning the secret loves of Spanish and English notables during years when hostilities were on between France and those countries. Lenglet-Dufresnoy deplored the fact that certain novels were condemned for the way in which they dealt with royalty, while Eustache Le Noble, a notoroious propagandist "armed with a good privilege from the king, was paid by his publisher to say that [Queen Elizabeth] was in love with Lord Courtenay."[49] When set in France, the official *nouvelle* may have revealed the secret loves of venerable historical figures as the real motivations behind events of the time, but it rarely overstepped the bounds of decorum in depictions of the protagonists. Vaumorière's *Diane de France* (1675) introduces love intrigues into the well-known rivalry between the Guise and Montmorency families, and manages to flatter everyone in the process, including of course Diane herself, a "natural" daughter of Henri II.

Most of the aforementioned *nouvelles* follow a pattern according to which the main and secondary characters are historical figures whose love lives are largely embroidered by the author. *La Princesse de Clèves* follows the other major pattern we have discerned in the *nouvelle,* in which a fictional protagonist intermingles with the historical characters. This is where Mme de La Fayette's novel got into trouble. The action is set in the court of Henri II. Although the author lists no sources, it is evident that she consulted much of the better known historical literature on the period.[50] Henri II, Catherine de Médicis, Diane de Poitiers, Mary Stuart, the Guises, the Montmorencys, and many other great names of the day come alive in her pages. But her heroine, Mlle de Chartres, later the Princesse de Clèves, appears nowhere in history books, and it was as a figment of the author's imagination that she particularly disconcerted contemporary readers. One of the more vehement critics, later identified as a certain Valincour, came out with some anonymous *Lettres à Madame la Marquise* *** on Mme de La Fayette's novel just after it was published. He went so far as to say that the presence of the Princesse de Clèves and some minor fictional characters spoiled the historical atmosphere of the whole

49. Lenglet-Dufresnoy, *De l'usage des romans.* pp. 149–51. He is referring to Eustache Le Noble, *Mylord Courtenai, ou histoire secrète des premières amours d'Elisabeth d'Angleterre* (Paris, 1697).

50. See H. Chamard and G. Rudler, "Les Sources historiques de *La Princesse de Clèves,*" *Revue du seizième siècle* 2 (1914): 92–131, 289–321. See also, by the same authors, "La Couleur historique dans *La Princesse de Clèves,*" *RSS* 5 (1917–18):1–20, and "L'Histoire et la fiction dans *La Princesse de Clèves,*" *RSS* 5 (1917–18):231–43.

book. He objected to the fictional modifications of historical figures such as the Prince de Clèves (who in reality married Diane de
Poitiers's granddaughter, and who was barely fifteen years old at
the death of Henri II). As far as Valincour was concerned, Mme
de La Fayette might just as well have chosen the period of Alexander the Great as that of Henri II. Everything in her novel is
false, he concludes. To add insult to injury, he declares that *La
Princesse de Clèves* evokes the "kingdom of Amadises" (the *Amadis
de Gaule* was an archetypal *roman de chevalerie* of the sixteenth
century).[51] Just about the worst thing you could say of a *nouvelle*
was that it *sent le roman"*—that it smacked of a *roman*.

The most frequent accusation that Valincour and other seventeenth-century readers directed at the Princesse de Clèves was
that she was *invraisemblable*. And not only because she stood out as
fictional in a historical setting. Her very actions and character
seemed improbable to them. *La Princesse de Clèves* is the story of a
young wife's love for a man who is not her husband. When she
was married at sixteen to the Prince de Clèves, Mlle de Chartres
did not even know enough to realize that she did not love her
husband. Thus when she meets the most sought-after man at
court, the Duc de Nemours, she is destined for unhappiness.
Struggling to live up to the lessons in virtue that her mother gave
her, she feels so guilty about a love expressed only in her own
mind or through involuntary glances and subtle innuendoes that
she confesses her passion for Nemours to her husband. This
scene takes place at their country home in Coulommiers. Nemours, who stalks her relentlessly, just happens to be nearby and
overhears the conversation. Through a subsequent series of misunderstandings, Clèves becomes unbearably jealous and finally
dies. Free at last to marry Nemours, who presses her insistently to
do so, she chooses instead to enter a convent, where she ends her
days.

This relatively simple plot is interwoven by Madame de La
Fayette with the historical life of Henri II's court. *La Princesse de
Clèves* follows the formulas of the secret history: it opens with the
traditional series of portraits (which Valincour found much too
long) of the principal figures of the court; it offers explanations
of certain events—the failure of negotiations for the marriage of
the Duc de Nemours with Queen Elizabeth, Catherine de

---

51. [Jean-Baptiste Du Trousset de Valincour], *Lettres à Madame la Marquise ****
sur le sujet de La Princesse de Clèves (Paris, 1678; facs. ed. Tours, 1972), pp. 88–89.

Médicis's dislike of the Vidame de Chartres and of Mary Stuart—
which we might not find in official histories. Yet the Princesse de
Clèves has a different functional relationship to the historical
characters from such relationships as we have observed in other
nouvelles. Theodorine in Catherine Bedacier's story, or the Comtesse de L. in *Le Grand Alcandre frustré*, as embodiments of virtue,
present such a contrast to the historical characters that they make
the latter look ludicrous or utterly vicious, or both. They serve as
a foil to the historical characters in order to expose their seamy
side. As they are obscure or completely imaginary figures, their
fictional status is not in question. The virtuous Princesse de Clèves
is very different from the historical characters surrounding her,
but, as one of the favorites at court, she is also like them. This was
what confused readers. They found the princess *invraisemblable*
both in her behavior and in the fact that, under a historical name,
she was entirely imaginary. At the same time that they seemed to
want the fictional to look more historical, they objected to what
they considered an overdose of history in the book. Critics chafed
at what are still looked upon as four "digressions" from the main
plot (in reality stories within stories), three of which have a historical basis. Valincour objected particularly to the first of these tales,
a brief history of the Duchesse de Valentinois (Diane de Poitiers),
as told by Mme de Chartres to her daughter. He said that it
reminded him of novels in which, under the pretext of writing a
history of one person, the author ends up writing about
everybody.[52]

The insertion of the fictional into the historical bothered
readers all the more because Mme de La Fayette gave none of the
traditional guarantees of authenticity for her tale. Préchac and
Vaumorière followed precedent and cited sources in their prefaces. The anonymity of Mme de la Fayette's omniscient narrator
was found to disorient a public eager for real histories. Since the
author apparently did not work from memoirs, Valincour said,
you could not read the book as a history. He was unable to understand how the narrator could have gotten certain information,
such as Mme de Clèves's inner feelings and her private conversations with Nemours. No wonder he thought that Mme de La

---

52. Ibid., pp. 19–20. On the relationship between frame and framed stories and
the importance of the framed stories for the entire narrative, see John D. Lyons,
"Narrative, Interpretation, and Paradox: *La Princesse de Clèves*," *Romanic Review* 72
(November 1981):383–400. Lyons' highly suggestive article touches on many
points that I attempt to elaborate in this chapter and elsewhere in this book.

Fayette was imitating a *roman!*[53] *Romanistes* devoted far too little attention to the authenticity of their narratives for modern tastes. Readers of novels were not yet ready to forsake the guarantees of authenticity which secret historians provided. Apparently the idea that fiction and history were separable did not circulate until the eighteenth century. The first definition of *histoire* in the 1690 edition of Furetière's *Dictionnaire universel* is: "Description, narration of things as they are, or of actions that have occurred, or that could occur." In the 1701 edition, the first definition of this word is limited to that of a description of *true* events.[54] The omniscient narrator announces the autonomy of fiction. It lets fiction assume the appearance of fact without apology or rationalization.

If the fictional Princesse de Clèves offended by masquerading as real under an assumed historical name, she compounded her faults by behaving quite unlike any of the historical characters in the novel, or, for that matter, unlike any real woman. The focus of accusations on this count was her confession to her husband. Valincour found this scene "tender" and "touching,"[55] but Bussy-Rabutin wrote to his cousin Mme de Sévigné that he thought it was "extravagant." Rarely, he said, does a woman tell her husband that someone is in love with her, and never does she reveal that she loves another man. He dismissed the whole scene at Coulommiers as something smacking of a *roman* ("pas vraisemblable et sent le roman").[56] The editor of the *Mercure galant*, Donneau de Vizé, organized an inquiry based on the confession just after the publication of Mme de La Fayette's novel. In the form of a *question galante*, he asked his readers if a virtuous woman in the Princesse de Clèves's situation would do better to keep quiet or to reveal her love to her husband. Respondents both for and against confession found the princess "extraordinary" and "inimitable."[57] One reader said that to confess was not *galant*.[58]

The standards of measurement for *vraisemblance* used by respondents to the inquiry were drawn both from the behavior of

---

53. Valincour, *Lettres à Madame la Marquise ****, pp. 117–18.

54. Antoine Furetière, *Dictionnaire universel* (The Hague, 1690), as compared with the 1701 edition. Cf. Claudette Delhez-Sarlet, "*La Princesse de Clèves:* Roman ou nouvelle?" *Romanische Forschungen* 80, no. 1 (1968):84–85.

55. Valincour, *Lettres à Madame la Marquise ****, p. 203.

56. Roger de Rabutin, comte de Bussy, *Correspondance*, ed. L. Lalanne (Paris, 1858–59), 4:141–42.

57. See excerpts from the inquiry in Maurice Laugaa, *Lectures de Mme de La Fayette* (Paris, 1971), pp. 27, 32–40.

58. *Le Mercure galant*, special issue, July 1678, p. 308.

the historical figures in the novel and from "real life," that is, an ideology that was at once aristocratic and male.[59] A lady in Mme de Clèves's position had the option of following one of two conventions of love. If she were to choose the path of the historical characters in the novel, who uniformly indulge in *galanteries*, she would be adopting what one historian views as a Neoplatonic, feminist code of love, which prevailed in the salons of the day. This code sanctioned the flowering of human love even outside of marriage, an institution that the circle of *précieuses* to which Mme de La Fayette belonged tended to dismiss as a mere convenience. The other convention, antifeminist and ascetic, confined sexual love to marriage.[60] The social circumstances of Mme de Clèves's life, not unlike those of her creator, made it far more probable that she would choose the Neoplatonic code. In either case, her option was limited by the primary desire prescribed to her by a male ideology: to fulfill her role as wife and/or mistress. Mme de Clèves simply did not live up to the expectations that this ideology raised in the minds of Donneau de Vizé's readers. In conserving to the end of her days her passion for the Duc de Nemours, despite her refusal of his marriage proposal, the princess crosses the boundary of the ascetic. In refusing to consummate her passion, she violates the Neoplatonic convention. Her idiosyncrasy is her freedom, for within an aristocratic, male ideological preserve, she asserts her individuality. In lightly grazing both amorous conventions, she conforms to social standards, but in evading both she deviates. As one critic has shown, her anomaly is that of women in their relationship to culture as both participants and outsiders.[61]

La Princesse de Clèves was in fact not a particularly successful novel. It did much less well than Mme de La Fayette's first *nouvelle*, *La Princesse de Montpensier* (1662), which was reprinted about fifteen times in Paris and twice in Lyon before the end of the century. *La Princesse de Clèves* was reprinted only three times in Paris and three times in Holland before 1700.[62] Was Barbin, the

59. Recent discussion of *vraisemblance* in *La Princesse de Clèves* generally take as their point of departure Gérard Genette, "Vraisemblance et motivation," in *Figures* (Paris, 1969), 2:71–99. Genette does not focus on the specifically male character of the behavioral code to which he refers.

60. See Carolyn C. Lougee, *Le Paradis des Femmes: Women, Salons, and Social Stratification in Seventeenth-Century France* (Princeton, 1976), pp. 36–37.

61. Nancy K. Miller, "Emphasis Added: Plots and Plausibilities in Women's Fiction," *PMLA* 96 (January 1981):38.

62. Martin, *Livre, pouvoirs, et société*, p. 823.

publisher of the *Mercure galant,* behind the paper's inquiry? He may well have felt that the publicity would do some good for the novel in which he had just invested. In 1679 he brought out what was almost certainly meant as a piece of publicity for Mme de La Fayette's novel, an anonymous *Conversations sur la critique de la Princesse de Clèves.* This reply to Valincour was attributed to a shadowy abbot named Charnes, who is generally supposed to have been a straw man for Mme de La Fayette herself.[63]

Reactions of seventeenth-century readers were, however, by no means uniformly negative. A respondent to Donneau's inquiry calling himself "Géomètre de Guyenne" (probably Fontenelle) said that *La Princesse de Clèves* was the only work of its kind that he was able to read four times.[64] But few readers seemed able or willing to articulate their positive views as clearly as their criticisms. Valincour had no reply to his interlocutor's objections other than: What does it matter, provided that the novel brings me pleasure?[65] It is this elusive "pleasure" that we must try to understand against the background of the criticisms in order to see the representational value of Mme de La Fayette's novel for the seventeenth century.

Like so many of the secret historians, Mme de La Fayette democratized her portraits. In deviating subtly from the traditional means of doing so, she managed to change the portrait's function and value, and ultimately to change the value of fiction. As in other *nouvelles,* the historical portraits at the beginning of *La Princesse de Clèves* serve as identifications of the dramatis personae. In this case, we have the definite impression that we are going through a roll call, like those that some editors or authors insert before such sprawling novels as *War and Peace,* whose double purpose is informative and mnemonic. The "Geómètre de Guyenne" said that many people found all the opening portraits of *La Princesse de Clèves* irrelevant to the story, but he believed that the author simply wanted to give "a bird's-eye view of the history of the times." He expressed a "small scruple" concerning the portraits in Mme de Chartres's story of the Duchesse de Valentinois: wasn't everything the princess' mother told her well known, since all of it was recorded in history books? Perhaps, he generously

63. See, for example, Antoine Adam, *Histoire de la Littérature française au XVIIe siècle,* vol. 4 (Paris, 1958), pp. 191.

64. *Le Mercure galant,* May 1678, p. 56.

65. Valincour, *Lettres à Madame La Marquise* ***, pp. 105, 119.

adds, these facts were not so well known at the time.[66] Like the secret historians, Mme de La Fayette writes of both known and unknown, or secret, history in her novel, but whereas the secret historian used the known as a pretext to reveal the unknown, Mme de La Fayette reveals the known along with the unknown.[67] She seems to give them both equal weight. Unofficial *nouvelles* especially dealt with the barest minimum of fact. But in her opening gallery of portraits and in the portraits of the historical stories within stories, it is as if Mme de La Fayette were saying, "In case you haven't read about these people in Davila or Le Laboureur or Mézeray, let me tell you about them." *Nouvelles* were for people who did not have the inclination or learning to pour over large erudite tomes. Mme de La Fayette democratized the historical portrait in transmitting genuine information in a more accessible form. For the reader, it was learning without tears. *La Princesse de Clèves*, unlike the *roman*, does not imitate the rhetoric of history. Like other *nouvelles*, it does away with the mediation of such rhetoric. Unlike other *nouvelles*, it conveys much genuine historical information. In so doing, it imitates the very stuff of history as it might be related by a living eyewitness. For external guarantees, Mme de La Fayette substitutes the authenticity of an omniscient reporter. Perhaps this is why her apologist Charnes says that *histoires galantes* (of which *La Princesse de Clèves* is his prime example) are "simple, faithful copies of true history, often so similar that you would take them for history itself." Madame de La Fayette had said that her own novel was "a perfect imitation of the world of the court and the manner of life there."[68]

Charnes remarked that Mme de La Fayette did not do her portraits "according to form,"[69] meaning that she dropped the exterior division. She did share the preference of the secret historians for the *caractère*. Her historical portraits, however, tend neither simply to expose nor to flatter, but rather to depict a believable personality composed of both good and bad. Of Charles de Guise, for example, she says: "The Cardinal of Lorraine . . . was born with unbounded ambition, a keen mind, and

66. See Laugaa, *Lectures de Mme de La Fayette*, pp. 23, 25.

67. Barbara Woshinsky rightly points out the mixture of official and secret history in the novel. See Woshinsky, *Princesse de Clèves*, pp. 66–70.

68. [Abbé de Charnes], *Conversations sur la Princesse de Clèves* (Paris, 1679), p. 135; Jean de Bazin, ed., *Lettres de Mme de La Fayette au chevalier de Lescheraine* (Paris, 1970), p. 1.

69. Charnes, *Conversations*, p. 154.

admirable eloquence, and he had acquired profound learning, which he used to gain eminence in defending the Catholic religion."[70] Even Diane de Poitiers, who is perhaps one of the least likable characters in the book, arouses some admiration. Mme de Chartres's history of her is inspired by her daughter's view of the duchess as a kind of marvel. How can it be, the young princess wonders, that the king is still in love with her after all these years, and how could he have fallen in love with "a person who was much older than he, who was the mistress of his father, and who is still that of many others, from what I've heard?" (p. 264). Mme de La Fayette's historical portraits do not serve mainly to expose hidden vice, as they so often do in unofficial secret histories. In presenting historical figures as compounds of virtue and vice, Mme de la Fayette above all makes them recognizable as fellow human beings. Her portrayals privilege the human nature that exceeds the bounds of historical specificity. She naturalizes her historical characters to the point where they are easily identifiable, thereby enabling her readers to identify with them. The secret historian subverted history by telling readers in effect that royal personage were just like anyone else, by bringing the high and mighty down to the level of ordinary folk. Mme de La Fayette further democratizes the principle of identification by showing that we are just as much like the royals as they are like us.

If Mme de La Fayette's historical characters did not serve primarily to expose vice, her fictional or highly fictionalized characters—Mme de Chartres, the Princesse and Prince de Clèves—were models of virtue. This is not to say that, particularly in the cases of the prince and the princess, Mme de La Fayette does not portray complexity of feeling, but that in the context of the other portraits the more fictionalized characters tend to be the more virtuous ones. The resulting pattern is a complicated variant of the one that we have remarked in some unofficial *nouvelles*, namely, virtue is to vice as the fictional is to the historical. In *La Princesse de Clèves*, the fictional characters are not completely opposed to the others in morality. They are simply more virtuous than the historical figures. But the "simply" is not so simple.

The princess, in her sincerity and in her absolute refusal to

70. Marie Madeleine (Pioche de La Vergne), comtesse de La Fayette, *La Princesse de Clèves*, in *Romans et nouvelles*, ed. Emile Magne (Paris, 1961), p. 243. Further references to *La Princesse de Clèves* will be to this edition and will be inserted in parentheses in the text.

indulge in any sexual adventure, is quite unlike any of the historical characters in the novel. All of the four stories within the frame story deal with miseries arising from the entanglements of love affairs. In the more dramatic of the historical tales, Diane de Poitiers is the despair of two kings and wreaks havoc at court, while Anne Boleyn loses her head on the scaffold. Politics at court, where rival cliques are led respectively by the king's mistress and the queen, seem to revolve around the vicissitudes of sexual alliances. In this atmosphere, the fact that M. de Clèves is in love with his wife seems bizarre and Mme de Clèves's confession to her husband even more peculiar. The princess herself, reflecting on her own behavior, finds no model for "the uniqueness of such a confession" (p. 337). Later, news of the confession leaks out through Nemours's indiscretion. Mary Stuart, without knowing the identity of the people involved, relates the story to Mme de Clèves, who replies that it does not seem at all *vraisemblable* to her (p. 345).

Mme de Clèves famous refusal of love is a refusal of social norms and of history.[71] According to a neo-Freudian analysis of the novel, the refusal constitutes a victory for Mme de Clèves and for the feminine as a rewriting of male history and ideology. In her subtle revision of masculine conventions of love, the princess, in this view, betrays a repressed impulse to power. Asserting her subjectivity, she rejects the traditional female role of object in the circulation of sexual commodities.[72] As in secret histories, the opposition of the fictional to the historical in *La Princesse de Clèves* serves to question the reality and the authority of history. In this text, however, which has been called "the first text of women's fiction in France,"[73] the questioning consciousness is female. Mme de La Fayette's princess subverts the male conventions that would keep her a slave of love and strives instead for mastery of the subject. The master/slave reversal in Courtilz' *Grand Alcandre frustré* functioned to heap ridicule on a male monarch in portraying him as dominated by a female subject and to belittle him by implying that he was so weak as to be ruled by the weaker sex. The meaning of this topos deepens in the hands of a serious female writer, where it serves to question a history shaped by male subjectivity.

To define the limits of this questioning is to clarify the dialectic

71. On the refusal of love, see Claude Vigée, "*La Princesse de Clèves* et la tradition du refus," *Critique*, nos. 159–60 (August–September 1960), pp. 723–54.
72. Miller, "Emphasis Added," pp. 39, 41.
73. Ibid., p. 36.

of feminine and masculine, fictional and historical in the novel. In refusing to consummate her passion, Mme de Clèves refuses the well-trod path of her historical counterparts. Significantly, she lavishes her love on a portrait of Nemours rather than on the man himself, as if she realizes that a love defined by male subjectivity is more satisfactory in art than in life.[74] Her love is nonetheless real, similar in its effects to any consummated affair. Like the Duchesse de Valentinois and other historical characters in the book, she spreads misery around her. Her mother dies with the anguish of seeing her daughter on the brink; her husband dies of jealousy. Mme de Clèves does deviate from social norms determined by men, but by only so much. She does not reject male conventions; she elides them. No matter how different she may be in character from the historical courtiers in the novel, her debut at court causes a flutter of admiration. She becomes Mary Stuart's favorite, and is petted and flattered by those who surround her. The boundaries of her fictitiousness are drawn within a historical arena. A male history allows her only a measured amount of female difference. In her difference she subverts the history that has formed her; in her sameness—as a "historical" figure like the others—she supports it.

There is no historical resolution of this dilemma in *La Princesse de Clèves.* Mme de Clèves never carries her contestation of history so far as to become a character in the historical dimension, struggling against social forces. She never fully defies society and her female role in it. The novel ends on a disturbingly irresolute note. The princess neither runs off with her now legitimate lover nor retreats completely into her convent (a stock literary, if not historical, solution of the time). She vacillates, dividing the remainder of her days between the cloister and a retired existence at home.[75] Perhaps this is an instance of Lucien Goldmann's notion of the tragic view of life, a rejection of the world within the world.[76] In any event, it marks a retreat from a fully historical confrontation of the problem.

Paradoxically, it is through her very historicity that Mme de La Fayettte's heroine ultimately transcends history. In her passion, the princess becomes like the other women at court, partially fulfilling her dying mother's fear that the daughter might "fall like

74. See ibid., pp. 42–43.
75. See ibid., p. 43.
76. I refer to Lucien Goldmann, *The Hidden God,* trans. Philip Thody (London, 1964).

other women" (p. 278).[77] Mme de Clèves herself, in a moment of disenchantment with Nemours, torments herself with the reproach: "It's . . . for this man, whom I believed so different from other men, that I find myself like other women, having been so unlike them" (p. 352). And in her final interview with Nemours, when she admits her love to him, offering it as an explanation for her refusal to marry him, she says, "Do men conserve their passion in an eternal commitment?" Again, "You reproach a lover; but do you reproach a husband for loving you no longer?" (pp. 387–88).[78] Mme de La Fayette effects a subtle but crucial evasion here. She abandons the realm of the historical for the universal. She transfers our attention from the behavior of people at court to the behavior of people in love. In love, Mme de Clèves becomes not only like every other woman at court, but, through the principle of identification, allowing her female nature to exceed its historical bounds, like all women. She is everywoman. Valincour says of her: "Her self-searching, her agitation . . . are things that happen every day inside ourselves, that everyone feels.[79]

In the secret history, the function of love was to motivate, therefore to revise history. This is only a secondary function of love in *La Princesse de Clèves*. Its primary function here is universalization. Love does not so much revise history as it dehistoricizes fiction. Rather than democratize history by showing that historical figures are just like everyone else, it universalizes a fictional history by transforming the princess into everywoman. The fictional absorbs the historical as the heroine is made to stand for all women—fictional, historical, and real. For the formula "fiction is to history as virtue is to vice," this novel substitutes the formula "fiction is to history as the universal is to the particular." The secret history was fictionalized history. *La Princesse de Clèves* begins to take on the characteristics of historical fiction.

In *La Princesse de Clèves*, fiction fully wrests the exemplum from history. It is the fictional character alone that has exemplary value. In this transfer, the exemplum renounces any historical

---

77. For a feminist-psychoanalytic appreciation of the importance of the mother's deathbed utterances, see Marianne Hirsch, "A Mother's Discourse: Incorporation and Repetition in *La Princesse de Clèves*," *Yale French Studies* 62 (Fall 1981):67–87.

78. See Jules Brody, "*La Princesse de Clèves* and the Myth of Courtly Love," *University of Toronto Quarterly* 38 (January 1969):124. See also Susan Tiefenbrun's discussion of what she calls the "uniqueness/sameness" structure of the *Princesse*, in *A Structural Stylistic Analysis of "La Princesse de Clèves"* (The Hague, 1976), pp. 26–29.

79. Valincour, *Lettres à Madame la Marquise ****, p. 199.

dimension it may still have had in the *roman* or secret history for a uniquely moral dimension. In the last phrase of the novel, Mme de La Fayette sums up her heroine's deeds in a telling oxymoron: "her life, which was rather short, left inimitable examples of virtue" (p. 395). An example that defies imitation is no longer a historical model; the rhetoric of history gives way to a rhetoric of fiction. In the eighteenth century, when fiction had definitely acquired a morality of its own, Lenglet-Dufresnoy reduced Mme de La Fayette's novel to a moral message: "*La Princesse de Clèves* leads only to a very fine moral principle, which is . . . that any love that attacks duty can never make us happy."[80] To capture morality from history is to take fiction a step further toward autonomy. The secret history said what history was not. It was the "real story"; official history was at best varnished. To make the fictional exemplary is to say that fiction has a moral value of its own.

Fiction, however, if it is not history, is nevertheless *in* history. This is a problem with which novelists did not come to terms until the nineteenth century. Mme de Clèves is not timeless, not without social class and historical context. Yet as everywoman she leaves her moorings. When the novel assumes responsibility for its historicity, it can be called modern. Only when it claims to have a historical truth of its own does it become generically independent of history. This is not to say that the nineteenth-century novel abandoned pretensions to universality. On the contrary, it would have a bourgeois truth be valid for all classes. Even when it subverts the history between its covers, it makes a positive historical claim to possess its own truth, to make a truthful statement about the world. *La Princesse de Clèves* strikes a classical compromise. It contests history only to transcend it in the universal. It fills in the ideological blank of the *nouvelles* with historically empty statements on human nature. Does Molière do otherwise? I think that in so-called classical literature this was and continues to be a principal source of the pleasure that Valincour could not define. In this literature, the universal achieves a balanced compromise between the subversive and the acceptable.

The classical compromise was like a pause in history. It is said to have occurred over the slenderest of time spans—some twenty-five years between Louis XIV's assumption of personal power and the Revocation of the Edict of Nantes. If it has never been forgotten, is this not in part because the literature of bourgeois democ-

80. Lenglet-Dufresnoy, *De l'usage des romans,* p. 14.

racy has continued the universalizing tradition? By the time of *La Princesse de Clèves*, as we have seen, a certain *embourgeoisement* had set into the *ut pictura poesis* representational system. By this time, the essentially aristocratic system had entered a critical phase. The universalizing tendency was a symptom of the system's progressive erosion through *embourgeoisement*. It emerged in the system as a historical phenomenon with a historical function. The erosion was truly progressive, for the universalizing function is also the system's link with the future and our link with the past. It transformed an unlikely princess into a timeless heroine and a historical compromise into classicism.

6

Mandarins Steal the Scene

Back in the reign of Louis XIII, when historians and novelists were scurrying to outdo each other in virtuosity, a pensive voyager discarded the art of both in favor of a new occupation—the pursuit of scientific truth. Neither fable nor history yields truth, wrote Descartes in his *Discourse on Method.* Fables make us see purely imaginary events as possible, while even the most accurate histories spoil whatever truth they may potentially contain by modifications or omissions for the purpose of moral edification. Travel serves almost the same purpose as history anyhow, Descartes argued. In teaching us about foreign customs, it gives us a better perspective on our own. It seemed to the wandering philosopher that he could learn much more about truth by observing people conduct their daily lives than by listening to some scholar theorize in his study. Ultimately, of course, Descartes rejected the traditional humanistic disciplines, as he tells us in the *Discourse.* The scholar, Descartes explains, must touch up his speculations with artifice in order to make them *vraisemblables,* whereas he himself was interested in disentangling truth from error. Thus Descartes's project was removed from concern with the *ut pictura poesis* system of representation, in which truth and untruth combined to form the verisimilitude of artful imitation, of that artifice which produced the illusion of truth. Descartes decided, in other words, to forsake the verisimilitude of art for the truth of science.[1]

1. René Descartes, *Discours de la méthode,* ed. Etienne Gilson (Paris, 1966), pp. 51–52, 55–56.

The arc described by Descartes's itinerary of methodical doubt as he recapitulates it in the first part of the *Discourse on Method*, from the art of letters to the truth of science by way of foreign travel, prematurely describes that of the entire *ut pictura poesis* system during the personal reign of Louis XIV. By the 1660s, voyage literature, a genre not wholly congenial to the representational system because of its strong documentary and scientific components, had willy-nilly become incorporated into the system. Between the 1660s and the death of the Sun King in 1715, the heterogeneous structure of voyages, a pasteboard amalgam of the artful and the scientific, gave way to a new fiction and a new truth, dividing the genre profoundly between the old and the new. In its division against itself, voyage literature abandoned the rhetorical truth of *romans* and *histoires*. Thus the whole representational system was split open. Voyage literature was the pivot in a dialectical process of disintegration and reintegration by which the verisimilitude of artful truth that had informed both *romans* and *histoires* in the *ut pictura poesis* system was separated into truthful fiction and truthful fact, and relocated in the respective domains of art and science. The introduction of voyage literature into the representational system in the 1660s proved therefore to be a symptom of the system's decline. During the long reign of Louis XIV, coherence in the system gave way to patchwork, which in the course of the eighteenth century gave way in turn to a new generic configuration and a new representational system.

Voyage literature was deeply implicated in two major institutional developments of the 1660s: Colbert's founding of the French West and East India companies and of the Académie des Sciences. Information brought home by overseas travelers was as indispensable to commercial expansion as the scientific and technological expertise that they utilized and often promoted. Voyagers and academicians tended to flock together in the same social and intellectual circles. The commercial expansion abroad which they helped to further was the necessary complement to industrial development at home in Colbert's mercantilist program. And so, with state economic planning and intervention sanctioned by Louis XIV, voyage literature was ever more firmly molded into the edifice of merchant capital.

Voyagers did not uniformly garner the power and prestige often conferred upon servants of the crown's new economic policies. Scientists, merchants, perhaps simply adventurers, they were all nonetheless connected, directly or indirectly, to the recently institutionalized centers of commercial and intellectual power. From the once humble quarters of trade and science mandarins were drawn. During the administration of Colbert, chief mandarin of them all, this new elite came to steal the scene from the official historiographers and men of letters who had won the favor of Louis XIV's forebears.

Voyagers of the Academic Circles

In the 1660s a new rage swept the French reading public. The *romans* that had been so eagerly devoured by salon society were now passé, and everyone, so it seemed, was reading voyage literature. That supreme arbiter of taste Jean Chapelain noted the trend in a letter of December 1663, dating its inception from the death a few months earlier of one of France's more successful novelists, La Calprenède.[2]

Like the other literary vogue of the 1660s, *nouvelles* and secret histories, voyage literature derived from a tradition with antecedents in classical antiquity. With the growth of European expansionist policies and increased sea travel in the sixteenth century, the tradition had lately been renewed.[3] The extraordinary illustrated cosmographies by the De Bry family of engravers were printed and reprinted in the late sixteenth and early seventeenth centuries. André Thévet, compiler of the *Vrais pourtraits et vies des hommes illustres . . .*[4] and royal cosmographer, had brought out an impressively engraved two-volume *Cosmographie universelle* in 1575. It was not until the middle of the seventeenth century, however, when more and more Frenchmen were engaged in official and unofficial travel abroad, that French voyage literature made considerable gains in volume and in popularity. From 1665 to 1745 about 150 *relations de voyage* appeared. After 1660, published accounts of travels to Asia were double the number they had been before this time. At the beginning of the eighteenth century the general production of voyages went up by a third.

2. Philippe Tamizey de Larroque, ed., *Lettres de Jean Chapelain* (Paris, 1883), 2:340.

3. See Arnaldo Momigliano, *Studies in Historiography* (London, 1966), p. 137. I am grateful to my former colleague William Higgins for this reference, and to him and to Leonard Muellner of Brandeis University for their enlightening comments on the voyage literature of classical antiquity.

4. See above, Chapter 3, pp. 75, 77.

Some booksellers, such as Barbin in Paris and Benoît Rigaud in Lyon, specialized in voyage literature.[5]

By the 1660s this literature had developed to the point where it could serve an important ideological function. Gone, with Louis XIV's assumption of personal power in 1661, was the "truth" of official history, a truth that had resided in a splendid glorification of the French monarchy. Louis rejected such tactics. For the reading public, moreover, such truth had worn thin. Nobles who had composed *romans* in imitation of history, to glorify themselves in the image of and against the monarchy, had lost ground in their struggle for preeminence during the conflicts of the Fronde and were ready to drop the literary model of official history. Secret histories and *nouvelles* contested the truth of official history by purporting to tell the real story, the truth never revealed by court historiographers, and thus a new truth began to circulate.[6] Voyage literature contemporaneously responded to the same ideological demand for a new truth, but in a different manner.

Whereas the writers of *nouvelles* and secret histories were by and large outsiders—disaffected nobles, bourgeois, adventurers and adventuresses, people who had no real power or access to power—from the 1660s on, voyagers began to constitute a new breed of insider. They might not have been privy to state secrets; they might never have set foot in royal chambers. But in general they possessed an expertise that was fast becoming the new basis of glory for the monarchy. They harbored a new scientific truth vital to the economic development of modern France.

This was a truth that thrived in the informal learned academies that the monarchy came to use as intellectual raw material for the Académie des Sciences. From 1657 to 1664, a group of illustrious *érudits* and savants frequented the home of Henri-Louis Habert de Montmor. The group included, among others, Samuel Sorbière, the Dutch scientist Christian Huygens, Jean Chapelain, Melchisédech Thévenot (uncle of the voyager Jean), the mathematician Roberval, the royal physician Abraham du Prat, the Cartesian Jacques Rohault, the scientists Frenicle and Pecquet, and the voyager Balthasar de Monconys. Montmor was one of several dissidents in the Académie Française who sought an erudi-

---

5. See Geoffroy Atkinson, *The Extraordinary Voyage in French Literature before 1700* (New York, 1920), p. 8. See also Pierre Martino, *L'Orient dans la littérature française au XVIIe et au XVIIIe siècle* (Geneva, 1970), pp. 39, 53–55.

6. See Chapter 4, above.

tion that they felt the official body did not provide.[7] The so-called Montmor Academy played a crucial role on the Parisian scholarly scene. In 1657, Sorbière, who was to be permanent secretary of the academy, drew up its first regulations. The society was soon torn by violent quarrels, principally between Cartesians and non-Cartesians. In April 1666, just before a journey to England during which he was admitted to the Royal Society, Sorbière suggested some reforms. In a speech before his fellow Montmorians, he proposed to limit discussion and to divide the meeting time between experiments and the reading of prepared papers. He also made an appeal for royal aid. Several days later he sent Colbert the printed text of his speech in pointed inquiry. Although Colbert was not responsive, Sorbière did not give up. In 1664 he sent the minister his latest plan for an "Académie Royale Colberto-Montmorienne" in another effort to gain royal aid. Colbert had a different idea. The Montmor Academy, itself a descendant of one of the first important scientific circles in France, that of Father Marin Mersenne, was to be the main intellectual repository from which Colbert drew in founding the Académie des Sciences in 1666. At least four of the official academy's members—Huygens, Roberval, Frenicle, and Pecquet—had been Montmorians.[8] Furthermore, Huygens was the single most important original member, if not the very raison d'être of the Académie des Sciences.

As early as 1658, the Montmorians had begun to use their expertise to reach for a treasure trove of scientific knowledge. In that year Montmor asked both Thévenot and Jean Chapelain to obtain for the academy the description of a new pendulum clock invented by Christian Huygens. Huygens accordingly sent a copy of his *Horologium* to Chapelain. The treatise made clear what was to be the immediate practical application of the clock: determination of longitudes at sea. A solution to the problem of longitude was crucial to the development of navigation during this period. Latitude posed no difficulties, for it involved the refinement or replacement of instruments then in existence, such as the astrolabe and the cross-staff, and the use of already established astronomical tables. But little headway had been made in finding an accurate method of determining longitude, and without one the navigator could not efficiently find his precise position on the ocean's surface. Jean Chapelain immediately realized the signifi-

7. Harcourt Brown, *Scientific Organizations in Seventeenth-Century France* (Baltimore, 1934), pp. 64–66.
8. See ibid., p. 117.

cance of the document that Huygens had placed at the disposal of the Montmorians. To keep them abreast of matters, he read aloud letters from Huygens to himself at their meetings. Chapelain had Colbert's ear, and it was ultimately to him that he referred the decision of how to use the scientific resources that Huygens had to offer. In 1663 he asked Colbert to subsidize the Dutch scientist. Chapelain was convinced that Huygens would eventually solve the problem of longitudes at sea, although he seems to have had some doubts as to the efficacy of the pendulum clock. Colbert was evidently swayed by Chapelain's confidence, for he soon advanced gratuities to Huygens. Negotiations to bring Huygens to Paris were begun by the spring of 1665. In 1666, Colbert called in Chapelain as a consultant on the matter of founding the Académie des Sciences.

It almost appears as if Colbert founded the Académie des Sciences for Huygens, so crucial was his expertise to the successful implementation of an economic program directly dependent on navigational skill. Before the establishment of the academy, Huygens had sent some of his clocks to the mathematician Pierre de Carcavi, another future member of the Académie des Sciences. Huygens wrote to Carcavi of a marine clock, which he had included among the others, that it would be of use to the French East India Company, and that he intended to work on perfecting it once he arrived in France. Colbert's establishment of the academy in this climate suggests that if Huygens was not the immediate pretext for it, nevertheless the prospect of finding solutions to problems of navigation was more than sufficient motivation. The inclusion of the Italian astronomer Giovanni Domenico Cassini among the members of the Académie des Sciences is significant in this respect. In 1668, a year before he was called to Paris as an academician, Cassini published one of the most accurate ephemerides of Jupiter's satellites to date. This table was the result of his work on an alternative method of determining longitude involving simultaneous observations, on land, of the eclipses of one or another of the four major satellites of Jupiter. The use of this method in the late seventeenth century was to have a dramatic impact on cartography, increasing significantly the accuracy of maps. Huygen's marine clocks never fulfilled their early promise. His "astronomical clocks," however, or those designed for use on land, when used in combination with other technological innovations developed by the members of the Académie des Sciences in the 1660s, were to bring revolutionary changes to observational astronomy, enabling it to enter the arena of modern science. Furthermore, the use of Huygen's method in conjunction with Cassini's eventually led to a successful solution to the problem of longitude in the eighteenth century.[9]

The scientific advances in navigation and astronomy made by the Académie des Sciences were invaluable aids to commercial expansion abroad, and Colbert's academy played just as critical a role in the development of industry at home. From its founding, the institution was charged with the task of screening technological projects eligible for a royal privilege. The greatest number of these projects involved technical inventions and machines: labor-saving devices, pumps, machines to clean harbors and to mill grains, among many others. More and more, the academy came to perform a consultative function, passing its reports on inventions directly on to the crown. In 1699 this function was formalized in Article 31 of the academy's revised regulations, according to which the body of scientists would examine for approval all machines for which a royal privilege had been requested. Even without a royal privilege, technicians and inventors came to benefit from the coveted stamp of approval, "approuvé par l'Académie."[10] Colbert took a direct personal interest in those machines that he judged particularly useful to industrial development. Because the textile industry was of utmost concern to him, he followed closely the progress of some ribbon-making machines for which a certain Antoine des Hayes had been issued privileges in 1668–69. In 1670 he sent a written request to Des Hayes for the dimensions of one of his looms that made several ribbons at once, in order to construct a model of it for the royal collections. Eight years later, La Reynie, head of the Paris police, had to order all the new looms in the city broken and the ribbons manufactured on them

9. For the importance of Huygens in the establishment of the Académie des Sciences, see John W. Olmsted, "The Voyage of Jean Richer to Acadia in 1670: A Study in the Relations of Science and Navigation under Colbert," *Proceedings of the American Philosophical Society* 104 (December 1960):612–34; Henri-L. Brugmans, *Le Séjour de Christian Huygens à Paris et ses relations avec les milieux scientifiques français* (Paris, 1935), pp. 54–70. One view concerning Colbert's eagerness to bring Huygens to France is that the monarchy wanted to deprive Holland of that scientist's services while France was at war with the United Provinces. See John M. Hirschfield, *The Académie Royale des Sciences (1666–1683)* (New York, 1981), p. 67. On the crown's interest in astronomy, see pp. 102, 169–93. For Chapelain's role in forming the academy, see Albert J. George, "A Seventeenth-Century Amateur of Science: Jean Chapelain," *Annals of Science* 3 (April 1938):217–36.

10. Roger Hahn, *The Anatomy of a Scientific Institution: The Paris Academy of Sciences, 1666–1803* (Berkeley, 1971), pp. 21–24.

confiscated. Des Hayes's exclusive right to use the looms in Paris had stirred violent opposition on the part of other ribbon makers, who had seized ribbons and looms and had persecuted the masters who were using the new process.[11]

It is unlikely that such incidents deterred Colbert from promoting technological innovations and new industrial practices. In order to implement his mercantilist aims of ensuring an inflow of gold and silver to France while simultaneously preventing their outflow to other nations, he tended to subordinate all considerations to that of increasing French productivity and production. He was willing to use almost any means to build up industries, although he does seem to have preferred guilds to independent masters and individual capitalists to companies. He was certainly not above lending support to Protestant manufacturers. His chief encouragement to enterpreneurs was the granting of a royal privilege for their manufactures which theoretically allowed them exclusive rights for the duration of its term, but he frequently lured them with noble status or a post as a royal domestic officer. The privilege was often accompanied by provisions for tax exemptions, for a noble's right not to derogate, for freedom from guild regulation and inspection, and other important prerogatives. Others of his policies were even more drastic. A memorandum of 1664 to the king reveals that he wanted all occupations limited to those four that he considered useful to the state: agriculture, trade, war on land, and war at sea. Concomitantly he advised a reduction in the number of subjects employed in law and finance. He was particularly eager to decrease the number of religious of both sexes, for he judged their occupation to be as unproductive as those of law and finance. To prevent "idleness" among workers, he even secured a reduction in the number of official annual holy days.

Essential to Colbert's goal of greater productivity was a large and healthy population. His assumption was that more people meant increased production. His interest in the progress of medicine, therefore, was due in large part to his desire to save France's population from decimation by the plague. In 1668, when the plague was ravaging important industrial cities in the north, he found himself torn between the conflicting desires of checking the spread of the disease by quarantining the cities and preventing

11. Charles Woolsey Cole, *Colbert and a Century of French Mercantilism* (Hamden, Conn., 1964), 2:193–94.

any interruption of commercial activity. A vast promotional and distributional campaign for the so-called Royal Remedy or Universal Remedy for the Poor foisted on an unknowing public three black, white, and yellow pills advertised as a cure for any and every ill, even though they in fact contained small doses of the poison antimony. If the "remedy" worked to reduce the number of malingerers and to decrease hospital expenses, as he hoped it would, it would serve the minister's purposes.[12]

Colbert's draconian measures seem to have met with success, for by his death in 1683 France is estimated to have become the world's leader in industrial productivity.[13] Nevertheless, his efforts to regulate industry through monopolies, chartered trading companies, and tariff restrictions were greeted by often intense resistance on the part of landowning aristocrats and merchants. Colbert encountered so much difficulty in launching the chartered companies that in many cases he practically had to force merchants to join. The merchants' resistance to mercantilist policies was largely muted during his administration, but it broke out into open hostility at his death. Tariff regulations posed the severest threat to merchants who wanted freedom from government regulation in their pursuit of capital. By the end of the century, merchants had made such immense gains in power and wealth from the War of the League of Augsburg that they were able to plead their self-interest from a position of strength. Benefiting from increased government reliance on their services, they had expanded their influence to such an extent that it was now in their interest to join the trading companies so as to exert even more effective pressure on the administration. By the closing years of the century, merchants, previously divided by a diversity of interests, began to cohere as a national group.[14] Colbert's efforts to subordinate commercial interests to those of the monarchy, like his effort to subordinate science to technology, ultimately liberated commerce and science from royal restraint.

Reinserted into the context of Colbert's mercantilist priorities, the establishment of the Académie des Sciences, like so many others of his projects, takes on a fundamental economic significance. The advice that the minister got from Jean Chapelain in

12. Ibid., pp. 133–36, 463–72.
13. Ibid., p. 362.
14. On merchant opposition to mercantilism, see Lionel Rothkrug, *Opposition to Louis XIV: The Political and Social Origins of the French Enlightenment* (Princeton, 1965), pp. 175–99, 211–33, 392–419.

1666 on the matter of the forthcoming academy shows that the former Montmorian understood Colbert's motivations. It also affords us an important insight into the implications of officially sanctioned scientific inquiry in seventeenth-century France.

Choose only professional scientists, Chapelain warned the minister in his note to him, not those who frequent the court and foster cabals. The professional scientist is unambitious in his single-minded pursuit of knowledge, whereas the scientist of the beau monde does not necessarily make the king's most obedient subject. Because the monarchy has not hitherto remunerated scientific work, the fashionable scholar is concerned only to gain favor at court, whereas the professional is disinterested. What more striking evidence of the shift in centers of power in France! Colbert was to follow Chapelain's advice and institutionalize the preference of professional over courtier by rewarding erudition— once the disdain of nobility—with money and royal favor. For the professional scholar, Chapelain implied, was the one whose talents could best be directed to meet the needs of the state. No potential frondeur, the scientist of Chapelain's dreams would be only too happy to put aside personal ambition in the service of the state. Leave literary judgments to the beau monde, Chapelain went on; scientific merit is another matter entirely. The choice of scientists suitable for the academy must not be left to any of the scientists themselves, but to those above all possible self-interest (meaning, undoubtedly, himself). Only in this way will we see fulfillment of the academy's goal: "to banish all prejudices from the sciences, basing them solely on experimentation; to find certainty, . . . and to open to scientists of the future as wide a road to truth as God may grant for our utility."[15]

Chapelain insistently stresses the words *utile* and *utilité* in his note to Colbert, indicating that if the individual academician was to be disinterested, the truth that he was to be paid to pursue was strictly in the interests of the state. The scientist's work had to be useful; it was just as essential to productivity as the development of commerce and industry, which it was meant to aid. Thus an ideology privileging objective, impartial scientific truth was born amid strict fetters institutionalized by the state.

Colbert's administration did not, of course, invent the concept of objective, scientific truth. But it did exploit and promote the

15. Pierre Clément, *Lettres, instructions, et mémoires de Colbert* (Paris, 1868), 5:513–14. Clément does not attribute the note to Chapelain, but later scholars do. See, for example, George, "Seventeenth-Century Amateur of Science," p. 234.

value of this concept when it took advantage of the development of France's productive forces in the historic attempt to launch a planned economy.[16] Technological and scientific advances in seventeenth-century Europe favored and accompanied these efforts. At the same time, the progress of Cartesian science in particular held out to scientists and scholars the promise of a truth accessible to anyone willing to employ methodical discipline. Voyagers, mandarins or not, often shared Chapelain's view of scientific truth. The moment was propitious to a marriage of erudition and administration. Suddenly the bourgeois—scholar, merchant, voyager—could gain dignity. His expertise was in demand; his values were validated by the state. Increasingly we will find that "truth" in voyage literature tends to exceed its rhetorical bounds as the voyagers strive for the precision of science.

Voyages produced by the Montmor circle are bathed in the light of new knowledge. Obsession with accuracy and impartiality haunts their writings. Some of the Montmorians were not chosen as members of the Académie des Sciences, and they met with varying degrees of royal bounty. Samuel Sorbière was among those not included in the official body. Although he was appointed as a royal historiographer in 1660 (strictly a sinecure in his case) and received some modest gratifications from the king, he never quite made it to official favor. Was it his English travel journal that disqualified him from admission to Colbert's academy, as one historian has suggested?[17] The *Relation d'un voyage en Angleterre* was first published by Billaine in 1664 without the author's name, although the dedicatory epistle to the king was signed "Sorbière." Louis XIV quickly ordered the book suppressed and Sorbière banished to Nantes. Thomas Sprat's *Observations on Monsieur de Sorbière's Voyage into England* (London, 1665), a vigorous outcry against Sorbière's report, may help to clarify Louis's reaction. Sprat was a member of the Royal Society, and he rather unjustifiably took offense at some less than glowing opinions that Sorbière interspersed among generally admiring comments on that society. Sorbière, who had recently renounced his Protestantism, also showed insufficient respect for English clerics. Louis was eager at this point not to alienate the British, and may

16. For an overview of industrial transformation in France from the period of Colbert to the French Revolution, see Fernand Braudel and Ernest Labrousse, eds., *Histoire économique et sociale de la France* (Paris, 1970), 2:217–66.

17. René Taton, *Les Origines de l'Académie Royale des Sciences* (Paris, 1965), p. 26.

have been responding to their protests in punishing Sorbière.[18]
There may have been other reasons. The *Relation* is at least every
bit as critical of France as it is of England. Ironically enough,
Louis XIV had on the eve of Sorbière's departure for England
given him a gratification, as the author of the *Relation* recalls in
his dedicatory epistle to the king. Little could Louis have recognized then the implications of Sorbière's travel plans! The journal
opens on a seemingly innocuous note: "I went to England to see
friends and learned people, to become informed about scientific
matters as well as to see the country and to learn about other
things."[19] "Seeing the country" and "learning about other things,"
interwoven as they were with the Montmorian's scientific curiosity, proved to be Sorbière's undoing. He could have been more
prudent in his implied criticisms of France. What separates him
from the original members of the Académie des Sciences is his
lack of discretion. For scholars and scientists within and without
the academy of necessity possessed critical minds. The critical
view of the voyager is inseparable from the notion of that objective, empirically verifiable truth which is the goal of science.
Sorbière's travel journal may have brought an unfortunate halt to
his career, but it marked him forever as one of the new scientific
elite.

No sooner did Sorbière arrive in England than, true to his
word, he looked up his friends Thomas Hobbes and Balthasar de
Monconys. Later he went to see Henry Oldenburg and Sir Robert
Moray of the Royal Society. He marveled to see the latter occupied in the humble task of adjusting telescopes in St. James Park.
Moray was after all an eminent statesman and military officer.
One would never find French nobles engaged in such tasks,
Sorbière remarks. Louis's courtiers, who never so much as cast a
glance at the heavens, "would consider themselves dishonored if
they dabbled in anything other than in dreaming up new fash-
ions." Now the Royal Society, he explains, started when nobles in
exile during the English Civil War decided to spend their time in
scholarly pursuits. Upon their return to London after the war,

---

18. See Vincent Guilloton, "Autour de la *Relation* du voyage de Samuel Sorbière
en Angleterre," *Smith College Studies in Modern Languages*, 11 (July 1930), 5–11.

19. [Samuel] Sorbière, *Relation d'un voyage en Angleterre, où sont touchées plusieurs
choses, qui regardent l'estat des sciences, et de la religion, et autres matières curieuses*
(Cologne, 1667), p. 47. The full title explicitly restates Sorbière's actual travel
project.

these nobles (English nobility is almost entirely "learned" and "enlightened," Sorbière says in a significant parenthetical comment) had no desire to abandon their pursuits and to fall back into the "customary idleness of courtiers."[20]

Here we have a good example of the generic complexity and ideological richness of seventeenth-century French voyage literature. These voyages break down into two main subgenres that are not necessarily indicated by their titles: the travel journal and the travel guide. In the journal, as in Sorbière's *Relation*, the voyager and his adventures serve as the unifying narrative thread. The travel guide, which was heir to the cosmography, is encyclopedic and claims to tell all there is to be told about the places in question.

Underlying both is the same ambiguity: the voyager at once reports and compares. He is at once dispassionate and displaced, but his displacement infringes on his claim of dispassionate observation. How can he observe foreign customs without implicitly or explicitly relating them to his own? Whether he knows it or not, he brings his full historical situation to his scientific inquiry. The objectivity of the reportage is undermined by the historicity of the reporter.[21]

As a Frenchman, Sorbière was impressed by the erudition of the British nobility, as well as by the prestige enjoyed by the learned in England. He admired the fact that the English monarch allocated funds to the Royal Society, thereby pursuing "solid glory." Better science than war, Sorbière concludes, in an implicit criticism of Louis's military ambitions. Similarly, if Sorbière was struck by the lack of secrecy and ceremonial in relations between the English monarch and his subjects,[22] was this not because his own king had so shrouded himself in both that only the secret historians could claim to penetrate to the real story?

Sorbière was seeking not the real story behind the facade but rather a truth accessible to all, verifiable by anyone. Deprived of the real story by his historical situation, he and his fellow voyagers set forth on a quest for a new truth that promised new power. Sorbière defends his bluntness by attacking inflated rhetorical discourse, which he compares to the frills and ribbons worn by the petty nobility. Words, he says, can be misleading, especially when they have been consecrated by authority. "You have to leave aside

20. Ibid., pp. 53, 57–58.

21. See Michèle Duchet, *Anthropologie et histoire au siècle des lumières: Buffon, Voltaire, Helvétius, Diderot* (Paris, 1971), pp. 13–14.

22. Sorbière, *Relation*, pp. 82–84, 87–88.

authority and words," he cautions, "to deal only with things, and to imagine them immediately."[23] Sorbière and his fellow voyagers were fond of variations on the "words and things" topos of classical antiquity. One such variation is the "plain-speaking" topos that decorates the prefaces of many voyages and that Sorbière draws on here. The voyagers were seeking a truth in which words transparently signified things, in which referent and meaning were one. They aimed at immediacy, a representation of the world unmediated by passion, partisan loyalty, and duplicity, a representation purged of the rhetoric of *romans* and *histoires*.

Yet just as the travelers were condemned to compare as they reported, so they were condemned to use rhetoric in their desire to abandon it. Plain speaking too is rhetoric, and the pursuit of scientific truth entails all the pitfalls of historical truth.[24] History, says Sorbière, seems more truthful than novels because not everything in it is made up; but like a novel, a history is composed by one person, who may rearrange facts formed by the actions of many according to personal taste. The historian writes with a bias—adds, subtracts, and arranges things subjectively—so that "truth is in his picture of it like the resemblance to the human subject is in those spoiled paintings that have something both of the human and of some other animal bearing a relation to the human. You see the traits of the one and the other, but the subject would not want to accept the painter's work as his true portrait." The truth of both *romans* and *histoiries* was transmitted by means of portraits that, just as Sorbière states, both resembled and did not resemble their models, for the portrait was as metaphorical as its truth was analogical. The voyagers' portraiture would be different. However, Sorbière continues, "I don't know if in our philosophizing on the material and intelligible world in physics and in mathematics we may not observe the same gradation that we find in passing from Fable to Truth via History." Our childish understanding is "completely novelish" (*romansque*), resolving easily as it does nature's greatest difficulties. What we learn in school is more historical, since it does not always involve

23. Ibid., pp. 147–54.
24. On this rhetoric of science, see Bernard Beugnot, "De quelques lieux rhétoriques du discours scientifique classique," *Revue de synthèse* 101–2, 3d ser. (January–June 1981):5–25. See also Bernard Tocanne, *L'Idée de nature en France dans la seconde moitié du XVIIᵉ siècle* (Paris, 1978). Tocanne finds that French classicism was characterized by a "natural style" (inherited from classical antiquity), which developed in opposition to ornate rhetoric. He calls this a *rhétorique du naturel* (p. 395). See pp. 371–75, 395–409.

recourse to miracles in solving problems; it teaches us that there is much we do not know. "But I find that there can be an even greater distance between this Philosophy and Truth than there is between History and its true subject. And all that natural philosophers have done in constructing new systems is to take us by another road several steps beyond where their Masters left them off."[25]

It would be all too easy to infer that Sorbière, like the freethinking scholars he frequented, fell victim to the "skeptical crisis" besetting European intellectuals in the seventeenth century. Like Descartes's methodical doubt, such skepticism can best be understood as part of a general intellectual project. Sorbière aimed at a truth that was other than historical, yet because he could not fully comprehend his historical situation, he was in part—but only in part—condemned to repeat it. Such was the voyagers' historical dilemma: how to report while yet comparing, how subjectively to arrive at objectivity, how to render things transparent in words that would yet remain the author's own? If the scientific truth they so urgently sought seemed at times elusive, was it not because they were only beginning the long, slow process of changing the very historical bases of the limitations on scientific truth as well as on the truth of historians, the same historical conditions that had denied the real story to the historian, leaving it only to the secret historian as a subject for fiction?

Although in our minds scientific and fictional truth may seem poles apart, in the early days of their development their motivations were similar. Just as eagerly as the secret historian, the scholar and the scientist sought the secret of things; they were *curieux*. Sorbière's friend and fellow Montmorian Balthasar de Monconys was a typical *curieux*. His son says of him that his curiosity verged on excess. Monconys was also a born wanderer. In 1628, at the age of seventeen, he had completed his studies in Salamanca and wanted to go to India and China, but his father made him come home to Lyon, where he acquired the office of *conseiller du roi*. From 1645 to 1649, however, he was off to Portugal, thence to Provence and Italy, and onward to the "Orient": Egypt, Palestine, Syria, and Turkey. In 1663–64 he was on the road again, this time across Europe, to England, Holland, Germany, Italy, and Savoie. Sorbière wrote to him urging him to

25. Sorbière, *Relation*, pp. 156–60.

publish his voyages, but by 1665 Monconys was dead, and the task of publication was left to his son, the Sieur de Liergues.

Monconys's three-volume, richly illustrated *Journal des voyages* (1665–66), published thanks to his son's efforts, is closer in genre to the travel guide than to the travel journal. Its full title promises savants "an infinite number of novelties: Calculating Machines, Experiments in Physics, Philosophical Reasonings, Curiosities in Chemistry, and Conversations with the Illustrious of this Century: and in addition the description of diverse Animals and rare Plants, several unknown receipts [*secrets*] for Pleasure and Health, Works of famous Painters, Habits and Customs of Nations, what is most worthy of a Gentleman's knowledge in the three Corners of the World." That the encyclopedic project of the travel guide should be dependent on scientific knowledge was expected, since the guide usually contained a "natural history" of the places visited. It is less apparent that the seemingly disparate elements of the travel guide were unified by the underlying assumption that the truths of natural history and social history are one. Social customs can be examined, inventoried, and documented as accurately as species of flora and fauna. The voyage of discovery was for the *curieux* above all an intellectual adventure. What they discovered was a region where all could be known, where truth merely lay in wait for its liberator. At home there were only those little islands of virgin territory for the mind formed by the banding together of savants, scientists, and other *curieux* into academies such as Montmor's. Travel opened the door to a much larger academy, as Monconys's son says in his preface. According to him, his father endeavored to shed his "vulgar prejudices" by becoming an "inspector of that which Nature has most hidden from man, and of that which men hide the most from Nature, that is, their customs and the object of their actions. . . . This is the voyage of a philosopher," the son announces to his father's readers.[26]

The truth proposed in Monconys's *Journal des voyages* is thus essentially documentary in character. The voyager would have us believe that he scans his field with the eye of a would-be camera, reproducing as faithfully as possible what he finds. To this end

---

26. [Balthasar] de Monconys, *Journal des voyages* (Lyon, 1665–66), "Advertissement au Lecteur . . . ," 1:1–2, 9. Sorbière's letter to Monconys follows the "Advertissement." For Liergues's remark on his father's excessive curiosity, see p. 3 of the "Advertissement." Further references to Monconys's *Journal* are placed in parentheses in the text.

voyagers, if they did not sketch themselves, often tried to take painters along with them in order to bring back visual records of their travels, which an engraver would then transpose to plates for the finished book. Monconys hired a Dutch painter to accompany him, and when the man disappeared, the author was forced to do his own sketching. He worried that an engraver would not be able to work from his amateurish efforts.[27] Because voyagers professed to be concerned chiefly with accuracy, engraved illustrations in voyages serve a different function from that of portraits in *romans* and *histoires*. Illustrations for voyages exploit more strikingly the photographic potential of copperplate engravings, for they aim not to imitate but to reproduce. The portrait had to imitate its subject with "artifice." Its viewers admired it less for the accuracy with which it reflected traits of the model than for the artistry with which the imitation was carried out. Between the representation and the represented is all the opacity of art. The illustrations for Monconys's voyage, on the other hand, purport to lend us the voyager's eye, recreating for us what the author himself saw. They would clarify and render immediate objects mediated in reality by space, time, and the perceiving subject. They have all the transparency of scientific illustrations.

The camera-like sweep of Monconys's eye reflects the encyclopedic range of his interests. Illustrations for his *Journal* include engravings of monuments, houses, costumes, trees, and machines. If the portraitist was preoccupied with art, the voyager was primarily concerned with technique, in both the objects of his observations and the manner in which he reproduced them. Thus Monconys, who is addressed as "Technophilus" in a letter written in Latin by a friend who signs himself in the same way (1:175–76), includes illustrations of mechanisms for drawing water with oxen (1:266, recto), of a machine used by members of the Royal Academy for their experiments on the vacuum (2:73, verso) (fig. 14), and of other technological innovations. Many figures in illustrations of voyages were close-ups or details of larger monuments or structures which the author added to clarify his textual descriptions and explanations. When Monconys shows us a device for cleaning and polishing the inside of a cannon which he saw in a Portuguese arsenal (1:5, verso) (fig. 15), or when he devotes two

27. Ibid., p. 2. On the documentary character of French literature in the late seventeenth century, see Roger Francillon, "Fiction et réalité dans le roman français de la fin du XVIIe siècle," *Saggi e ricerche di letteratura francese* n.s. 17 (1978):99–130.

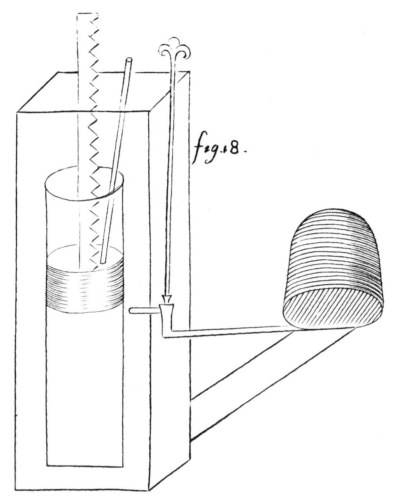

fig.18.

14. Experimental machine. From Balthasar de Monconys, *Journal des voyages* (1665–66). By permission of the Houghton Library, Harvard University.

plates to different types of mechanisms for lamps (1:65, verso; 66, recto) (figs. 16 and 17), he is making use of this close up technique. By the careful attention to detail and to technique which these illustrations display, they seem to serve not merely as clarifications of the text but as proof of the voyager's accuracy in reporting. Like the photograph the tourist brings home to show to friends, the illustration in effect says, "You see, I was really there."

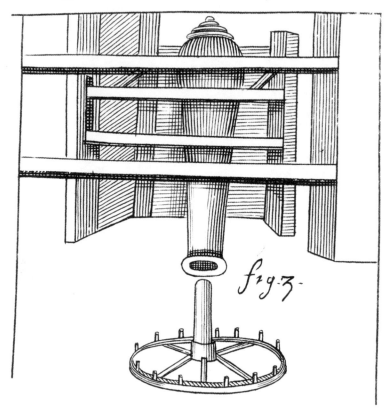

15. Device for cleaning cannon. From Balthasar de Monconys, *Journal des voyages* (1665–66). By permission of the Houghton Library, Harvard University.

Monconys and Sorbière were primarily technophiles writing to satisfy their own curiosity and that of their readers. Their friend and colleague in the Montmor Academy Melchisédech Thévenot published a collection of voyages whose erudition was much wider in scope and in implications. Thévenot, an extremely learned orientalist, was appointed curator of the Royal Library in 1684. When Montmor's academy broke up in 1663, Thévenot briefly sponsored a continuation of it. Around the same time he was busily drawing up plans, together with the scientists Adrien Auzout and Pierre Petit, for a Compagnie des Sciences et des Arts which they subsequently submitted to Colbert. It was not the first such grandiose idea. Richelieu seems to have been pondering schemes for a Pansophic College before his death, but by 1650

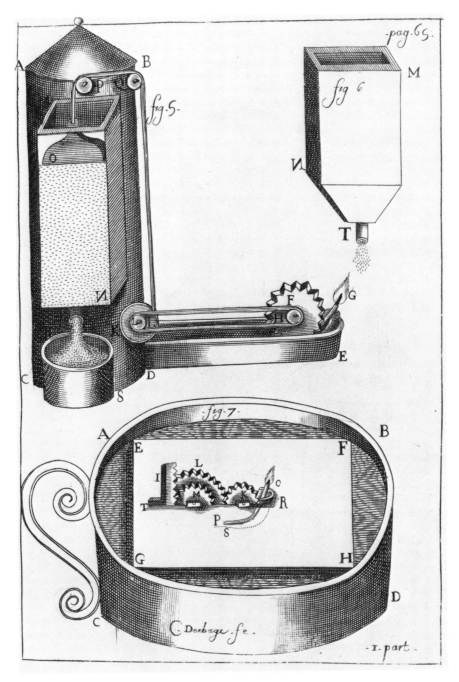

16. Lamps. From Balthasar de Monconys, *Journal des voyages* (1665–66). By permission of the Houghton Library, Harvard University.

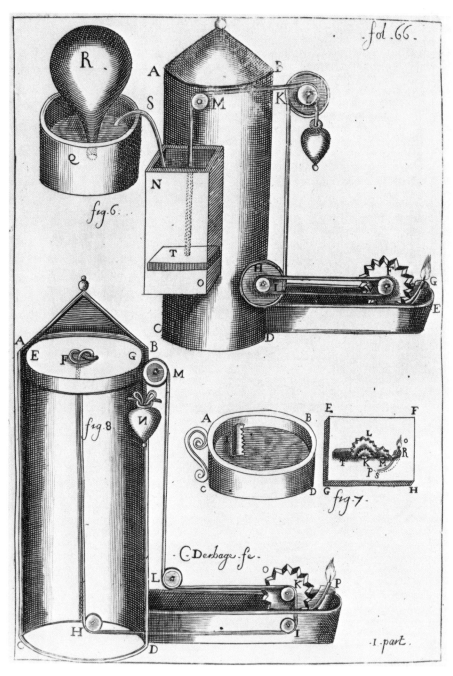

17. Lamps. From Balthasar de Monconys, *Journal des voyages* (1665–66). By permission of the Houghton Library, Harvard University.

242

nothing was left of his dream. The purpose of the projected Compagnie des Sciences et des Arts was nothing short of the betterment of humanity. This aim was to be achieved by scientific experimentation; by the study of chemistry, anatomy, and medicine; by technological development and improvements in trade, navigation, and agriculture; and by the advancement of meteorology, astronomy, and natural history. The plans were never implemented in their original form, yet the needs that they were designed to meet were real, as Colbert recognized. If when he founded the Académie des Sciences in 1666 he did not follow the blueprint for the Compagnie des Sciences et des Arts, he nevertheless established an organization that would meet similar needs and attend to similar concerns. Thévenot's *Relations de divers voyages* (1663–72) continued the encyclopedic, "pansophic" tradition that helped to inspire Colbert in forming the first French academy to contribute materially to the economic goals of the modern nation-state.[28] In addition, the *Relations* provides us with valuable evidence as to how academic interests functioned to serve new material, economic interests.

In the preface to the second volume of his *Relations*, Thévenot noted that since publication of the first volume, an event of considerable importance had occurred: the establishment of commercial companies for overseas trade. He was undoubtedly referring to Colbert's founding in 1664 of the French West India Company and the French East India Company. The creation of these companies strengthened Thévenot's conviction that France was destined to lead the way among European nations in commercial expansion. At the same time it strengthened the case that he had been making since the appearance of the first volume of the *Relations* for the importance of his scholarly contribution to commercial and colonial enterprise. His premise was that the collection of voyages had an overriding pedagogic value as so many *exempla* that would teach the French how to emulate and surpass their European neighbors in colonial and commercial endeavors and how to avoid their errors. In the preface to volume 1, after briefly recalling the vicissitudes of the Spanish, Portuguese, and Dutch empires, he says: "I think that examples of our Neighbors' Conquests and of the riches that they have brought may someday

---

28. For the developments leading to the founding of the Académie des Sciences and Thévenot's role, see Albert J. George, "The Genesis of the Académie des Sciences," *Annals of Science* 3 (October 1938):372–401; Brown, *Scientific Organizations*, pp. 61–62, 146–47; Hirschfield, *Académie Royale*, pp. 1–29.

inspire Frenchmen to undertake similar efforts, and to sail the faraway Seas under the French flag; furthermore, that reading Voyages for inspiration may serve as instruction in foreign travel." Moreover, he adds, would King Ferdinand have spent 17,000 écus to send Christopher Columbus to America without the knowledge of navigation which they both obtained from a treatise on the subject by a Basque voyager? Or would the king of Portugal have sponsored a voyage of discovery to the East Indies without first having read Marco Polo? Thévenot continues with a string of historical examples illustrating the utility of voyage literature for colonial expansion.[29]

In underlining the utilitarian value of his work, in citing exempla from the past, Thévenot was following a rhetorical tradition common to histories and voyage literature. He seems to echo André Thévet, who in the dedication to Henri III preceding his *Cosmographie universelle* (1575) had invoked shades of those obscure voyager-scribes who facilitated the conquests of emperors and rulers of old. For Thévet, the practical utility of a cosmography was counterbalanced by its moral dimension. "You will . . . see," Thévet informs his king, "by what types of government foreign kingdoms and provinces have been and are still ruled: some by Tyrants, others by civil laws, others by kings, some of whom are given over entirely to vice, others to virtue. But the kingdom that can be counted as perfectly happy is the one ruled by a Prince devoted to knowledge and to virtue."[30] A history book, in accordance with conventions dating from classical antiquity, distilled moral lessons through exempla. It was also often conceived as a "mirror of princes," a pedagogical tool—always cast in a flattering light—for the reigning monarch. The cosmography and later the voyage conserved something of this rhetoric. The conventional rhetoric shared by histories and voyages was meant to

29. Melchisédech Thévenot, *Relations de divers voyages qui n'ont point esté publiées; ou qui ont esté traduites d'Hacluyt; de Purchas et d'autres voyageurs anglois, hollandois, portugais, allemands, espagnols; et de quelques persans, arabes et autres auteurs orientaux* (Paris, 1664–66), "Avis," vol. 1, unpaginated. I consulted a two-volume set consisting of parts 1 and 2 of the first four parts, which were published during Thévenot's lifetime, of a projected five-part series. The first part appeared in 1663, the second in 1664, and the two were reissued in 1666 by Cramoisy. In the volumes to which I refer, the second part is the original of 1664, the first is Cramoisy's reprint of 1666. See Armand Gaston Camus, *Mémoire sur la collection des Grands et petits voyages* [de Théodore de Bry] *et sur la collection de voyages de Melchisédech Thévenot* (Paris, 1802), pp. 280–92.

30. André Thévet, *La Cosmographie universelle* (Paris, 1575), I, dedication to Henri III, unpaginated.

provide the combination of pleasure and utility found in all genres of the *ut pictura poesis* representational system.

Nearly a century had passed since the publication of Thévet's cosmography. Thévenot dedicated his work to Louis XIV under very different historical conditions from those that prevailed when Thévet wrote his dedication to Henri III. By the mid-seventeenth century, France was well into its struggle for commercial supremacy in Europe. The utility of Thévenot's *Relations* was more practical than moral, since it was to be a learning manual for commercial and colonial enterprise. Therefore Thévenot says that an account of travels in the East Indies, for example, which he included in volume 2, would be primarily a kind of colonial bulletin, informing readers which territories are held by the Dutch, which by the Portuguese, and where the two nations had common or exclusive trading rights. Volume 2 also contains a Dutch report on their East Indian trade and an extract of a letter from the governor general of the East Indies concerning trade with Japan. Thévenot's moral message to Louis XIV is the practical necessity of imperialism:

> These Relations will make [your subjects] see that other European peoples who have undertaken to populate parts of these vast territories have exhausted their supply of men in the effort. They will see that France alone can meet the demand for people, that she alone can send enough men to plant the Faith and to maintain Colonies. Possession of these lands belongs to her by natural right, and has been reserved for the time of your reign, under which no exaltation of France is too high. The glory, Sire, of having won battles, conquered provinces, and given laws to the Princes of Europe is something you share with other Conquerors, distinguishing yourself only in the number and grandeur of your victories. But that of obliging Your entire age, or rather the entire human Race, is worthy of the efforts of a Prince as elevated above all others as you are.[31]

The encyclopedic knowledge offered by Thévenot's *Relations* was therefore harnessed to economic ends. Discovery and the art of navigation on which it depended were for the purpose of conquest. Technological innovations observed by the voyagers would

---

31. Thévenot, *Relations de divers voyages qui n'ont point estées publiées,* "Au Roy," vol. 2, unpaginated. See the "Advis" of vol. 2, also unpaginated, for the description of the contents of this volume. The idea that France was destined to become the leader of all Christendom, if not of the globe, was not new. See Rothkrug, *Opposition to Louis XIV,* p. 95. In Thévenot it has a peculiarly colonialist, mercantilist ring.

be used to develop industry at home; the natural history of plants and animals would serve medical, industrial, and agricultural needs. Thévenot explicitly stated in the "Avis" to volume 1 that he was interested in perfecting the knowledge of those "arts" that were useful to society: geography, navigation, commerce, natural history. It is easy to understand why Colbert subsidized and protected voyagers.[32] Thévenot's *Relations* responded perfectly to Colbert's double-faceted mercantilist mandate as he transmitted it to the commercial companies and to the Académie des Sciences: develop industry and commerce through both expansion abroad and the acquisition of scientific knowledge.

Thévenot was a natural mandarin. Born into an era when erudition began to have an immediate economic value for the monarchy, he must have glimpsed at least from the beginning of his association with the Montmor Academy what future benefits could accrue from the practial application of the knowledge that he and his associates were pursuing. Especially at the time of the founding of the East India Company, he must have sensed the future that lay ahead for orientalists: Colbert was giving them subsidies, chairs in the Collège de France, and positions as royal interpreters, while at the same time he was allocating funds for archeological missions and the purchase of oriental antiquities and manuscripts.[33] Moreover, Thévenot's participation in planning the Compagnie des Sciences et des Arts indicates that he did not need to wait for the founding of the Académie des Sciences to be convinced that scientific knowledge was henceforth to be inseparable from and indispensable to the mercantilist priorities of the emerging modern state.

As traveler and *érudit,* Thévenot sought for his *Relations* the accuracy of the new science. Like Monconys, he assured his readers that the engravings in his collection were done from authentic, original drawings.[34] In fact, the engravings in the enlarged, posthumously published 1696 edition betray a conscious endeavor to maintain standards of precision. Brief, numbered descriptions correspond exactly to a series of thirty-three numbered illustratons for the "Relation du voyage des Hollandois à Pekin" (vol. 2). Others of the voyages that Thévenot collected for this edition are sprinkled with marginalia referring the reader to illustrations corresponding to the descriptions in question. Such

32. See Martino, *L'Orient,* p. 42.
33. Ibid., p. 145.
34. Thévenot, *Relations,* "Avis," vol. 1.

visual documentation had become common practice in voyage literature of this period. Sometimes the illustration passed from the status of documentation to that of document, as in the remarkable "Histoire de l'Empire mexicain representée par figures" (vol. 2).

This "history" is a version of Samuel Purchas' reproduction of the Codex Mendoza (the original is in the Bodleian Library, Oxford). Thévenot includes a translation of part of Purchas' preface, which relates how the pictorial history of the Mexican empire, commissioned for Charles V by the first viceroy of New Spain, happened to fall into the English traveler's hands. The engravings, which Thévenot reproduced after Purchas, are quite accurate in their detail (fig. 18). Only the brilliant color of the original is lacking, and the Spanish translator (the text was retranslated into English for Purchas and here into French) frequently interpolates references to the original colors. The intricate, densely packed pictographs aim to portray the entire civilization of the Mexican empire according to a tripartite division into chronicles, economic history, and social history. The alphabetized key to each figure forms a separately appended, continuous explanation of the illustrations, but the reproduced glyphs, not the translated Spanish commentary, provide the narrative of the history. In Purchas the key is separate from the narrative, whereas in Thévenot the two are collapsed into one running text, and the narrative is reduced.[35] The "Histoire de l'Empire mexicain" seems to attain the status of absolute document in Thévenot's collection. No matter if the document is the reproduction of an original. The aim is clear: the voyage as document will be coextensive with an original truth.

Although court historiographers had claimed that the portraits and medals that accompanied their histories were accurate, the accuracy of these images was that of a re-presentation of a representation, for the portrait or medal, not always authentic, had metaphorical value. The image was just as metaphorical as its text.

35. Thévenot, *Relations de divers voyages curieux . . .* (Paris, 1696), vol. 2, each voyage separately paginated. The pictorial part of the "Histoire de l'Empire mexicain" runs from p. 1 to p. 46, the textual explanation from p. 47 to p. 58. This posthumous edition of the *Relations* includes the four parts published during Thévenot's lifetime and various pieces that he had assembled for a fifth part. See Camus, *Mémoire*, pp. 283–84. For a full appreciation of the accuracy of the engravings, compare fig. 18 with a reproduction of the original in James Cooper Clark, ed. and trans., *Codex Mendoza: The Mexican Manuscript, known as The Collection of Mendoza and preserved in the Bodleian Library, Oxford* (London, 1938), 3:fol. 63. See also Samuel Purchas, *Purchas, His Pilgrimes* (London, 1625), 3:1109.

18. Priestly occupations. From Melchisédech Thévenot, "Histoire de l'Empire mexicain," in *Relations de divers voyages* (1696). Courtesy of the Harvard College Library.

The illustrations of voyages reproduce documents or documentation from original sketches by the traveler or his painter. These voyages aim to efface themselves as representations in order to pass as pure document. But despite every effort to reproduce the truth as its document, the voyage cannot overcome the mediation of representation. Whence both the profound ambiguity and the versatility of voyage literature. As representation, making use of a rhetorical fund common to historical and fictional narrative, the voyage could replace the latter in the *ut pictura poesis* system. As would-be document, reproduction of a transparent truth, it was inherently hostile to the system. As voyages increasingly strove for a documentary truth as immediate as scientific proof, they moved farther and farther away from a representational system that they helped to destroy even as they maintained it.

To the extent that the voyage endeavors to promote its truth as documentary, it attempts to flee the rhetoric of a truth that it rejects, the truth of historical and fictional narratives. To the extent that it is still representation, the voyage draws on the rhetorical tradition of these genres in creating its own rhetoric. As this voyage literature cannot overcome the mediation of representation, so it cannot escape rhetoric. Thus Thévenot accuses previous voyagers, Marco Polo among them, of inaccuracy, just as historiographers laid rhetorical claim to greater accuracy than that of their predecessors. Now, asserts Thévenot, France possesses accounts by merchants, simple men who do not disguise the truth in their eyewitness accounts.[36] Court historiographers might have claimed eyewitness accuracy, but they would not have associated truth with the status of merchant. Thévenot, in linking the plain-speaking topos to the merchant, lets us see the historical dimension of that rhetorical development which negated rhetoric. Documentary truth belonged to the bourgeois merchant and scientist who brought home the documents from their travels. But their mode of expression was not yet fully their own, for it did not blend with the consciousness of a fully formed class. Even the scientific truth of the scientist was not yet his own. How could it be when the interests that he was working to serve were as yet only potentially those of his developing class? Although Colbert's attempt to harness scientific, technological, and mercantile resources to interests of state furthered the autonomous develop-

36. Thévenot, *Relations de divers voyages curieux*, "Avis sur le voyage des ambassadeurs de la Compagnie Hollandoise des Indes Orientales vers le Grand Chan de Tartarie, à Pekin," vol. 2, unpaginated.

ment of the bourgeoisie in the long run, during his administration bourgeois expertise was limited by royal constraints. Only for a brief moment did it seem that the respective interests of the bourgeoisie in formation and of the monarchy might coincide. The story of Louis XIV's mandarins is also the story of ever sharpening tensions between these interests.

Sébastien Le Clerc and Tensions of Scientific Representation

It is not surprising that, since voyagers were often scientists and scientists voyagers, and both were ordinarily bourgeois, scientific literature of Louis XIV's reign should display some of the same representational ambiguities as voyage literature. Science was as yet still representational; it had not yet become disengaged from an encyclopedic tradition in which the arts included scientific thought. Frances Yates has pointed out the error in thinking of Fontenelle's *Entretiens sur la pluralité des mondes* (1688), for example, as a "vulgarization" of science. Fontenelle—who was a secretary of the Académie des Sciences as well as a member of the Académie Française and the Académie des Inscriptions et Médailles, which Colbert founded in 1663—wrote of science in the same manner as he wrote of a fictional voyage in his *Relation de l'isle de Bornéo* (1686), or of anything else, for that matter.[37] Even the more serious scientific works of this period are marked by the same hesitation between imitation and reproduction which we have seen in voyage literature.

In 1752 Voltaire could satirize the representational character of this scientific literature. His Micromégas rejects the metaphorical language that a thinly disguised Fontenelle uses to talk about nature. "I don't want to be pleased," Micromégas protests, "I want to be instructed."[38] During the reign of Louis XIV, voyages and scientific literature alike began to lay emphasis on their utility as they moved away from the aesthetic of the *ut pictura poesis* system, satirized by Voltaire, in which pleasure and instruction were inseparable. The very necessity that scientists and voyagers felt to

37. See Frances A. Yates, *The French Academies of the Sixteenth Century* (London, 1947), pp. 304–8.

38. Voltaire [François-Marie Arouet], *Micromégas*, in *Oeuvres complètes*, ed. Louis Moland (Paris, 1877–85), 21:108.

stress this aspect of their work, however, indicates how closely the literature they produced was still linked to a representational system whose values were becoming obsolete.

Sébastien Le Clerc's *Pratique de la géométrie* (1668) quite literally illustrates the tension between pleasure and instruction, imitation and reproduction in scientific literature. In a prefatory section titled "De son utilité," Le Clerc enumerates the uses of geometry: for astronomical measurements, for geography, architecture, drawing, and the study of perspective, for engineering, fortification, and military purposes.[39] The treatise's dedication to Colbert's son, the Marquis de Seignelay, is concrete evidence that the utility that Le Clerc claimed for his work fully coincided with Colbert's notions of what was useful to the state. The little volume was enormously successful. It seems to have been used as an instructional manual in schools. At the same time, it brought great pleasure to the court.[40] Now this pleasure was undoubtedly in instruction itself, for the simple, clearly written axioms and theorems, with their accompanying demonstrations, were, like Descartes's method, meant to be accessible to anyone. Equally important was the pleasure afforded by the illustrations. Sébastien Le Clerc was by profession an engraver, the most prolific book illustrator of the seventeenth century after François Chauveau,[41] and the eighty-three plates in the 1669 editon of his *Pratique de la géométrie* are among his finest works.

A frontispiece portraying Geometry teaching the elements of her art to a young noble soldier (fig. 19) continues the tradition of the allegorical portrait as it renews it. Whereas the function of the allegorical portrait was to glorify a ruler, prince, or noble through identification with a mythological figure, this portrait in allegorizing abstractions places in question the object of the glorification. Even though the young soldier may also be a vehicle for flattering Seignelay, he personifies something fully as abstract (the military) as the member of the quadrivium personified by Dame Geometry. In the dedicatory epistle and prefatory section, which correspond to the frontispiece as the written text corresponded to the allegorical portrait, Le Clerc suggests that the knowledge of geometry

---

39. [Sébastien Le Clerc], *Pratique de la géométrie, sur le papier et sur le terrain* (Paris, 1669), pp. 3–4.

40. Se Edouard Meaume, *Sébastien Le Clerc et son oeuvre* (Paris, 1877), pp. 62–64.

41. E. C. Watson, "The Early Days of the Académie des Sciences as Portrayed in the Engravings of Sébastien Le Clerc," *Osiris* 7 (1939):559.

19. Geometry. From Sébastien Le Clerc, *Pratique de la géométrie* (1669). By permission of the Houghton Library, Harvard University.

252

is a precondition for military glory. The Geometry of Le Clerc's frontispiece seems to hold out to her noble soldier-pupil a promise of future military glory for the entire reign. Does the portrait glorify that reign which has the wisdom to honor geometry, or the geometry that honors a wise reign with military victories? Obviously both. The implications of this portrait, in which erudition and interests of state seem to weigh equally in the balance, are interesting. Surely Colbert would have accorded priority to interests of state, to glorification of the reign. Le Clerc's portrait exudes the optimism of that moment when mandarins came to court, when the impossible marriage of science and the ancien régime seemed about to occur.

It is in the plates inserted into the text proper, however, that the tension between pleasure and instruction is most striking. These plates have a uniform vertical division into an upper portion consisting of the drawings for the demonstrations of the axioms and theorems in the text and a lower portion containing an illustrative vignette. The demonstrations in the upper portion are often bordered by frames of the type commonly found in contemporary engraved portraits; sometimes they are held aloft by putti. It is not clear to what the vignettes below refer. Certainly they do not document the written text—that is the function of the demonstrations in the upper portion, which offer examples of the axioms and theorems. Yet they may bear a more general relationship to the upper portion. The demonstrations are abstract; the vignettes are concrete. They portray such diverse scenes as ships being loaded with merchandise in a harbor, people on a walk in a formal garden, two Persians engaged in conversation, a combat with drawn swords among four men (fig. 20), the ruins of an amphitheater in classical style, and an artillery officer commanding soldiers about to fire some cannon (fig. 21). A number of the vignettes depict military scenes. Thus they give pictorial expression to geometry's various applications—astronomy (consequently, navigation and commerce), architecture, the military—as outlined in the dedicatory epistle and prefatory section. Thus they complement the demonstrations above them. If the demonstration is theoretical, as the division implies, the vignette suggests an eventual practical use for the theory. Even in those scenes that seem far removed in subject matter from the applications of geometry, there remains a connection to utility. The illustration for Book I, Theorem II, for example, shows a hermitage atop a mountain with a hermit below (fig. 22). In the background is a

253

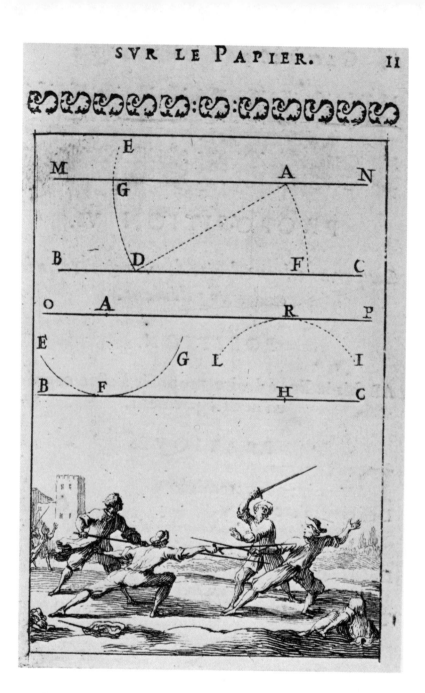

20. Combat with drawn swords. From Sébastien Le Clerc, *Pratique de la géométrie* (1669). By permission of the Houghton Library, Harvard University.

254

21. Artillery officer and soldiers. From Sébastien Le Clerc, *Pratique de la géométrie* (1669). By permission of the Houghton Library, Harvard University.

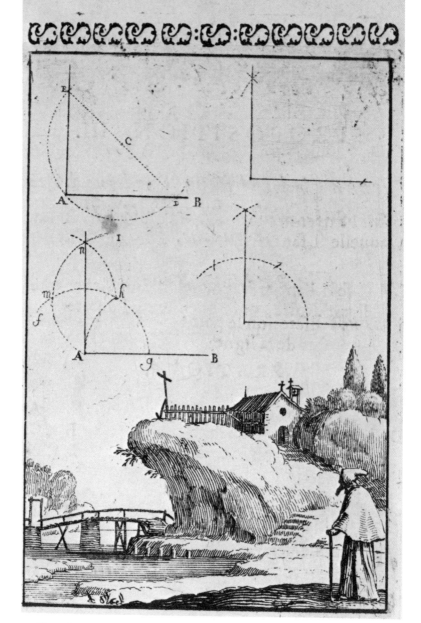

22. Hermitage. From Sébastien Le Clerc, *Pratique de la géométrie* (1669).
By permission of the Houghton Library, Harvard University.

river spanned by a wooden bridge.[42] Finely wrought, sometimes elaborate backgrounds are a distinguishing feature of Le Clerc's work. As in this particular vignette, they emphasize the perspective that the knowledgeable engraver included in the uses of geometry. Together, the upper and lower portions of the engravings correspond perfectly to the full title of Le Clerc's treatise, which promises a method of geometry "on paper and on earth." The theoretical and the practical, although divided, are united in their juxtaposition on each full-page plate. The vignette actualizes "on earth" the demonstration above "on paper."

The utility of the vignette is, nonetheless, subordinate to the pleasure it affords the eye in counterbalancing the rigorous instruction of the demonstration above. Even the demonstrations are offset in their starkness by those vestiges of conventional portraits—frames, borders, putti—which contrast somewhat awkwardly with the geometrical matter they enclose. It is as if, not content to let the drawings for the demonstration simply reproduce examples of the axiom or theorem, Le Clerc had to surround them with the trappings of conventional imitation. At the same time, the vignettes below remind us that no matter how instructive Le Clerc intended his treatise to be, it was still very much the product of a representational system in which the *agréable* and the *utile*, pleasure and instruction, were one.

The prodigious output of Sébastien Le Clerc during his long and successful career records a historically significant attempt to integrate the divergent demands of science and representation in accordance with specific standards set by the monarchy. Le Clerc's engravings appear in an impressively vast array of scientific, historical, fictional, religious, and travel works. Beneath the seeming diversity of many of these books is a unifying set of representational demands informing the conception of official and unofficial publications alike. Following Le Clerc's engravings from scientific and historical works back to voyage literature will provide us with an understanding of the representational and historical conditions for the ultimate modifications of the *ut pictura poesis* system.

Le Clerc was a technician and an artist. Trained in Metz as an engraver by his father, a jeweler, he had also managed to establish himself as an engineer before he left the town for Paris in 1665 at

42. Still the most complete descriptive catalogue of Le Clerc's works is Charles-Antoine Jombert, *Catalogue raisonné de l'oeuvre de Sébastien Le Clerc* (Paris, 1774), 2 vols. Edouard Meaume has made corrections of Jombert's listings, in *Sébastien Le Clerc*, pp. 259–62.

the age of twenty-eight, still uncertain as to which of his two careers to pursue. In Paris he met Charles Le Brun, who became his sponsor. When the miniaturist Jacques Bailly completed his painted manuscript, *Devises pour les tapisseries du roy,* after designs by Le Brun, Le Clerc was hired to do the engravings for the printed edition. Bailly, like the powerful Le Brun, was a member of the Académie Royale de Peinture et de Sculpture and had also been named *peintre ordinaire des bâtiments du roi* in 1667. He worked at the royal manufacture of the Gobelins on ornamental motifs for royal furnishings. The king had commissioned Bailly's *Devises* for the "Cabinet du Roi," his growing collection at Versailles consisting of manuscripts, medals, luxury books, and other treasures. The miniatures in the *Devises* illustrated Latin maxims invented by the "Petite Académie," the Académie des Inscriptions et Médailles (later the Académie des Inscriptions et Belles-Lettres), whose principal charge was to design medals and compose inscriptions glorifying the monarchy. Le Clerc's entry into this academic enterprise responding to the royal command marks the launching of his career. In 1670 Colbert appointed him engraver to the king and gave him lodgings at the Gobelins—all sorts of artisans were housed there—along with a pension of 1800 livres. In 1672 Le Clerc became in turn a member of the Académie de Peinture and its professor of geometry and perspective, a position that he held for the next thirty years.

Shortly after his marriage in 1673 to the daughter of the chief dyer at the Gobelins, Le Clerc gave up his official title of engraver and took a reduced pension, because he felt that he could earn more money working on private commissions. He maintained his residence at the Gobelins and continued to teach there until his death in 1714.[43] Although he did much work for private booksellers and individuals, he continued to make important contributions to a coherent program of official publications of printed books destined for specific uses. The program had been outlined in a decree issued by the King's Council on December 22, 1667, stating Louis's intention to sponsor a large-scale production of engravings. The engraving was to be strictly supervised by Colbert, and the subjects would include views of royal dwellings, paintings and sculptures decorating the interiors of these buildings, paintings and antiquities in the Cabinet du Roi, and figures

43. For biographical data on Le Clerc, see Meaume, *Sébastien Le Clerc,* and Watson, "Early Days."

of all species of plants and animals. Owing to Colbert's efforts, the engravings were collected into large luxury editions bound in Moroccan leather. These volumes were put on display in the Cabinet du Roi, deposited in the Royal Library on the rue Vienne, and sent abroad as gifts through foreign ambassadors. A foreword to the 1670 printed edition of Bailly's *Devises*, the one for which Le Clerc did the engravings, clarifies the intentions of the program. One of the advantages that moderns have over the ancients, we read, is the art of printing and engraving. "These are two marvelous means of multiplying infinitely a given discourse and of displaying the image of one thing in various places." Not everyone can see the buildings, paintings, statues, tapestries, and so on which the king is erecting to celebrate his glory. Printed reproductions will make them visible to those who cannot come to see the originals. The engravings will serve posterity as "precious monuments to everything that is being accomplished today."[44]

Engraving was essential to a propaganda campaign that exploited the universality of the visual image. More eloquent than the history books that Louis XIV did not care to commission, the engraved image transcended linguistic, cultural, and social barriers. Foreigners and illiterates alike could get the message. The function of engraving in this context is just as much the reproduction of a representation as it is representation itself. Engraving, like its sister art of printing, was beginning to democratize representation. Its function was beginning to be just as much that of a medium as that of an art.

One of Louis's most prized treasures in the Cabinet du Roi, *Médailles sur les principaux evenements du regne de Louis le Grand* (1702), is a good example of this propaganda, which both renewed and undermined the *ut pictura poesis* representational system in orienting it toward reproduction, in privileging the visual over the verbal, and in subordinating the pleasure of art to the utility of instruction. The most important work produced by the Petite Académie in the seventeenth century (and one that used an entirely new typeface),[45] the collection of *Médailles* was a huge

---

44. As quoted in André Jammes, "Louis XIV, sa Bibliothèque, et le Cabinet du Roi," *The Library* 20, 5th ser. (March 1965):5. This article contains invaluable information on Louis XIV's official publication program and the Cabinet du Roi. Arnold Hauser has noted the industrial, repeatable character of art under Louis XIV in *The Social History of Art* (New York, [1961–62?]), 2:196–97.

45. See Stanley Morison, *The Typographic Arts* (Cambridge, Mass., 1950), pp. 27–30.

collaborative effort involving, among others, the poets and royal historiographers Jean Racine and Nicolas Boileau. Sébastien Le Clerc contributed both the design and the engraving for 33 of the 286 medals in the collection; for 56 others in the collection he did just the design.

Like the portrait books to which they are closely related, "metallic histories" were, by the time the Petite Académie began its task, a well-established genre in the royal literature of praise. They purported to be a kind of emblematic history of a reign or a monarchy. In the preface to the *Médailles,* its authors claim the superiority of their metallic history over previous ones, owing to the rational ordering of its material. Previous histories (were they thinking of Mézeray's *Histoire de France depuis Faramond?*) relied on medals made by diverse individuals working unmethodically and without inspiration. But all the medals for this collection, they declare, wre designed by the members of the Petite Académie in accordance with strict rules. History, in other words, had come under official regulation.

Portrait books and metallic histories were, of course, regulated by the monarchy—though not strictly enough for the tastes of Louis XIV. He preferred no history at all to history of the type written by seventeenth-century France's last great historiographer, Francois Eudes de Mézeray.[46] Mézeray had placed as much emphasis on textual commentary—some of which could be and was construed as critical—as he had on portraits and medals. In the *Médailles,* this difficulty is overcome by the simple procedure of drastically reducing the text. The preface informs readers that care has been taken to limit the number of words in the text so that they never run over the one page allotted to each medal. Thus "the Reader may constantly have the Medal before his eyes." The same spatial constraint, the authors continue, has necessitated occasional cutting of the text and, especially, great selectivity in subject matter. Many aspects of Louis's reign have been omitted in favor of only the most glorious: military conquests, commercial and navigational achievements, the establishment of charitable and academic institutions, the justice, piety, clemency, and so on of the monarch. In fact, the focus of the book is the image; there is very little text at all. The authors rightly state that the reader will see "the image of a great event" and then read its "abbrevi-

46. See above, Chapter 4.

ated particulars."[47] The entire collection is an abbreviated history, one in which the visual censors the verbal.

The care taken by the Petite Académie to limit each medal and its explanation to one page may also have resulted from an attempt to follow the instructions on engraving which Colbert had issued on February 22, 1670 as part of the new propaganda campaign. At that time, the minister stipulated that all engravings of animals, plants, medals, statues, tapestries, royal buildings, and anything else should be of the same size so that they could subsequently be collected into large volumes of uniform size. He suggested ways in which material could be reduced or expanded so as to conform to the uniform size requirement. For about ten or twelve years, all these engravings would go into one comprehensive annual volume. After this period of time, the engravings would be redistributed into separate volumes according to subject matter. Thus, for example, the natural history of plants, the natural history of animals, and so on would eventually be extrapolated from the comprehensive annual volumes to form separate, specialized volumes.[48] The collection of *Médailles* seems to have been designed as one such separate volume. Uniformity in the size of these volumes was not actually achieved until much later, but the Petite Académie probably followed a rigorous set of guidelines for the format of the *Médailles* in order to meet the requirements of publications for the Cabinet du Roi.

Colbert does not seem to have waited ten or twelve years to start ordering separate, specialized volumes. In 1671 the Académie des Sciences, with the collaboration of Sébastien Le Clerc, among other leading engravers, produced two large folio volumes: the *Mémoires pour servir à l'histoire des plantes,* supervised by Denis Dodart, and the *Mémoires pour servir à l'histoire naturelle des animaux,* supervised by Claude Perrault. In 1676 there followed a second volume of the animal collection.

The same frontispiece by Sébastien Le Clerc heads both the plant and animal collections (fig. 23). It depicts Louis XIV and Colbert, with some princes from the court, visiting a meeting of the Académie des Sciences in its quarters on the rue Vivienne, which were furnished with the apparatus of scientific research. Through two windows in the background we see a view of the

47. *Médailles sur les principaux evenements du regne de Louis le Grand, avec des explications historiques* (Paris, 1702), Preface, unpaginated.

48. Jammes, "Louis XIV," p. 6.

23. Louis XIV visits the Académie des Sciences, by Sébastien Le Clerc. From *Mémoir pour servir à l'histoire des plantes* (1671). By permission of the Houghton Library, Harvar University.

Paris Observatory, then under construction (in reality, the site was several miles away). This engraving renews the Renaissance tradition of the group portrait, which typically represented biblical scenes with characters bearing the traits of recognizable contemporary notables. Like a roman à clef, the group portrait required a key (the viewer's ability to identify the contemporary figure in biblical dress) to be fully appreciated. But Le Clerc's portrait required no key. Its characters, like those of the *nouvelles* and secret histories so popular during this period, are dressed as themselves and are meant to be immediately recognizable.[49] The mediation of a metaphorical key, of biblical or mythological representation, is not necessary to the portrait's purposes, which have traces of the ambiguity in Le Clerc's frontispiece to his *Pratique de la géométrie:* glorification of the monarchy through the scientific research it encouraged, glorification of science through its services to the monarchy.

Once again, as in the *Pratique de la géométrie,* the effort to dispense with the mediation of art in order to approach the immediacy of science does not result in mere reproduction. This portrait, one of Le Clerc's most powerful works, renews imitation in orienting it toward reproduction. It re-presents what was undoubtedly an actual, historic meeting without the mediation of metaphor, it is true, but with recourse to well-established conventions of portraiture. Thus, for example, Le Clerc renews the convention of the inner portrait, or portrait within a portrait, by quoting from himself. In the background to the right is a drawing of a gazelle, with anatomical details, similar to a plate that Le Clerc did for the animal collection.[50] Now the function of the inner portrait in the days of Richelieu had usually been glorification of a living or dead person. Here the glorification takes on the abstract quality that it had in the frontispiece to the treatise on geometry. Surely Le Clerc used the device of the inner portrait less as a glorification of his own work than as homage to anatomy and to science itself. The entire group portrait focuses not on the individual Louis XIV but on his reign (both he and Colbert occupy the center of the portrait), not on individual scientists but on the collective insti-

49. The various princes and scientists in the portrait are identified in Watson, "Early Days," pp. 566–70.

50. [Claude Perrault], *Mémoires pour servir à l'histoire naturelle des animaux* (Paris, 1671–76), 1:41. Vols. 1 and 2 are bound together and continuously paginated in this edition. See Watson, "Early Days," p. 570.

tution of the academy, composed of individuals. In the integration of Louis, his minister, and the princes of the blood in the academic setting, in the intermingling of scientists, statesmen, princes, and monarch, Le Clerc's portrait transcends the ambiguity of the frontispiece of his mathematical treatise. The plant and animal collections were, after all, official publications. Here it is clear that the object of glorification is, precisely, the interrelationship of science and the state. In all its elements the portrait signifies the dawn of a new era (construction of the observatory in the background is not yet complete; the Académie des Sciences has just been founded) in which the monarchy and science will progress together, in which scientific progress is the ever greater glory of the state.

It seems that the scientific transparency that in Le Clerc's frontispiece was of necessity subordinated to representational demands would have been better achieved in the illustrations accompanying the texts of the plant and animal collections. These are among the outstanding scientific illustrations produced in seventeenth-century France. Yet here, too, the representational demands are evident. The preface to the *Mémoires pour servir à l'histoire des plantes* informs us that the authors ordered the largest plates possible for the engravings; consequently, certain plants of medium size are drawn to exact scale. When a plant is twice as tall as the page, its two halves are split and shown on the same page. In the case of much larger plants, the authors state, a detail drawn to exact scale is added to the illustration as a scale for the representation of the whole plant.[51] This preoccupation with fitting material for the engraving to page size betrays the authors' concern to adhere to the specifications set by Colbert for the Cabinet du Roi collection as much as it does their concern for scientific accuracy. Or, in other words, they were concerned that the accuracy of the drawings conform to the dimensions prescribed for representation of the monarchy's achievements.

Illustrations for the animal collection correspond just as closely to Colbert's instructions of 1670. In order that each engraving fill up the whole page and leave no blank space, the minister advised, it would be necessary to add landscapes and ornamental skies to figures that would otherwise be too small for the page, or else to

---

51. [Denis] Dodart, *Mémoires pour servir à l'histoire des plantes* (Paris, 1676), p. 6. On the plant collection, see Hirschfield, *Académie Royale*, pp. 146–62.

have two figures on one page.[52] The enormous size of the plant
and animal folios seems to have necessitated the adoption of both
solutions at once in the animal collection. Thus, as in the inner
portrait of the gazelle for Le Clerc's frontispiece, the upper portion of the animal engravings contains anatomical drawings, the
lower portion the portrait of the animal itself. Especially in the
illustrations by Le Clerc, landscape backgrounds and skies in the
portraits are elaborated with great care. His otter (p. 72) (fig. 24)
is shown in its natural swampy habitat. In the background to the
right we see a mill surrounded by trees against a chain of moun-
tains. To the left are ruins of a Roman aqueduct. Le Clerc shows
his dramatically dark, magnificent ostrich (p. 164) (fig. 25) against
a light, delicate, almost magical background of cliffs bordering a
lake. On cliffs jutting from the middle of the lake are Roman-style
ruins. Footbridges span the rocky islands, and boats wend their
way in between. One of the most stunning of Le Clerc's animals is
the lion (preceding p. 1) (fig. 26). He is shown against a wild,
rocky valley terrain. Sharp contrasts in the shading of the landscape correspond to a theatrical, stormy, cloud-filled sky.

The animal portraits precede their textual description, calling
attention to the animals first by their images. On the left-hand
page facing each portrait is a brief explanation corresponding to
the alphabetized key to the anatomical drawings in the upper
portion of the engraving on the right hand page. These keys, like
those in many illustrations for voyages, have a function diametrically opposed to that of keys to the portraits in the old romans à
clef. Keys to the latter were not available to the general public; if
they were published at all, they were generally revealed by someone other than the author, someone who professed special
knowledge. The key opened secret doors, known only to that
privileged, aristocratic circle of insiders who could recognize
themselves in their portraits. Keys to scientific illustrations, on the
other hand, aim to open doors to everyone; they aim to make the
portrait intelligible to all. They aim to clarify, not to mystify.

This democratized key was strictly in line with Colbert's thinking on propaganda. To exploit engraving as a medium for the
reproduction of images glorifying the monarchy was to make
those images accessible to as wide an audience as possible. Keys to

---

52. Jammes, "Louis XIV," p. 6. On the animal collection, see Hirschfield,
Académie Royale, pp. 121–28, and Francis Joseph Cole, *A History of Comparative
Anatomy from Aristotle to the Eighteenth Century* (London, 1944), pp. 394–424.

24. Otter, by Sébastien Le Clerc. From *Mémoires pour servir à l'histoire naturelle des animaux* (1671–76). Courtesy of the Beinecke Rare Book and Manuscript Library, Yale University.

25. Ostrich, by Sébastien Le Clerc. From *Mémoires pour servir à l'histoire naturelle des animaux* (1671–76). Courtesy of the Beinecke Rare Book and Manuscript Library, Yale University.

26. Lion, by Sébastien Le Clerc. From *Mémoires pour servir à l'histoire naturelle des animaux* (1671–76). Courtesy of the Beinecke Rare Book and Manuscript Library, Yale University.

scientific illustrations aim at the same accessibility. Yet these keys point to an important contradiction. The scientific illustration requires a key in order to make accessible its essential inaccessibility. For propagandistic purposes, it is quite unlike the engraving of a royal palace, painting, or tapestry, which has immediate accessibility. To be understood by the layperson, the scientific illustration must always have a gloss. The authors of the plant collection found it necessary to append an actual linguistic gloss to their work. They apologize for their use of technical words. Such words form a vocabulary that departs from "polite language," the authors say, but it is the only appropriate one for scientific descriptions.[53] Propagandistic science aims at a large public. Yet in order to reach this public it must make available an expertise possessed by the few. In the propaganda, then, is diffusion of a knowledge. For science to progress, however, the few must gain an ever more specialized expertise. Between the comparatively few experts and the general public the gap widens. The democratic metamorphosis of artistics forms into media cannot begin to bridge the gap between an ever growing knowledge of the few and diffusion to the many. The incipient tension between democratization and specialization in Colbert's propaganda campaign was symptomatic of a newly developing concentration of economic power in the form of merchant capital. This tension would eventually be an expression of a fundamental contradiction in bourgeois democracy between liberal political forms and wealth in the hands of the few.

It is noteworthy that Colbert's propaganda campaign rested on the foundations of this contradiction, as the period of Colbert founded conditions for the contradictions of the bourgeois democracy that was so distantly to follow it. Louis's minister wanted to transmit both an undifferentiated, encyclopedic corpus of information and products of highly specialized, developed branches of knowledge. The encyclopedic project was, however, conceived by him as a preparation for the specialized products in that the comprehensive annual volumes of engravings were to serve as the common fund for the later separate volumes. But inherent in the initial project was a specialization marking a radical departure from the older encyclopedic tradition in which all branches of knowledge were organically linked in the arts. How indeed were the engravings for the comprehensive volumes linked, other than

53. Dodart, *Mémoires*, p. 5

by the unsubstantial thread of their propagandistic purpose? The developing division between art and science had in fact already helped to categorize these engravings. They fell much more naturally into specialized volumes such as the plant and animal collections. By encouraging such specialization Colbert unwittingly undermined his own goals, because he was encouraging the concentration of knowledge in the hands of bourgeois intellectual elites, giving them the means to further acquisition of such knowledge, and therefore control of it, enabling them to diffuse it as democratically as they needed for their own purposes. He was, ultimately, encouraging consolidation of power in a forming class. It has been suggested that Colbert's plans for the Cabinet du Roi collection seem to outline the eighteenth-century *Encyclopédie*.[54] In the *Encyclopédie*, too, the alphabetical link is not organic but superficial. It is the divisions—technological, scientific, philosophical— that are real, not the unifying thread. The development from the Cabinet du Roi to the *Encyclopédie* is not, however, linear but rather dialectical. It occurred through contradictions in the economic, political, and ideological demands of a monarchy that relied ever more heavily on a developing bourgeoisie that it both encouraged and restricted. With the *Encyclopédie* the development from an organic inclusion of science among the arts to scientific specialization is complete.[55] As those who developed commercial, scientific, and technological expertise came to use it increasingly in the interests of their own class, their knowledge became truly their own, an expression of their own needs. Summa of bourgeois accomplishments, as Colbert wanted each of his comprehensive annual volumes to be a summa of the monarchy's accomplishments, the *Encyclopédie* is an intellectual monument to the acquisition of power by the bourgeois mandarins.

Nowhere in the literature of Colbert's period is the movement from "the arts" to art and science so clearly delineated as in the preface to the *Mémoires pour servir à l'histoire naturelle des animaux*.[56] This preface is like a manifesto of the mandarins. Marked by a contradiction between conventional imitation and reproduction, it heralds the triumph of science over history, of scientific truth over historical verisimilitude. It suggests the ultimate collapse of

54. Jammes, "Louis XIV," p. 9.
55. See Yates, *French Academies*, pp. 275–316.
56. All references are to the Preface (unpaginated) to vol. 1 of Perrault, *Mémoires*.

an aristocratic, organic representational system into the discrete units of a democratized, bourgeois knowledge.

Since classical antiquity, natural history had been a historical genre, so it is not surprising to find in this preface the topoi of many prefaces to histories written in seventeenth-century France. Yet the topoi in this preface indicate just as much the distance of the academy's work from historical writing as they do its continuity with such writing. The authors of the Académie des Sciences continue in their preface the historiographers' tradition of competing with each other in claims of truth. Almost every historiographer claimed special eyewitness knowledge as the basis of greater accuracy than any to be found in the histories of his colleagues or predecessors. The academicians claim that, as memoirs have greater truth value than general histories, so their *mémoires* (records, reports) have greater truth value than, for example, the general histories of Aristotle and Pliny or the particular accounts of voyagers. Because the general natural histories and the particular *relations* of voyagers are often based on secondhand knowledge, the authors of the preface declare, these works may have "symmetry" but no "true solidity." Voyagers especially come under the academicians' fire. Often simple merchants or soldiers, voyagers, they assert, have neither the patience nor the expertise to do the necessary research for a natural history. Their sincerity and accuracy cannot be trusted, since they often embroider on what they themselves have seen or else bring in material from other authors. Voyagers, in other words, are not specialists.

Now the contrast between "symmetry" and "solidity," between the work of an individual historiographer or voyager and the work of a body of specialists, is the basis for the academicians' implicit distinction between art and science in their preface. Although court historiographers, to emphasize their impartiality, frequently disclaimed self-interest, they were unable to muster much evidence for the disclaimer. The academicians have a stronger basis: working as a group precludes seeking individual glory. The truth of their *mémoires* will have, according to them, the certainty of the empirically verifiable, having already been verified by all the members of the academy before publication. An individual writer "considers less the truth of facts, which are not his production, than his arrangement of them." The academicians, on the other hand, have attempted in their description a "natural painting," executed "with simplicity and without ornament," in order to "show things as we have seen them, as in a mirror, which puts nothing of itself into the image and represents only what was presented to it." They have, so they suggest, chosen the solidity of science over the symmetry of art.

We are here at the very limits of representation, the precarious boundary that separates science from scientific representation. The academicians turned the voyagers' plain-speaking topos against them in an attempt to cross the border from the encyclopedic, organically linked knowledge of the travel guide, with its natural history, social and economic history, lexicon, and so on, to the specialized knowledge of the scientist as embodied in this discrete work on animals. Like the members of the Académie des Inscriptions et Médailles, who worked together on the *Médailles* collection, these authors were well aware that "each Academy working on its own specialty" was the new road to glory for the monarch and his subjects.[57] But, like the voyagers, the academic scientists were still struggling to escape the rhetoric that they rejected, to attain a transparent system of signification. They had not yet sloughed off the "painting" at the heart of the *ut pictura poesis* system; they merely wanted the painting to be self-effacing. In descriptions and illustrations for a natural history such as theirs, the authors advise, "the important thing is less to represent well what you see than to see properly and well what you want to represent."

Notice that this formula does not get rid of representation, but subordinates it to seeing. Accordingly, as in the *Médailles* collection, commentary of the type found in histories is drastically reduced. The authors declare that they have shied away from generalizations, that they have advanced only a few tentative "reflections," that any "reasonings" they may have added to their experiments are less important than their "facts." As in the *Médailles* collection, the visual is privileged over the verbal. Again, the dangerous commentary of history books is replaced by images, or by facts, which are supposed to speak for themselves. The authors of the animal volumes state explicitly that they will take responsibility only for their facts, as if they, as natural historians, still feared all the pitfalls of historical writing which such unfortunates as Mézeray did not escape.

What constitutes a fact is not at issue here. The problem for the mandarins was to find facts different in nature from those of historians in a regime where factual writing on French history was

57. See *Médailles*, Preface.

no longer tolerated. This demand in part explains the representational character of seventeenth-century French science, which had to define itself against the representation of history. It had to define itself against a history to which it was generically related, but which it replaced as a beneficiary of royal patronage, and which it therefore strove to disown. Its facts had to be nonhistorical according to the standards of history with which scientists were familiar. Such facts, then, had to be empirically verifiable, immediately recognizable by anyone, presented without the rhetoric of "art." The most transparent mode of presenting facts which the official scientists could come up with was what they called "exact description," in effect a rigorous taxonomy according to which no one species of plant or animal could be confused with any other. In these taxonomies a Cartesian truth was distinguishable from error, as the right classification is distinguishable from the wrong. At the same time, description aims at a mirror image; it "impresses better the image of things," as the preface states. It aims to form a language drained of representational rhetoric, where words will immediately signify things.

In their facts, the academicians found the basis of a much more grandiose claim than that of the court historiographers, who had wanted only to emulate their rivals in the rhetoric of truth. The authors of the animal collection assert that their search for truth distinguishes them as moderns from the ancients, whose errors they correct in a scientific disregard for authority. At the very end of the preface, the authors express the hope that their *mémoires* will furnish material for a natural history "that will not be unworthy of the greatest king ever; and that if to equal Alexander in this respect . . . he lacks a personage as great as Aristotle . . . this Work that he wanted undertaken will perhaps not be inferior to that which was done for Alexander." The "modern" platform, as outlined here and as elaborated, for example, in Charles Perrault's *Paralelle* [sic] *des anciens et des modernes* (1688), is inseparable from the premise that Louis's reign is greater than all that preceded it. The most convincing evidence for this position is always the scientific accomplishments that Louis promoted, both because he indeed promoted them and because it seemed that scientific progress was as measurable as longitudes at sea or right angles on land.

There is no mistaking the glorifying function of Charles Perrault's *Paralelle*, just as the glorifying function of the animal collection that his brother directed is made evident in the preface of that work. Both brothers were powerful men in Louis's regime. Charles, in addition to his position as head of the Surintendance des Bâtiments, was a member of both the Académie Française and the Académie des Inscriptions et Médailles. His *Paralelle*, modeled on Plutarch's "parallel lives," shows how "modern" achievements—that is, those of the present reign—both parallel and surpass the ancients'. The dialogues are framed by an excursion to Versailles, thus by the contemplation of Louis's most dazzling monument. The heart of Perrault's argument for the moderns is Louis's protection of the sciences and his founding of academies. Perrault at times waxes lyrical in his praise of machines. He describes in some detail and with much wonderment Des Hayes's disruptive ribbon-making machine, which so captivated Colbert's fancy.[58]

The authors of the *Mémoires pour servir à l'histoire naturelle des animaux* were resolute moderns. But the moderns' very existence as a "party" was possible only in relationship to the ancients. Far from repudiating the *ut pictura poesis* system, with its roots in classical antiquity, Perrault's *Paralelle* uses it even in its Plutarchan conception. It is therefore not unexpected to find Perrault calling painting a "mute poem" and a painter an *historien*.[59] Similarly, even the most scientific aspect of the animal collection, the drawings of the anatomical details in the upper portion of the engraved plates, do not lose their representational value. Like engraved personal portraits with elaborate frames, reminding the viewer that an engraved portrait was often the representation of a painted original, the drawings are represented on scrolls of paper held in place by pins. That is to say that they are not drawings at all, but representations of drawings. And if the animal portraits were conceived as transparent images of animals (yet we saw that they were far from transparent in their careful attention to Colbert's specifications), ready for insertion into a precise taxonomy, Sébastien Le Clerc's *lettres grises* balance the portraits' would-be transparency with a most intricate representation. Le Clerc was a master of this miniaturizing art, which packed as much pictorial virtuosity as possible into the engraved illustration of a letter. The

58. Charles Perrault, *Paralelle* [sic] *des anciens et des modernes; en ce qui regarde les arts et les sciences. Dialogues* (Paris, 1688), pp. 77–78. Like Colbert, Perrault utterly disregarded any questions of labor posed by such machines. In passing, he mentions that the ribbon-making machine can easily by handled by a child. He obviously considers it an advantage of the machine that it can facilitate the use of child labor.

59. Ibid., pp. 223, 225.

27. Noah and the animals, by Sébastien Le Clerc. From *Mémoires pour servir à l'histoire naturelle des animaux* (1671–76). Courtesy of the Beinecke Rare Book and Manuscript Library, Yale University.

block initial *L* for the preface represents Noah looking at the various animals leaving the ark (fig. 27). The block initial *A* for the description of the lion (p. 1) shows Adam and Eve in earthly paradise surrounded by all the animals (fig. 28). Le Clerc's *lettres grises* remind us that the animals that the academic scientists dissected in their laboratories still held for them another, analogical value as God's creatures. The combination of Le Clerc's *lettres grises* with the other engravings in the collection suggests that the nature of which the animals are a part is both divine creation and object of scientific investigation. The representation of nature as both sacralizes science as much as it desacralizes the animals.

In volume 2 of the animal collection, Le Clerc's *cul-de-lampe* of

275

Le Clerc in. et f.

28. Adam and Eve in earthly paradise, by Sébastien Le Clerc. From *Mémoires pour servir à l'histoire naturelle des animaux* (1671–76). Courtesy of the Beinecke Rare Book and Manuscript Library, Yale University.

Apollo discovering truth (p. 139) (fig. 29) perfectly captures the value of scientific truth for the authors of the *Mémoires*. It depicts Apollo quite literally dis-covering Truth in lifting a drapery from her nude, reclining body. Apollo has about him the symbols of culture and power—his lyre, books, a globe, and the like. Juxtaposed with the image, the inscription from Ovid's *Metamorphoses* (1:518), "Per me quod eritque fuitque, estque patet," suggests that it is Truth just as much as Apollo (the conventional figure of Louis XIV) that makes clear (*patet*) everything in the past, present, and future. The French alexandrines correspond more closely than the Latin to the image, for they have Apollo's/Truth's glances un-cover what the past hides, what the future "yet covers in its shadows," as

29. Apollo discovering truth, by Sébastien Le Clerc. From *Mémoires pour servir à l'histoire naturelle des animaux* (1671–76). Courtesy of the Beinecke Rare Book and Manuscript Library, Yale University.

well as what happens in the present. The truth represented in the *cul-de-lampe* is the uncovering of a secret: Apollo lifts the lady's draperies. In modifying the conventional allegorical representation of Truth as a nude woman, Le Clerc portrays a scientific truth not far removed in value from that of the secret historians, who, deprived of the real historical facts, chose to invent a "true story" and to expose the less glorious aspects of Louis's reign.[60] In fusing Apollo and Truth, the engraver fuses the truth of classical antiquity with that of the new science. As scientists unwittingly renewed

60. See above, Chapter 4, pp. 152–153. The French verses in Le Clerc's *cul-de-lampe* read: "Tout ce que le Passé cache en ses replis sombres / Tout ce que le Present produit de toutes parts / Tout ce que l'Avenir couvre encor de ses ombres / Est decouvert par mes regards." I am indebted to Leonard Muellner of Brandeis University for his help in locating the source of the Latin inscription. On portrayals of the Sun King as Apollo, see Nicole Ferrier-Cavarivière, *L'Image de Louis XIV dans la littérature française de 1660 à 1715* (Paris, 1981), pp. 73–80.

the canons of representation and the rhetoric of historical narrative, they adapted traditional truth to their own purposes. The meeting of Apollo and Truth is a confrontation of the arts and science, of the old and the new, as much as it is a blending of old and new into one still allegorical representation of Louis as a patron of science. The *cul-de-lampe* celebrates a scientific truth that is continuous with a rhetorical, historical, and artistic truth from which it is nevertheless distinct. It summarizes all the ambiguity of scientific representation.

Toward a New Representational System: Ideological Development of Voyage Literature

The truth of Le Clerc's *cul-de-lampe* is the same as that which informs much of "real" voyage literature. Voyage literature of the late seventeenth century betrays a development of social contradictions which resulted finally in the obsolescence of the *ut pictura poesis* system. The heavily fictionalized "real" voyage and the imaginary one were, traditionally, literary neighbors. During this period, the imaginary voyage, in consciously parodying the real, pushed its contradictions to the point of subversion. The outcome was an autonomous fictional truth for those who would claim as their own what the monarchy had endeavored to expropriate. In the imaginary voyage we see the outline of a new set of contradictions proper to the bourgeoisie: ideals of human justice founded on the exploitation of others for profit.

The ideological contradictions of the official publications for the Cabinet du Roi appear more sharply in a voyage by a Dominican misisonary priest, which was illustrated by Le Clerc. Jean-Baptiste Du Tertre's *Histoire générale des Antilles* is like a signpost indicating two opposing directions. It points back to a feudal history now in the throes of capitalist transformation, forward to the development of a capitalism unconstrained by the monarchy. As a mercantilist-colonialist manual that should have warmed Colbert's heart, it was also the expression of economic interests that were to gain autonomy from the ancien régime. Values linked to those interests were embodied in growing criticism of a regime that placed fetters on the free development of capitalism. In Du Tertre's voyage we can discern the glimmer of these new values within the setting of Colbertism.

The Montmor Academy had taken a special interest in Du

Tertre's work. In 1658 a certain Rochefort had published a pla-
giarized version of an earlier voyage to the West Indies by Du
Tertre. Montmor had somehow gotten wind of Rochefort's game,
and he offered to pay for publication in Holland of Du Tertre's
voyage. The priest felt that he did not have the time to accept. He
chose instead to go on another mission to the Antilles, and subsequently published an account of this voyage in the three volumes
of his *Histoire générale* (1667–71).[61]

It was undoubtedly the scientific aspect of Du Tertre's voyage
that attracted Montmor's attention. The second volume, the one
that Le Clerc illustrated, is an *histoire naturelle*. Its comprehensive
character conforms to the encyclopedic conception of the entire
work. The three volumes comprise respectively a history of
French colonization in the Antilles, the natural history of the islands, and a specific account of the establishment and governance
of the French West India Company. In its division into eight
separate treatises, the second volume, on natural history, aims also
at a more scientific specialization. The titles of the treatises in this
volume are as follows: (1) "Description of the Antilles Inhabited
by the French," (2) "Of My Travels to the Antilles and Back to
France: Of Tides, Air Temperature, and the Precious Stones and
Minerals of the Antilles," (3) "Of the Plants and Trees of the
Antilles," (4) "Of Fish," (5) "Of Flying Animals," (6) "Of Land
Animals," (7) "Of the Inhabitants of the Antilles," and (8) "Of the
Slaves of the Antilles." The inclusion of social and natural history
in this one "natural history" is a typical feature of the travel guide
genre of voyages. In applying the descriptive apparatus of specialized science to social customs, the natural history of the travel
guide aims at objective reportage that confers the same documentary status of fact upon nature and society alike.

Le Clerc's engravings clarify the intentions that undermine the
documentary appearance of the priest's account. Along with engravings of the various plants and animals that Du Tertre describes in his third treatise, we find two plates on facing pages
(2:106–7) devoted to the production of indigo (fig. 30), in
which the basic steps of the process are shown along with the
necessary machinery. A numbered key refers us to the textual
description. There is a similar illustration of sugar refining
(2:122–23) (fig. 31). Although Du Tertre informs us at the

61. Jean Baptiste Du Tertre, *Histoire générale des Antilles* (Paris, 1667–71),
1:Preface, unpaginated.

30. Indigo production. From Jean-Baptiste Du Terre, *Histoire générale des Antilles* (1667–71). By permission of the Houghton Library, Harvard University.

1. *Moulin.* 2. *Fourneaux.* 3. *Formes.* 4. *Vinaigrerie.* 5. *Cannes* **SVCRERIE.** 6. *Gros* 7. *Latanir.* 8. *Pajomirioba* 9. *Choux* 10. *Cases* 11. *Figuir. : 138.*
et Chaudieres. *de Sucre.* *Cocos, p. 128.* *p. 92.* *Carraibes* *de Negres*

31. Sugar refining. From Jean-Baptiste Du Tertre, *Histoire générale des Antilles* (1667–71). By permission of the Houghton Library, Harvard University.

beginning of this treatise that plants on the islands contain "treasures of marvels," he modestly denies any expertise as a "doctor, philosopher, or naturalist" and claims to offer nothing more than a "simple, naive account of things I noticed during my stay on the Islands."[62] Nevertheless, Du Tertre's descriptions of plants are generally accompanied by precise indications as to their uses. An entire chapter (2:115–18) is devoted to cassava products. Le Clerc's engravings of the animals that Du Tertre describes in his fourth, fifth, and sixth treatises depict flora and fauna in their natural settings. At the same time, humans are shown engaged in local industries involving the use of the animals. Thus the tortoise is portrayed in a scene of tortoise fishing (2:246–47) (fig. 32); land animals are portrayed in a hunting scene (2:288–89) (fig. 33).

It has been said that Du Tertre composed all of his descriptions with the goal of attracting new colonists to the Antilles.[63] Certainly both Colbert and religious missionary orders felt the need of such advertisement. Colbert engaged the French Academician François Charpentier to write propaganda for his French East India Company in order to win over investors.[64] Jesuit travel accounts dating back to the sixteenth century were designed to raise money for the order's missions.[65] By the 1660s, moreover, missionary interests had dovetailed with Colbert's, for the minister knew how to turn his resources to mercantilist advantage. Thus Jesuits were sent to Siam and to China in order to set up an observatory and to pursue work on the astronomical measurements so necessary to advances in navigation. For Colbert's purposes, the Jesuit-astronomers were a double asset: they could be used to propagate the faith as well as to gain trading policies favorable to France by ingratiating themselves with foreign rulers.[66] Du Tertre himself, in a dedicatory epistle (vol. 1) to the kingdom's attorney general, Achille de Harlay, emphasized the utility of his voyage. Like Thévenot, he viewed his account as a compilation of so many *exempla* instructing prospective colonists in the art of colonization. Newcomers can learn from him, he says, how to maintain their colonies by "considering the accidents and the dangers that

62. Ibid., 2:82. Further references to Du Tertre's voyage appear in the text.
63. Gilbert Chinard, *L'Amérique et le rêve exotique dans la littérature française au XVIIᵉ et au XVIIIᵉ siècle* (Paris, 1934), p. 47.
64. Cole, *Colbert*, 1:484–86. Cf. Martino, *L'Orient*, p. 80.
65. Martino, *L'Orient*, pp. 109–13.
66. See *Mémoires de l'Académie royale des sciences. Depuis 1666 jusqu'à 1699* (Paris, 1730), 8:51–52. Cf. George, "Genesis of the Académie des Sciences," p. 392.

Tortue faisant son trou pour pondre. 3 Verre de la Tortue. xvi. 7 Arras p. xxx. 8 R. Esmer. xvi. 9 Chasse des poissons volants xii. 11 Pesta au cul ou oiseau du tropique. xvi. 13 Crabier.
Comme on la retourne p. xxv. 4. Courbaril p. vii. 6. Fir Onde. 8. Peroquets xx. 10. Fregate p.xiv. 12. Flamant xvi. 14 Grand pissier. p xx

32. Tortoise fishing. From Jean-Baptiste Du Tertre, *Histoire générale des Antilles* (1667–71). By permission of the Houghton Library, Harvard University.

33. Hunting. From Jean-Baptiste Du Tertre, *Histoire générale des Antilles* (1667–71). By permission of the Houghton Library, Harvard University.

the first settlers were unable to avoid." Yet the zealous missionary and loyal partisan of Colbert reveals another aspect of himself when he describes the native inhabitants whom he would proselytize. Here the ambiguity of his voyage comes to light.

The first chapter of Du Tertre's treatise on the inhabitants of the islands (2:356–58) seems an echo of Montaigne's essay on cannibals, another version of the myth of the noble savage. Like Montaigne, Du Tertre plays on the French word *sauvage* in order to show that the so-called savages are merely as wild or natural as the plants and fruit on the island. It is we, he asserts in the style of Montaigne, that corrupts the savage, uncultivated growth of the tropics by planting it with artifice in our gardens.

Such praise of the West Indians was not inconsistent with religious and mercantilist propaganda. Du Tertre says that as he has shown that the islands have the best climate on earth, so it is "appropriate" that he prove the natives to be the happiest, healthiest, most virtuous people on earth. After all, the colonists would have to live among them. In the interests of populating the colonies, Colbert even encouraged the intermarriage of French men with Indian women (converts, of course). In 1673 the king established a royal bounty of 150 livres to be paid to every French colonist who married an Indian woman. In 1669, in order to strengthen the colony by integrating the French and Indian populations, he had allocated money for the education of Indian children.[67]

So Du Tertre compares as he reports. And in his implicit comparison of Indian society with the French he distances himself from the regime whose goals he would propagandize. To suggest the superiority of natives over colonizers he draws on many commonplaces of the noble savage myth: the natives are all equals; they have no rich and poor; they have no laws; they know no want, and they are content with the necessary, feeling no need to seek the superfluous; they are uncorrupted by learning. The features of this myth are always historicized; they are not eternal. To be understood properly, Du Tertre's use of the myth has to be placed in its historical context. His myth is neither simply a rehashing of Montaigne's nor an anticipation of the philosophes'. If Du Tertre reduced the "savage" to a tractable person living in an egalitarian society, it is because his rose-colored lenses blotted out the inequalities and damage that the colonists brought with

67. Cole, *Colbert*, 2:72–73.

them. It is, historically speaking, a prelapsarian vision. As the social-economic inequalities of the ancien régime came to be replaced by those that characterized the development of merchant capital, voyagers began to compare what they saw abroad more and more favorably with what they saw at home, forgetting that they were serving the Old World in exploiting the New. Their comparison was a vehicle of criticism for policies that, consciously or unconsciously, they helped to carry out. With Du Tertre we are at the moment of developing contradiction. The priest's criticisms are a counterweight to his endorsement of the regime. They are like the obverse of his enthusiastic inventory of the islands' commercial resources. Both sides of the voyage—criticism and endorsement—point up the contradiction of a monarchy that in attempting to appropriate these resources to serve its own interests was restraining the development of the bourgeoisie, which it needed in order to do so. In voyage literature, criticism of the monarchy begins at the moment when royal encouragement of the mandarins is perceived as a constraint on the interests of the voyagers. When bourgeois power was consolidated in the eighteenth century, criticism was fully integrated with an underlying endorsement of the regime's colonial policies, which then served the interests of the class.[68]

At the beginning of Du Tertre's first chapter in the treatise on the islanders is a full-length portrait by Le Clerc of a nude Indian couple set against a fertile landscape (2:356) (fig. 34). Between the man and the woman is a lush, fruit-laden papaya tree. The man holds a bow and arrows; the woman covers her genitalia with a leaf. Du Tertre had called the Indians' land a "little Paradise, ever verdant" (2:357). Le Clerc's portrait is an obvious reference to Adam and Eve in terrestrial paradise, thus a projection of a biblical utopia onto the West Indian society of the New World. As a utopian vision, it is a negation of the reality that Du Tertre saw. It replaces the inequality of the colonized with the equality of all divine creatures before God. A fitting image for the work of a

68. On the noble savage myth in relation to European colonialist policy, see Duchet, *Anthropologie et histoire*, pp. 9–12, 14–18, 217. Duchet's point is that the savage has meaning only in relation to the civilization that is its dialectical opposite. Once the savages have survived the devastation of colonialization, they will nobly submit to the exploitation of the civilizing process. Her thesis is that social criticism in the literature of the philosophes betrays an underlying solidarity with the neo-colonialism of the French monarchy. See especially pp. 125–36 and 145–60. See also Hayden White, "The Noble Savage Theme as Fetish," in his *Tropics of Discourse: Essays in Cultural Criticism* (Baltimore, 1978), pp. 183–96.

34. West Indian couple. From Jean-Baptiste Du Tertre, *Histoire générale des Antilles* (1667–71). By permission of the Houghton Library, Harvard University.

missionary priest! But here too there is a distancing. If Du Tertre makes use of Christian imagery to criticize the inequities of colonialism, he wishes to dissociate his values from those of the Christan colonizers. Chapter 13 of this same treatise on the West Indians is titled "Of the Obstacles Encountered in the Conversion of the Savages." The "first and almost only" such obstacle, the priest says, is the "evil life of Christians." Indians have seen in them "men who came to seize their land ... with unheard-of cruelty, who came only for gold, and whose life had something much more barbarous about it than theirs" (2:413–15).

The same ambivalence formed of criticism and endorsement of the ancien régime which characterizes Du Tertre's treatise on the West Indians also characterizes his treatise on slaves in the Antilles. Any pity he may express for the "frightful misery" of the Africans, or for their "misfortune" (2:493), is counterbalanced by the racism that inevitably accompanies slavery. Thus he deplores sexual relations between French men and black women, whose "hideous" appearance and "unbearable odor" he disdains (2:511). He applauds the segregated living quarters that remove the blacks' odor from the nostrils of the whites (2:517). Yet he comments with some bitterness on exploitation of black labor for white gain (2:523). Le Clerc's illustration for this treatise (fig. 35) is much more eloquent than all of Du Tertre's text. It shows black slaves at work on various household tasks—the preparation of cassava, tobacco, and meal. In the background, standing next to his proper, well-groomed house, is a Frenchman. Arms folded, he looks on as the Africans perform his chores. There could be no more appropriate illustration of the contradictions underlying Du Tertre's voyage. These were the contradictions that by the eighteenth century were to turn the voyagers from endorsement of an exploitative regime that both protected and alienated them to implicit endorsement of exploitation by their own class in the interests of their own class, accompanied by explicit criticism of the regime that served their ends.

Sometime between 1661 and 1715, voyagers took a decisive turn in this direction, for by the death of the Sun King the intellectual forces of an emergent bourgeoisie had begun to gather. As early as the 1670s, the fragility of the marriage between mandarins and the state became apparent in travel literature. It was a marriage threatened by those mandarins or would-be mandarins who saw their power alienated from them by the alliance. A new group of voyagers as outsiders began to produce its own litera-

35. Slaves at work. From Jean-Baptiste Du Tertre, *Histoire générale des Antilles* (1667–71). By permission of the Houghton Library, Harvard University.

ture, whose fictional character responded to their unfulfilled aspirations. Like the authors of *nouvelles* and secret histories, this group was a potpourri of disaffected characters. Gabriel de Foigny, whose *Terre Australe connue* first appeared in 1676, was a renegade Franciscan monk who went to Geneva and converted to Protestantism. In Switzerland he got into repeated trouble for drunkenness and immorality. He was dismissed from his teaching post at the Collège de Morges in 1671. He and his printer, La Pierre, were hauled off to prison for the *Terre Australe connue*, which they published without permission, under a false imprint. Denis Vairasse, or Veiras, author of the *Histoire des Sevarambes*, whose two parts first appeared in French in five volumes from 1677 to 1679, was a Protestant from the town of Alais, or Alès. After leaving the army to pursue a doctorate in law, he went to England, where he became involved in political intrigue, and where the first part of his imaginary voyage was published in English, under the title *The History of the Sevarites* (1675). In 1674 he returned to France, where he gave private French and English lessons, as well as lectures on history and geography. After the Revocation of the Edict of Nantes, he emigrated to Holland. A number of French editions and translations of his voyage were published abroad well into the eighteenth century, indicating the success of his work. Foigny's voyage also went through several editions before the early eighteenth century, and appeared in 1693 in English translation.[69] In 1703 Louis-Armand de Lom d'Arce, baron de Lahontan, published his *Nouveaux Voyages dans L'Amérique septentrionale*. Lahontan left his native Béarn at the age of seventeen to go to Canada with the navy. In Canada he participated in military campaigns, became a military officer and companion to the French governor, Frontenac, but continually deserted his posts to take off on impromptu travels. He wasted much of whatever time he spent in France in fruitless lawsuits, always disappointed in his efforts to regain the fortune that had been expropriated from his father's estate. His *Nouveaux Voyages*, however, were very successful: they went through fourteen editions in his lifetime.[70] Although not all of these authors were bourgeois, all had reason to resent the concentration in the hands of the mandarins of power that they themselves would have liked to possess. Foigny and Vairasse were learned men. Lahontan had a

69. See Atkinson, *Extraordinary Voyage*, pp. 36–37, 87–91.
70. On Lahontan, see Joseph-Edmond Roy, "Le baron de Lahontan," *Proceedings and Transactions of the Royal Society of Canada* 12 (1894):63–192.

basic formal education, and he was able to amass a good amount of knowledge as an autodidact. The success of their voyages indicates that the authors found a public whose interests were becoming consolidated in opposition to a regime that did not wish to recognize the autonomy of those interests.

The *Histoire des Sevarambes* is a counterfeit travel guide, Foigny's *Terre Australe* more a counterfeit travel journal. Earlier in the century, nobles had attempted to emulate royalty in romances, or trompe l'oeil histories, which imitated royal history. Now voyagers subverted mandarins in fictional voyages during the same period when writers of *nouvelles* and secret histories were subverting *romans* and *histoires* alike. Unlike the *nouvelles*, which created a new genre in subverting older ones, the fictional voyage as a French genre began as a subversion of itself. When voyagers began to subvert the mandarins with whom they had so much in common, they took a paradoxical step toward declaring the solidarity of their interests with the mandarins' over against the monarchy's. The fictional voyage is both a division against itself as a voyage and an autonomous expression. It subverts the solidarity of the mandarins and the monarchy in suggesting a new solidarity of interests independent of the monarchy. Unlike the *nouvelle*, which expresses only a negative truth, a truth against the monarchy, the fictional voyage expresses a positive truth for an emerging class, pointing to a convergence of hitherto diverse interests. The double function of the subversive voyage is even more evident in Lahontan's *Nouveaux Voyages*, where fictional and real voyages combine to form one work.[71]

Du Tertre had pointed the way toward the fiction of the subverted voyage. The most fictional aspect of his *Histoire générale des Antilles* (an aspect that is also typically found in Jesuit relations) was the treatise on native inhabitants with its noble savage myth. This is the starting point for the fiction of the subversive voyage. For both Foigny and Vairasse, the Terre Australe is the land of the noble savage. For Lahontan it is North America. Foigny relates the adventures of a European hermaphrodite shipwrecked off the coast of an Australian hermaphrodite society, which

71. My notion of the fictional voyage as a subversion of the voyage genre differs significantly from Atkinson's "extraordinary voyage." My analysis of the development of voyage genres also differs from that in Jacques Chupeau's important article, "Les Récits de voyages aux lisières du roman," *Revue d'histoire littéraire de la France* 77 (May–August 1977):536–53. I have found Chupeau's efforts to develop a poetics of the voyage particularly valuable.

adopts him. Vairasse's story of a group of shipwrecked Europeans is a pretext for his lengthy description of the fictional Sevarites. All voyagers inevitably inserted some fiction into the accounts of their travels, even if at times their fiction was only the almost imperceptible locus on their subjectivity. Du Tertre's fiction blends with the more objective observations that he recorded on his actual voyage. In the work of such authors as Foigny, Vairasse, and Lahontan, fiction, in subverting the real, acquires autonomy.

Foigny and Vairasse parody the encyclopedic pretensions of travel literature by claiming to tell all there is to be told about their fictionalized Austral lands. Vairasse includes a little treatise on the language of the Sevarites, recalling the lexicons that commonly accompanied voyage books; Foigny includes sections on native animals and rarities, recalling natural histories. Both announce intentions to deal with the customs, religion, and government of the Australians. Their parodies discredit the truth of the voyages that they imitate in order to establish a higher fictional truth. Yet there is also a seriousness to the imitation in some borrowings from real voyages, suggesting continuity in the value of truth for all the voyagers.

In his foreword, Vairasse says that merchants traveling only for self-interest have brought back scanty, insufficient information on foreign lands. How nice it would be, he muses, if peace would give rulers the revenues to commission young travelers specially trained in sciences and mathematics to write up much more accurate reports than those of ignorant merchants and sailors. Such a policy would bring their benefactors "solid glory."[72] Vairasse echoes Sorbière's criticism as he adds to it implicit criticism of officially sponsored voyagers. Yet what truth was there to his accusation? The Huguenot jewel merchant Jean Chardin, knighted Sir John by Charles II of England, in whose kingdom he finally decided to settle, was hardly an ignorant man. In the accounts of his travels to Persia in the *Couronnement de Soliman* (1671) and in his later *Voyages*, the wealth of description, translations of inscriptions, and detailed information of all kinds reveal an impressively wide-ranging learning. The same can be said of the *Six Voyages* to the Orient (1676–77) by Jean-Baptiste Tavernier, a jewel mer-

---

72. [Denis Vairasse], *Histoire des Sevarambes, peuples qui habitent une partie du troisième continent, communément appellé la Terre Australe. Contenant une relation du gouvernement, des moeurs, de la religion, du langage de cette nation, inconnuë jusques à present aux peuples de l'Europe* (Amsterdam, 1702), 1:"Au Lecteur," unpaginated. Further references to Vairasse appear in the text.

chant ennobled by Louis XIV. Vairasse's objections to the merchants' "ignorance" are largely rhetorical; what really bothered him was their "self-interest," that is, the fact that they benefited from royal benevolence in their commercial dealings abroad. Vairasse must have been delighted by the review of his book in the official academic *Journal des sçavans* (March 7, 1678). Not only did the reviewer point out that some readers assumed that the *Histoire des Sevarambes* was a real voyage; he also noted that the author's learning would attract the interest of savants. Vairasse's fictional voyage had succeeded: in truth and in learning it could rival the voyages of the mandarins.

In the mandarins' voyages, any comparison between French and foreign societies undermines the narrative's character as reportage. Such comparison is what veers Du Tertre's *Histoire générale des Antilles* toward fiction. In the subversive voyage, on the other hand, comparison is the form of the fiction as well as the vehicle for a new truth. The plots of Vairasse's and Foigny's voyages are structured on the confrontation of the European with the primitive. In both cases, the European "goes native" for a while (Foigny's hero has a strong tie with the Australians in his hermaphroditism), but in the end leaves Australian society to return home. One wonders why, if the Europeans have found an ideal society of noble savages, they should choose to leave it. The answer lies partly in the ambiguous nature of the savage. Like the European who goes native, the savages, through parody, also have a European side. They are both noble savages and parodies of Europeans. The story of Sevarias, the Sevarites' first ruler, clarifies the implications of the European/native Australians.

Sevarias was by birth a Persian noble who acquired immense learning through travel and under the guidance of his Venetian tutor, Giovanni. He established his authority in Australia through a ruse. At the opening of a temple in honor of the sun, he arranged for an oracle quite like those that Fontenelle exposed in his *Histoire des oracles*,[73] to proclaim his rule. The European voyager and narrator, Captain Siden, approves the strategem, comparing it to those of "several other great legislators who in order to legitimate their laws say that they have received them from some Divinity" (1:269–71). The suggestion that Louis XIV's claim to rule by divine right is as flimsy as Sevarias' is patent. Other allusions make it clear that

---

73. See Frank E. Manuel and Fritzie P. Manuel, *Utopian Thought in the Western World* (Cambridge, Mass., 1979), p. 372. The authors see in this passage a reference to divine right rule, with no parodic intent.

there are significant parallels between the Sevarites and the French. Sevarias instituted his rule after winning a military victory over "barbarians" who were engaged in a religious war that sounds suspiciously like European conflicts between Protestants and Catholics. Sevarias himself appears on the scene like a European missionary-colonist, spreading terror among the natives with his firearms (1:226–36). The present-day sovereign lives in a Palace of the Sun that has all the magnificence of the Sun King's Versailles (1:186–89), with its furnishings and formal gardens strictly in the style of Louis XIV (2:66–71). But the regime instituted by Sevarias, far from being a copy of the ancien régime, was a firm rejection of it. At first Sevarias and Giovanni concocted a plan to divide the Sevarites into various classes that would reproduce exactly all the inequities of class structure in seventeenth-century France (1:273–75). Siden remarks that he thinks Giovanni was the real author of this plan (1:276). Is the Italian Giovanni an allusion to Mazarin? If not, he certainly evokes the figure of any one of the royal ministers whom such authors as Vairasse routinely blamed for the evils of French society. Sevarias chose instead a system of state communism in which there were no riches, taxes, or poverty. Before his death Sevarias provided that his successors could modify the system, but he forbade them to institute any legislation "contrary to natural law" or to "recognize any sovereign other than the Sun" (2:276–81).

The metamorphosis of the private Persian citizen Sevaris into the Sevarite ruler Sevarias (the -as ending in the Sevarites' language is reserved for notables) marks the transition in the voyage from divine right to natural law, from Catholicism to a naturalist sun worship, from parody to utopia. The transition is never complete, since Sevarite society retains throughout the narrative many features reminiscent of seventeenth-century France, or at least of the France that Vairasse would have liked to see, with its well-developed technology and public works and its rehabilitated divisions in rank. The European is both identified and contrasted with the utopian. Parallels and contrasts between the European leader Siden and the utopian leader Sevarias follow parallels and contrasts between their two societies. Both are rulers who at first refuse to rule (1:39–41, 259); but the little European society of shipwrecked passengers which Siden governs is as ridden with strife as the Sevarites are orderly and peaceable. Denis Vairasse divides the anagram of his name between "Siden" and "Sevarias," unifying the European and the utopian by his subjective identification with both leaders. Du Tertre and other voyagers had glimpsed a better life elsewhere. The subversive voyager, merging his European identity with the primitives of his imagination while comparing their society with his own, wants to bring the utopia home.

Comparison between the European and the primitive in Foigny's *Terre Australe* is structured on a reversal. The hermaphrodite voyager Sadeur was considered a monster in Europe; in the Australia he supposedly discovers, anyone who is born *not* a hermaphrodite is smothered at birth "as a monster."[74] In making the hero a hermaphrodite, Forigny identifies him with the other, the non-European, the utopian. His Australian natives have many characteristics of the noble savage. They wear no clothes in an ideal climate, their property is communal and they know no "mine" or "thine," they live in perfect equality, they do not accumulate wealth, they have no ambition or avarice, they are free from servitude and so on. (pp. 90–95, 106). Foigny's reversal is thus a variant of the word play on *sauvage:* the monster hermaphrodites are much more human than the European humans, who are the monsters in this setting. As noble savages, the hermaphrodites are parodies of the monsters that figure in real voyage literature. Foigny explicitly derides the tall tales about monsters commonly found in such literature (pp. 79–80). The implication is that his fictional monsters have more truth than that of monsters in real voyages. In his deliberate confusion of the fictional and the real lies a demystification: Foigny's fictional voyage will express a truth that is obscured in real voyages. Similarly, Denis Vairasse, in the foreword to his *Histoire des Sevarambes*, warns his public

74. [Gabriel de Foigny], *La Terre Australe connue, c'est-à-dire la description de ce pays inconnu jusqu'ici, de ses moeurs et de ses coûtumes, par M. Sadeur, avec les avantures qui le conduisirent en ce Continent et les particularitez du séjour qu'il y fit durant trente-cinq ans et plus, et de son retour*... (Vannes, 1676), in Frédéric Lachèvre, *Les Successeurs de Cyrano de Bergerac* (Paris, 1922), p. 95. I have also consulted the 1692 edition of this work, revised presumably by Foigny himself. The omissions and corrections of 1692 frequently tend to modify the *libertinage* of the original, as Lachèvre has shown, yet the 1692 text also contains some political implications not present in the earlier version. Further references to Foigny appear in parentheses in my text. When I have wanted to cite the 1692 edition, I have referred to the variants (indicated by small letters) which Lachèvre includes in his volume. Unless otherwise noted, therefore, all references will be to the 1676 edition as it appears together with the variants in Lachèvre. It is interesting that a reviewer of the 1692 edition of Foigny's voyage in the *Journal des sçavans* mistook it for a real voyage (see Francillon, "Fiction et réalité," p. 124). This was the same journal that had pointed out a similar error in the case of Vairasse's *Histoire des Sevarambes* (see above, Chapter 6, p. 293).

neither to disbelieve the contents of utopias nor to believe the contents of real voyages.

The subversive parody of voyages functions as a denial of their truth. Foigny's natural history sections repudiate the value of natural histories in real voyages. As we have seen in the case of Du Tertre, natural histories of colonial territories were often guides to commercial and industrial exploitation of their natural resources. Chapter 11 of the *Terre Australe,* "On Rarities Useful to Europe Which Are Found in the Australian Land," is a satire on the secrets or receipts that voyagers typically included in their natural histories. Sadeur thinks, for example, that an Australian soporific fruit (perhaps also reminiscent of the biblical forbidden fruit) could be used as a "universal remedy" in Europe (pp. 138–39). He remarks that Australia contains all kinds of resources that France could put to profitable use. The only difficulty would be in establishing trade with Australians, "because since they desire nothing, it is not likely that you could attract them with the lure of profit, remuneration, or pleasure. . . . Besides, . . . all the things that we bring to newly discovered lands in order to ingratiate ourselves with their inhabitants are considered by the Australians to be bagatelles and children's toys. For them, our cloth is like spiders' webs; they don't understand the meaning of gold and silver, and everything we value as precious they find ridiculous. Our only recourse would be to arms" (p. 140, k, l, m). In addition to all the other obstacles, physical access to Foigny's Australia is very difficult. Like Voltaire's Eldorado, utopias in subversive voyages tend to be topograhically inaccessible, as if their geographic isolation were one more instance of their invulnerability to colonial exploitation for mercantilist and capitalist ends.

How subversive these utopias are may be measured by the mandarins' open endorsement of mercantilism in their voyages. The learned physician and philosopher François Bernier (lionized as "le Mogol" in such Parisian salons as Madame de la Sablière's)[75] includes in his Indian voyage a letter to Colbert on the circulation of coins in Hindustan. The thesis of his letter is that gold and silver coming from America are "lost" in India, because as a result of oriental trade they do not leave the Hindustani kingdom. Moreover, Bernier's conclusion to the long comparison between French and Indian economic systems which forms the body of the letter is

75. Martino, *L'Orient,* p. 57; Menjot d'Elbenne, *Mme de la Sablière* (Paris, 1923), pp. 72–73.

an apology for private property, of the "mine" and "thine" that subversive voyagers abolish in their utopias.[76] Jean Chardin includes in his Persian *Voyages* an appropriately documented account of the formation of the French East India Company. He praises Colbert's enlightenment in valuing "manufactures and commerce above all things."[77] Jean-Baptiste Tavernier expressed to Louis XIV the hope that an "exact, faithful" account of his travels to the Orient would be as useful to France as the "rich merchandise" he brought back. He was especially proud of the diamonds that he secured for the king.[78]

Foigny opposes incipient French capitalism to utopian communism, civilization to "nature," the "monstrous" heterosexual European to the noble Australian hermaphordite, supernatural religion (that is, Christianity) to "natural reason." Science and learning do not enter into this scheme of oppositions, for Foigny's Australians devote much of their time to education (pp. 126, 131). Similarly, in the *Histoire des Sevarambes,* science and technology serve the interests of an enlightened nation. It is as if Vairasse would remove science from the grasp of the mandarins, whose interest in serving the monarchy was a focus of his parody, to transfer it to Sevarias-Vairasse for quite different uses. Although both Foigny and Vairasse parody the scientific, encyclopedic structure of real voyages, neither one rejects a science separable from the monarchical ties of such voyages. On the contrary, science is the very fabric of their works, which are cut from the cloth of scientific voyage literature. What the subversive voyage does is to change the value of the science that it imitates. In so doing, it subverts the entire *ut pictura poesis* system.

The "truth" of both the *Histoire des Sevarambes* and the *Terre Australe connue* is purportedly documentary. In his preface, Vairasse claims to have gotten Siden's papers from a physician who treated the mortally wounded captain after his return home on a Dutch ship that was attacked by the British. Not knowing the various languages in which Siden wrote his papers, the physician gave them to Vairasse to translate and put in order. Vairasse "proves" the authenticity of Siden's papers by citing wit-

76. [Francois Bernier], *Histoire de la dernière Revolution des Estats du Grand Mogol* (n.p., 1671), 1:130–201.

77. [Sir John Chardin], *Voyages de monsieur le chevalier Chardin, en Perse, et autres lieux de l'Orient* (Amsterdam, 1711), 1:224.

78. [Jean Baptiste Tavernier], *Les Six voyages de Jean Baptiste Tavernier, ecuyer baron d'Aubonne, qu'il a fait en Turquie, en Perse, et aux Indes . . .* (Paris, 1676–77), 1:"Au Roy," 3–5.

nesses' testimony and by including a documentary letter. Foigny in his preface (pp. 65–66) claims to have aided the debilitated Sadeur when he fell into the sea while disembarking at Leghorn in 1661. Before dying, Sadeur supposedly bequeathed his manuscript to Foigny. In both voyages, the "discovered manuscript" topos functions to confer on the subversive voyage the documentary character of real voyages and scientific literature. It borrows the mandarins' plain-speaking topos in order to challenge them: do they speak as plainly and truthfully as their imitators? Siden's theory, Vairasse says in his preface, is "written in such a simple manner that no one, I hope, will doubt the truth of its contents. . . . It has all the features of a true History." Admittedly a fake—Vairasse allows that Siden's story has only the *features* (*caractères*) of a true story—the subversive voyage imitates the artlessness of the voyage it subverts in order to speak a new truth. It announces itself as a fake in order to denounce the fraudulent truth of real voyages. Its fiction is the vehicle for a truth that it wishes to establish over against the mandarins' facts.

Subversive voyages parody the "impartiality" of science and voyage literature produced in the interests of the state. If the mandarins were under the illusion that they could attain objectivity while working for the monarchy, subversive voyagers cherished the illusion that they could reclaim truth as their own by transforming empirically verifiable fact into fiction. For the universality of a science that the few experts wanted to open to everyone, they substituted the universality of a utopian message: *liberté, égalité, fraternité*. Their is an *embourgeoisement* of the noble savage myth. It is an attempt to wrest from the service of the monarchy a democratizing science and a democratized scientific representation developed by the emerging bourgeoisie.

The mandarins inevitably undermined the facts of their voyages with an unconscious fiction proper to their historical situation. Their facts were facts for the monarchy and were therefore still dressed in the trappings of the *ut pictura poesis* system. Both fictional and real voyages retained certain narrative and rhetorical features of the old system, such as stories within stories (sometimes transformed into voyages within voyages), descriptions, and *harangues*. Such features are not organic to voyage literature; they are mere vestiges. The real voyage uses these devices seriously, whereas the fictional voyage parodies them. The real voyage still found a place in the old system, because it was still partly tied to its rhetoric of glorification. Du Tertre in his preface advises the reader to skip documentary material on the French West India Company in the first volume of his voyage if it is too boring in order to get on with the story. *Romanistes* and historians alike had issued such warnings to their readers. The ambiguity of the real voyage gave it an ambiguous yet recognized status in the old system. As fiction, it could be identified with *romans;* as truth, with *histoires.* The publisher of a real travel journal precisely defined its ambiguous status for contemporary readers. Voyages, he said, are a "middling genre" between novels and histories, because they "deal with the adventures of individuals, as do Novels, but with as much truth and more exactitude than Histories." He thought that voyages could be called "Novels for those who scruple to read them, and History for those who don't want to bother studying it."[79]

Du Tertre's endorsement of the ancien régime led him to fictionalize his colonialist-mercantilist catalogue of natural resources as facts of natural history. His criticism of the ancien régime led him to fictionalize facts concerning the West Indians as the myth of the noble savage. The contradiction between criticism and endorsement of the ancien régime was fundamental to the real voyage. Sorbière, who compared as he reported, leaned more toward criticism, which developed naturally from the comparison. Chardin openly endorsed the ancien régime, yet there is also implicit criticism in his comparisons. The real voyage and official scientific literature contemporaneous with it were similarly linked to the *ut pictura poesis* system: representation attempted to pass itself off as science, while science was still representational. The subversive voyage overcomes this contradiction by fully developing the comparative and critical side. It is frankly representational. As fiction, it imitates the document, which real voyages tried to be, in order to re-present nature as truth. It aims not at scientific investigation, but rather at the nature that science wanted to investigate. Its naked noble savage has the value of a universal human nature, of a human being descended like all others from Adam. That its truth was also its myth is another matter. Here it leaves the contradictions of a scientific representation still enmeshed in the *ut pictura poesis* system for a new set of contradictions proper to seventeenth- and eighteenth-century utopias.

Lahontan goes a step further in developing the critical side. He

---

79. [François Bertaut], *Journal du Voyage d'Espagne* (Paris, 1669), "Le Libraire au Lecteur," unpaginated.

uses the features of both real and fictional voyages to make explicit the criticism that was implicit in the former, veiled by parody or satire in the latter. The *Nouveaux Voyages* are a report of Lahontan's observations on North America. As such, they are accompanied by engravings often as dry and technical as Monconys's, as precise as a remarkably intricate series on Persepolis in Chardin's Persian voyages. Lahontan has sections on natural history; he has a glossary of navigational terms and a dictionary of the natives' language. His account of native customs and society is interspersed with criticisms of the French treatment of the Indians and of their profit-making motives, with a letter inveighing against the injustice and corruption of French ministers and the sale of offices, and with a denunciation of the science that develops a technology of war and destruction. Lahontan also inserts in his account reports of his conversations on religion with a Huron chief called Rat by the French. Here fact slides into fiction, as it becomes evident that Rat is largely a vehicle for the expression of Lahontan's freethinking, which profoundly shocked the French reading public. The native chief also delivers a speech against war, which is set off from the reportage, as the *harangues* Lahontan here parodies were set off from the narrative thread of the old histories and novels. Elsewhere in the *Voyages* Lahontan completely fictionalizes such conversations. His *Dialogues ou Entretiens entre un Sauvage, et le baron de Lahontan* follow the standard utopian form of the conversation or dialogue. Foigny devoted a section of his *Terre Australe* to *entretiens* between Sadeur and an old Australian man on life in Europe and Australia.[80] Lahontan uses this comparative vehicle par excellence to elaborate his criticisms of Christian doctrine and the French system of justice.[81]

The *Nouveaux voyages* is in the form of letters, which an anony-

---

80. Foigny, *Terre Australe connue*, pp. 96–124. On Lahontan's *Dialogues*, see Baron de Lahontan, *Dialogues curieux entre l'auteur et un sauvage de bon sens qui a voyagé, et mémoires de l'Amérique Septentrionale*, ed. Gilbert Chinard (Baltimore, 1931), pp. 1–72. Michèle Duchet says that Lahontan in his *Dialogues* was the first person to give form to a true "contestation of the civilized world." She observes the suitability of the dialogue form in allowing the reasoning native an equal role with the European. See Duchet, *Anthropologie et histoire*, p. 102.

81. [Louis-Armand de Lahontan], *Nouveaux voyages de Mr. le baron de Lahontan dans L'Amerique Septentrionale* (The Hague, 1703–4), 2 vols. Vol. 1 contains two tomes bound in one, the second of which includes Lahontan's voyages in Portugal and Denmark. Vol. 2 contains the *Dialogues* and the dictionary of the native language in the continuation of the North American voyage. Chinard (*Dialogues curieux*, pp. 37–44) has disproved Roy's thesis that Nicolas Gueudeville was the author of the original *Dialogues* (Roy, "Baron de Lahontan," pp. 119–22).

mous third person claims to have found.[82] Is this a real or a fictional discovered manuscript? It is as difficult to know as it was for contemporary readers to know that Lahontan's reported discovery of the Long River was a tale he invented.[83] What we do know is that Lahontan himself lived the fiction of Foigny's Sadeur and Vairasse's Siden. He actually found a better life in the New World. In his voyages, he reports his experience as he uses it to construct concrete criticisms of French society and a utopian dream. In so doing, he explodes the fiction of real voyages as he exposes the truth of the subversive voyage.

Like the fictional heroes of Foigny and Vairasse, Lahontan discovered in the New World that he felt closer in identity to the Indians than to Europeans. "I've spent the happiest days of my life with the Savages of America," he says (1:Dedicatory Epistle). His enemies do not insult him, he points out, when they call him a "savage," because in this designation they honor him with "the character of the finest gentleman" [*le plus honnête homme*] in the world" (2:Preface to *Dialogues*). As Vairasse criticized merchants' voyages, so Lahontan criticizes the errors in missionaries' reports of the savages. Missionaries, he charges, wrote only with an eye to conversion, whereas through open-minded talks with the Indians he has acquired a much more accurate knowledge of their life (2:91–92). Engravings depicting various scenes of Indian life—hunting, child care, and so on (2:95)—which correspond to textual descriptions of these scenes (2:94–96), seem to bear out his claim. But in the following section, "Customs and Manners of the Savages," fact once more slides into fiction as description of the Indians merges with the noble savage myth, and Lahontan's identification with them is transformed into the identity of all humans as equals.

Lahontan's noble savage is set in relief against criticisms of the Europeans. The savages have no "mine" and "thine"; only the Christians use money, which native Americans call "the French serpent." The Americans are amazed at all the crimes that Europeans commit for money, and they cannot comprehend the concept of unequal distribution of wealth. Their society has no crime. They see the French as enslaved to one man "who has no law

82. Lahontan, *Nouveaux voyages*, 1:Preface, unpaginated. Further references to Lahontan appear in the text.

83. On Lahontan's fabrication of the Rivière Longue episode, see Roy, "Baron de Lahontan." Roy makes the interesting suggestion that Lahontan may have been motivated by a desire to obtain the customary rewards for voyages of discovery.

other than his will." They themselves are each one equally "master" in their society, since "all men being formed of the same clay, there should be no distinction or subordination among them" (2:97–99). The savages scorn the religious faith of the Europeans, holding that "writings from the past are false, made up or changed, since Histories of our own day have met with the same fate" (2:118). The history of Foigny's Australians was, similarly, their weak point, filled as it was with "fabulous" events and "prodigies."[84] The monarchy had encouraged the mandarins in their use of a scientific representation that replaced an obsolete history needed neither by the protector nor by the protégés. Subversive voyagers, reacting especially against colonization in the name of conversion, tend to identify history and the Christian religion, and to replace both with "natural reason."

It seems odd that the same Lahontan who discovered in the native Americans the equality of all human beings should have owned slaves. Yet he refers quite ingenuously to the ones he kept in North America (1:158). And the same man who said, "It seems to me that you have to be blind not to see that private property is the single source of all disorders troubling European society" (2:Preface to *Dialogues*) spent a good part of his life trying to recover his father's property. The contradiction between his interests as a disaffected noble, which coincided paradoxically with some of the interests of the emerging bourgeoisie, and the myth that he helped to promulgate are no longer the same contradictions as those that inform the real voyage. Whether or not they perceived it, the mandarins were divided between the interests of their emerging class and those of the monarchy that protected them. Lahontan, who was no longer tied to the monarchy's interests, was nonetheless a Frenchman who wanted to believe that his self-interest as a European was in the interest of humanity. Both bourgeois and disaffected nobles such as Lahontan chafed at a monarchy that placed constraints on their exploitation of economic resources. Lahontan's *Nouveaux voyages* are something of an anomaly. They give us a rare opportunity to see both sides of the contradiction. In his voyages, Lahontan specified his individual self-interest as he universalized the aspirations of the rising class

84. Gabriel de Foigny, *Les Avantures de Jacques Sadeur dans la decouverte et le voiage de la terre australe. Contenant les coûtumes et les moeurs des australiens, leur religion, leurs exercices, leurs études, leurs guerres; les animaux particuliers a ce païs, et toutes les raretez curieuses qui s'y trouvent* (Paris, 1692), pp. 224–26 (Lachèvre, *Successseurs de Cyrano de Bergerac* p. 132, variants *a* and *f*).

in the myth of a utopian society where *liberté, égalité,* and *fraternité* would be valid for everyone.[85]

Like the court historiographers and the mandarins, Lahontan nonetheless used the rhetoric of impartiality to convince himself and his readers that his work was not inspired by self-interest. He claims to write without partisan feelings: "I neither flatter nor spare anyone," he declares (2:4). His variant of the plain-speaking topos has a distinctly moralistic tone. His speech is so plain, he would have us believe, that the light of a truth higher than any personal feelings everywhere shines through it. He advises his correspondent that his letters from the New World contain nothing but "truths clearer than day." "I sacrifice everything to the love of truth," he announces (2:4). At the same time, he points explicitly to his enemies—for example, the minister Pontchartrain, who was enraged by the first volume of the *Nouveaux voyages* and impervious to the author's efforts to recover his patrimony. Injecting a note of militancy into a favorite commonplace of the bourgeois *érudits,* Lahontan warns that he will "make war with my pen, since I can't do it with my sword" (2:Preface to *Dialogues*). Deprived of the hereditary rights of his class, abandoned by a monarchy indifferent to his pleas, the baron cuts a solitary figure in the wilderness. Having deserted the nation that deserted him, Lahontan felt that he had risen above all national ties. His putative publisher says of him that he writes "as if he had neither homeland nor religion" (1:Preface).

Such bitterness helps to account for the streak of anarchism in the universality of the *Nouveaux voyages.* Adario, the Indian interlocutor of Lahontan's *Dialogues,* is as eloquent in his denial of the value of civil laws (which he sees as dependent on a money economy) as he is in defense of his society's natural law. Lahontan fictionalized in Adario's society what he thought he saw in Canada: freedom from the constraints imposed by Louis XIV on France's nobility. This imagined freedom, a product of Lahontan's concrete dissatisfactions, is the basis of his identification with the Indians. "I envy the lot of the poor savage," he says, "who *leges et sceptra terit,* and I would hope to spend the rest of my life in his

---

85. My treatment of the *liberté, égalité, fraternité* message differs fundamentally from Geoffroy Atkinson's. See his *Relations de voyages du XVIIᵉ siècle, et l'évolution des idées* (Geneva, 1972), esp. pp. 181–95. Another critic has remarked that Lahontan's purpose was less to oppose natural and civil society than to defend a political ideal for civil society. See Jean Ehrard, *L'Idée de nature en France dans la première moitié du XVIIᵉ siècle* (Paris, 1963), pp. 491–92. See also pp. 747–49.

hut, so as no longer to be obliged to bow before people who sacrifice public good to private interest, who are born to enrage decent people [*les honêtes* (sic) *gens*]" (2:Preface to *Dialogues).*

Disembodied from the text in the inscription of an engraved portrait for the frontispiece to the *Nouveaux voyages,* the Latin phrase reflects a transition from the particular to the universal which unifies the real and the fictional in Lahontan's work. The portrait (fig. 36) depicts a naked Indian warrior, with the conventional fig leaf, holding a bow and arrow. Under his left foot is a code of laws, under the right a crown and a scepter. On the left-hand facing page is another engraving depicting a globe in a circular frame bordered by stars, with the legend "Orbis Patria" (fig. 37). Here Lahontan rises above his particular identification with the Canadian Indians to proclaim his identity with all humans as a citizen of the world. His Indian savage is metamorphosed into the naked warrior proclaiming his triumph over domination and unjust laws in the name of a universal liberty.

Lahontan's warrior tramples underfoot symbols of the very values originally glorified by the *ut pictura poesis* representational system. These symbols had been the voyagers' last ties to that system. It was for the crown that the mandarins brought back their precisely documented, "impartial" reports of life in faraway lands, for the crown that scientists recorded their "exact descriptions" of empirically verifiable fact. An ornament on the title page of the 1711 edition of Chardin's *Voyages* depicts Minerva surrounded by books (fig. 38). Above her a legend reads, "Libertas sine scientia Licentia est." *Scientia* is here the mediating term between a liberty that the mandarins wanted to believe they possessed and a disorder that they perhaps glimpsed on their travels. Their *scientia* was a principle of "law and order" which Lahontan's warrior rejects. Adario is illiterate. He is a naked denial that any freedom exists within the monarchy. The American native squashes the mandarins' hope that scientific work for the monarchy could have a liberating value.

And yet it did. Without the science of the mandarins, Lahontan could never have produced his *Nouveaux voyages.* His real voyage relies on the scientific and documentary apparatus perfected by the mandarins. And if Adario is illiterate, he nonetheless subscribes to the truth of empirically verifiable fact. He rejects the Christian faith because he can believe only when persuaded by the "clear, solid proof" of empirical evidence (*Dialogues,* 4). Subversive voyagers retained what they could of the objective, documentary

ET LEGES ET SCEPTRA TERIT.

36. "Et leges et sceptra terit." From [Louis-Armand de Lahontan], *Nouveaux Voyages de Mr. le Baron de Lahontan dans L'Amérique Septentrionale* (1703–4). By permission of the Houghton Library, Harvard University.

Orbis Patria.

37. "Orbis Patria." From [Louis-Armand de Lahontan], *Nouveaux Voyages de Mr. le Baron de Lahontan dans L'Amérique Septentrionale* (1703–4). By permission of the Houghton Library, Harvard University.

38. "Libertas sine scientia Licentia est." From [Sir John Chardin], *Voyages de Monsieur le Chevalier de Chardin, en Perse, et autres lieux de l'Orient* (1711). By permission of the Houghton Library, Harvard University.

scientific paraphernalia in real voyages, for they recognized it as their own. In the science developed by the mandarins was the technology of capitalism which was to liberate the bourgeoisie as a class.

The subversive voyager transformed the truth of the mandarins' scientific fact into the truth of fiction. In such fact there had been an alienation: it was fact found by the bourgeoisie for the monarchy. The truth of scientific and voyage literature was split by this division in its function. It had to be the truth of a democratizing science for the few who controlled the uses of science. The subversive voyager, in substituting the truth of fiction for the truth of fact, makes the truth fully his own. In the substitution, however, we see the identity of the same truth. Produced largely by bourgeois or by people whose interests coincided with bourgeois interests, the truth of fiction and the truth of fact have the same abstract, universal character. For the universality of a science that the subversive voyager could not use freely in his own interests he substituted the universality of a myth produced by him for his own ends.

Du Tertre's portrait of the West Indian couple was still overlain with the embellishments of the mythological portrait. His noble savages were as innocent and pure as Adam and Eve before the fall. As Adam's descendants, they also bespoke an equality of all humans before God. The missionary priest was caught in the ambiguities of scientific representation. To reproduce true American natives, he needed the trappings of the conventional portrait. To suggest the equality of all human beings, he needed the analogy furnished by the religion of France. Lahontan's portrait is a rejection of mythological representation. It projects a new metaphor: the savage as universal man, the naked warrior as universal human nature. For the abstract glorification of science, as in the Minerva on the title page of Chardin's *Voyages* or in Sébastien Le Clerc's Geometry, it substitutes the abstraction from the noble savage myth of the message *liberté, égalité, fraternité*. The subversive voyager produces both myth and message as the truth of his own fiction.

This is the point at which the subversive voyager leaves the *ut pictura poesis* system to go his own way. He abandoned an artful truth, still used by the mandarins, for a new fictional truth continuous with the scientific truth that mandarins had not yet disengaged from the old system. The subversive voyager established a fictional truth for the bourgeoisie as autonomous as its counterpart in scientific truth. The substitution of objective for rhetorical truth and its division into fictional and factual vehicles of expression announce a new representational configuration in which art and science go their separate ways yet share the features of a democratized truth.

Voyage literature, unlike *nouvelles* and secret histories, has a positive ideological content, an early expression of bourgeois consciousness. The function of *nouvelles* and secret histories was to subvert the truth of *romans* and *histoires,* but in their subversion they bore no positive ideological truth. They merely contested the value of the older genres. As parodic imitations and nothing more, they could slip as it were unnoticed into the representational system. They could "pass." Real voyages maintain an ambiguous status with respect to conventional representation. Their utopian notion of a better life elsewhere suggests a positive truth, yet this truth is undercut by their endorsement of the ancien régime and their adoption of conventional modes of representation. In the subversive voyage, negation is unified with a positive ideological truth. The subversive voyager reclaims his freedom against the monarchy, in his own interests. He proclaims the utopian myth of the bourgeoisie over against the rhetorical truth of the ancien régime. As the seemingly divergent interests of nobles and bourgeois slowly converged in opposition to a regime that they no longer needed, the *ut pictura poesis* system fell into disuse. The subversive voyager turned from the mandarins to find a new mode of expression for a new consciousness. When this consciousness acquired maturity in the eighteenth century and the subversive voyager was metamorphosed into philosophe, the interests of the bourgeoisie had begun to solidify. How short, then, was the distance from subversion to revolution!

7

Conclusion

The year 1789 is a convenient sign whose discursive function is to seal an alliance between political institutions and social reality achieved at a historical moment that we have termed revolutionary. It marks not the definitive victory of bourgeois ideology, but rather a concatenation of political conditions of possibility for the bourgeois hegemony that has prevailed to our own day. The uneven erosion and displacement of aristocratic hegemony concealed the interrelationship of seemingly disparate events. Just because the social and ideological conditions of bourgeois dominance in France had become visible by 1715, it does not follow that they "prepared" the French Revolution in a logical sequence. It does mean that these conditions were in themselves revolutionary, and that the events of 1789 form another phase in the development of a new society. Both the disintegration of the *ut pictura poesis* representational system and the storming of the Bastille were, in other words, part of the same process of revolutionary social change.

It was a process that permitted the eventual triumph of those cultural values that emerged from the debris of the old representational system: fictional realism and scientific truth. Although specializations that arose with merchant capital and early modern science and technology had the effect of severing science from art, the two new values proved to be complementary aspects of one ideological truth. Underlying both is the premise that an objective truth is attainable by any disinterested observer capable of grasping it.

In the seventeenth and eighteenth centuries, objective truth wore subversive garb. Its champions had to struggle in order to make it prevail over an aristocratic, rhetorical truth that they saw as a mystification, because it obstructed their interests. The utility of conventional representation derived from a princely glorification. Its morality was the exemplary standard set by royalty and the highborn. Its art was opaque; truth was concealed in the folds of mythology and metaphor. Its pleasure lay in the discovery of its utility, for representation acquired full meaning only with the paring away of allegorically allusive layers that concealed the core of aristocratic morality. Verisimilitude supported the particularism of a society in which politics was inseparable from the individual dynastic or familial representative. The monarch seemed a living Hercules; Hercules seemed as real as the contemporary figure embodying him. The original coherence of the *ut pictura poesis* system was formed of the unity of truth and its semblance.

When artists, writers, and intellectuals began to pry apart truth and semblance, they loosened the consistency of the *ut pictura poesis* system. The confrontation between a new moneyed elite and a still dominant landowning nobility introduced a negative mode into conventional representation. Rhetorical truth was exposed as mere semblance, or as the negation of what it seemed. Apollo was dethroned from his palace at Versailles and made to reside among ordinary mortals. The challenge was to break through the opacity of representation, to reduce the mediations of artistic imitation to a transparently immediate signification. The aim was to represent the world not as it seemed to be but as it was.

Implicit in this project was the construction of a new, positive truth. For the hierarchy of aristocratic privilege bourgeois ideology substituted the equality of all human beings in their fundamentally identical nature, regulated by laws as objective and discoverable as those that govern the natural world and the physical universe. With the obsolescence of princely dominance, history as a "mirror of princes" and a fiction that imitated this history in romance were no longer functional. The mirror of princes gave way to a mirror of the human nature that princes shared with their subjects. For a history verifiable only by consent of the rulers, if at all, the new elite substituted a science verifiable by empirical investigation. Fiction acquired the documentary character of a travel report; the portrait relinquished mythological costume for the transparency of scientific illustration.

A new mode of cultural production based on individual gain

rather than on the dependency of patronage broke down conventional genres and ultimately established forms appropriate to the new ideology. When fiction and fact were separated from each other and reorganized into autonomous domains of a verifiable, objective truth, novels, histories, and science were relocated to the respective spheres that they now occupy. When the *nouvelle* ceased to provide the "news" that was censored by official history, it asserted its integrity as a novel with a realism proper to it alone. History freed of its celebratory function reappeared as an independent genre when the research once consigned to the special purview of *érudits* was reunified with a broadly humanistic inquiry into the past, and both were placed under the jurisdiction of fact. Under the impetus of mercantilism and colonialism during the ancien régime, science refined and pursued it own specializations. The mythological and metaphorical portrait at the center of conventional representation no longer served to unite all genres in an organic system of correspondences between past and present. Revolutionary France wanted to turn its back on the past, confident in its ability to progress toward a better future.

But social change is as bound to the past as it is committed to the future. Just as the assertion that a divinely appointed king is father to his people served the needs of the ruling aristocracy, so the assertion that all human beings share an identical nature came to serve the needs of a bourgeoisie that could mask its exploitation of others behind the promise of political equality. The scientific heritage of the ancien régime came to be used by a dominant bourgeoisie that wanted to develop and preserve its power with a license granted to the disinterested pursuit of scientific truth. French classicism's mirror of human nature survived in the mirror that the realistic novel claimed to hold up to all of society, while abstracting the bourgeois observer from its scene. Bourgeois ideology preserved what it needed from the past for the construction of its future dominance.

If we now look back with a critical eye to the prehistory of that dominance, it is because we are witnessing the moment of its decay. With today's ubiquitous challenge to bourgeois society, its ideology and culture have come under a vigorous critical scrutiny. We are living a much later crisis in the continuous dialectical process of social and cultural change that established the conditions of bourgeois hegemony several centuries ago. An understanding of the origins and early development of this hegemony may help us to understand its eventual demise.

Bibliography

The extensive theoretical literature on ideology and cultural and social change, the vast amount of secondary materials on seventeenth-century France, and the wealth of primary sources make it impractical to include all works consulted in the following list. The interested reader is advised to consult specialized bibliographies in the various fields covered by the subject of this book.

PRIMARY MATERIAL

Académie Royale des Sciences (Paris). *Mémoires. Depuis 1666 jusqu'à 1699.* Vol. 8. Paris: Compagnie des Libraires, 1730.

Amyot, Jacques. *Les Vies des hommes illustres grecs et romains. Comparees l'une avec l'autre par Plutarque de Chaeronee.* Paris: Abel l'Angelier, 1584.

Barthélemy, Edouard de, ed. *Galerie des portraits de Mademoiselle de Montpensier.* Paris: Didier, 1860.

————, ed. *Gazette de la Régence* (January 1715–June 1718). Paris: Charpentier, 1887.

[————, ed.] *Nouvelles de la cour et de la ville.* Paris: Edouard Rouveyre, 1879.

Bayle, Pierre. *Dictionnaire historique et critique.* 16 vols. Paris: Desoer, 1820–[24].

[————.] *Nouvelles de la République des Lettres* (October 1684, September 1686).

————. *Nouvelles lettres de l'autheur de la Critique generale de l'Histoire du Calvinisme.* In *Oeuvres diverses,* vol. 2. The Hague: P. Husson, T. Johnson, 1727.

[Bedacier, Catherine.] "Les Amours du pape Gregoire VII et de la comtesse Mathilde." In *Histoire des amours de Gregoire VII, du cardinal de Richelieu, de la princesse de Condé, et de la marquise d'Urfé*. Cologne: Pierre Le Jeune, 1700.

Bellegarde, abbé Morvan de. *Lettres curieuses de littérature et de morale*. The Hague: Adrian Moetjens, 1702.

[Bernier, François.] *Histoire de la dernière revolution des estats du Grand Mogol*. 3 vols. bound in 2. [N.p.], 1671.

[Bertaut, François.] *Journal du voyage d'Espagne*. Paris: Denis Thierry, 1669.

Bie, Jacques de. *Les Vrais portraits des rois de France: Tirez de ce qui nous reste de leurs monumens, sceaux, médailles ou autres effigies, conservées dans les plus rares et plus curieux cabinets du royaume*. Paris: chez l'Autheur . . . and au Palais, chez Pierre Rocolet . . . , 1634.

Boileau-Despréaux, Nicolas. "Dialogue des héros de roman." In *Oeuvres complètes*. Paris: Gallimard, 1966.

Bussy, Roger de Rabutin, comte de. *Correspondance*. Ed. Ludovic Lalanne. 6 vols. New ed. Paris: Charpentier, 1858–59.

———. *Histoire amoureuse des Gaules*. Ed. Georges Mongrédien. 2 vols. Paris: Garnier, 1930.

———. *Histoire amoureuse des Gaules*. Ed. Francis Cleirens. Paris [Club du meilleur livre, 1961].

[——— and Courtilz, Gatien, sieur de Sandras.] *La France galante, ou Histoires amoureuses de la cour*. Cologne: Pierre Marteau, 1689.

[Caumont de la Force, Charlotte Rose de.] *Anecdote galante, ou Histoire secrette de Catherine de Bourbon, duchesse de Bar, et soeur de Henry le Grand. Avec les intrigues de la cour durant les regnes de Henry III et de Henry IV*. Nancy, 1703.

Chapelain, Jean. *Lettres*. Ed. Philippe Tamizey de Larroque. 2 vols. Paris: Imprimerie Nationale, 1880–83.

Chardin, [Sir John]. *Voyages en Perse, et autres lieux de l'Orient*. 3 vols. Amsterdam: Jean Louis de Lorme, 1711.

[Charnes, abbé de.] *Conversations sur la Princesse de Clèves*. Paris: Claude Barbin, 1679.

Clark, James Cooper, ed. *Codex Mendoza: The Mexican Manuscript, Known as the Collection of Mendoza and Preserved in the Bodleian Library, Oxford*. 3 vols. London: Waterlow, 1938.

Claude, Isaac. *Les Amours de Madame d'Elbeuf: Nouvelle historique*. Amsterdam: Westein & Smith, 1739.

Claudin, Anatole, ed. *Diverses pièces curieuses et extraordinaires*. 3 vols. Lyon: Perrin & Martinet, 1875.

Colbert, Jean-Baptiste. *Lettres, instructions et mémoires*. Ed. Pierre Clément. Vol. 5. Paris: Imprimerie Impériale, 1868.

Corneille, Thomas. *Le Berger extravagant*. Ed. Francis Bar. Geneva: Droz, 1960.

[Courtilz, Gatien de, sieur de Sandras.] *Les Conquestes amoureuses du grand Alcandre dans les Pays-Bas. Avec les intrigues de sa cour*. Cologne: Pierre Bernard, 1684.

[———.] *Le Grand Alcandre frustré ou Les derniers efforts de l'amour et de la vertu*. Cologne: Pierre Marteau, 1696. Reprint ed. P. L. Jacob [Paul Lacroix]. San Remo: J. Gay, 1874.

Daniel, père Gabriel, *Histoire de France*. 17 vols. New ed. Paris: Libraires Associés, 1755–57.

Descartes, René. *Discours de la méthode*. Ed. Etienne Gilson. Paris: J. Vrin, 1966.

Dodart, [Denis]. *Mémoires pour servir à l'histoire des plantes*. Paris: Imprimerie Royale, 1676.

[Donneau de Vizé, Jean.] *Nouvelles nouvelles*. 3 vols. Paris: Pierre Bienfaict, 1663.

Du Plaisir. *Sentiments sur les lettres et sur l'histoire avec des scrupules sur le style*. Ed. Philippe Hourcade. Geneva: Droz, 1975.

Dupleix, Scipion. *Histoire de Louis le Juste, XIII du nom, roy de France et de Navarre*. Paris: Claude Sonnius, 1635.

Du Tertre, Jean Baptiste. *Histoire générale des Antilles*. 3 vols. Paris: Thomas Jolly, 1667–71.

[Félibien, André.] *Conférences de l'Académie Royale de Peinture et de Sculpture pendant l'année 1667*. Paris: Frederic Leonard, 1669.

[Foigny, Gabriel de.] *La Terre Australe connue, c'est-à-dire la description de ce pays inconnu jusqu'ici, de ses moeurs et de ses coûtumes, par M. Sadeur, avec les avantures qui le conduisirent en ce Continent et les particularitez du séjour qu'il y fit durant trente-cinq ans et plus, et de son retour . . .* Vannes: Jaques Verneuil, 1676. In Frédéric Lachèvre, *Les Successeurs de Cyrano de Bergerac*. Paris: Honoré Champion, 1922.

————. *Les Avantures de Jacques Sadeur dans la decouverte et le voiage de la terre australe. Contenant les coûtumes et les moeurs des Australiens, leur religion, leurs exercices, leurs études, leurs guerres; les animaux particuliers à ce païs, et toutes les raretez curieuses qui s'y trouvent*. Paris: Claude Barbin, 1692.

Furetière, Antoine. *Dictionnaire universel*. 3 vols. The Hague: Arnout & Reinier Leers, 1690, 1701.

————. *Le Roman bourgeois*. Ed. Georges Mongrédien. Paris: Club du Meilleur Livre, 1955(?).

[Gomberville], Marin le Roy [de]. *Discours des vertus et des vices de l'histoire, et de la manière de la bien escrire*. Paris: Toussainct Du Bray, 1620.

Gournay, Marie de Jars de. *L'Ombre*. Paris: Jean Libert, 1626.

Huet, [Pierre Daniel]. *Traité de l'origine des Romans*. In [La Fayette, Marie Madeleine (Pioche de La Vergne), comtesse de], *Zayde: Histoire espagnole*. Paris: Claude Barbin, 1670.

La Bruyère, Jean de. *Oeuvres complètes*. Ed. Julien Benda. Paris: Gallimard, 1951.

La Calprenède, Gautier de Costes de. *Faramond, ou L'Histoire de France*. 12 vols. Paris: Antoine de Sommaville, 1664–70.

La Fayette, Marie Madeleine (Pioche de La Vergne), comtesse de. *Lettres au chevalier de Lescheraine*. Edited by Jean de Bazin. Paris: Nizet, 1970.

————. *Lettres à Gilles Ménage*. Ed. Harry Ashton. Liverpool: University Press of Liverpool, 1924.

————. *La Princesse de Clèves*. In *Romans et nouvelles*, ed. Emile Magne. Paris: Garnier, 1961.

Lahontan, Louis-Armand de. *Nouveaux voyages dans L'Amérique Septentrionale*. 2 vols. The Hague: Honoré, 1703–4.

La Mothe le Vayer, François de. *Discours de l'histoire*. Paris: Jean Camusat, 1638.

————. "Du peu de certitude qu'il y a dans l'histoire." In *Oeuvres*. New ed. Dresden: Michel Groell, 1757.

La Serre, Jean Puget de. *Le Portrait de la reyne*. Paris: Pierre Targa, 1644.

————. *Le Portrait de Scipion l'Africain: ou l'image de la gloire et de la vertu, représentée au naturel dans celle de Monseigneur le cardinal, duc de Richelieu*. Bordeaux: Guillaume Millanges, 1641.

Le Clerc, Sébastien. *Pratique de la géométrie, sur le papier et sur le terrain*. Paris: Thomas Jolly, 1669.

Le Moyne, père Pierre. *De l'histoire*. Paris: Louis Billaine, 1670.

[Lenglet-Dufresnoy, Nicolas.] *De l'usage des romans, où l'on fait voir leur utilité et leurs differens caracteres: Avec une bibliothèque des romans, accompagnée de remarques critiques sur leur choix et leurs editions*. 2 vols. Amsterdam: Veuve de Poil Ras, 1734.

Lusinge, René de. *La Manière de lire l'histoire*. Paris: Toussainct Du Bray, 1614.

Matthieu, Pierre. *Histoire de France*. Paris: I. Metayer, 1609(?).

Médailles sur les principaux evenements du regne de Louis le Grand, avec des explications historiques. Paris: Imprimerie Royale, 1702.

Mercure galant, Le. May 1678; July 1678 (special issue).

Monconys, Balthasar de. *Journal des voyages*. 3 vols. Lyon: Horace Boissat & George Remeus, 1665–66.

Montpensier, Anne Marie Louise d'Orléans, duchesse de. *Divers portraits*. In *Mémoires*, vol. 8. Maestricht: Dufour & Roux, 1776.

————. *Mémoires*. Ed. A. Chéruel. 4 vols. Paris: Charpentier, 1858–68.

Nicéron, père Jean Pierre. *Mémoires pour servir à l'histoire des hommes illustres*. Vol. 6. Paris: Briasson, 1728.

"Nouvelles burlesques portées par le duc de Chastillon à l'Empereur des Tenebres, aux affreuses cavernes de sa domination." N.p., 1649. Houghton Library Collection, Harvard University.

Pasquier, Estienne. *Choix de lettres*. Ed. D. Thickett. Geneva: Droz, 1956.

Perrault, Charles. *Paralelle* [sic] *des anciens et des modernes; en ce qui regarde les arts et les sciences. Dialogues*. Paris: Jean Baptiste Coignard, 1688.

[Perrault, Claude.] *Mémoires pour servir à l'histoire naturelle des animaux*. 2 vols. bound in 1. Paris: Imprimerie Royale, 1671–76.

"Portrait (Peinture)." In *Encyclopédie, ou Dictionnaire raisonné des sciences, des arts, et des métiers*, vol. 13. Neuchâtel: Samuel Faulche, 1765. Facs. ed. Stuttgart: Friedrich Fromman, 1966.

Purchas, Samuel. *Purchas, His Pilgrimes*. Vol. 3. London: William Stansby–Henrie Fetherstone, 1625.

Rapin, père René. *Instructions pour l'histoire*. Paris: Sébastien Mabre Cramoisy, 1677.

Renaudot, Théophraste. *Recueil des Gazettes de l'année 1631*. [*Gazette de France*.] [Paris]: Bureau d'Adresse, 1632.

Retz, Jean François Paul de Gondi, cardinal de. *Mémoires*. Ed. Maurice Allem and Edith Thomas. Paris: Gallimard, 1956.

Saint-Réal, abbé César Vichard de. "De l'usage de l'histoire." In *Oeuvres*. New ed. Amsterdam: François L'Honoré, 1740.

Scudéry, [Madeleine de]. *Almahide, ou L'Esclave reine*. Paris: Augustin Courbé, 1660.

————. *Artamène ou le Grand Cyrus*. 10 vols. Paris: Augustin Courbé, 1654.

————. *Clélie.* 5 vols. in 15. Paris: Augustin Courbé, 1656–62.

————. *Ibrahim, ou L'Illustre Bassa.* Paris: Antoine de Sommaville, 1641.

Segrais, Jean Regnault de. *Les Nouvelles françoises, ou les divertissemens de la princesse Aurélie.* 2 vols. The Hague: Pierre Paupie, 1741.

Sévigné, Marie [de Rabutin Chantal], marquise de. *Lettres.* Ed. M. Monmerqué. 14 vols. Paris: L. Hachette, 1862–68.

Sorbière, [Samuel]. *Relation d'un voyage en Angleterre, où sont touchées plusieurs choses, qui regardent l'estat des sciences, et de la religion, et autres matières curieuses.* Cologne: Pierre Michel, 1667.

Sorel, Charles. *Le Berger extravagant.* Paris: Toussainct Du Bray, 1627–28. Facs. ed. 3 vols. bound in 1. Geneva: Slatkine Reprints, 1972.

————. *Le Berger extravagant.* 3 vols. Rouen: Jean Osmont, 1646.

————. *La Bibliothèque françoise.* Paris: Compagnie des Libraires du Palais, 1664; 2d ed. 1667.

[————.] *De la connoissance des bons livres.* Paris: Andre Pralard, 1671.

————. *Histoire de la monarchie française.* Paris: Louys Boulanger, 1632.

[————.] *Le Tombeau des romans.* Paris: Claude Morlot, 1626.

[Tavernier, Jean Baptiste.] *Les Six voyages de Jean Baptiste Tavernier, ecuyer baron d'Aubonne, qu'il a fait en Turquie, en Perse, et aux Indes . . .* 2 vols. Paris: Clouzier & Barbin, 1676–77.

Tessereau, Abraham. *Histoire chronologique de la Grande Chancelerie de France.* Paris: Pierre le Petit, 1676.

Thévenot, Melchisédech. *Relations de divers voyages qui n'ont point esté publiées; ou qui ont esté traduites d'Hacluyt; de Purchas et d'autres voyageurs anglois, hollandois, portugais, allemands, espagnols; et de quelques persans, arabes et autres auteurs orientaux.* Vols. 1 and 2. Paris: Sébastien Cramoisy & Sébastien Mabre-Cramoisy, 1664–66.

————. *Relations de divers voyages curieux . . .* 2 vols. Paris: Thomas Moette, 1696.

Thévet, André. *La Cosmographie universelle.* 2 vols. Paris: Pierre L'Huillier, 1575.

————. *Les Vrais pourtraits et vies des hommes illustres grecz, latins et payens . . .* Paris: Veuve I. Keruert & Guillaume Chaudière, 1584.

Urfé, Honoré d'. *L'Astrée.* Ed. Hugues Vaganay. 5 vols. Lyon: Pierre Masson, 1925–28.

[Vairasse, Denis.] *Histoire des Sevarambes, peuples qui habitent une partie du troisiéme continent, communément appellé la Terre Australe. Contenant une relation du gouvernement, des moeurs, de la religion, du langage de cette nation, inconnuë jusques à present aux peuples de l'Europe.* 2 vols. Amsterdam: Estienne Roger, 1702.

Valdor, Jean. *Les Triomphes de Louis le Iuste, XIII du nom, roy de France et de Navarre.* Paris: Imprimerie Royale, 1649.

[Valincour, Jean-Baptiste Du Trousset de.] *Lettres à Madame la Marquise *** sur le sujet de La Princesse de Clèves.* Paris: Sébastien Mabre-Cramoisy, 1678. Facs. ed. Tours: Université de Tours, 1972.

Varillas, Antoine. *Les Anecdotes de Florence, ou L'Histoire secrète de la maison de Médicis.* The Hague: Arnout Leers, 1685.

Voltaire [François-Marie Arouet.] *Micromégas.* In *Oeuvres complètes,* ed. Louis Moland, vol. 21. Paris: Garnier, 1877–85.

Vulson, Marc de, sieur de La Colombière. *Les Portraits des hommes illustres françois qui sont peints dans la gallerie du palais Cardinal de Richelieu.* Paris: Henry Sara, 1650.

SECONDARY MATERIAL

Adam, Antoine. *Histoire de la littérature française aux XVIIe siècle.* 5 vols. Paris: Del Duca, 1958–62.
Althusser, Louis. *For Marx.* Trans. Ben Brewster. New York: Vintage Books, 1970.
Anderson, Perry. *Lineages of the Absolutist State.* London: New Left Books, 1974.
Apostolidès, Jean-Marie. *Le Roi-machine; Spectacle et politique au temps de Louis XIV.* Paris: Minuit, 1981.
Ariès, Philippe. *Le Temps de l'histoire.* Monaco: Du Rocher, 1954.
Atkinson, Geoffroy. *The Extraordinary Voyage in French Literature before 1700.* New York: Columbia University Press, 1920.
———. *Relations de Voyages du XVIIe siècle, et l'évolution des idées.* Paris, 1924. Reprint ed. Geneva: Slatkine Reprints, 1972.
Backer, Dorothy Anne Liot. *Precious Women.* New York: Basic Books, 1974.
Bardon, Françoise. "Fonctionnement d'un portrait mythologique: La Grande Mademoiselle en Minerve par Pierre Bourguignon." *Colóquio* 26, 2d ser. (February 1976):4–17.
———. *Le Portrait mythologique à la cour de France sous Henri IV et Louis XIII: Mythologie et politique.* Paris: A & J. Picard, 1974.
Bates, Blanchard W. *Literary Portraiture in the Historical Narrative of the French Renaissance.* New York: G. E. Stechert, 1945.
Bellanger, Claude, Jacques Godechot, Pierre Guiral, and Fernand Terrou. *Histoire générale de la presse française.* Vol. 1. Paris: Presses Universitaires de France, 1964.
Beugnot, Bernard. "De quelques lieux rhétoriques du discours scientifique classique." *Revue de synthèse* 101–2, 3d ser. (January–June 1981):5–25.
Bilezikian, Monique A. "La Triple écriture dans les *Mémoires* du Cardinal de Retz." *Symposium* 34 (Summer 1980):91–106.
Bitton, Davis. *The French Nobility in Crisis, 1560–1640.* Stanford, Calif.: Stanford University Press, 1969.
Bollème, Geneviève. *Les Almanachs populaires aux XVIIe et XVIIIe siècles: Essai d'histoire sociale.* Paris: Mouton, 1969.
Braudel, Fernand, and Ernest Labrousse, eds. *Histoire économique et sociale de la France.* Vol. 2. Paris: Presses Universitaires de France, 1970.
Brody, Jules. "*La Princesse de Clèves* and the Myth of Courtly Love." *University of Toronto Quarterly* 38 (January 1969):105–35.
———. "Saint-Simon, peintre de la vie en déclin." *Marseille,* no. 109 (2d trimester, 1977), pp. 185–92
Brown, Harcourt. *Scientific Organizations in Seventeenth-Century France.* Baltimore: Williams & Wilkins, 1934.
Brugmans, Henri-L. *Le Séjour de Christian Huygens à Paris et ses relations avec les milieux scientifiques français.* Paris: Pierre André, 1935.

Buci-Glucksmann, Christine. *Gramsci and the State.* Trans. David Fernbach. London: Lawrence & Wishart, 1980.

Camus, Armand Gaston. *Mémoire sur la collection des grands et petits voyages* [de Théodore de Bry], *et sur la collection des voyages de Melchisédech Thévenot.* Paris: Baudoin, 1802.

Canivet, Diane. *L'Illustration de la poésie et du roman français au XVIIe siècle.* Paris: Presses Universitaires de France, 1957.

Chamard, H., and G. Rudler. "La Couleur historique dans *La Princesse de Clèves.*" *Revue du seizième siècle* 5 (1917–18):1–20.

——— and ———. "L'Histoire et la fiction dans *La Princesse de Clèves.*" *Revue du seizième siècle* 5 (1917–18):231–43.

——— and ———. "Les Sources historiques de *La Princesse de Clèves.*" *Revue du seizième siècle* 2 (1914):92–131.

Chinard, Gilbert. *L'Amérique et le rêve exotique dans la littérature française au XVIIe et XVIIIe siècle.* Paris: Droz, 1934.

———. Introduction to *Dialogues curieux entre l'auteur et un sauvage de bon sens qui a voyagé et Mémoires de l'Amérique septentrionale,* by Louis-Armand de Lahontan. Ed. Gilbert Chinard. Baltimore: Johns Hopkins Press, 1931.

Chupeau, Jacques. "Les Récits de voyages aux lisières du roman." *Revue d'histoire littéraire de la France* 77 (May–August 1977):536–53.

Church, William F. *Richelieu and Reason of State.* Princeton, N.J.: Princeton University Press, 1972.

———. "France." In *National Consciousness, History, and Political Culture in Early Modern Europe,* ed. Orest Ranum. Baltimore: Johns Hopkins University Press, 1975.

Clark, Sir George N. *The Seventeenth Century.* Oxford: Oxford University Press, 1969.

Cole, Charles Woolsey. *Colbert and a Century of French Mercantilism.* 2 vols. Hamden, Conn.: Archon Books, 1964.

Cole, Francis Joseph. *A History of Comparative Anatomy from Aristotle to the Eighteenth Century.* London: Macmillan, 1944.

Cousin, Victor. *La Société française au XVIIe siècle, d'après "Le Grand Cyrus" de Mlle de Scudéry.* 2 vols. Paris: Didier, 1858.

Couton, Georges. "Effort publicitaire et organisation de la recherche: Les gratifications aux gens de lettres sous Louis XIV." *Le XVIIe siècle et la recherche.* Actes du 2eme Colloque de Marseille (January 1976), pp. 41–55. Centre Méridional de Rencontres sur le XVIIe Siècle.

Crozet, René. *La Vie artistique en France au XVIIe siècle.* Paris: Presses Universitaires de France, 1954.

Culler, Jonathan. *Structuralist Poetics: Structuralism, Linguistics, and the Study of Literature.* Ithaca: Cornell University Press, 1975.

Darnton, Robert. *The Literary Underground of the Old Regime.* Cambridge: Harvard University Press, 1982.

Davies, Donald W. *The World of the Elseviers, 1580–1712.* The Hague: Martinus Nijhoff, 1954.

Davis, Lennard J. "A Social History of Fact and Fiction: Authorial Disavowal in the Early English Novel." In *Literature and Society,* ed. Edward W. Said, pp. 120–48. Selected Papers from the English Institute, 1978, n.s. no. 3. Baltimore: Johns Hopkins University Press, 1980.

Davis, Natalie Z. "Ghosts, Kin, and Progeny: Some Features of Family Life in Early Modern France." *Daedalus* 106 (Spring 1977):87–114.

Delavaud, L. *Quelques Collaborateurs de Richelieu: Rapports et notices sur l'édition des "Mémoires" du Cardinal de Richelieu*, ed. Jules Lair and the Baron de Courcel. Vol. 2. Paris: Renouard, 1907–14.

Delhez-Sarlet, Claudette. "*La Princesse de Clèves*: Roman ou nouvelle?" *Romanische Forschungen* 80 (1968):53–85, 220–38.

Deloffre, Frédéric. *La Nouvelle en France à l'âge classique*. Paris: Didier, 1968.

Demoris, René. "Le Corps royal et l'imaginaire au XVIIᵉ siècle: *Le Portrait du Roy* par Félibien." *Revue des sciences humaines* 172 (December 1978):9–30.

———. *Le Roman à la première personne*. Paris: A. Colin, 1975.

Di Corcia, Joseph. "*Bourg, Bourgeois, Bourgeois de Paris* from the Eleventh to the Eighteenth Century." *Journal of Modern History* 50 (June 1978): 207–33.

Dijkstra, Sandra. "La Grande Mademoiselle and the Written Portrait: Feminine Narcissism, Aristocratic Pride, or Literary Innovation?" *Pacific Coast Philology* 13 (October 1978):19–28.

Dimier, Louis. *Histoire de la peinture française du retour de Vouet à la mort de Lebrun (1627 à 1690)*. 2 vols. Paris: Librairie Nationale d'Art et d'Histoire, 1926–27.

Dowley, Francis H. "French Portraits of Ladies as Minerva." *Gazette des beaux-arts* 45 (May–June 1955):261–86.

Duccini, Hélène. "Regard sur la littérature pamphlétaire en France au XVIIᵉ siècle." *Revue historique* 528 (October–December 1978): 313–37.

Duchet, Michèle. *Anthropologie et histoire au siècle des lumières: Buffon, Voltaire, Helvétius, Diderot*. Paris: Maspero, 1971.

Dulong, Gustave. *L'Abbé de Saint-Réal: Etude sur les rapports de l'histoire et du roman au XVIIᵉ siècle*. Paris: Champion, 1921.

Duportal, Jeanne. *Etude sur les livres à figures édités en France de 1601 à 1660*. Paris: Champion, 1914.

Eagleton, Terry. *Criticism and Ideology*. London: Verso, 1978.

Ehrard, Jean. *L'Idée de nature en France dans la première moitié du XVIIᵉ siècle*. 2 vols. Paris: S.E.V.P.E.N., 1963.

Eisenstein, Elizabeth L. *The Printing Press as an Agent of Change*. Cambridge: Cambridge University Press, 1979.

Elbenne, Menjot d'. *Mme de la Sablière*. Paris: Plon, 1923.

Elias, Norbert. *The Civilizing Process: The History of Manners*. Trans. Edmund Jephcott. New York: Urizen Books, 1978.

Escarpit, Robert. "La Définition du terme 'littérature.' " In *Le Littéraire et le social*, ed. Robert Escarpit. Paris: Flammarion, 1970.

Evans, Wilfred H. *L'Historien Mézeray et la conception de l'histoire en France au XVIIᵉ siècle*. Paris: J. Gamber, 1930.

Ferrier-Caverivière, Nicole. *L'Image de Louis XIV dans la littérature française de 1660 à 1715*. Paris: Presses Universitaires de France, 1981.

Foucault, Michel. *The Order of Things*. New York: Vintage, 1973.

Fournel, Victor. *Les Contemporains de Molière*. Paris, 1863–75. Reprint ed. 3 vols. Geneva: Slatkine Reprints, 1967.

Francillon, Roger. "Fiction et réalité dans le roman français de la fin du XVIIe siècle." *Saggi e ricerche di letteratura francese* n.s. 17 (1978):99–130.

Frye, Northrop. *Anatomy of Criticism*. Princeton, N.J.: Princeton University Press, 1973.

Fumaroli, Marc. "Les Mémoires du XVIIe siècle au carrefour des genres en prose." *XVIIe Siècle* 94–95 (1971):7–37.

Funck-Brentano, Frantz, with Paul d'Estrée. *Figaro et ses devanciers*. Paris: Hachette, 1909.

——— with ———. *Les Nouvellistes*. Paris: Hachette, 1905.

Gebelin, François. *L'Epoque Henri IV et Louis XIII*. Paris: Presses Universitaires de France, 1969.

Genette, Gérard. *Figures*, vol. 2. Paris: Seuil, 1969.

George, Albert J. "The Genesis of the Académie des Sciences." *Annals of Science* 3 (October 1938):372–401.

———. "A Seventeenth-Century Amateur of Science: Jean Chapelain." *Annals of Science* 3 (April 1938):217–36.

Gérard-Gailly, Emile. *Bussy-Rabutin: Sa vie, ses oeuvres et ses amies*. Paris: Champion, 1909.

Godenne, René. "L'Association 'Nouvelle-petit roman' entre 1650 et 1750." *Cahiers de l'Association Internationale des Etudes Françaises* 18 (March 1966):67–78, 249–53.

———. *Histoire de la nouvelle française aux XVIIe et XVIIIe siècles*. Geneva: Droz, 1970.

Goldmann, Lucien. *The Hidden God*. Trans. Philip Thody. London: Routledge & Kegan Paul, 1964.

———. *Marxisme et sciences humaines*. Paris: Gallimard, 1970.

Goubert, Pierre. *L'Ancien Régime*. Vol. 1 Paris: Armand Colin, 1969.

Gramsci, Antonio. *Selections from the Prison Notebooks*. Ed. and trans. Quintin Hoare and Geoffrey Nowell Smith. New York: International Publishers, 1971.

Grand-Mesnil, Marie-Noële. *Mazarin, La Fronde et la presse, 1647–1649*. Paris: Armand Colin, 1967.

Guiffrey, Jules. *Comptes des bâtiments du roi sous le règne de Louis XIV*. 5 vols. Paris: Imprimerie Nationale, 1881–1901.

Guilloton, Vincent. "Autour de la *Relation* du voyage de Samuel Sorbière en Angleterre." *Smith College Studies in Modern Languages* 11 (July 1930):1–29.

Hahn, Roger. *The Anatomy of a Scientific Institution: The Paris Academy of Sciences, 1666–1803*. Berkeley: University of California Press, 1971.

Harth, Erica. "Classical Disproportion: La Bruyère's *Caractères*." *L'Esprit Créateur* 15 (Spring–Summer 1975):189–210.

———. "The Ideological Value of the Portrait in Seventeenth-Century France." *L'Esprit Créateur* 21 (Fall 1981):15–25.

Hatin, Eugène. *Histoire politique et littéraire de la presse en France*. Paris: Poulet Malassis et de Broise, 1859.

Hauser, Arnold. *The Social History of Art*. 4 vols. New York: Vintage, [1961–62?].

Hilton, Rodney, ed. *The Transition from Feudalism to Capitalism*. London: New Left Books, 1976.

Hipp, Marie-Thérèse. *Mythes et réalités: Enquête sur le roman et les mémoires.* Paris: Klincksieck, 1976.

Hirsch, Marianne. "A Mother's Discourse: Incorporation and Repetition in *La Princesse de Clèves.*" *Yale French Studies* 62 (Fall 1981):67–87.

Hirschfield, John M. *The Académie Royale des Sciences (1666–1683).* New York: Arno Press, 1981.

Hobsbawm, Eric J. "The General Crisis of the European Economy in the Seventeenth Century." *Past and Present* 5 (May 1954):33–53; (November 1954):44–65.

Howard, William G. "Ut Pictura Poesis." *PMLA* 24, n.s. 17 (1909):40–123.

Huppert, Georges. *Les Bourgeois Gentilshommes.* Chicago: University of Chicago Press, 1977.

———. *The Idea of Perfect History.* Urbana: University of Illinois Press, 1970.

Jacquiot, Josèphe. "La Littérature et les médailles." *Cahiers de l'Association Internationale des Etudes Française* 24 (May 1972):201–13.

Jameson, Fredric. *The Political Unconscious: Narrative as a Socially Symbolic Act.* Ithaca: Cornell University Press, 1981.

Jammes, André. "Louis XIV, sa Bibliothèque, et le Cabinet du Roi." *The Library* 20, 5th ser. (March 1965):1–12.

Janmart de Brouillant, Léonce. *La Liberté de la presse en France aux XVII͏ᵉ et XVIII͏ᵉ siècles: Histoire de Pierre du Marteau, Imprimeur à Cologne.* Paris: Maison Quantin, 1888.

Jombert, Charles-Antoine. *Catalogue raisonné de l'oeuvre de Sébastien Le Clerc.* 2 vols. Paris: Chez l'Auteur, Libraire du Roi, 1774.

Kelley, Donald R. *Foundations of Modern Historical Scholarship.* New York: Columbia University Press, 1970.

Klaits, Joseph. *Printed Propaganda under Louis XIV: Absolute Monarchy and Public Opinion.* Princeton, N.J.: Princeton University Press, 1976.

Kossmann, Ernst H. *La Fronde.* Leiden: Leiden University Press, 1954.

Kuhn, Thomas S. *The Structure of Scientific Revolutions.* 2d ed. Chicago: University of Chicago Press, 1970.

Laugaa, Maurice. *Lectures de Mme de La Fayette.* Paris: Armand Colin, 1971.

Lee, Rensselaer W. "Ut Pictura Poesis: The Humanistic Theory of Painting." *Art Bulletin* 12 (December 1940):197–269.

Lever, Maurice. *La Fiction narrative en prose au XVII͏ᵉ siècle.* Paris: Centre Nationale de la Recherche Scientifique, 1976.

Lombard, Jean. *Courtilz de Sandras et la crise du roman à la fin du grand siècle.* Paris: Presses Universitaires de France, 1980.

Lorris, Pierre-Georges. *La Fronde.* Paris: Albin Michel, 1961.

Lougee, Carolyn C. *Le Paradis des Femmes: Women, Salons, and Social Stratification in Seventeenth-Century France.* Princeton, N.J.: Princeton University Press, 1976.

Lough, John. *Writer and Public in France from the Middle Ages to the Present Day.* Oxford: Clarendon Press, 1978.

Lublinskaya, Aleksandra Dmitrievna. *French Absolutism: The Crucial Phase, 1620–1629.* Cambridge: Cambridge University Press, 1968.

Lyons, John D. "Narrative, Interpretation and Paradox: *La Princesse de Clèves.*" *Romanic Review* 72 (November 1981): 383–400.

McGowan, Margaret. *L'Art du ballet de cour en France, 1581–1643.* Paris: Centre National de la Recherche Scientifique, 1963.

Macherey, Pierre. *Pour une théorie de la production littéraire.* Paris: Maspero, 1974.

Macpherson, Harriet D. *Censorship under Louis XIV, 1661–1715.* New York: Institute of French Studies, 1929.

Magendie, Maurice. *Du Nouveau sur "L'Astrée."* Paris: Champion, 1927.

——. *La Politesse mondaine et les théories de l'honnêteté en France, au XVIIe siècle, de 1600 à 1660.* Paris: Alcan, 1925.

Magné, Bernard. *La Crise de la littérature française sous Louis XIV: Humanisme et nationalisme.* Paris: Champion, 1976.

Magne, Emile. *La Vie quotidienne au temps de Louis XIII.* [Paris]: Hachette, [1948].

Malandain, Pierre. "Ecriture de l'histoire dans 'La Princesse de Clèves.'" *Littérature* 36 (December 1979):19–36.

Mandrou, Robert. *Classes et luttes de classes au début du XVIIe siècle.* Messina: G. D'Anna, 1965.

Mansau, Andrée. *Saint-Réal et l'humanisme cosmopolite.* Paris: Champion, 1976.

Manuel, Frank E., and Fritzie P. Manuel. *Utopian Thought in the Western World.* Cambridge: Belknap Press of Harvard University Press, 1979.

Marin, Louis. *Le Portrait du roi.* Paris: Minuit, 1981.

Martin, Henri-Jean. *Livre, pouvoirs, et société à Paris au XVIIe siècle (1598–1701).* 2 vols. Geneva: Droz, 1969.

Martino, Pierre. *L'Orient dans la littérature française au XVIIe et au XVIIIe siècle.* Paris, 1906. Reprint ed. Geneva: Slatkine Reprints, 1970.

Marx, Karl. *Capital.* Vol. 1. Trans. Samuel Moore and Edward Aveling. London: Lawrence & Wishart, 1970.

——. *Capital.* Vol. 3. New York: International Publishers, 1967.

——. *Grundrisse.* Trans. Martin Nicolaus. New York: 1973.

——. *Pre-Capitalist Economic Formations.* Trans. Jack Cohen. Ed. E. J. Hobsbawm. New York: International Publishers, 1965.

May, Georges. *Le Dilemme du roman au XVIIIe siècle.* New Haven: Yale University Press, 1963.

Mayer, Denise. "Recueils de portraits littéraires attribués à la Grande Mademoiselle." *Bulletin du bibliophile* (1970):136–74.

Meaume, Edouard. *Sébastien Le Clerc et son oeuvre.* Paris: Baur & Rapilly, 1877.

Miller, Nancy K. "Emphasis Added: Plots and Plausibilities in Women's Fiction." *PMLA* 96 (January 1981):36–48.

Momigliano, Arnaldo. *Studies in Historiography.* London: Weidenfeld & Nicolson, 1966.

Mongrédien, Georges. *Madeleine de Scudéry et son salon.* Paris: Tallandier, 1946.

Moote, Alanson Lloyd. *The Revolt of the Judges: The Parlement of Paris and the Fronde, 1648–1652.* Princeton, N.J.: Princeton University Press, 1971.

Morison, Stanley. *The Typographic Arts*. Cambridge: Harvard University Press, 1950.

Mousnier, Roland. *La Vénalité des offices sous Henri IV and Louis XIII*. Rouen: Maugard, [1945].

Olmsted, John W. "The Voyage of Jean Richer to Acadia in 1670: A Study in the Relations of Science and Navigation under Colbert." *Proceedings of the American Philosophical Society* 104 (December 1960):612–34.

Pagès, Georges. *Les Institutions monarchiques sous Louis XIII et Louis IV*. Paris: Centre de Documentation Universitaire, [1961].

Peterson, Richard A., ed. *The Production of Culture*. Beverly Hills, Calif.: Sage, 1976.

Pope-Hennessey, John. *The Portrait in the Renaissance*. New York: Bollingen Foundation, Pantheon Books, 1966.

Porshnev, Boris. *Les Soulèvements populaires en France de 1623 à 1648*. Paris: S.E.V.P.E.N., 1963.

Pottinger, David T. *The French Book Trade in the Ancien Régime, 1500–1791*. Cambridge: Harvard University Press, 1958.

Prévost, Claude. *Littérature, politique, idéologie*. Paris: Editions Sociales, 1973.

Ranum, Orest. *Artisans of Glory: Writers and Historical Thought in Seventeenth-Century France*. Chapel Hill: University of North Carolina Press, 1980.

Reed, Gervais E. *Claude Barbin, Librarie de Paris sous le règne de Louis XIV*. Geneva: Droz, 1974.

Reiss, Timothy J. *The Discourse of Modernism*. Ithaca: Cornell University Press, 1982.

——— "Power, Poetry, and the Resemblance of Nature." In *Mimesis: From Mirror to Method, Augustine to Descartes*, ed. John D. Lyons and Stephen G. Nichols, Jr. Hanover, N.H.: University Press of New England, 1982.

Rothkrug, Lionel. *Opposition to Louis XIV: The Political and Social Origins of the French Enlightenment*. Princeton, N.J.: Princeton University Press, 1965.

Roy, Émile. *La Vie et les oeuvres de Charles Sorel*. Paris: Hachette, 1891.

Roy, Joseph-Edmond. "Le baron de Lahontan." *Proceedings and Transactions of the Royal Society of Canada* 12 (1894):63–192.

Schapiro, Meyer. *Words and Pictures*. The Hague: Mouton, 1973.

Serroy, Jean. *Roman et réalité: Les Histoires comiques au XVIIe siècle*. Paris: Minard, 1981.

Servois, Gustave. "Notice biographique." In Jean de La Bruyère, *Oeuvres*, vol. 1. Paris: Hachette, 1882.

Seznec, Jean. *The Survival of the Pagan Gods*. Trans. Barbara F. Sessions. Princeton, N.J.: Princeton University Press, 1972.

Smith, David Nichol. *Characters from the Histories and Memoirs of the Seventeenth Century*. Oxford: Clarendon Press, 1929.

Smith, Hallet. *Elizabethan Poetry*. Cambridge: Harvard University Press, 1952.

Soman, Alfred. "Press, Pulpit, and Censorship in France before Richelieu." *Proceedings of the American Philosophical Society* 120 (December 1976):439–63.

Spingarn, Joel E. *A History of Literary Criticism in the Renaissance.* New York: Burlingame–Harcourt, Brace & World, 1963.

Stanton, Domna C. *The Aristocrat as Art: A Study of the Honnête Homme and the Dandy in Seventeenth and Nineteenth-Century French Literature.* New York: Columbia University Press, 1980.

Steegmuller, Francis. *The Grand Mademoiselle.* New York: Farrar, Straus & Cudahy, 1956.

Stierle, Karlheinz. "L'Histoire comme exemple, l'exemple comme histoire: Contribution à la pragmatique et à la poétique des textes narratifs." In *Critique et création littéraires en France au XVIIe siècle.* Colloques Internationaux du Centre National de la Recherche Scientifique, no. 557. Paris: Centre National de la Recherche Scientifique, 1977.

Tallemant des Réaux, Gédéon. *Historiettes.* Ed. Antoine Adam. 2 vols. Paris: Gallimard, 1960–61.

Tapié, Victor L. *La France de Louis XIII et de Richelieu.* Paris: Flammarion, 1967.

Taton, René. *Les Origines de l'Académie Royale des Sciences.* Paris: Palais de la Découverte, 1965.

Taylor, George V. "Noncapitalist Wealth and the Origins of the French Revolution." *American Historical Review* 72 (January 1967):469–96.

Thomas, Thomas Head. *French Portrait Engraving of the XVIIth and XVIIIth Centuries.* London: G. Bell, 1910.

Thuillier, Jacques. "La Notion d'imitation dans la pensée artistique du XVIIe siècle." In *Critique et création littéraires en France au XVIIe siècle.* Colloques Internationaux du Centre National de la Recherche Scientifique, no. 557. Paris: Centre National de la Recherche Scientifique, 1977.

Tiefenbrun, Susan. *A Structural Stylistic Analysis of "La Princesse de Clèves."* The Hague: Mouton, 1976.

Tocanne, Bernard. *L'Idée de nature en France dans la seconde moitié du XVIIe siècle.* Paris: Klincksieck, 1978.

Todorov, Tzvetan. *The Poetics of Prose.* Trans. Richard Howard. Ithaca: Cornell University Press, 1977.

Trotsky, Leon. *Literature and Revolution.* Ann Arbor: University of Michigan Press, 1975.

Tyvaert, Michel. "L'Image du roi: Légitimité et moralité royales dans les histoires de France au XVIIe siècle." *Revue d'histoire moderne et contemporaine* 21 (October–December 1974):521–47.

Varga, A. Kibédi. "Pour une définition de la nouvelle à l'époque classique." *Cahiers de l'Association Internationale des Etudes Françaises* 18 (March 1966):53–65, 249–53.

———. "La Vraisemblance—problèmes de terminologie, problèmes de poétique." In *Critique et création littéraires en France au XVIIe siècle.* Colloques Internationaux du Centre National de la Recherche Scientifique, no. 557. Paris: Centre National de la Recherche Scientifique, 1977.

Vernier, France. *L'Ecriture et les textes.* Paris: Editions Sociales, 1974.

Vigée, Claude. *"La Princesse de Clèves* et la tradition du refus." *Critique,* nos. 159–160 (August–September 1960), pp. 723–54.

Watson, E. C. "The Early Days of the Académie des Sciences as Portrayed in the Engravings of Sébastien Le Clerc." *Osiris* 7 (1939):556–75.

White, Hayden. *Tropics of Discourse: Essays in Cultural Criticism.* Baltimore: Johns Hopkins University Press, 1978.

Williams, Ralph Coplestone. *Bibliography of the Seventeenth-Century Novel in France.* New York: Century, 1931.

Williams, Raymond. *Marxism and Literature.* Oxford: Oxford University Press, 1977.

Wolf, John B. *Louis XIV.* New York: W. W. Norton, 1974.

Woodbridge, Benjamin M. *Gatien de Courtliz, sieur du Verger: Etude sur un précurseur du roman réaliste en France.* Johns Hopkins Studies in Romance Literatures and Languages no. 6. Baltimore: Johns Hopkins University, 1925.

Woshinsky, Barbara R. *"La Princesse de Clèves": The Tension of Elegance.* The Hague: Mouton, 1973.

Yates, Frances A. *The French Academies of the Sixteenth Century.* London: Warburg Institute, University of London, 1947.

Index

Page references to illustrations appear in italics.

Library of Congress Cataloging in Publication Data

Harth, Erica.
    Ideology and culture in seventeenth-century France.

    Bibliography: p.
    Includes index.
    1. French fiction—17th century—History and criticism. 2. Literature-and soci-
ety—France—History—17th century. 3. France—Civilization—17th century. I.
Title. II. Title: Ideology and culture in 17th-century France.
PQ645.H37   1983   843'.4'09355   83-5352
ISBN 0-8014-1527-6